Luminos is the Open Access monograph publishing program from UC Press. Luminos provides a framework for preserving and reinvigorating monograph publishing for the future and increases the reach and visibility of important scholarly work. Titles published in the UC Press Luminos model are published with the same high standards for selection, peer review, production, and marketing as those in our traditional program. www.luminosoa.org

The publisher and the University of California Press Foundation gratefully acknowledge the generous support of the Constance and William Withey Endowment Fund in History and Music.

The Divo and the Duce

CINEMA CULTURES IN CONTACT

Richard Abel, Giorgio Bertellini, and Matthew Solomon, Series Editors

The Divo and the Duce

*Promoting Film Stardom and Political
Leadership in 1920s America*

———

Giorgio Bertellini

UNIVERSITY OF CALIFORNIA PRESS

University of California Press, one of the most distinguished university presses in the United States, enriches lives around the world by advancing scholarship in the humanities, social sciences, and natural sciences. Its activities are supported by the UC Press Foundation and by philanthropic contributions from individuals and institutions. For more information, visit www.ucpress.edu.

University of California Press
Oakland, California

Suggested citation: Bertellini, G. *The Divo and the Duce: Promoting Film Stardom and Political Leadership in 1920s America*. Oakland: University of California Press, 2019. DOI: https://doi.org/10.1525/luminos.62

Cover illustrations: *(Above)* Valentino, posing before his bust-in-progress and unidentified sculptress. Rudolph Valentino, no. 194, Core Collection Biography Photos, Academy of Motion Pictures Arts and Sciences. Courtesy of AMPAS. *(Below)* Mussolini, posing before his bust-in-progress and American sculptor Jo Davidson, ca. 1927. Archivio Centrale dello Stato, Partito Nazionale Fascista, Ufficio Propaganda (Fotografie Istituto Luce), b.1, 90. Courtesy of ACS.

Author photo by Mary Lou Chlipala.

Library of Congress Cataloging-in-Publication Data

Names: Bertellini, Giorgio, 1967– author.
Title: The Divo and the Duce : promoting film stardom and political
    leadership in 1920s America / Giorgio Bertellini.
Description: Oakland, California : University of California Press, [2019] |
Series: Cinema cultures in contact ; 1 | Includes bibliographical references
    and index. | This work is licensed under a Creative Commons CC-BY
    license. To view a copy of the license, visit: http://creativecommons.org/
    licenses |
Identifiers: LCCN 2018033486 (print) | LCCN 2018036816 (ebook) |
    ISBN 9780520972179 (ebook) | ISBN 9780520301368 (pbk. : alk. paper)
Subjects: LCSH: Publicity—United States—History—20th century. |
    Valentino, Rudolph, 1895–1926. | Mussolini, Benito, 1883–1945. | Mass
    media and publicity. | Communication in politics. | Celebrities in mass
    media. | Motion picture industry—United States—History—
    20th century.
Classification: LCC HM1226 (ebook) | LCC HM1226 .B48 2019 (print) |
    DDC 305.5/2--dc23
LC record available at https://lccn.loc.gov/2018033486

26   25   24   23   22   21   20   19   18
10   9   8   7   6   5   4   3   2   1

To Leila

CONTENTS

ILLUSTRATIONS

ACKNOWLEDGMENTS

This study took (way) more than a decade of research, writing, conference presentations, and rewriting. Out of curiosity and, admittedly, inertia, I could have gone for a few more, but it was time to share my findings with readers. What follows may offer an indication of the volume of my debts.

A large-scale research project requires large institutional shoulders, and I feel privileged to work at the University of Michigan. I would like to thank the College of Literature, Science, and the Arts (LSA); the Office of the Vice President for Research; and my two departments, Film, Television, and Media (FTVM), formerly known as Screen Arts and Cultures, and Romance Languages and Literatures (RLL), for their steady financial support and multiple accommodations. The generous resources of an associate professor fund enabled me to acquire primary materials (i.e., microfilms) and scores of secondary sources, as well as to travel to archives in the United States and Europe. An ADVANCE faculty summer writing grant allowed me to hire two amazingly competent copyeditors, Ken Garner and Rebecca Grapevine, who polished my prose. Three spring and summer grants from the Rackham Graduate School were also fundamental for compensating three remarkable graduate students, Courtney Ritter, Pierluigi Erbaggio, and Roberto Vezzani, who assisted with research and with compiling the bibliography. Outside funding came from a Radcliffe Fellowship at Harvard University and a Franklin Research Grant from the American Philosophical Society (APS). I wish to thank Barbara J. Grosz, then dean of the Radcliffe Institute; Judith Vichniac, director of its Fellowship Program; and Linda Musumeci, director of Grants and Fellowships for APS.

In Ann Arbor, I was also spoiled by an incredibly efficient library system that delivered in-house and interlibrary-loan volumes practically to my office door. I am grateful to all the indefatigable librarians at Michigan for making research such a pleasurable adventure. This system could be improved only if, say, after the delivery of every ten books, they served an espresso macchiato. Over the years, I relied on the unwavering support and enthusiasm of different department chairs, Markus Nornes, Caryl Flinn, Johannes von Moltke, and Yeidy Rivero of Film, Television, and Media, and Michèle Hannoosh and Cristina Moreiras-Menor of Romance Languages and Literatures. In FTVM I have also been blessed to count on the exceptional professionalism and, most importantly, the friendship of Mary Lou Chlipala, the carpooler from "Up North" and a perfect house guest, the archivist-librarian-cum-magician Phil Hallman, and our departmental grand master Marga Schuhwerk-Hampel. I also wish to thank all my colleagues in FTVM and RLL for their support and help with bibliographic and scholarly suggestions, particularly Richard Abel, Matthew Solomon, and Johannes von Moltke, as well as Vincenzo Binetti, Alison Cornish, Karla Mallette, and Paolo Squatriti. A special thank-you also to Dario Gaggio, from Michigan's Department of History, for the generosity of his insights.

The research for this project accompanied me for years in the classroom and in many exchanges with both graduate and undergraduate students. I am deeply grateful to the Undergraduate Research Opportunity Program at the University of Michigan. Under its aegis, I benefitted throughout the years from the help of a tremendous group of undergraduate students. I would like to mention here some of the most dedicated ones, including Jessica M. Oyler, Sara Cecere, Olivia Glowacki, Katharine Rose Allen, Nicolette De Simone, and, especially, James Hamzey. James continued to work after his employment ended and helped me with the bibliography before Roberto Vezzani completed the task. Roberto Vezzani and Pierluigi Erbaggio also enlightened me with their doctoral dissertations on, respectively, the American circulation of Italian fiction and of nonfiction films produced during Fascism. I am also grateful to other students who took my seminars American Cinema and Race, Screening Fascism, Stardom, and Cinema and Propaganda. I am happy to mention Jim Carter, Syed Feroz Hassan, Vincent Longo, Simonetta Menossi, Dimitrious Pavlounis, Emily Saidel, and Marissa Spada. A very special thanks to the graduate students at NYU–Italian Studies during my tenure as a Tiro a Segno Fellow. Their contributions to our seminar on 1920s masculinity were extraordinary. I am happy to single out particularly Noelle Griffis, Karen Graves, Marcella Martin, and Jacobus "Jaap" Verheul.

Tracking film prints and photographs has not been terribly difficult because I have been aided by talented and professional researchers and archivists. I wish to thank Nico de Klerk, Ronny Temme, Jan-Hein Bal, Leontien Bout, and Annette Schulz from the EYE Filmmuseum (Amsterdam); Gabrielle Claes, Jean-Paul Dorchain, Jill De Wolf, and Clémentine De Blieck at the Cinematek (Brussels); the archivists at the Cinémathèque française (Paris) and the Centre national du cinéma et de l'image animée (CNC; Bois d'Arcy); and Maria Chiba and Serge Bromberg of Lobster Films (Paris). I am grateful also for the help I received from the Cineteca di Bologna, especially Andrea Meneghelli; and from the Museo del Cinema (Turin), especially Roberta Basano, Paola Bortolaso, Carla Ceresa, and Donata Pesenti Campagnoni. At the Margaret Herrick Library of the Academy of Motion Picture Arts and Sciences, I was lucky to be aided by Stacey Behlmer, Marisa Duron, Faye Thompson (who went out of her way to be of help), Jonathan Wahl, and Elizabeth "Libby" Wertin. In Los Angeles I also worked fruitfully at the UCLA Film & Television Archive Research and Study Center (ARSC) and at the University of Southern California's Cinematic Arts Library. At the Museum of Modern Art, I relied on the superb professionalism of Ashley Swinnerton. At the Motion Picture, Broadcasting and Recorded Sound Division (MBRS) at the Library of Congress, Rosemary C. Hanes suggested a wealth of titles and research paths.

For research into paper documents, I am also grateful to the archivists at the Special Collections at UCLA, USC, the University of Chicago, the Center for Oral History at Columbia University, the Baker Library at Harvard University, the Sterling Memorial Library at Yale, the Seeley G. Mudd Manuscript Library at Princeton, and the Bancroft Library at Berkeley. My research was also fruitful at the Center for Migration Studies (Staten Island), thanks to Mary Elizabeth Brown, and at the Archivio Prezzolini (Biblioteca Cantonale, Lugano), with the help of Diana Rüesch and Karin Stefanski. In Rome, I spent an amazingly productive summer because of the generous assistance of Loredana Magnanti, Vincenzo Troianiello, and Alberto Cau of the Archivio Storico Capitolino; Caterina Arfè of the Archivio Centrale dello Stato, Stefania Ruggeri and Paola Busonero of the Archivio Storico Diplomatico of the Ministero degli Affari Esteri. They went out of their way to accommodate my endless requests and my often difficult schedule.

For help with the process of reproduction and publication permissions, I am grateful to Giuseppe D'Errico of the Biblioteca Nazionale Centrale of Rome; Nicola Immediato of the Archivio Storico Capitolino (Rome); Daniela Loyola and Paolo Danilo Audino of the Archivio Centrale dello Stato; Jean-Paul Dorchain of the Cinematek (Brussels); Kristine Krueger and Faye Thompson of Academy of Motion Picture Arts and Sciences; Thomas Lisanti and Jeremy Megraw of the New York Public Library; Rosemary Hanes of the Library of Congress; and Ashley Swinnerton of MoMA.

I began giving talks on the subject back in 2001, at Berkeley, when I was invited by Barbara Spackman. That initial talk became my first essay on the topic, which I published in the *Journal of Urban History* in 2005 in a special issue edited by Donna Gabaccia, who had also invited me to present it at the University of Pittsburgh. Barbara and Donna, along with Gaylyn Studlar, Jacqueline Reich, Ruth Ben Ghiat, and Giuliana Muscio, taught me in countless ways how to research male stardom and political authority. Gaylyn also generously gifted me her splendid collection of photographs of Valentino. Over the years, I presented various iterations of my research at different institutions and conferences at Harvard University, the Calandra Institute for Italian American Studies, the Columbia Film

Seminar, New York University, Tiro a Segno Club (New York), the University of Turin, the University of Maryland, Ohio State University, the University of Notre Dame, Michigan State University, Oxford University, the University of Southern California, and the Columbia University Seminar in Modern Italian Studies. I wish to thank the organizers of these invited talks, particularly Krin Gabbard and William Luhr; Stefano Albertini and Ruth Ben Ghiat; Anthony J. Tamburri, Fred Gardaphé, and Joseph Sciorra; Silvio Alovisio and Giulia Carluccio; Saverio Giovacchini and Elizabeth Papazian; Lucy Fisher and Mark Lynn Anderson; Gaoheng Zhang; Joseph Francese and Joshua Yumibe; Dana Renga; Zygmunt Baranski and John P. Welle; Alessandro Carlucci, Guido Bonsaver, and Matthew Reza; and Ernest Ialongo. I also had the fortune of presenting my work at a few Society for Cinema and Media Studies meetings. I wish to thank the participants for their cogent questions, which made me rethink assumptions, arguments, and conclusions in ways that I treasure as models of scholarly exchange and growth.

A number of colleagues and friends have provided encouragement, information, and advice. They may not know, but their contributions at different stages have helped me in no small measure to complete the work. For this, I wish to thank Mark Lynn Anderson, Jennifer Bean, Guido Bonsaver, Francesco Casetti, Sue Collins, Mark Garret Cooper, Kathryn Cramer-Brownell, Raffaele De Berti, Simone Cinotto, Yvonne Elet, Jane Gaines, Ken Garner, Lee Grieveson, Charlie Keil, Rob King, Marcia Landy, Emily Leider, Denis Lotti, Stefano Luconi, Giovanni Montessori, Burton Peretti, Ivelise Perniola, Francesco Pitassio, Matteo Pretelli, Dana Renga, Steven J. Ross, and Matthew Solomon. In particular, Silvio Alovisio, Luca Mazzei, and Giuliana Muscio have been extraordinarily generous with their time and knowledge in replying quickly to my innumerable queries. Gian Piero Brunetta has been unwavering in his support of this project and a model of research curiosity and argumentative lucidity through his many essays on Hollywood and Fascist Italy. Needless to say, however, whatever is on the page is my sole responsibility.

A very special thank-you goes to Richard Abel, who read the manuscript twice (!) and provided masterful feedback and much needed encouragement. Thank you also to Ferdinando "Nando" Fasce (University of Genoa), whom I contacted for his inspiring research on American business and cultural history (and its relationship with Italy). Without ever meeting with me, Nando offered very productive feedback and was a model of long-distance scholarly collegiality. I am also grateful for the productive feedback I received from two anonymous reviewers who read the manuscript for the University of California Press. To put it simply, this book would not exist without Raina Polivka. As the acquisition editor for Film Studies at the University of California Press, she showed an immediate appreciation of the project's design and appeal, as well as its significance in our fraught media and political climate. I feel very lucky that our collaboration, which started long ago, will continue with the series Cinema Cultures in Contact, coedited with Richard

Abel and Matthew Solomon, for which this study constitutes the opening volume. At the Press I also relied on Jessica Moll and Elena Bellaart, who did a superb job in overseeing the production process, and on Barbara Armentrout for a truly masterful copyediting. I am grateful to Jessica, Elena and Raina for shepherding the volume through the complex, but most rewarding, process of digital publication. The volume appears in the open-access platform Luminos thanks to a generous Open Access Monograph Publication Initiative Subvention from the University of Michigan.

For personal hospitality, I am grateful to Stefano Bottoni, who provided a Mantuan haven in Brussels, to Ingalisa Schrobsdorff, who arranged for my stay in Washington, DC, to C. Paul Sellors and Ken Garner, who accompanied me in my Dutch and Parisian travels, and to Pierluigi Ercole for being always there. These close friends constantly encouraged me. In particular, Giovanni Cocconi foresaw the existence of a book after hearing me talk about this project nearly twenty years ago and never stopped demanding that his prophesy become reality. I wish to thank my families: Argia Lavagnini, Davide and Elena Presutti, Enzo and Benedetta Bertellini, Irma and Teresa Lavagnini, and Giorgio Cattapan for countless errands and forms of support. Your affection continues to sustain me. Thank you also to Jennifer, Mark, Mayya, and Suheil Kawar for welcoming me into their lives and for their splendid hospitality in Washington, DC, and Beirut. Finally, my greatest debt is to my wife, Leila Kawar, who has not only taught me about politics and public life but also showered me with love, loyalty, and trust while pretending that my prose was always fine and my cooking amazing.

Introduction

"Nothing Like Going to an Authority!"

This element of "Caesarism" is ineradicable (in mass states).
MAX WEBER, 1918[1]

What problems does foreignness solve for us? [. . .] Is foreignness a site at which certain anxieties of democratic self-rule are managed?
BONNIE HONIG, DEMOCRACY AND THE FOREIGNER, 2001[2]

STARS' SOVEREIGNTY

In February 1927, in a photograph published in *Motion Picture Magazine*, Mary Pickford and Douglas Fairbanks appeared in the pleasurable company of friends and colleagues amidst ocean breezes on sun-kissed sands at their beachfront property near Laguna Beach. It seemed a serene and much-deserved escape from their bustling careers. Yet, even a casual magazine reader likely could not help but notice that the image told more than the story of two stars' belated vacation at their second home. Most of the individuals, including Pickford and Fairbanks, smiled for the camera while proudly raising their right arm and stretching their hand to the sky (figure 1).[3] A long caption identified their distinct gesture as the "Fascisti salute" and explained that "Doug" and "Mary" used it to "greet visitors at their beach camp in true Italian style" after learning it in Italy during a meeting with none other than Benito Mussolini.

Less than a year earlier, in the spring of 1926, the two Hollywood royals had paid a much-advertised visit to Italy, with stops in Florence, Naples, and Rome, where they expressed enthusiasm for Fascism.[4] In the capital, they met with the Italian dictator, and Pickford greeted the press with what a local daily described as a "saluto fascista." Likewise, before readying himself for the camera, Fairbanks "proudly placed the fascist pin in his buttonhole, promising to carry it in and out of Italy, as long as he was in Europe," to his wife's approving nod.[5] Their various public engagements, including a visit to the Circus Maximus and the Imperial Fora, where they posed doing the Fascist salute, were the subject of intense coverage and visual display (figures 2 and 3).[6]

The meeting with the Duce most likely occurred on May 10, 1926.[7] It lasted only fifteen minutes, from 4:30 p.m. to 4:45 p.m., but it gained wide (albeit brief) notoriety on both sides of the Atlantic.[8] At Palazzo Chigi, the headquarters of the

The Fascisti salute. Mary and Doug learned it in Italy from Mussolini. There's nothing like going to an authority! And now with their camping party they greet visitors at their beach camp in true Italian style. Right to left are Mary, Doug, Betty Bronson, Doug Junior, Ted Reed, of the Fairbanks production department, Mrs. Elizabeth Cameron, Mary's secretary, and Roger Lewis of the Fairbanks' scenario department

FIGURE 1. Pickford, Fairbanks, and friends giving the Fascisti salute, 1927. "Mrs. Doug," *Motion Picture Magazine*, February 1927, 58.

FIGURE 2. Douglas Fairbanks in Rome at the Circo Massimo. Douglas Fairbanks Collection, General Publicity, Academy of Motion Pictures Arts and Sciences. Courtesy of AMPAS.

FIGURE 3. On a visit to the Roman Forum, Mary Pickford and Douglas Fairbanks give the Fascist salute. *Il Messaggero*, April 29, 1926, 5. Courtesy of Archivio Storico Capitolino, Rome.

Italian government, Mussolini received the two celebrities and conversed with them about moving pictures. He also asked them to use their contacts with the American press to publicize that, contrary to rumor, he and the Italian nation were in great physical and economic health. Italian and American newspapers reported the participants' mutual displays of respect and exquisite courtesy. They made it clear that the Duce was no less a star than the Hollywood couple, as his guests had recognized when they arrived in Italy. To Italian reporters, Fairbanks confessed his awe of the Duce's exceptionally energetic personality ("like an airplane propeller") and charisma ("all you need is to look at him to realize that").[9] Similarly, the *New York Times* duly reported that Fairbanks expressed admiration for "the progress and modernity of Italy" but was much more expansive in recounting how the American actor treated the Duce like a film star. "I have seen you often in the movies," Fairbanks allegedly gushed, "but I like you better in real life."[10] For his part, Mussolini did not hesitate to treat his celebrity guests as *his* fans and offered them a Hollywood-like gift: his autographed photograph.[11]

In 1927, the *Motion Picture Magazine* caption reminded readers of that special moment and included the memorable line "There's nothing like going to an authority!" Historians may not be able to identify who uttered the striking phrase; it may have even been an editorial flourish. Considering the arranged unanimity of the gestures and that Pickford and Fairbanks were the hosts, parents, or employers of the scene's other participants, it is likely that the caption expressed the sentiments of one or the other. No matter who signed off on the caption, in theory, the image and the well-documented Roman meeting with Mussolini should have disturbed contemporary observers. After all, just a few years earlier, Pickford and Fairbanks had raised millions of dollars for Woodrow Wilson's "war for democracy" against Europe's autocratic regimes. Something had changed; now they were publicly flaunting their personal encounter with Europe's most flamboyant dictator. The unusual pairing of the erstwhile democrats with the authoritarian leader did not provoke outrage or protests—except among a few antifascist dissenters. Instead, the visit summoned curiosity and marvel, as if it were a natural meeting of like-minded celebrities.

The meeting did not have the same meaning for the two parties. The pro-regime Italian press was enthusiastic about the Hollywood duo's visit since it meant a Hollywood homage to both the archeological beauty of old Italy and Mussolini's modernizing aspirations. It was an endorsement that the Italian dictator took great pride in, considering the couple's international fame. Yet, what was the meeting's significance for Pickford and Fairbanks as American celebrities? What exactly could the notion of "authority," conventionally associated with political leadership, bestow upon them in the Hollywood context?

In this study, I assume that what occurred in Rome had much more than anecdotal significance. Instead, it revealed a morphological kinship between the *popularity* of the Hollywood royals and the *authority* of the Italian dictator. It was a newsworthy event that, I argue, rested on two converging historical phenomena: the rising political import of celebrity culture and the growing popularity of authoritarian political leadership. Even in their contingency, the widely advertised Roman meeting, the Los Angeles beach scene, and the caption reveal the increasing public significance of both film stars and political leaders *beyond* their respective realms of screen and political culture. This contention begs several questions. How was it possible that in apparently nativist and isolationist 1920s America, a foreign leader like Mussolini, who never set foot in the country, could become a paragon of authoritative leadership? Why did the praise for a foreign dictator's authority in political *and* popular culture develop at the same time when access to suffrage and civil rights (i.e., the passing of the Nineteenth Amendment), employment opportunities, and consumer choices were expanding? When and how did film stardom and political leadership, as apparently distinct institutions of mass governance, become comparable, parallel, and analogous? Was this phenomenon *specifically* linked to the immediate postwar period and to the 1920s? After all, about a dozen years later, when the Duce had become widely seen as "a blowhard whose strutting often inspired derisive cackles," the more ominous Hitler was widely known in America but almost invisible on American screens. U.S. newsreel editors declared taboo most shots of Hitler, not just the close-ups, as his chilling and provocative authority was not to be publicized.[12]

One approach to comparing Mussolini with 1920s Hollywood stars would rely on a tempting, but limiting, side-by-side analysis of personal charm and appealing performative style. Inherent in this celebrity-centered comparative reading is a top-down approach to stars' relationship to their followers. Cultural historians might instead argue that personal charisma and performances matter a great deal, but they ought to be placed in dialogue with the social and cultural circumstances that enable certain individuals to emerge as popular authoritarian figures. While I find both the top-down and the culturalist approaches to be productive, I argue that what is needed is a third, complementary one. Comparisons of famous and charismatic individuals in different countries, in fact, overlook the most consistent factor of their popularity: namely, how distinct publicity practices shape stars' media representations. The effectiveness of these practices is itself informed both by the stars' charisma and broad social and cultural dynamics, but their mediating role deserves close attention.

Preliminary definitions of publicity are in order. In 1968, historian Alan R. Raucher noted that as a modern profession publicity "sprang from multiple antecedents [. . .] not entirely separate, including press-agentry and advertising, from which in the early 1920s it sought to assert itself."[13] Press agentry was a theatrical, ostensibly vulgar, Barnum-like mode of influencing the press with free publicity, often by way of monetary compensation, and was already being practiced during election campaigns. Advertising, in contrast, was a much more explicit strategy of conveying information toward a straightforward commercial goal: promoting and selling products or services. By the early twentieth century, these activities, as well as their names, oscillated between information and commerce, news and products, facts and promotion. At the same time, while indebted to practices of press agentry and advertising, the dissemination of information for promotional purposes also represented a reaction to the news-making practices of Progressive muckraking. Initially Progressives had denounced corporate "secrecy" as detrimental to the public interest. Reacting to these charges, corporations began making use of publicity strategies to defend themselves against damaging criticism.[14] They hired publicity specialists, variously known as "publicity experts" or "specialists in relations with customers," and "came to sponsor the largest and most important experiments in publicity before 1917."[15]

This date was not a random choice. Raucher points to the start of a process that was eventually affected by a watershed moment in American media history. The U.S. government's 1917 decision to enter World War I mobilized a massive institutional and commercial apparatus of pro-American initiatives both domestically and internationally. Publicity was not unknown to the film industry or to political campaigning, of course. Even before there was a Hollywood, moving picture companies had realized that publicity practices could expand the popular aura of screen actors beyond their film roles. Similarly, since the turn of the century, presidential contenders, from the publicity-obsessed Theodore Roosevelt to the media-shy Woodrow Wilson, had turned to publicity strategists to manufacture and broadcast narratives, images, and slogans about their politics and about themselves. The publicity machine of the Great War, however, generated an entire repertoire of new practices of mass communication and public opinion management. In the short term, the war-fueled publicity machine engaged Mary Pickford, Douglas Fairbanks, Charlie Chaplin, and William S. Hart into serving the national interest by selling Liberty Bonds and promoting Wilson to new heights of domestic and, especially, international celebrity. This was a safe, patriotic—and thus virtually unanimous—cause, but a political one nonetheless. In the longer term, such innovations taught the burgeoning film and public relations industry that, through skillful publicity, stars and public leaders could sell a whole range of political and cultural ideas to the public in America and overseas.[16] In ways that became more systematic, institutionalized, and transnational after the Great War, the success of stars' and politicians' public management brought mass entertainment, politics, and news ever closer and inaugurated the familiar crisscrossing of attributes between popular and political stardom on both domestic and international ground.

The Divo and the Duce studies how the public notoriety of Hollywood actor Rudolph Valentino, the "Divo," and Fascist dictator Benito Mussolini, the "Duce," indexed and shaped a broad range of 1920s celebrity-centered publicity initiatives that interwove news-making, media economics, and political communication. While it is attentive to their distinct career trajectories, my approach shows that, despite never having met each other, the Divo and the Duce form a productive pairing. For a few years, from the very early 1920s to Valentino's untimely death in 1926, the two Italian-born icons showcased a comparable type of fame that exceeded each man's respective domain. With the 1921 release of *The Four Horsemen of the Apocalypse* and *The Sheik*, the ideal and passionate lover Valentino was promoted as Hollywood's first truly foreign star. His fame was not limited to fantasies of screen romance. In carefully managed pronouncements to the press, he spoke against women's rights, democracy, the Hollywood industry, and even American masculinity. At first glance, these were not advisable positions to hold due to the potential of alienating the moviegoing public. At the same time, however, Valentino did not touch upon what Thomas Doherty defines as "the controversial issues and *causes célèbres* of the 1920s—immigration restriction, labor strikes, or [the long public trial against] the anarchists Sacco and Vanzetti."[17] And neither did Mussolini, who, whatever his domestic agenda, was careful not to meddle in American politics, which would have risked damaging his political and diplomatic relationships with U.S. officials.[18] Still, after the October 1922 March on Rome, the large-jawed, Caesar-like Duce was widely promoted in America not just as anti-Communist exemplar but also as a paragon of antidemocratic male leadership. His fame lasted for little more than a decade, until Italy's imperial campaigns in East Africa in 1935–36 and his concurrent formation of the Axis alliance with Hitler. Throughout the 1920s, though, Mussolini's name, image, and opinions pervaded American media through interviews, syndicated columns, (auto)biographical accounts, books, and films. Popular media broadcast his authoritative pronouncements—which Valentino appeared to share—about modern leadership and the importance of traditional gender roles.

With different degrees of success, official and unofficial publicity agents—whether filmmakers, journalists, ambassadors, or newspapers editors—established and managed the Italian duo's public personas. By repurposing the public relations practices used during World War I and working in the service of press syndicates, Hollywood studios, and business conglomerates, these publicity enablers had diverse purposes that ranged from journalistic self-advocacy to studio advertisements to political and financial gain. I shall refer to them as the architects of ballyhoo, to use a 1920s expression popularized by writer and publicist Silas Bent.[19] Whatever their individual agendas, their work shared a common repertoire of journalistic and narrative techniques. Of these, the most sensational and Boorstinian one—the publicity stunt—bestowed upon the Divo and the Duce the authority to shape consumer choices and manage modern crowds at home and abroad.[20]

Focusing on the promotional activities around these two foreign-born celebrities provides significant advantages. First, by looking at Valentino and Mussolini *as a pair*, and not as representatives of the distinct domains of entertainment and politics, I aim to foster a dialogue between the usually divergent disciplines of film and political studies. These scholarly disciplines have looked at the Divo and the Duce, respectively, as a subversive model of masculinity (film and cultural studies) and as a popular anti–Red Scare icon (history; political studies). Pairing them offers new insights into one of the earliest interweavings of film stardom and political leadership in the emerging celebrity-centered media economy that shaped advertising, news-making, and political communication. As Graeme Turner has noted, the success of celebrity culture is rooted in its ability to "generate large amount of content" and "secure a relationship of interdependency between media outlets."[21] Over the course of my research, the popularity of Valentino and Mussolini, especially in their outspoken endorsement of antidemocratic governmentality, revealed the emergence of a novel public discourse about authority and citizenship.

A second advantage of my focus on the interweaving of stardom and political leadership is that it also foregrounds two other historical dynamics—antinativism and anti-isolationism—one opening America to its own national diversity, the other opening it to the world. On the one hand, even before America's participation in the Great War, growing misgivings about the melting pot ideal were at least in theory legitimizing the foreign culture of immigrant communities within the country's popular and political scene. In 1916, the intellectual Randolph Bourne characterized the country's great democratic experiment as "a transnationality."[22] A few years later, despite the passage of anti-immigration legislation, American film culture witnessed a dramatic internationalization. "In the roaring converter of war more than nations are fusing," *Photoplay* boasted. "The Iowa lad is learning that the French aren't frog-eaters, nor are the Italians 'Ginnies.'"[23] The acceptance of international diversity in America opened the way to novel formulations of male character, personality, and leadership. The Divo and the Duce, I will argue, became popular not despite, but because of their widely advertised national and racial otherness. Their diversity offered license for daringly authoritarian political statements, most pointedly against women and the democratic process, while still enabling them to remain as charming and exotic specimens, ready-made for news and photographic coverage.

As for opening the United States to the world, the war catalyzed the country's political, financial, and cultural engagement with other nations. The assistance provided by American financial centers to European nations, banks, and film industries enabled Wall Street and Hollywood to achieve financial and commercial dominance. The worldwide fame of Hollywood's stars alerted U.S. financial and government leaders about the impact of celebrities' transnational branding for America's commercial and geopolitical reach.[24] The postwar collaboration between the industry's top organization, the Motion Picture Producers and Distributors of America (MPPDA), and the U.S. State Department, even if their economic and political interests were not always precisely aligned, warrants the consideration of the role the international framework played in the Divo's and the Duce's rise to fame. In brief, America's growing domestic acceptance of foreign cultures and their divergent ideas of leadership and gender relationships went hand-in-hand with the expanded projection of American culture onto the world.

A third advantage of focusing on both stars, and specifically of reading them through the lens of publicity practices, is that it allows us to avoid the teleological temptation to simply match celebrities' personas with the popular enthusiasms of 1920s America. Instead, I follow promotional mediators' deeds along a historical trajectory of personal and institutional agendas and continuous adjustments, rather than postulating the somewhat ahistorical closed circuit between charismatic figures and popular reception.[25] Stars' popularity was not a fait accompli but the result of actions taken by individuals on the basis of institutional imperatives, guesswork, and artful manipulation of popular rituals and preferences.[26] If celebrity culture is a given phenomenon today, it was not during and after World War I, when women and men made decisions that would create a new public, political role for film stars and a new cultural import for political figures.

Overall, this publicity-centered historiographical framework has enabled me to unearth new evidence related to the Italian duo's intersecting trajectories, such as Valentino's ghostwritten political pronouncements and Mussolini's rarely studied biographical exposés and screen appearances. It has also led me to new archival repositories that reveal the "Pink Powder Puffs" scandal as a publicity stunt and identify its architects. Ultimately, research into the promotion of each man's celebrity has enabled me to recognize links in film history to 1920s debates about public opinion management and propaganda in democratic America.

This volume consists of three parts and a conclusion. In the three chapters of part 1 ("Power and Persuasion"), I reconstruct the historical context of publicity practices that first informed the wartime alliance between Hollywood and the White House and that after the war affected the relationship between American cinema and U.S. public culture at home and abroad. In the five chapters of parts 2 ("The Divo, or the Governance of Romance") and 3 ("The Duce, or the Romance of Undemocratic Governance"), I detail the promotional strategies deployed to shape and maintain the popularity of Valentino and Mussolini.

In chapter 1 ("Popular Sovereignty, Public Opinion, and the Presidency"), I start from the 1915 Supreme Court decision that ruled that motion pictures were "not to be regarded [. . .] *as organs of public opinion*" but as "a business pure and simple."[27] Yet, the history of how the Wilson administration worked with Hollywood to shape public opinion during America's participation in World War I shows how the executive branch embraced cinema as a legitimate force in public discourse. The Wilson-appointed Committee on Public Information (CPI) worked with Hollywood to advertise the nation's war effort to domestic and foreign audiences alike. The Treasury Department engaged such Hollywood superstars as Mary Pickford and Douglas Fairbanks to market its Liberty Bonds. These new displays of patriotic persuasion and authority were extremely influential; not only did they promote Wilson's visionary leadership and Hollywood stars' political credibility, but they also inaugurated a powerful new correlation of national political ideals with celebrity culture.

As many observers noted, however, the wartime explosion of publicity activities by a small group of government officials, media operators, and businessmen constituted a challenge to the core democratic principle of popular sovereignty. In chapter 2 ("Cultural Nationalism and Democracy's Opinion Leaders"), I trace the intellectual debates about the impact of public opinion management on the fabric of American national identity, U.S. democracy, and political leadership. Concerned intellectuals, editorialists, and political scientists—most notably Walter Lippmann and John Dewey—reflected on the surprising efficiency with which unscrupulous private management of public opinion—in which cinema stood out as a paragon of visual suggestiveness—could end up dominating the nation's political discourse. Public relations operatives such as Edward Bernays embraced the role of public opinion managers as fundamental to advertising and consumer education—practices he saw as utilitarian and democratic.

In chapter 3 ("Wartime Film Stardom and Global Leadership"), I return to the wartime collaboration between Hollywood and the U.S. government, but this time from the perspective of the film industry. Specifically, I examine the effects of war propaganda on two of Hollywood's most important stars: Mary Pickford and Douglas Fairbanks. Their widely reported participation in the Liberty Loan drives in 1917 and 1918 turned them into on- and off-screen icons of both the Hollywood film industry and U.S. democracy. Pickford became the nation's sweetheart and a model of resilient and evergreen Americanness, and Fairbanks became a flashier update of Theodore Roosevelt's ideal of the athletic and strenuous life. After the war, the film industry and its Wall Street backers recognized in film stardom the key vector for the industry's financial capitalization, market consolidation, and global hegemony. In conjunction with the growing global alliance between Hollywood and Washington, Pickford's and Fairbanks's American branding promoted the country and its interests around the world. By the middle of the 1920s, however, both began to age out of their juvenile personas. Other charismatic idols sporting a more exotic flair, such as Greta Garbo, Ramon Novarro, and Rudolph Valentino, were exciting a younger generation of film audiences.

Part 2 (chapters 4, 5, and 6) focuses on how film roles and publicity often failed to match in the ways they shaped Valentino's public image from the beginning of his career in the late 1910s to the immediate aftermath of his death in 1926. In chapter 4 ("The Divo, New-Style Heavy"), I focus on the years before and immediately after Valentino's breakout role in *The Four Horsemen of the Apocalypse* (March 1921). His pre-1921 performances, including the one as seductive exotic villain in *The Married Virgin* (1918), help us to understand how his persona was made to attract sympathy so much that later screenwriters and publicists used it in tales of either moral conversion or Americanization (or both). June Mathis's script for *The Four Horsemen* created the role of the charming but vulnerable (and thus sympathetic) seducer, who initially displays a kind of primal sexual desire but eventually sacrifices himself to authentic love. Still, Mathis did not control the film's publicity and its impact on the broader American public. The film's studio, Metro Pictures, and Valentino's unofficial publicist, Herbert Howe, promoted his image as a "new style heavy," that is, as an exotically unrepentant lover, which became particularly resilient and found its most complete cinematic embodiment in *The Sheik* (November 1921).

In chapter 5 ("The Ballyhooed Art of Governing Romance"), I focus on the production and reception history of *The Sheik*, whose construction of Valentino as an assertive, authoritarian male type belied the evidence of his earlier screen roles and his known lifelong dependency on strong women. The film's release also coincided with political pronouncements, possibly ghostwritten by Howe, in which the Divo insisted on the necessity of a "leader for a nation, for a state, for a home" in ways that intertwined antidemocratic rhetoric with opposition to women's new civic and cultural freedom.[28] The chapter juxtaposes this political stance with a series of on- and off-screen occurrences aimed at expanding, but also taming, the quickly clichéd image of the Sheik. In such films as *Camille, Blood and Sand*, and *Monsieur Beaucaire*, written or managed by Mathis or his wife, art director Natacha Rambova, he was turned into as an unselfish lover willing to embrace sacrifice and defeat. Similarly, the articles that novelist and publicist Elinor Glyn ghostwrote for Valentino portrayed him as part caveman, part inveterate romantic. Reviews and letters to editors of film magazines were dismayed at how these productions compromised his more popular image of an authoritarian ruler of women's and spectators' romantic longings.

In chapter 6 ("Stunts and Plebiscites"), I detail the ways in which promotional experts sought to resurrect Valentino's stardom following the lull in his popularity beginning in 1924. United Artists publicity men Harry Reichenbach and Victor Mansfield Shapiro sought to restore his prospects by designing publicity stunts that cast him as a Sheik-like romantic figure. Shapiro presided over the "Pink Powder Puffs" scandal, which started with an anonymous editorial in July 1926 that challenged Valentino's heterosexual masculinity. The actor's response garnered newspapers' front pages and a massive attendance for his latest film, *The Son of the Sheik*. Valentino's sudden death in late August, moreover, would not bring an end to this publicity. His handlers collaborated with the funeral home's publicity manager to stage and manage a media display of unanimous grief. Few in America could remain indifferent; even Fascist representatives residing in New York sent Blackshirts to place a wreath on his flower-covered bier as if Mussolini himself were paying patriotic homage to the Divo. By then the American press had already turned the Duce into a competing version of the Sheik.

Part 3 turns to similar publicity processes across the Atlantic, looking at the thoroughly modern efforts to craft Mussolini's public appeal. This section also challenges the culturalist approach that posits an unmediated rapport between the Duce's virile image and his American audiences. In American political and diplomatic circles, Mussolini represented the perfect anti-Bolshevik ally, but his celebrity status resulted from the contributions of a range of mediators, including diplomats, journalists, editorialists, and writers. Chapter 7 ("Promoting a Romantic Biography") details the actions of these individual promoters, who were variously affiliated with the Italy America Society (IAS), a lobbying group with links to the U.S. State Department, Wall Street, and the press. Created in 1918 to promote American financial and geopolitical interests in Italy, from industrial investment to postwar debt compliance, IAS became an influential PR agency for Mussolini in America. One of its members was the U.S. ambassador to Italy during the March on Rome, William Washburn Child, who contributed significantly to Mussolini's acceptance in America, initially in high government circles and later in the court of public opinion, particularly through his ghostwriting services and connections. The Duce's image in financial circles and in the press also benefitted greatly from the work of Thomas W. Lamont, a founding member of IAS and J. P. Morgan's chief executive, and from the tireless mediation of the Italian ambassador, Prince Gelasio Caetani. Their public relations efforts, together with the publication of *The Life of Benito Mussolini* (1925) by the Duce's former lover, Margherita Sarfatti, and largely ghostwritten autobiographies like Child's *My Autobiography* (1928), filtered any discussion of Mussolini's despotism through a celebratory exposé of his personal life that romanticized his humble upbringing, iron discipline, and popular charm.

In chapter 8, I detail the specific ways in which the few film productions featuring Mussolini emerged out of this network of Italian and American mediators. *The Eternal City* (1924), shot in Rome by George Fitzmaurice and featuring Mussolini as himself, resulted from the contacts between the U.S. State Department, MPPDA's chief Will Hays, IAS's factotum secretary Irene di Robilant, and Ambassador Caetani. Despite their collective effort, the film proved disappointing and led Mussolini to demand control over future projects. The opportunity came when Fox, in search for a world-renowned celebrity to test its new proprietary sound technology, cast the Duce as himself in an address to Americans and Italian Americans in a Movietone News short entitled *The Man of the Hour* (1927). The results appeared remarkable: never before had Americans heard the Duce speak in English directly to them (he also addressed Italian immigrants in Italian). Critics' praise focused on his acting style and star quality, as if his plebiscitarian appeal trumped any questions about his antidemocratic domestic politics. At the same time, American newsreel companies enhanced Mussolini's cinematic visibility in America as an exemplar of undemocratic governing.[29] Fox and Hearst, for instance, edited the newsreel footage of the Istituto LUCE, the cinematographic arm of the Fascist state, and inserted it into their own effective distribution networks from the mid-1920s to the mid-1930s. A collage of LUCE footage was also the basis for Columbia's much-promoted *Mussolini Speaks* (1933).

The danger of these productions, as Caetani's most eloquent communications described it, was that the Duce ended up as a character actor in someone else's story and not the protagonist of his own.

The question of Hollywood's historical relationship with powerful political players, from mainstream American parties to totalitarian regimes, has received a great deal of scholarly attention in recent years. Although researchers have begun to study studio moguls' contacts with the Wilson administration during World War I,[30] most scholars have chosen to focus on the 1930s relationship of Hollywood to aspiring California governors and U.S. presidents[31] and the menace of Nazi Germany.[32] In the 1920s, however, Hollywood and Washington began to partner with each other to regulate and institutionalize forms of public coexistence and mutual benefit. The familiar narrative that sets up Hollywood scandals in opposition to the Hays Office tells an important but only partial history of personal confrontations, institutional regulations, and occasional collaborations. What is left out are other significant convergences that emerged after World War I on the basis of a shared, pressing need: the management of ever-increasing and diverse crowds capable of accessing film theaters, consumer goods, and voting booths.

Hollywood's euphoric self-mythologizing as America's progressive and democratic arena par excellence emerged concomitantly with the consolidation of film stardom as an effective technique of cultural and commercial regimentation. The industry's self-serving promotion of moviegoing as a democratic practice postulated film audiences' *spontaneous* preference for stars or films within the conveniently self-celebratory notion of cinema as a universal and democratic art.

The selling of the Great War and of star-studded Hollywood films at home and abroad educated government officials, film studios, and public relations specialists on both coasts about the political potential of charismatic male personalities and film stars. What ensued was a striking gathering of ideals about men's personalities and views on authoritative leadership that prevailed over mass conformism and challenges of modern life like women's rights and labor strife. As such gendered ideals pervaded political and film discourses, political figures were made to exude celebrity-like charisma while film stars came to be seen as masters of public opinion and social mobilization, at least for patriotic causes if not yet for social justice campaigns. Celebrity-centered publicity was key to the articulation of an apparently un-American attitude: a suspicion of the inadequacy of liberal democracy. At a time when ideas about dictatorship were preferable to the chaos of "mobocracy," Hollywood and Washington began to converge—sometimes haphazardly—on the promotion of public figures capable of effectively managing public opinion. Film celebrities emerged, on- and off-screen, as imagined authorities and leading men (i.e., sheiks, barons, Zorros, industry captains) capable of turning threatening crowds into well-managed consumers. Similarly, politicians emerged as iconic leaders capable of turning citizens, whether recently enfranchised or not, into identifiable targets for political campaigns. In a tumultuous decade marked not only by social protests, nativism, and radical immigration restrictions but also by the rise of a multiclass consumer base and the expansion of civic and employment opportunities for women, the Divo and the Duce were similarly branded as captivating authority figures and charismatic male models of mass governance. This book tells the story of the remarkable hits and misses of their mass promotion.

PART ONE

Power and Persuasion

1

Popular Sovereignty, Public Opinion, and the Presidency

Any discussion of the political laws of the United States has to begin with the dogma of popular sovereignty. [. . .] When a man or party suffers from an injustice in the United States, to whom can he turn? To public opinion? It constitutes the majority.

ALEXIS DE TOCQUEVILLE, *DEMOCRACY IN AMERICA*, 1835[1]

IN THEORY

Alexis de Tocqueville's systematic examination of U.S. political institutions devoted several pages to the issue of popular sovereignty and came to celebrate it as one American democracy's master tenets. Written a few decades after the presidencies of George Washington and Thomas Jefferson, *Democracy in America* surprisingly did not include a section on the presidency. For the French observer, the figure of the president was "an inferior and dependent power" before the legislature, "not a part of the sovereign power" but simply "its agent."[2] Half a century later, in a different media environment, a little-known political scientist named Woodrow Wilson translated Tocqueville's diagnosis into a denunciation. Wilson lamented the weakness of the executive office vis-à-vis not just Congress but also the new, dramatically expanded power of public opinion, by which he meant newspapers' much expanded commercial and political import. In *Congressional Government*, Wilson critiqued the American system for its parceling of power and lack of personal accountability, saying that it resulted in a presidency that was "too silent and inactive" and unable to represent "real leadership" against the press's " 'government by declamation' and editorial-writing."[3] In 1893, exactly two decades before becoming president, Wilson was still describing the executive exactly as Tocqueville had, as "the agent, not the organ, of sovereignty."[4] At the same time, however, Wilson was also devising an alternative approach to governance by articulating a critical difference between "the powers or processes of governing," lodged in the presidency, and the people's "relations of *assent* and *obedience*" to those powers and processes. The appreciation of "the degree of assent and obedience" as "the limits, that is, the sphere, of sovereignty" would eventually change the perception of his office as executive in chief and ultimately mark his own presidency.[5] The effectiveness of the chief executive, he came to argue, rested on its ability to *control* public opinion and thus to counter the "revolution in journalism," which was dangerously and arbitrarily "assuming the leadership in opinion."[6] Similarly, in *Constitutional Government in the United States* (1908), he argued that the "part of the government [that] has the most direct access to opinion has the best chance of leadership and mastery; and at present that part is the President."[7]

Together with the revolution in journalism, another major change was affecting presidential elections and politics. Although incomplete, by 1912 a new system of state primaries was gaining national significance by taking nominating power away from the party bosses and replacing their smoke-filled back rooms with the apparent openness of party conventions.[8] For decades, aspiring or established political leaders had to master individual relationships inside the party machine through personal favors and exchanges that patterned their political life from nomination to governance. Steadily operating in the background, lifelong political professionals preferred unremarkable and easily controllable candidates who stood out for their personal honesty and ordinariness (so-called dark horses). The new primary system changed the game. "Direct popular choice of candidates has arrived," George Kibbe Turner of *McClure's Magazine* noted in 1912, "and candidates, not parties, must introduce themselves directly to the voters."[9] In the new system, the press became something of a platform: newspapers had to explain and popularize candidates' personalities as much as their policies. "The democracy of the printing-press had come," boasted Turner, with Theodore Roosevelt's mastery of publicity in mind.[10]

Although to many observers the press was a force controlled by political and financial elites, its role in public opinion's free exchange of ideas was undisputable. The First Amendment to the Constitution recognized and protected free speech and the press's independence from government interference. In the mid-1910s the same right was explicitly denied to motion pictures even though by then cinema had been used for the propagation of news and opinions (and not just entertainment) and had already played a significant role in presidential politics. It is worth referring here to a very famous legal decision that included a specious and often overlooked assessment of cinema's status in American society.

In early January 1915, the U.S. Supreme Court agreed to hear the appeal of the interstate film exchange Mutual Film Corporation, which had lost its case against the State of Ohio's decision to create a censorship board. Motion pictures may be harmless per se, state judges had argued, but their effects were not. Before the highest court in the land, the Mutual lawyers retooled what had been their ancillary argument, an unconstitutional curtailing of free speech, behind their main charge of a curtailing of interstate commerce and thus of property rights. Censoring motion pictures, the Mutual lawyers now forcefully claimed, equaled censoring such comparable "publications" as works of art and the press.[11] The Supreme Court unanimously rejected the moral and educational rhetoric linked to motion pictures, describing them as "insidious in corruption," prone to rely on "prurient interest" for things that "should not have a pictorial representation in public spaces," and thus rightly subject to government restriction. The formula that the U.S. Chief Justice Joseph McKenna used to reject the proposed equation of motion pictures with free speech and the press, has become quite well-known. "The exhibition of moving picture is a business, pure and simple," Justice McKenna wrote, "originated and conducted for profit, like other spectacles." Less cited, at least by film scholars, is the remainder of the sentence, which ruled that moving pictures could not be regarded "as part of the press of the country or *as organs of public opinion.*"[12] In refuting their status as a legitimate or responsible force in public discourse, the Supreme Court denied moving pictures protection from state or federal censorship. The court's rejection impinged upon the deceptively neat but historically variable, knotty, and ultimately inaccurate distinction between private enterprise, represented by the film companies, and public interest or, to put it simply, between private gain and public benefit.[13]

While an obvious counterargument could stress that newspapers, like moving pictures, were private businesses created for a combination of private gain and public benefit, a whole range of actual practices had already contradicted and were about to challenge head on the Supreme Court ruling. Promotional synergies between cinema and political campaigning had already emerged at the turn of the twentieth century, but in the 1910s the same process underwent a remarkable development. During his tenure, President Wilson exploited motion pictures not only for his election campaigns but more significantly to secure support for his war policies. The film industry's involvement in the war effort raised both the president's favorability and Hollywood's stature in American public opinion. During his presidency, the U.S. engagement in World War I effectively disproved any legal theory limiting cinema's role to merely business and introduced new and enduring means of enhancing its political effectiveness. The office that the government instituted for its propaganda activities, the Committee on Public Information (CPI), did not bother to distinguish between motion pictures and the press. Instead, it sought to coordinate all sorts of mass communication media—including newspapers, periodicals, cartoons, photography, and advertising—to convey its wartime messages and shape America's public opinion. In turn, the film industry relentlessly sought to contribute to the war effort by claiming that its business and cultural activities fulfilled a national necessity.

PRESIDENTIAL LEADERSHIP AND PUBLICITY

Up to the late 1880s, political campaigns consisted mainly of public rallies and staged political oratory that limited candidates' geography of reach and influence no matter the newspaper coverage. At the turn of the twentieth century, presidents exploited the much-expanded circulation of print and, especially, visual media to elevate the power of the executive over the legislature and to expand their cultural currency. Quite significant in this regard were the 1892 and the 1896 presidential elections. The introduction of illustrated lectures using magic lanterns (or stereopticons) in 1892 visualized party platforms and extended candidates' familiar political oratory without the need for their physical presence. Even more remarkably, the introduction of motion pictures in 1896 shifted public attention away from candidates' policy positions and political eloquence toward their biography and personality. The case of the Republican candidate William McKinley is most symptomatic of this emerging trend of effective communication in absentia. His handlers staged a "front porch campaign" from his home in northern Ohio; produced illustrated lectures about his life, filled with cartoons; and hired the famous Edison inventor W. K. L. Dickson to film *William McKinley at Home* (American Mutoscope and Biograph Co., 1896). If until then, "political theater and theatrical entertainments were rivals of sorts," the few dozen feet of this film constituted an utter novelty: they gave the stationary McKinley visual ubiquity throughout the nation.[14] Furthermore, the short one-shot film could produce a compelling personal narrative that the press expanded upon, contributing to what Charles Musser has defined as a "*politicized feedback loop* between vaudeville screenings and the press."[15] Turning a campaign's planned effect into spontaneous reporting would become a decisive dynamic in media politics even outside the context of presidential elections.[16]

After McKinley's assassination six months into his second term, on September 6, 1901, Vice President Theodore Roosevelt was sworn in as president. Already a national icon thanks to his unique ability to manage press and publicity, which included the celebratory filming, real and not, of his Rough Riders' heroic feats in Cuba, Roosevelt soon became "the first U.S. president to have his career and life chronicled on a significant scale by motion picture companies."[17] His ability consisted in cultivating personal relationships with top reporters inside and outside the White House, as well as in experimenting with press agentry, which up to that point had been the exclusive domain of the theater, the opera, and the circus.[18] Sooner than any other politician, he began to appreciate how motion pictures could offer a novel and expansive mode of mass communication beyond electoral campaigns. His life on screen amounted to more than one hundred films recorded from 1898 to his death in 1919, including his political campaigns, troop parades, and world trips. Roosevelt's experience of strenuous life on the frontier and his writings, filled with illustrations by Frederic Remington, inspired numerous Western films. On the other hand, his manipulative relationship with the press even inspired a few satirical films. Edwin S. Porter's *The Terrible Teddy, the Grizzly King* (Edison, 1901), which was based on a cartoon, parodied Roosevelt's management of publicity by featuring him as a hunter followed by two characters carrying signs reading "My Press Agent" and "My Photographer."[19] With him, the link between motion pictures and presidential figures reached a novel level of mythopoetic intensity. In 1910, *Moving Picture World* described him, with typographical emphasis, as "A PICTURE MAN."[20] Roosevelt's celluloid performances enabled his swaggering personality, warrior temperament, and international fame to reach the widest possible audience. Before than any other politician, he realized that the film medium's all-embracing appeal would enable him "to fuse polyglot audiences into a single mass following, albeit at the box office rather than the ballot box."[21]

In 1912, in fact, while mired in a mutually destructive competition with his former protégé William Howard Taft for the Republican presidential nomination and being forced to run on the Progressive Party ticket, Roosevelt lost the election to a Democratic candidate who was temperamentally his opposite. Woodrow Wilson knew very well that he lacked TR's personal magnetism and mass appeal. "He is a real, vivid person," the then New Jersey governor wrote a friend before the elections. "I am a vague, conjectural personality, more made up of opinions and academic prepossessions than of [. . .] red corpuscles."[22] Yet, within a few years, Wilson managed to bring cinema to a level of partnership with the government that Roosevelt never managed to reach.

The 1912 campaign reveals how the co-optation of new media affected the reserved Wilson. Initially, he limited himself to the use of pamphlets that reproduced his printed speeches and magazine articles. Yet, to compete with Roosevelt, Wilson began to rely on phonographic recordings and motion pictures. The reproduction of his distinct oratorical talent for "modulated tones and precise selection and pairing of words" popularized the impression that Wilson was "a voice of reason and reform."[23] It was a performative advantage that his campaign exploited by ensuring that newspapers advertised the phonographic records and sent them out along with motion pictures "in order to have him both seen and heard in theaters."[24]

These new media practices inaugurated a new campaign style. It did not matter that Wilson scorned the recordings as "canned speeches" nor that he felt uneasy before movie cameras to the point that *Motography* described him as "an involuntary actor in the 'photo-play.'"[25] Over time he grew into being a media-savvy political candidate, particularly appreciative of the power of the moving image. In between his two elections, in fact, the rise of his political reputation was intertwined with the emergence of early newsreels, such as *Pathé Weekly* (aka *Pathé Weekly Review*), *Gaumont Weekly, The Mutual Weekly,* and *Universal Animated Weekly.*[26] With a multimedia campaign insisting on his level-headed temperament and rhetoric, Wilson gained the support of newspaper editors and common citizens and scored a landslide victory. More than a hundred still and motion-picture cameras captured his inauguration in March 1913. As a sign of things to come, Wilson enjoyed how the film cameras portrayed him like a royal dignitary, towering over cheering crowds before a Congress adorned in American flags.[27]

Ultimately, Roosevelt's cinematic visibility, while intense, did not augment his "bully pulpit" in ways that radically affected his well-known public persona. On the other hand, Wilson began his presidential campaign without a national profile, but during his time in office, he intertwined politics and motion pictures in such a way that his political leadership came to complement what he once described as cinema's universal language.

Such intertwining took time. Before examining the propaganda machine that Wilson set in motion during the U.S. involvement in the First World War, two series of events alerted him to the cinema's extraordinary power as a tool of public relations. The first began with the White House screening of D. W. Griffith's *The Birth of a Nation* on February 18, 1915, ten days after its release and a week before the Supreme Court's *Mutual Film Corporation* decision (February 23).[28] News of the screening elicited accusations of racism against the president at a time of much-needed national solidarity, and the ensuing controversy possibly constituted one of the most glaring counterarguments to the justices' ruling. The second series of events relates to the rarely documented approaches that filmmakers, producers, distributors, and exhibitors made to Wilson in the form of letters, telegrams, and meeting requests on the subject of the war between 1914 and 1917. This unrelenting pressure and, at times, Wilson's own response reveal that industry representatives clearly understood the potential role film could play in the country's public life, as well as in their industry's future, if they could somehow personally involve the president.

POLITICS WRITTEN WITH LIGHTING

Film historians have often referred to D. W. Griffith's controversial blockbuster as one of the first motion pictures, if not the first one, to be screened at the White House. President Wilson allegedly commented on the screening with a memorable remark: "It is like writing history with lighting. And my only regret is that it is all so terribly true." Historians have repeatedly reported this unconfirmed comment since the 1930s, possibly the decade that saw the most systematic convergence between Hollywood and Washington.[29] Historian Mark E. Benbow and biographer A. Scott Berg have recently noted that Wilson almost certainly never said it.[30] What is true, however, is that the screening did take place and animated a huge controversy. When several commentators publicized the president's alleged endorsement, Wilson tried to deny it, both publicly and privately, without much conviction or success.

The decision to screen *Birth of a Nation* at the White House resulted from a unique set of overlapping factors. On a personal level, Thomas Dixon, the white supremacist author of the film's source novels, was a friend of Wilson's from Johns Hopkins University's graduate school. On a cultural level, while most screenings at the White House in 1915 were proposed in conjunction with pressing issues of national neutrality and preparedness, a much-anticipated colossal production by the likes of D. W. Griffith was likely to have appeared capable of fostering national solidarity.[31] As for the film's racist narrative and depictions—which should have been recognized as inciting divisions rather than unity—they could not have been a novelty to Wilson, who knew Dixon's personal convictions and work. What may have balanced them out was Wilson's fondness for a very attractive representation of President Lincoln as a compassionate and reconciliatory national figure, which Ida Tarbell had first popularized in a 1897 serialized biography and which Dixon had continued to expand upon in his works.[32] A few months into the European war and a year before the heated 1916 presidential campaign, the image of Griffith's Lincoln as reuniting national figure and "a reaffirmation of the values of an older America" was also supposed to mute the divisive national loyalties of European immigrants on U.S. soil.[33]

Yet, as soon as news of the event reached the press, Wilson began to receive countless requests of official confirmation from individuals and civic groups that opposed the film's racial politics and called for its ban from circulation.[34] He first hesitated to respond. When the volume of protests did not subsidize, he instructed his secretary Joseph Patrick Tumulty in early March 1915 to answer any letter on the topic with this standard, self-justifying rejoinder that denied prior knowledge or later approval of the film's ideological perspective:

> It is true that *The Birth of Nation* was produced before the President and his family at the White House, but the President was entirely unaware of the character of the play before it was presented and has at no time expressed his approbation of it. Its exhibition at the White House was a courtesy extended to an old acquaintance.[35]

The statement encapsulated what many came to consider the sad truth about his position: his public denial of an endorsement was not the same as a condemnation.[36] It would take years for Wilson to express publicly reservations about the film, and when he did, it was out of concern for the reactions of African Americans as both loyal civilians and U.S. soldiers and for the needs of the war effort, not because of the film's racist and manipulative historical revisionism.[37]

The story of protests, disorders, and attempted bans of *The Birth of a Nation* is well known to film historians.[38] One of its less known but significant wrinkles is how the incessantly self-promoting Dixon, in his several contacts with Wilson, was both perceptive and boastful about cinema's unprecedented influence on Americans' electoral choices. In May 1915, he wrote a letter to the White House in response to the public controversy over Griffith's film. After describing cinema as not just "a new art" but "the mightiest engine for molding public opinion," he contended, exaggerating the figures, that when a political message reaches the screens of thirty thousand theaters, "no group of politicians can resist the onslaught."[39] He arrogantly claimed to have collaborated with Griffith not just to produce a revisionist account but also and ultimately to execute a major electoral design. The film's *"real big purpose,"* he contended, *"was to revolutionize Northern sentiments by a presentation of history that would transform every man in my audience into a good Democrat!"* He concluded by claiming to be the first person able to conjoin mass entertainment and electoral politics: "The next political campaign," he asserted with obvious reference to the coming elections, "will witness a revolution in political methods."[40]

The archival record does not include Wilson's response, but the president likely recognized in Dixon's argument the familiar self-promoting efforts of several film industry representatives who had been pounding on Wilson's office door since 1914 with all sorts of requests for collaboration. Pressed by the risk of censorship legislation and engaged in lifting cinema's public moral stance in response to the discrediting charges of civic and religious groups, film industry representatives articulated an insightful awareness about cinema's role in the new climate of mediated mass politics. Meanwhile, while the nativist Wilson was not immediately concerned with the European war, others were, or appeared to be.

PREPAREDNESS

After the early May 1915 sinking of the ocean liner *Lusitania*, which cost 128 American lives, and ahead of the 1916 election campaign, months of lively public debates about U.S. intervention shaped Wilson's public stance about the European war. In late 1915, the president began to promote domestic policies centered on "preparedness" or "armed neutrality." The new stance did not contradict his former pacifist one, but, given the post-*Lusitania* discussions about the state of America's military defense, it was better suited to his ambition for a second term. The subject of preparedness had newfound domestic relevance and was affecting ideas about the future of America's national unity, democracy, and, in Roosevelt's words, its "virility and moral fiber."[41]

The motion picture industry saw Wilson's need to communicate his new position on preparedness to the nation as a unique public relations opportunity. It was a critical time for an industry in search of responses to the threat of censorship, particularly after the Supreme Court's *Mutual Film Corporation* decision in 1915.[42] The studios viewed gaining national relevance as one such response. To achieve it, they sought to expand their commercial reach through incorporations and alliances and through a full professionalization of their business practices. These restructuring efforts paralleled broader dynamics that were changing the country's social and cultural landscape. Since the turn of the century, America's transformation from a continent of discrete and scattered communities to broader, interconnected ones had radically altered processes of production, delivery, and consumption. From 1914 to 1917, the film industry sought to establish a national film distribution system, institutionalize a star system at all levels of its business activities, and, as the European war persisted, expand its markets in Europe and

South America. While the war was raging in the Old World, the film industry was experimenting with ways to instill the Wilson administration's neutrality and preparedness policies through a "mass produced and nationally marketed product."[43] These packaging efforts permeated both fiction and nonfiction productions and were intended to obviate any state-directed censorship initiatives. They were also meant to counter the flood of letters from representatives of local censorship boards and civic and religious groups petitioning for a federal motion picture censorship bill in response to what they viewed as films' pernicious influence on the country. To achieve their goals, film industry representatives sought Wilson's endorsement of their plan for Hollywood's self-regulation by making explicit promises of electoral votes and broad support for the president's new war-related position—from passive pacifism or neutrality to preparedness.[44]

Two 1916 productions, *The Eagle's Wing* (Bluebird Photoplay) and *Civilization* (Thomas H. Ince Corp.), are key examples of the ways the film industry sought to aid the president's consensus building for his new policies. At the center of the production of *The Eagle's Wing* was the Motion Picture Board of Trade of America (MPBTA), an association created in September 1915 to represent the business of the entire film industry, in both internal and external matters. Chaired by J. Stuart Blackton, with Carl Laemmle as the manufacturers' vice president, the board met with Wilson, who granted it national recognition in late January 1916.[45] Fraught with internal divisions, however, the MPBTA was eventually disbanded, and in its place the industry created a new protective league, the short-lived National Association of the Motion Picture Industry (NAMPI), chaired by stage impresario and sports promoter William A. Brady.[46] Before its dissolution in June 1916, MPBTA had planned filming Wilson "in a speaking attitude" to illustrate a speech he had delivered in Cleveland the previous January.[47] The result was a fictionalized five-reel tale of war preparedness, entitled *The Eagle's Wing*, which Universal distributed for its subsidiary Bluebird Photoplay in early December. The film helped secure appropriate legislation.[48]

Even more helpful to the president's cause was Thomas H. Ince's pacifist epic, *Civilization* (1916), a moral parable telling of the conversion of a brilliant inventor of deadly submarines whose losses turn his king from warmongering sovereign to servant of a greater power and thus of human civilization. Produced by Ince, the film signaled the ideological partnership of a producer-director with the president, rather than a rapprochement between the White House and a film trade association. In the spring of 1916, John H. Blackwood of the New York Motion Picture Corporation proposed screening *Civilization* for the president since the film, as he wrote in his letter, "is an eloquent and tremendous preachment in favor of peace, along the identical lines that President Wilson has been following for the past twenty months."[49] A year after the *Lusitania* tragedy, Wilson was still publicly supporting a pacifist stance even while promoting industrial and military buildup. Not only did the White House grant Blackwood's request, but the president also invited Ince to his home in New Jersey and agreed to be filmed for what became the film's new prologue.[50] The new publicity emphasized how Wilson, as "Chief Director of the United States," warmly congratulated Ince, "Chief Director of the Cinema." In return, Ince publicly offered his vote for the president "because he is saving civilization by keeping us at peace."[51] And he offered much more. The film's intertitles matched Wilson's rhetoric about peace and preparedness and became its cinematic feedback loop, propagating the president's message in a most effective way. A decade later, Terry Ramsaye, owner and editor-in-chief of the *Motion Picture Herald*, reported the Democratic National Committee press representative William Cochrane's comment on this novel synergy. *Civilization* had "a large influence in the Wilson victory at the polls," Cochrane declared. "It put pictorial meaning into the slogan 'He Kept Us Out of War' on which Wilson was re-elected."[52]

Beyond fiction films, requests of public partnership from companies and individuals specializing in newsreels were particularly intense in this period. Paramount/Famous Players, Hearst, and Universal, for instance, were seeking endorsement for their commercial efforts, which they masked as patriotic. In spelling out the rationale for these schemes, industry representatives were quite articulate about the difference between films' and newspapers' modes of influence and about publicity's personalizing effects more broadly. For instance, in a March 1916 letter to Tumulty, noted war correspondent and *Paramount Pictographs'* editor Edward Lyell Fox stressed how, in contrast with the print press, newsreels compel viewers to consume their content and as such secure a much wider reach.

> A man opens his newspaper or magazine; he reads an article, the subject of which he is prejudiced against, and he turns the page; he avoids it. In a moving picture theater he pays to get a seat; he finds our magazine reel sandwiched in the bill between plays and he cannot get away from it no matter how prejudiced he may be against a certain subject. In other words, when we run animated cartoons showing President Wilson to be doing big things for this country [, . . .] 2,000,000 people a day are looking at them.[53]

Fox's letter also included the suggestion of closely associating the Wilson administration's policy with the *personality* of its chief executive. Beyond the use of animated diagrams about the European and American situation, the proposed film was to consist of "a day with the President" to reveal to all Americans what kind of man he was and what kind of challenges he faced on a daily basis. For the shrewd Paramount official, a production like this would achieve "a better culminating effect by Election Time." Possibly out of temperamental reservations, Wilson rejected the offer of turning Paramount's publicity department into a presidential public relations office, but his decision did not stop others from making the same kind of proposal. In the summer of 1916, two weeks before being elected as NAMPI's first president, Brady sent an original proposal to the White House. His plan was to film President Wilson delivering "kindergarten" speeches on peace, prosperity, "or any of the other slogans of the campaign" and interweave the footage with intertitles of the speech's content and with "illustrations carrying out what he is talking about."[54] As he did before, Wilson declined the offer, lamenting to Tumulty his "self-consciousness in the face of the camera" and limiting his personal involvement to writing rhetorical pronouncements that film companies could use as intertitles in their newsreels.[55] Still, he must have appreciated these professional suggestions detailing what cinema could do for his policies and governance. Barely a year later, he instituted the most effective public relations office ever established by an American president.

The following spring, in fact, while the censorship issue remained a preoccupation for the entire American media landscape, its critical and much-less-talked-about counterpart, *expression,* began to emerge. Designated as acceptable governmental publicity, expression implied a serviceable convergence of friendly political narratives with popular ones. As such it signaled a momentous change for political communication, one that duplicated what was occurring in the arena of corporate public relations. In the early twentieth century, as Karen Russell and Carl Bishop have noted, " 'publicity' moved from being something that newspapers gave to a person, event or issue, to being something that businesses and industries provided" in response to charges of monopoly and lack of trans-parency.[56] Such a turning point led to the rise of corporate publicity programs and initiated the careers of many public relations consultants—beginning with Ivy Lee.[57] The emergency of the European war forced the Wilson administration to also enter the public relations business through strategies that were based on a systematic propaganda effort that ultimately trained countless individuals in the new promotional craft. On April 6, 1917, the U.S. Congress approved Wilson's declaration of war against Germany. Shortly thereafter, the government mobi-lized the food, manufacturing, and weapons industries and passed mandatory conscription laws. It also instituted a public relations office that sought to shape the ways the war and the president's actions were communicated and received. The once media-shy president was media shy no more.

WILSON AND WARTIME FILM PUBLICITY

I am no expert in publicity, as you know, but [. . .] deeply concerned about the apparent growth of the mob spirit in the country.
WOODROW WILSON TO GEORGE CREEL, JULY 21, 1918[58]

About a week after the U.S. declaration of war against Germany, the president signed Executive Order No. 2594, which established the government's first propaganda office, the Committee on Public Information (CPI). At its helm was one of his most loyal and combative campaign supporters, the journalist George Creel. "The idea of the Committee," as the usually well-informed political scientist

Elmer E. Cornwell noted in 1959, "was the President's so far as one can tell."[59] It was not. But the attribution of its creation to Wilson perfectly dovetails with the views of the relationship between active leader and passive electors that the president had laid out as a political scientist.

Rhetorically aimed at broadcasting the "gospel of Americanism," the CPI was given a vital and demanding goal: persuading the United States and other nations that the war had become tragically necessary and that *all* Americans and allied populations needed to appreciate and support the president's plan for victory. In order to achieve its purpose, the CPI set out to control the flow of information domestically and internationally.[60] While Creel would regularly deploy the formulaic explanation that the CPI was interested in the "expression" of information and not in its "repression," the specter of federal censorship raised fierce objections and harsh personal criticism—against him and the president. Nothing remotely comparable to the CPI had ever been created before in America.[61] As Tocqueville had understood in the mid-1830s, the country had always taken pride in the free public circulation of information.[62] Censorship appeared to many as an antidemocratic, European perversion. Participation in the European war, however, created new scenarios. At stake, according to the pro-war advocates, was the question of the country's national defense, which justified the CPI's raison d'être. In the letter to the president that allegedly led Wilson to sign the CPI executive order, the secretaries of state, war, and navy clarified the new organization's dual purpose:

> It is our opinion that the two functions—*censorship* and *publicity*—can be joined, in honesty and with profit, and we recommend the creation of a Committee on Public Information.[63]

At first, great attention was given to the issue of censorship. Anticipating a press backlash against what could be viewed as an all-powerful censorship commission, the CPI's first-issued document was the "Preliminary Statement to the Press" (May 28, 1917). It included a quote from President Wilson meant to appease the press and the country:

> I can imagine no greater disservice to the country than to establish a system of censorship that would deny to the people of a free republic like our own their indisputable right to criticize their own public officials. While exercising the great powers of the office I hold, I would regret in a crisis like the one through which we are now passing to lose the benefit of patriotic and intelligent criticism."[64]

The same document explained the use of censorship specifically in relationship to information that either would directly aid the enemy or was "likely to cause anxiety, dissent or distress." Like a phenomenological treatise, the document distinguished between different categories of news and subtypes of censurable information.[65] Still, the justification for censorship went hand in hand with its constructive counterpart: publicity. In modern conflicts, the gathering and circulation of news is key since "public opinion is a factor in victory no less than ships and guns," the document read. The fighting role of the press was then "the creation and stimulation of a healthy, ardent national sentiment."[66]

More surprisingly, the justification for the entire enterprise seemingly challenged the foundation of democratic participation. "The motive for the establishment of this internal censorship," the document stated, "is not merely fear of petty criticism, but *distrust of democratic common sense*. The officials fear that the people will be stamped by false news and sensational scare stories."[67] By investing the notion of "democratic common sense" with such negative connotations, Creel's apparent dismissal of the basic tenet of democracy—"the will of the people"—may appear shocking today. In truth, his statement relied on the even more popular (and recent) theory of "crowd psychology," which many of his readers knew quite well. Elaborated in Europe by Gabriel Tarde, Scipio Sighele, and, most famously, Gustave Le Bon, crowd psychology held that popular masses were drawn like "primitive beings" to impressionable images and analogies, ignored "logical argumentation," and thus did "not reason or [. . .] reason[ed] falsely."[68] Not only was the CPI in a position to tame the herdlike impressionability of democratic common sense, but it had to for the nation's security. Referring to the 1914–1917 period, Creel later argued that after three years of "divisive prejudices," the CPI could finally replace selfish and irrational inclinations with a "mass instinct of fraternity, devotion, courage, and deathless determination."[69]

To reach his goal, Creel shaped the CPI into a multidimensional public relations agency, with several divisions all aimed at fostering national unity, the righteousness of the cause, and revulsion for the enemy. With $100 million to spend at its own discretion, the CPI promoted various initiatives that were greatly facilitated by its institutional alliance with the Association of National Advertisers. The committee printed a daily diet of government news and pronouncements, known as the *Official Bulletin*. With a print run of 100,000 copies per issue, it effectively constituted America's first national daily newspaper. The CPI also printed over 75 million pamphlets, mostly of Wilson speeches, as well as posters and cartoons to be given to the press or distributed freely. Furthermore, Creel oversaw a speakers' bureau of 75,000 individuals, the so-called Four-Minute Men, in charge of delivering talking points in movie theaters during intermissions. Their speeches were printed in more than 750,000 copies and reached about 5,000 communities.[70] And, of course, the committee entered the business of visual communication by playing all sorts of roles in producing and commissioning posters, illustrations, still photographs, and motion pictures. Its Division of Pictorial Publicity relied on the work of established illustrators including Charles Dana Gibson, Joseph Pennell, and James Montgomery Flagg, the creator of the famous Uncle Sam recruiting poster *I Want You for U.S. Army*.[71] The CPI also produced photographs and films about military preparedness and European battles, and it did so while maintaining close relations with a film industry that was keen to please the government.

From the start, the choice of Creel raised questions. *Collier's Weekly* writer Mark Sullivan initially found that, for a job that he believed required effective and smooth diplomacy, Creel was "the most unsuitable of men."[72] Why would the allegedly media-wary Wilson choose an acrimonious muckraker who had brought trouble wherever he worked, from Kansas City to Denver, with his sanctimonious anti-vice and pro-suffrage crusades? The answer requires an understanding of the specific job demands that Creel helped design and that Wilson gladly endorsed knowing with whom he was dealing.

Creel was a long-standing reformist, extremely loyal, and quite resourceful; most importantly, he was both well connected and fearless about managing the press. Although he personally knew several media players, he was not compromised by cozy business relationships with them. Over the years, instead, he managed to remain both inside and outside of the country's small community of public opinion operators.[73] In the early 1910s, he raised his national profile by publishing books in favor of suffrage and against child labor and by writing muckraking articles for *Everybody's Magazine* and *Century Magazine*. In 1916, he strengthened his political prominence as a member of the Democratic National Committee's publicity division and as a *New York Times* contributor.[74] A loyal Wilson supporter for years, he also published a pro-campaign volume, *Wilson and the Issues,* praising the president "as a leader, as a nucleating force." On trial in the electoral competition that pitted the reasonable Wilson against what Creel called the "bonfires of jingoism" was one of democracy's key values: *"the capacity of a people for self-government."*[75] A few months later as head of the CPI, Creel found himself challenging that very tenet.

In his many prewar articles, Creel advocated the mobilization of all national resources, not just the armies, and maintained that, while updating the president's older political diagnosis, "confusion and indirection are not so much an indictment of President Wilson, as they are an indictment of our governmental system."[76] While his reputation for being confrontational followed him, he also developed new imaginative and practical ideas about leadership that boldly combined political management and celebrity appeal. In December 1916, Creel wrote about one of Hollywood's biggest stars in relation to what the country's mood ought to have been and rarely was. "The Government ought to hire Douglas Fairbanks," he noted in *Everybody's Magazine,* "and send him over the country as an agent of the Bureau of Grins."[77] These inventive and ironic public expressions of party loyalty and support for strong and idealized leadership did not go unnoticed.

The evidence suggests that the CPI was probably his idea. Wilson, in fact, accepted the proposal that Creel had sent him a few days after the declaration of war. In that letter the journalist stressed the need "for expression not repression"—as he recounted years later.[78] Publicly, however, to give the CPI maximum political leverage, Wilson wanted to convey that the CPI was his idea and responsibility: "I would suggest that Creel say that the Committee on Public Information was created by me," he wrote in a letter to Tumulty.[79] On April 13, while officially acting on the recommendation of the secretaries of the State, War, and Navy Departments for the creation of an "authoritative agency to assure the publication of all the vital facts of National defense," the president announced that he had selected Creel for the agency's top job.[80]

Immediately criticized as "the censor" and the "publicity manager of the war," Creel was "repeatedly damned by a large portion of the press and distrusted by a certain portion of the public."[81] It must be noted that what also fueled widespread opposition to the issue of voluntary and involuntary censorship were the public debates and Congressional negotiations about the Espionage Act (June 1917) and the Sedition Act (May 1918), which covered wartime expressions of opinion. The persistence of those debates on the un-American character of censorship kept informing arguments against Creel during the war and long after its end.[82]

WASHINGTON TURNS TO HOLLYWOOD

The initial institutional rapprochements between the film industry and the government were not difficult. NAMPI's recently appointed director, Brady, had friends everywhere and was acquainted to both Creel and Tumulty. Brady was quick to realize that an alliance with the government was a unique opportunity for the film industry. In June 1917, after meeting Creel and several Hollywood representatives in his New York office, he wrote the White House with a remarkable pledge. He had a plan to "bring the motion picture [industry] under full control," without the interference of any political or private interest, and turn it into "the most wonderful system for spreading the National propaganda at little or no cost." The industry, he boasted, "could in two weeks to a month place a message in every part of the civilized world." It had a method in place that was "far more effective than the newspapers."[83] It was an impressive pitch.

Satisfied by the pledge, Wilson wrote back and asked Brady to "organize the motion picture industry in such manner as to establish direct and authoritative co-operation" with the CPI.[84] Wilson's stated intention was not just to bring Hollywood "into fullest and most effective contact with the nation's needs" but also "to give a measure of official *recognition* to an increasingly important factor in the development of our national life."[85] While Brady understood the proposed recognition as legitimation for the industry, it was Creel who had first suggested the concept and it was Wilson who gave it a broad cultural articulation that matched his policies' idealism and universalism. In his response to Brady, the president noted:

> The film has come to rank very highly as a medium for the dissemination of public intelligence, and since it speaks the universal language it lends itself importantly to the presentation of America's plans and purposes.[86]

This memorable characterization would soon be published in both American and British film periodicals.[87] On June 30, Brady telegrammed the president his appreciation for the U.S. government's invitation to the motion industry to "throw its weight to the last ounce into the task confronting the American people," and he pledged the "undivided conscientious and patriotic support of the industry in America."[88] Brady did not reveal the tensions that NAMPI had experienced with key members of the Motion Picture Exhibitors' League of America. Instead, in an effort to give leverage and prestige to NAMPI and prevent individual member producers from establishing independent relationships with the White House, he preferred to show a unified industry front.[89] Initially, the trade periodicals expressed some caution about the convergence between film and government, but they did not deny their support. The commercial and public relations advantages promised to be significant.[90] What Hollywood continued to request was to be classified by the U.S. government as one of the "essential industries," a recognition that the War Industries Board apparently granted in the winter of 1917.[91] Notwithstanding this recognition, the archival record shows that the industry continued to press the government to declare movie theaters critical to the war effort—even by way of rebranding them "temples of democracy."[92]

NAMPI's first institutional actions were forming the War Cooperating Committee (WCC) and supporting the First Liberty Loans. The WCC, whose illustrious membership included William Fox, Thomas Ince, Jesse Lasky, Carl Laemmle, Marcus Loew, Joseph Schenck, Lewis Selznick, and Adolph Zukor, made a significant public assurance to work with several government branches. Several initiatives were put into place in conjunction with the War, Navy, and Treasury Departments; the Departments of Agriculture and Labor; the United States Food Administration (USFA); and the United States Civil Service Commission.[93] For instance, the USFA collaborated with the War Cooperation Committee in producing and distributing short-subject films, including newsreels of Wilson and USFA director Herbert Hoover, and involving film exhibitors in screening slides and filmed advertisements about food conservation under the motto "Food will win the war."[94]

Still, the most popular form of collaboration between NAMPI and the government was the series of Liberty Loan campaigns, which received exceptional newspaper coverage due to the involvement of Mary Pickford, Douglas Fairbanks, Charlie Chaplin, and Sessue Hayakawa. This initiative was not under the purview of the CPI. Treasury Secretary William A. McAdoo had devised it a month before the WCC's formation.[95] The Liberty Bond drives were extraordinarily successful: four were held during the war and one, the Victory Bond drive, afterwards. The film industry participated in all of them by cooperating in the production and exhibition of posters, slides, and star-studded short films. It also planted advertisements in trade papers and newspapers and solicited stars to speak on behalf of bond sales at so-called Liberty Bond rallies.[96]

Covered nationwide by the press, the Liberty Loan campaigns represented the most sensational face of the alliance between Hollywood and the government, united in the effort of selling the war to a largely isolationist American public. Alliances between politicians and performers were nothing new. Notable precedents included Lincoln's celebrated trips to Matthew Brady's photographic gallery during the Civil War. What was new, however, was that through the Liberty Bond drives a new generation of politicians "were able to view their constituencies as audiences," as Leo Braudy famously put it.[97]

The democratic appeal to the crowd meant a reliance more on leaders' symbolic draw than on their actual policies. The intertwining of film and government publicity infused both American moviegoing and everyday life. Advised by trade periodicals, movie theaters began advertising the war effort by plastering their lobby and outside walls with portraits of Wilson and posters of Liberty Bond campaigns and war films; allowing Four-Minute Men to speak during intermissions; instructing musicians to play the national anthem or other patriotic tunes; and screening patriotic slides that celebrated both the war effort and motion pictures' contribution to the cause. The goal of these initiatives was to make sure audiences viewed movie theaters not only as sites of relief from the inconveniences of the war but also as places where they could contribute, in a pleasurable communal gathering, to the material and moral needs of the nation. The ultimate aim of the film industry was to ensure its essential relevance to the cause.

While several governmental agencies dealt with motion pictures, the CPI sought to centralize and coordinate most film initiatives through its Division of Films, established by presidential order on September 25, 1917. Under the direction of Charles S. Hart, a former advertising manager of *Hearst's Magazine,* the CPI Division of Films developed five major tasks: turn the footage provided by the Navy and Signal Corps—the government agencies for still and motion picture war documentation—into weekly film releases; write pro-government scenarios for commercial film productions; produce documentaries; distribute and promote war films, whether produced by the CPI, the Allies, or private companies; and coordinate their international distribution with the Foreign Film Division.[98]

It became increasingly clear that the Wilson administration, even with all its agencies, could not act alone from both production and distribution standpoints. While the photographic section of the Signal Corps, as Creel later maintained, produced "an enormous amount of material [of] the very highest propaganda value," its one-reel films were widely deemed to be of inferior quality.[99] They were not made by professional cameramen, did not have high production values, and were repetitive in the choice of subject (i.e., military parades, domestic preparedness, behind-the-frontline preparations). While screened for free, they rarely found exhibition in regular movie theaters.

In 1918 the CPI produced a few feature films of distinction, including the most successful of them, *Pershing's Crusaders,* an eight-reeler that secured more than four thousand bookings, as well as the five-reelers *America's Answer* and *Under Four Flags*.[100] The Signal Corps's best footage, with additional material provided by the United Kingdom, France, and Italy, was used for the *Official War Review*, also known as the *Allied War Review*. By the end of the conflict, the CPI's official newsreel output amounted to thirty-one weekly issues and about seven thousand domestic bookings. Its distribution, however, was the source of distressing negotiations with Pathé, Universal, Mutual, Gaumont, and other foreign newsreel companies.

No matter their lengths, the CPI productions exuded a recognizable patriotic idealism, which was greatly heightened in the feature-length films. For instance, *Pershing's Crusaders,* which focused on war preparations from weapon production and the arrival of U.S. soldiers in France to Liberty Loan rallies, opened with an intertitle that deployed pure Wilsonian rhetoric to echo its religious title. Its final section read as follows:

> The young men of America are going out to rescue Civilization. They are going to fight for one definite thing, to save Democracy from death. [. . .] This mighty exodus of America's manhood to the plains of Europe may well be called "the Eight Crusade."[101]

Unsurprisingly, the film's last intertitle was devoted to Wilson, "Champion of Humanity's Cause."[102] Similarly hagiographic, another feature, *America's Answer,* opened with a montage of the build-up to the war—"a glowering sky, men of different walks of life poised for action"—and of Wilson simply introduced as "Our Leader."[103]

By the late 1910s, at least until Congress's refusal to ratify the peace agreement and the U.S. entry into the League of Nations, Wilson had established himself as a familiar and reassuring presence to American and international audiences alike. His explicit cinematic visibility was mostly in newsreels, produced with different promotional purposes. As he grew more comfortable in front of the cameras, he appeared in numerous short films while signing laws, taking part in the draft lottery, inspecting military equipment and troops, and attending parades.[104] Also, Wilson's image had circulated extensively in still pictures, advertisements, and postcards. By the war's end, his media ubiquity had allowed him to reap the remarkable political benefits of a strengthened executive office.[105]

On his way to the Paris peace conference in 1919, several newsreels documented his journey to Europe, entertained on board the ship by the films of Griffith, Pickford, Fairbanks, and Chaplin; being greeted as a hero in France, London, and Rome; and finally meeting heads of state in Versailles. One of the few postwar dramas dedicated to him, *The Great Victory, Wilson or the Kaiser* (Screen Classics, January 1919), dramatically juxtaposed the American and the German leaders, from youth to mature age, and the forms of government they stood for—autocracy versus democracy.[106] It did not document his deteriorating health. Four months

FIGURE 4. Mary Pickford sending Liberty Bond films to President Wilson, 1919. Photograph from the Mary Pickford Collection (General, 1911–1920), Academy of Motion Pictures Arts and Sciences. Courtesy of AMPAS.

after his death, on February 3, 1924, the Woodrow Wilson Memorial Society released a compilation documentary, *The Woodrow Wilson Film Memorial*. It alternated views of the president giving speeches, signing documents, and meeting world's leaders with, among others, images of Pickford directly delivering the latest propaganda film to the president during the fifth Liberty Bond drive (figure 4). Boasting intertitles filled with laudatory narratives and eulogies, the film praised him as "world-known authority" and "model of intelligence, sobriety and determination." Beyond the moral and intellectual tribute, however, the film also advanced a notion of charisma that combined Francis Galton's eugenics with Gustave Le Bon's crowd theory: "The personal magnetism of the man [. . .] the light of his gray eyes—the fine poise of his well-shaped head—the beautiful rhythm of his vigorous sentences—held audiences breathless under their mystic spell." In the end, the film proposed a clear rationale for Wilson's failure to have the Republican-held Congress approve the peace treaty and the U.S. membership in the League of Nations in 1920: "While foreign peoples were idolizing him," a final intertitle read, "our own yellow press kept stabbing at him with cutting headlines."[107]

Wilson's indirect management of publicity initiatives affected the presidency in ways that Theodore Roosevelt's physical and oratorical skills did not. On Wilson's behalf and to his advantage, the CPI and the Treasury Department mobilized loyal journalists, editors, speakers, artists, publicists, advertisers, celebrities and film-makers capable of devising novel ways to reach vast sections of the electorate and influence their opinion. As political scientist Elmer Cornwell noted, these pervasive publicity activities "were a major factor underlying this growing public tendency to see the Federal Government personified in Presidential terms."[108] Neither Warren Harding nor Calvin Coolidge would set in motion anything comparable. Despite Wilson's reserved and intellectual temperament, he became, at least for a brief period, a celebrity in his own right in the United States and an even bigger one beyond the national borders.

During the nineteen months of the United States' involvement in the First World War, Hollywood played a direct and indirect role in heightening the status and appeal of presidential leadership. The film industry produced fiction films that were sympathetic to the war effort but also contributed to expanding the reach of Wilson's moral and military decisiveness. In a sort of cultural loop, both war films and stars' off-screen patriotic engagement infused a disparate range of moving pictures with a nationalistic dimension. On the ground, the range of collaborations between Hollywood and the executive branch anointed cinema as an organ of public opinion, akin to the press. As such, they strikingly contradicted the pronouncements of another branch, the judiciary. The CPI distinguished motion pictures from the printed press and other journalistic venues not according to juridical categories that separated commercial activities from civic ones but in medium-specific terms—News Division, Films Division, Pictorial Publicity Division. On a more speculative level, from the late 1910s the pressing issue of public opinion and its relationship to the changing, multinational face of American democracy came to dominate key public debates. Even the most learned observers could not avoid looking at cinema as a paragon of mass-mediated public opinion influence and management. It is to these debates that we shall turn to identify the political frameworks at stake in how observers and practitioners viewed the increasingly dominant role of public opinion—and of moving pictures—in American society.

2

Cultural Nationalism and Democracy's Opinion Leaders

Probably not one man in a thousand is geared with sufficient heart action to run counter to a false public opinion. [. . .] There are just two such men in our hundred and odd millions today.

DOUGLAS FAIRBANKS, WRITING ABOUT T. ROOSEVELT AND W. WILSON, 1918[1]

Any description in words, or even any inert picture, requires an effort of memory before a picture exists in the mind. On the screen the whole process of observing, describing, reporting, and then imagining, has been accomplished for you.

WALTER LIPPMANN, *PUBLIC OPINION*, 1922[2]

NATIONAL DEMOCRACY

The war taught many lessons to American politicians and intellectuals. Past progressive understandings of what nationalism entailed gave way to more aggressive ones in the thick of novel practices of public opinion management. When in 1910 Roosevelt unveiled the program that came to be known as the "new nationalism," his politics of countering the era's profit-driven individualism and mobilizing a national sentiment for novel forms of welfare amounted to an inspiring platform for constructive, progressive change.[3] The program also shared a surprising ideological convergence with *The Promise of American Life*, a volume that progressive intellectual Herbert Croly had written in 1909, four years before cofounding the *New Republic*. To today's readers, the word *nationalism* conveys ideological fanaticism and military belligerency. In Croly's analysis, nationalism was as a powerful unifier for a stronger *democratic* America. "It may discover," he argued, "that the attempt to unite the Hamiltonian principle of national political responsibility and efficiency with a frank democratic purpose will give [. . .] a new power to democracy."[4] Together with the *New Republic*'s other two cofounders, Walter Weyl and Walter Lippmann, Croly was rather blind to nationalism's domestic and, especially, international implications. Leading up to the war, ideas about America's power in the world, largely associated with Roosevelt's nationalist democracy, appeared to many progressive intellectuals to be legitimate and benign, notwithstanding an implicit advocacy for imperialist expansion. A prideful rhetoric of national democracy pervaded *New Republic* editorials and Wilson's speeches. But it also informed the publicists' and the president's efforts to shape public opinion about America's place in the world and about the war's meaning for America. Over time, the *New Republic* intellectuals came to disapprove of the unilateralist and imperialist policies first promoted by Roosevelt and then enacted by Wilson. Instead, they came to advocate a more restrained exercise of power politics. For his part, Wilson's actions showed publicists and readers alike how to discriminate "between those who would make *power* and those who would make *democratic persuasion* the ruling force in world politics."[5] It was a move away from Rooseveltian power politics toward a strategy that viewed "world opinion" as the most effective "guarantee of peace."[6]

The CPI's management of public opinion led many intellectuals to recognize disturbing occurrences of jingoistic manipulation and near-autocracy in the modern democratic experience. Until the sinking of the *Lusitania,* they hardly regarded nationalism as a conceptual rival to internationalism, but when they joined the country's war chorus, they realized that nationalism could acquire aggressive military connotations and sharp xenophobic edges. Randolph Bourne, a *New Republic* contributor and one of the most lucid voices in American intellectual life, saw the difference between the cultural nationalism he advocated and the destructive political nationalism prevalent in Europe and spreading across the Atlantic. In a June 1917 issue of the *Seven Arts,* he reproved his *New Republic* colleagues' "leadership for war" and their alignment "with the least democratic forces of American life." In his view, the government's systematic and effective management of public opinion, aided by illiberal forces, urged a pressing examination of world liberalism and world democracy. His article also called for a long-overdue investigation about the meaning of nationalism and democracy in America.[7] Bourne died prematurely in 1918, but his calls did not go unanswered.

In this chapter I discuss some of the period's critical contributions about political power and mass-mediated persuasion particularly, but not exclusively, among the influential editors of the *New Republic*. I examine the positions of Walter Lippmann and John Dewey on the delicate balance between democratic life and public opinion management, and I also discuss pervasive and glaring blind spots about alternative, transnational appreciations of America's exceptionalism. Cinema was not extraneous to these debates. Motion pictures became, especially in Lippmann's work, a paradigmatic form of powerful and manipulative knowledge: he referred to crowds' lingering prejudices as "pictures in their head" to bemoan the irrational process of mass communication and reception. The war decade saw more than the intervention of dystopian intellectuals, however. Enthusiastic publicity supporters were seeking ways to grant civic and commercial validation to public opinion management. History proved them right.

UNIVERSALISM AND PLURALISM

We are provincials no longer.
WOODROW WILSON, SECOND INAUGURAL ADDRESS, MARCH 1917[8]

On paper, Wilson's eloquent rhetoric was not especially straightforward, but his message was compelling and became even more so during wartime. Key to his communicative success was the mediating role of personal emissaries and CPI activists. With great efficacy, they projected his charismatic presence and oratory into the exclusive circles of America's intellectual and business elites and the more expansive national press. They translated and broadcast Wilson's widely repeated phrase that Americans entered World War I "for no selfish advantage" and that the U.S. troops were "the armies of God" sent on a mission to redeem the continent.[9] Wilson's own communication armies divulged his high-minded millenarian and transcendent rhetoric about America as a paragon of democracy for mankind.[10] Ultimately, his Fourteen Points appeared as a covenant of peace, drafted to grant justice to weak nations and stateless minorities through the recognition of all peoples' legitimate interests under universal justice.

At war's end, America and the Allied powers continued to view the conflict through Wilson's eyes: as the Old World's "final emancipation" from "autocratic authority" and as America's way "to *redeem* [it] by giving it liberty and justice."[11] Wilson's civic religion led to morally inflected international policies that achieved very practical results. As Daniela Rossini put it, "Wilson led the United States in the transition from its provincialism and isolationism toward international engagement and world political leadership."[12] Not only was he the first "statesman to propose a supranational political organization, the League of Nations," but he was also "the first American president to urge his compatriots to become citizens of the world."[13] No other president had ever achieved such intense ideological mass mobilization in America or the world. It should not be surprising that when comparing Roosevelt with Wilson, Croly thought of the former as a "hero" and the latter as a "saint," which contributed to a sacralized political legitimation of the modern statesman.[14] Only in retrospect did Croly, Lippmann, and even Dewey see how their "cant of idealism" had blinded them to Wilson's "autocratic and coercive methods," which had led to the creation of an artificial national enthusiasm and unity.[15]

By turning the war into a crusade for democracy, Wilson's political millenarianism represented a universalistic, apparently all-inclusive aspiration. In truth, it was not. On the one hand, it was fraught with divisiveness as it presented a remarkable undercurrent of social Darwinism. Wilson's Anglo-Saxonism informed his notion of American exceptionalism, which compromised not only his internationalist democratic program but also his view of national differences in America. Even though he twice opposed immigration restriction bills that called for a literacy test, he abhorred "hyphenated" immigrants because, in Hans Vought's words, "they acted as groups, and put selfish group interests blindly above the national interest."[16] On the other hand, Wilson's millenarianism informed a distinct notion of American exceptionalism, which hindered his internationalist program because it sanctioned, paternalistically, the call for collective security to "restrain national egoism."[17]

The peace conference and its aftermath shattered these aspirations and provoked disturbing realizations. Wilson wanted a people's peace, and instead what he and his American supporters were forced to accept was a punitive one. Versailles put into question the meaning and promise of Wilsonian Americanism and defeated the idealism of Wilson's brainchild, the League of Nations. The Republican Senate did the same by blocking U.S. entry into the league in 1920, as many former supporters turned against the president. The *New Republic* rejected the Versailles Treaty, claiming it "merely [wrote] the future specifications for revolution and war."[18] Wilson's suppression of all dissent during the war years and his postwar betrayal of his idealist and internationalist principles shattered the remnants of American progressivism, marginalized new liberalism until the Depression reintroduced some of its principles, and disillusioned the new liberals' longing for a great reformist leader, "something of a saint and something of a hero."[19]

Over time, historians and commentators have posited that Wilson himself contributed to the defeat of his own idealistic policies. As Lippmann observed in 1919, Wilson's decision not to promote the League of Nations prior to the end of the war led to his failure to design a world community. But his racially isolationist ideology may have also contributed to the failure of his global politics. Under his presidency, the CPI sought to address the country's various national constituencies by targeting the ethnic press with news, bulletins, and various propaganda communications, all published in translation. But Wilson, like Roosevelt before him, dealt with immigrants either as outsiders or as subjects to be Americanized and, as such, as a domestic problem seemingly divorced from foreign policy.[20] While domestic pluralism was not an easy option for the president, in the mid-1910s progressive intellectuals had elaborated alternative views that would find fertile ground in 1920s film culture. Two in particular deserve mention.

In his influential essay "Democracy versus the Melting-Pot," published in the *Nation* in 1915, the Jewish American philosopher and academic Horace M. Kallen identified in "the practical fact of ethnic dissimilarity among the whites of the country" a subject unknown to authors of the Constitution.[21] Writing against the primacy of the pure "English American," Kallen explicitly critiqued the nativist positions embraced by the prominent sociologist E. A. Ross and President Wilson, among others. He judged their "resentment of the 'hyphenated' American" as "righteous and pathetic"[22] and sought to disengage Americanism from Anglo-Saxonism. Once in America, he argued, immigrants had found economic prosperity, but they also turned their ethnic and national differences "from disadvantage to distinctions."[23] This was possible, he continued, because "on the whole, Americanization has not repressed nationality. Americanization has liberated nationality."[24] He thus compared American society to a symphonic orchestra in which "each ethnic group is the natural instrument, its spirit and culture are its theme and melody, and the harmony and dissonances and discords of them all make the symphony of civilization."[25]

This conclusion both anticipated and influenced the work of the aforementioned Randolph Bourne, whose famous essay "Trans-National America" appeared a year later in the *Atlantic Monthly*. "The failure of the melting-pot," Bourne argued, "far from closing the great American democratic experiment, means that it has only just begun." By admitting the necessity for "a clear and general readjustment of our attitude and our ideal,"[26] Bourne recognized that America's "unique sociological fabric" could open a path to a new kind of cosmopolitan unity and interchange and avoid the dangers of European nationalism. Calling for "a higher ideal than the 'melting pot,'" whose long predominance had inspired an Americanism conjugated mainly in the past tense, he concluded with this sentence:

> *America is coming to be, not a nationality but a trans-nationality,* a weaving back and forth, with the other lands, of many threads of all sizes and colors.[27]

Rare among intellectuals of the time, Bourne understood that the notion of immigrants' isolation from their homelands matched Americans' widely held belief of their own nation as isolated. "To stigmatize the alien who works in America for a few years and returns to his own land," he wrote, "is to ignore the cosmopolitan significance of this migration."[28] The war in his view made untenable the isolation from Europe as well as the tradition of remaining "aloof and irresponsible."[29] On the constructive side, Bourne maintained that the work of the "younger *intelligentsia* of America" was to aim at a "higher cosmopolitan ideal[, . . .] a spiritual welding, which should make us, if the final menace ever came, not weaker, but infinitely strong."[30]

Even though the discursive emergence of a "trans-national" and cosmopolitan America did not overcome the competing racial discourses and anti-immigration policies, it nonetheless revealed the highbrow formulation of *cultural pluralism*—later expanded upon by John Dewey—that saw parallel reverberations in American popular culture.[31] Eventually, lowbrow versions of cultural pluralism emerged in the performative arts and sanctioned an attraction to foreign personalities and their elevation as testimonials for a new America. One question remains: in a cultural environment where large, powerful sections of American public opinion viewed transnational exchanges as miscegenational, how could any embrace of foreign performers' masculinity be possible and even desirable? A possible answer lies in reframing the question. Rather than considering foreignness as a problem, it may be helpful to regard the foreigner, to quote Bonnie Honig, "as a device that allows regimes to import from outside (and then, often, to export back to outside) some specific and much-needed but also potentially dangerous virtues, talent, perspective, practice, gift, or quality that they cannot provide for themselves."[32] As we shall in the remainder of this study, in the context of lively debates about public opinion management as both a growing cultural phenomenon and as a controversial political instrument, foreignness could be regarded as "a site at which certain anxieties of *democratic* self-rule are managed [. . .] as a way to frame other issues of democratic theory and citizenship."[33]

POWER AND PERSUASION

Before the end of the war, while some commentators praised Wilson's ability to avoid democratic inaction or, even worse, "mobocracy," others accused him of bypassing the authority of Congress and autocratically manipulating the will of the people. Implicitly attacking the president, a *Chronicle* editorial from 1918 called CPI director George Creel America's "publicity dictator."[34] After the war, many progressives and former Wilson supporters expressed fears that wartime propaganda practices were not about to end. "Shaping public opinion has become an essential industry," wrote John Dewey in 1918. A year later Progressive journalist William "Will" Henry Irwin, who had directed the CPI's program of overseas propaganda, warned that special interests continued "to slant, to bias, to color the news," well after the armistice was signed.[35] From the left, Socialists attacked Creel's promotion of Wilson as enhancing a dangerous "HERO WORSHIP" that "leads a mad stampede away from an orderly movement toward concentration of power, in order to follow some Messiah."[36] Toward the end of the 1910s, a few political cartoons in the *New York Tribune* depicted Wilson with a good dose of sarcasm. One of them captured the president as a farmer planting the seeds of the peace treaty, watered by his oratory, in the garden of public opinion, not far from the U.S. Senate (figure 5).

Because the press's exposure of party corruption required candidates to present themselves directly before their electors, politicians understood that their ability to influence the press was the only antidote against an out-of-control public opinion determining government policies. The challenge was to limit the "questions to which public opinion can apply," as Harvard president Abbott Lawrence Lowell had put it.[37] In other words, since in principle most scholars equated democracy with popular sovereignty and understood democracy as "government by public opinion," the challenge was to distinguish proper public *opinion* from crowds' irrational *beliefs* without denying legitimate demonstrations of popular will.[38]

FIGURE 5. President Wilson planting the seeds of his peace treaty. *New York Tribune*, September 2, 1919, 1.

One of the volumes most explicitly stressing the dangers of "crowd-mind" and "crowd-behavior" was Everett D. Martin's *The Behavior of Crowds*. In contrast to the antidemocratic stance of Le Bon but mindful of Tocqueville's warning about the tyranny of democratic majorities, Martin argued that "democracy has indirectly permitted, rather than directly caused, an extension in the range of thought and behavior over which the crowd assumes dictatorship."[39] His solution relied on the Deweyan empowerment of education, which he viewed as the prerogative of a select group of individuals, "men capable of philosophical tolerance, critical doubt and inquiry [. . .] who can rise above vulgar dilemmas and are deaf to crowd propaganda."[40] It was an elitist view that several public figures openly supported, including most famously Walter Lippmann, oftentimes on the basis of their direct experience of mass-mediated war propaganda.

At the center of these ideas was the concern that the massive expansion of the means and venues capable of informing public opinion challenged old formulations of popular sovereignty. Since the mid-1910s, as Progressivism was retreating from mainstream political discourse, Lippmann had begun to reflect on the relationship between public opinion and political action within democratic life. His war experience as columnist, assistant to the secretary of war, and general secretary of a secret intelligence unit, the War Data Investigation Bureau, informally known as the Inquiry, shaped his understanding of information's critical role for policy making.

Based at the New York Public Library on 42nd Street and made of historians and geographers, the Inquiry was entrusted with drawing Europe's postwar internal borders ahead of the peace conference. Between late 1917 and early 1918, Lippmann and his associates drafted a memorandum that "delineated the new European frontiers, explained how each decision was made, and illustrated the points with maps." Wilson "added six general principles of his own on the territorial points," and the Inquiry memorandum became the basis of the president's historical Fourteen Points speech to Congress on January 8.[41] After this initial success, the rest of Lippmann's war experience as propagandist and as a member of the American entourage in Paris was disheartening.[42] His immediate superior, Edward M. "Colonel" House was demoted, and the press bureau was handed to Creel. Lippmann despised the CPI director's approach to propaganda as a means to win the war but not to secure long-lasting peace. Disappointed at how Wilson's concessions at Versailles had profoundly undermined the principles of the peoples' war, he returned to the States and in the *New Republic* excoriated the treaty as a "prelude to quarrels in a deeply divided and hideously embittered Europe."[43]

In the following years, he published three dystopian volumes that reflected not only on the dangers of propaganda but also on the distorting effect of the press in contemporary democracy. Against the faith in the press as a necessary component of democratic governance, in *Liberty and the News* Lippmann denounced what he called the "plebiscite autocracy, or government by newspapers." The result of the current situation, he wrote, is that political decisions "tend to be made by the interaction, not of Congress and the executive, but of public opinion and the executive."[44] In this scenario, private interest groups shape, or even produce, mainstream public opinion and in so doing control the government's policy and actions. "This shift in the locus of sovereignty," he somberly concluded, "has placed a premium upon the manufacture of what is usually called consent."[45]

Lippmann directed his warning at the "protection of the sources of [. . .] opinion," which he hailed as "the basic problem of democracy. Everything else depends upon it."[46] His rather elitist solution was the employment of "expert organized reporters," who were not just individuals but also "institutes of government research" and "private agencies" assessing the technical work of government branches.[47]

Postulating that "the real enemy is ignorance," Lippmann advocated a disinterested news service impervious to special interests. Without it, he foresaw a country's degeneration into a dictatorship of the Left or of the Right. He redefined the traditional notion of "liberty," rejecting its traditional meaning as "permission" and reformulating it instead as "a system of information increasingly independent of opinion."[48]

Two years later, Lippmann's outlook grew darker. The issue was not just the quality of the press or the legitimacy of government intervention in the production of news but the precarious assumption that human beings receive and process opinions through their rational faculties. In *Public Opinion,* he articulated his anxieties about the possibility of governing an ever-expanding mass citizenry democratically. Democratic theory, he contended, rested on the "doctrine of the omnicompetent citizen."[49] In truth, in his view, common citizens did not necessarily make intelligent judgments even when presented with objective information. His wartime experience had taught him that facts could be manipulated and distorted and that human reception was not solely governed by rational faculties but operated on the basis of stereotypes formulated to confirm previous judgments and guarantee self-respect. Knowledge is ultimately linked not to experience but to preconceptions, which he aptly labeled "pictures in our head." These mental representations affect our physical perceptions: "We do not first see and then define, we define first and then see."[50] Humans' first impetus is not the search for the truth itself, particularly if such pursuit means abandoning the comfort of familiar stereotypes. Referring to the famous allegory of Plato's cave, Lippmann argued that newly unchained prisoners, after a lifetime of mistaking shadows for real entities, decline resolutely to turn their heads.[51]

Lippmann's dystopian notion of mediated democracy was dependent on his growing recognition of the imperfect workings of human knowledge. Rather than the traditional binary model of individual subjects responding to the outside world, human knowledge resulted in his view from "the insertion between man and his environment of a pseudo-environment" to which "his behavior is a response." Thus, Lippmann argued, "the analyst of public opinion must begin, then, by recognizing the triangular relationship between the scene of action, the human picture of that scene, and the human response to that picture." The ensuing conclusion was politically troublesome: "what each man does is based not on direct and certain knowledge, but on pictures made by himself or given to him."[52]

As his lexicon and discussion reveals, *Public Opinion* was not a mere academic exercise, but its references to moving pictures showcased a connection to popular culture as a most effective model of human knowledge and a most pervasive one of mass experience. The expression "pictures in our head," in fact, while long associated with Lippmann's analysis, had appeared in comparable forms in trade and film periodicals. A *Photoplay* editorial from September 1918, "War and the Fifth Estate," had self-servingly praised cinema for providing Americans with the only true understanding of the war. "As they gained a first-hand knowledge of events from the physical pictures on the screens," the editorial read, "their mental pictures of the war broadened into a true perspective of its overwhelming importance."[53] Whether or not Lippmann read film magazines, he was quite sensitive to the power of films as sources of mental pictures. "The moving picture," he argued, "often emphasizes with great skill this double drama of interior motive and external behavior."[54] When viewed as part of the history of visual representation, nothing could be "comparable to the cinema" because "photographs have the kind of authority over imagination to-day, which the printed word had yesterday, and the spoken word before that. They seem utterly real." In a point that recalls the politicized feedback loop discussed earlier, he also noted that "the moving picture is steadily building up imagery which is then evoked by the words people read in their newspapers."[55] To illustrate moving pictures' cultural and political import, Lippmann turned to the most glaring example of his time, Griffith's racist blockbuster.

> Your hazy notion, let us say, of the Ku Klux Klan, thanks to Mr. Griffith, takes vivid shape when you see the *Birth of a Nation*. Historically it may be the wrong shape, morally it may be a pernicious shape, but it is a shape, and I doubt whether anyone who has seen the film and does not know more about the Ku Klux Klan than Mr. Griffith will ever hear the name again without seeing those white horsemen.[56]

Four decades before Daniel Boorstin's dystopian notion of "pseudo-events," Lippmann's identification of pseudo-environments rested on a denunciation of the fallibility of human knowledge and, with it, of democracy. In a modern world that is "hurried and multifarious," he argued, citizens can make no judgments about the world based on firsthand knowledge but have to rely on facts and prejudgments, or stereotypes, created by them or created for them.[57] The author of *Public Opinion* thus recognized that the original dogma of democracy, that rational knowledge should inspire policy, is but an impossible dream. No trustworthy press could ultimately cure the structural defects of democracy: the average man is unable or unwilling to process the barrage of information in order to formulate a competent opinion about a subject. Rather than just press bureaus, always subject to possible stereotypes and agendas, what Lippmann advocated were "intelligence bureaus," transparent and accountable, whose modus operandi was largely technical. "Representative government," he argued, "cannot be worked successfully, no matter what the basis of election, unless there is an independent, expert organization for making the unseen facts intelligible to those who have to make the decisions."[58] Disillusioned with mass democracy and the press, Lippmann envisioned an insurmountable gap between well-informed *insiders,* who ultimately run the country, and distracted *outsiders* who think their opinion matters. In one of *Public Opinion*'s last chapters, Lippmann struck a final blow to democratic theory when he contended that "the common interest very largely eludes public opinion entirely, and can be managed only by a specialized class."[59] John Dewey famously described *Public Opinion* as "perhaps the most effective indictment of democracy as currently conceived ever penned."[60]

In 1925, Lippmann painted an even darker view of democracy, if that was possible. In *The Phantom Public* he sought to "bring the theory of democracy onto somewhat truer alignment with the nature of public opinion."[61] After positing that public opinion is "not the voice of God, nor the voice of society," he identified it as simply the voice of spectating common citizens, who have neither the time nor the preparation to attend to their government's affairs. They have to place their trust in the hands of actors, whose opinions and goals are not an "emanation of some common purpose."[62] Liberalism, he admits with a mea culpa, had been contributing to this mistaken judgment.

> For when public opinion attempts to govern directly it is either a failure or a tyranny [. . .] The theory of democracy has not recognized this truth because it has identified the functioning of government with the will of the people. This is fiction.[63]

By positing a "radical difference between the experience of the insider and [that of] the outsider," Lippmann was endorsing a conception of elitist democracy.[64] He knew he was not alone. In *The Phantom Public* he referred to works that also regarded popular sovereignty as a fiction and that endorsed an elitist approach of modern democracy.[65] He expressed particular sympathy for the German sociologist Robert Michels, whose *Political Parties,* published in the United States in 1915, popularized the concept of the inevitability, or iron law, of oligarchy in democratic societies. In later years, together with Alfredo Pareto and Gaetano Mosca, Michels became known as one of the key exponents of elitist theory and a supporter of the political experiment of Italian Fascism.[66]

Against Lippmann's elitist conception of politics, the philosopher, psychologist, and educational reformer John Dewey strove to defend the pragmatist wisdom of participative democracy. A widely known public intellectual versed in many disciplines and a public voice in matters of psychology, education, and aesthetics, Dewey had always expressed a profound belief in the values and practices of democracy. Pressed by Lippmann's writings on the unfeasibility of any democratic project, Dewey responded with the 1927 volume *The Public and Its Problems.* In it, he vehemently advocated for citizens' active role in shaping social issues and affecting decision-makers through communication and education. "Only through constant watchfulness and criticism of public officials by citizens," he maintained, "can a state be maintained in integrity and usefulness."[67] Propaganda may not be eliminated, but a possible alliance of sound pedagogy and psychology with the scientific method could guide citizens, students, and workers along the path of correct reasoning. With the aid of communal life and "communicated experience," Dewey argued, "the cure for the ailments of democracy is more democracy."[68] In contrast to Lippmann, he viewed modern media not as the arena where questions of public interest could potentially be accurately framed and structured but as a domain that generally distracts citizens from such questions. "The movie, radio, cheap reading matter and motor car," he argued, "did not originate in deliberate desire to divert attention from political interests," but that "does not lessen their effectiveness in that direction." He then concluded that "it is hard work to sustain conversation on a political theme; and once initiated, it is quickly dismissed with a yawn."[69]

To sum up, after the war experience, a renewed interest in public opinion became a major subject for editorialists as well as social and political scientists, no matter their ideological stance. At the start of the 1920s, attention to public opinion shifted from political and institutional concerns to the broad spectrum of social life, often touching upon the effects of manufactured consensus on political institutions. The co-optation of the disciplines of social psychology and, later, sociology led to public opinion being considered not strictly as political opinion but more as set of popular beliefs, including their formation, logic, and impact.

This interdisciplinary recasting affected the discipline of political science. The range of interests of Charles E. Merriam, founder of the behavioral approach to political science and a notable professor at the University of Chicago, was paradigmatic.[70] A pragmatic supporter of educating the citizenry, local participation, and representative democracy, Merriam had been the CPI's director of propaganda in Italy in 1918. A vehement supporter of scientific rigor, he promoted the study of political phenomena in the early 1920s through the intersection of a wide range of research methods.[71] Merriam saw the still rising and imperfect discipline of social psychology, more than individual psychology, as opening up the field to what he called "political psychology."[72] After observing in a 1920 survey of the Progressive era's political debates that, "of the three powers of government, the executive was the greatest gainer in public esteem," he became interested in the question of leadership.[73] Rather than juxtaposing civic incompetence and rational leadership, he advanced an enlightening methodological insight according to which "the attractiveness of the leader and the attraction of the follower are the same phenomena, viewed from different sides."[74] Notable scholars responded to his call for "studies of the qualities of political leadership." They included political historian, presidential advisor, and later member of Roosevelt's brain trust William Yandell Elliott of Harvard, who looked at European examples for modern leadership and found Mussolini to be the "prophet of the pragmatic era in politics."[75]

The end of the purely political approach to the study of public opinion took several directions. Armed with new scientific ambitions, some scholars began focusing on voting behavior and explored an alliance with psychological methods for the "measurement of public opinion."[76] The intersection of propaganda analysis and scientific method saw its most transformative impact in the 1930s and

1940s work of communication theorist Harold D. Lasswell.[77] On the other hand, outside the domain of political discourse, the ongoing reflections over the use of war propaganda prompted the emergence of cross-disciplinary interests in social behavioral techniques. Once the assumption of *rational* human conduct was bracketed off, a whole host of disciplines, including anthropology, sociology, and psychology, began to investigate the rational *and* irrational aspects of human behavior. Most remarkable, however, was the work conducted outside academic walls among the communication professionals in the emerging domain of the consumer economy.

DEMOCRACY AND CONSUMER CULTURE

Unlike concerned political observers and theorists, a whole class of profession-al journalists, press agents, and publicity experts argued that Germans' coarse approach to propaganda was giving the term a bad name. In their view, propaganda was "an essentially harmless refinement on the traditional American marketplace of ideas."[78] As Jackson Lears has noted, for them "advertising the war effort was an exercise in democratic social engineering, not Prussian regimentation."[79] The post-war years were momentous: advertising saw an unprecedented explosion of rele-vance and visibility in American business and social life. Publicists and advertisers began to see themselves as part of the same legitimate and effectual profession. By the 1920s the idea of audience manipulability had well-established academic, political, and professional currency. At the annual meetings of the professional advertising association, it was quite common "for heads of prestigious universities and national leaders [. . .] to enthusiastically hail advertising as 'an agent of civili-zation,' and 'the producer of desires which ends in creating demands.' "[80] What was in certain circles a doctrine of influence, in others could be "professionalized into the psychology of suggestion, which cast the consumer as an easy mark for the informed marketing strategist."[81]

The emergence of publicity as a legitimate profession did not occur in a vacuum but sprang from multiple antecedents, including the often-overlapping practices of theatrical press agentry and commercial advertising. In broad terms, publicity embodied the Progressives' opposition to corporate "secrecy," which they con-demned as detrimental to the public interest.[82] Even before the creation of the CPI, early twentieth-century American corporations realized that the best way to fight the charges of the muckraking press was to use the press to disseminate positive publicity about themselves.

In theory, news making and plain advertising or publicity were separate endeavors at odds with each other. In 1906, however, the *Bookman* had accused publicity practitioners of manufacturing "tainted news," and in 1914 the *New York Times* had described the conflict in Europe as the "the first press agents' war."[83] In the mid-1920s, accusations against publicity adopted a novel formula: public relations were not only akin to propaganda but were also described derogatively as "higher hokum"—a ploy, that is.[84] Yet, the press never came to condemn publicity or the PR profession for long or to distance itself from these practices. As Alan R. Raucher noted long ago, "the publicity's men's desire to have material printed and the editor's need for copy produced a marriage of convenience."[85]

The most outspoken and self-promoting representative of the rising public relations industry was a young Cornell graduate named Edward Bernays. He had served as press agent for Enrico Caruso and the Ballets Russes, worked for the CPI's Foreign Press Bureau, and attended the Paris Peace Conference as a member of the press team. His knowledge of the psychology of influence came from experience, readings, and a prominent family connection: he was Sigmund Freud's nephew twice over.[86] Shrewd and ambitious, in 1919 he established his own business in New York, promoting himself as "public relations counsel," and acquired academic credentials by teaching courses on public relations at New York University in the early 1920s. He published one of the first books on public relations in 1923, *Crystallizing Public Opinion,* which he followed in 1928 with the even more ambitious volume *Propaganda.*[87] While engaging critically with Lippmann's views about the dangerous manipulability of public opinion, Bernays did not often acknowledge his debts to the writings of the *New Republic* editor and at times turned him into an apologist for public relations.[88]

At the center of Bernays's understanding of the opportunities associated with publicity and public opinion management was his experience with the Creel Commission. In his recounting, it had "opened the eyes of the intelligent few in all departments of life to the possibilities of regimenting the public mind."[89] In contrast to German wartime practices, "modern propaganda," Bernays wrote in 1927, "is a consistent, enduring policy of creating or shaping events to influence the relations of the public to a given enterprise. Perhaps 'public relations' is a more accurate term than propaganda."[90] Whatever the name, he argued, "the conscious and intelligent manipulation of the organized habits and opinions of the masses is an important element in democratic societies."[91] In a chapter in *Crystallizing Public Opinion* entitled "Propaganda and Political Leadership," he lamented that "the methods of our contemporary politicians, in dealing with the public, are as archaic and ineffective as the advertising methods of business in 1900 would be today." The great challenge of our modern democracy, he remarked, "is how to induce our leaders to lead [. . .] When Napoleon said, 'Circumstance? I make circumstance,' he expressed very nearly the spirit of the public relations counsel's work."[92] To Bernays, the affinities between the Corsican leader's brilliance and the emerging professional field were obvious. After all, he remarked, "good government can be sold to a community just as any other commodity. True, it is an intangible product [. . .] but not more intangible than the creation of a desire for breakfast foods or a new style of hats or a new philosophic thought or theory."[93] The modern principles and practices of "universal education" for the common man have only expanded the possibilities of manipulation, not reduced them. "Instead of a mind, universal literacy has given him a rubber stamp [. . .] inked with advertising slogans [. . .] but quite innocent of original thought" because of propaganda's "organized effort to spread a particular belief or opinion."[94]

Due to his success and his reputation, it is not surprising that Bernays worked also for Hollywood, albeit briefly. Possibly recognizing how his talent best fit the task of promoting studio stars, William Fox assigned him in 1917 "the special handling of Theda Bara in *Cleopatra*." He devised catchy slogans and sought to appeal to respectable spectators by stressing the film's educational value (i.e., Egyptomania, Roman history, art history). But his plans clashed with an industry culture that in the case of Bara preferred "an easy stimulation of the senses and their imagination by powerful mass effects [and] by voluptuousness."[95] In publications and personal documents, he denounced Hollywood's sensationalist schemes as part of "a crude, crass, manufacturing business."[96] In a career that spanned decades, he rarely worked again for the film industry, preferring instead to collaborate with *Cosmopolitan* magazine, the publisher Bernarr MacFadden, and several large corporations.

Still, Bernays succeeded in his goal of redeeming the business of publicity from associations with Barnum-like trickstering to a semirespectable profession, one that he helped popularize as public relations. While his critics viewed his tactics as evidence of opportunism and deception, Bernays sought to invest his role with a serious intellectual status and an allegedly responsible social goal—as an opportunity to expand the knowledge of a busy public. He had learned valuable lessons about the critical role of established opinion leaders from the prince of publicity men, Ivy Lee. He had applied them as early as 1913, when he managed to have medical and religious authorities endorse a controversial stage play on syphilis, which eventually led to a widely publicized performance at Wilson's White House. What he ultimately perfected was the codification of strategies for the creation of newsworthy *events* and their widespread popularization through the use of experts or celebrities who provided "leader approval." In his view, even presidents could benefit from endorsement. In 1924 he organized a promotional event for President Coolidge's election bid. Asked to reverse the widespread opinion that Coolidge was "weaned on a pickle," Bernays thought of co-opting Broadway dancers and actors, including Al Jolson, for an official breakfast at the White House.[97] The pseudo-event aimed to produce stories and photographs of the president in the company of individuals who "symbolized warmth, extroversion and Bohemian camaraderie." At the event Jolson sang "Keep Coolidge." The headline on the *New York Times* front page read "Actors Eat Cakes with the Coolidges: President Nearly Laughs."[98] Bernays used these testimonials as part of a much-emulated strategy of publicity stunts, which he called "over acts," which secured free news coverage.

If advertising was an explicit plan to convey information to sell products or services, what Bernays practiced and later theorized was something that a 1926 study identified as "news publicity"—an oblique and much more effective way to market an idea, a product, or an individual.[99] "The intrinsic nature of news publicity material is news [. . .] News publicity is information, not argument," its authors asserted. "It educates, but does not sell. [It] is not directly concerned with merchandising, despite the fact that there is an occasional element of news in what is for sale."[100] Publicity, in other words, constituted a most effective form of information strategy when it masqueraded as news.

Bernays's celebration of "special pleaders" pervaded the 1920s. Notwithstanding Lippmann's eloquent and legitimate concerns for their impact on democracy, the practices that Bernays adopted, reworked, and endorsed became the modus operandi of film and political promotion and played no small role in shaping and enhancing the fame of Valentino and Mussolini. In a decade often derogatorily known as the age of ballyhoo, the industry could count on several Bernays-like figures who, albeit largely unknown and operating in the background, had no moral qualms about stunts and pseudo-events. In a two-part article, entitled "The Business of Motion Pictures" and published in 1927 in the *Saturday Evening Post*, Carl Laemmle commented on the role of "press agents' stunts" and the bad reputation that "exploitation" had attracted in the press and elsewhere. Defending the actions of "ballyhoo men" against moralistic detractors, Laemmle argued that "no matter what are the various views and definitions, exploitation, as I take it, is merely advertising the picture to the public in an unusual and convincing manner."[101] It was actually more than that.

To assess how Bernays's exemplary work contributed to the changes affecting film and press cultures, one has to go back to the Supreme Court's *Mutual Film Corporation* decision discussed in chapter 1. The stark distinction between the motion picture business, which for the court had no value as public interest, and the press was doubly contradicted by the facts. Griffith's radical and influential approach to motion pictures from 1915 on, together with the CPI's co-optation of Hollywood in 1917–1918, revealed that cinema was both a business *and* an organ of public opinion very much like the press—not one at the expense of the other. The press itself, in fact, was more than a mere conveyer of information and public opinion. It was also a private business and a fast-expanding one. Mainstream observers of the press's changes and workings were quite vocal about the illusion of any neat distinction between journalistic ideals and commercial realities.

In the late 1920s, journalist and author Silas Bent gave an enlightening public talk on the disturbing changes that had recently informed American journalism. Entitled "A Menace to Democracy: The Press in America—Is It Free?" and published in a 1929 volume, Bent's talk began by detailing the striking technological changes, from the introduction of economical pulpwood papers and photographic reproduction to transatlantic cables, that had turned a limited commercial enterprise into a mass industry with inevitable links to powerful commercial and financial interests.[102] The profitable partnership with advertising had dramatically lowered the cost of newspapers, inflamed harsh competition, and tilted news coverage toward sensationalism. While pro-reform editorialists may have launched crusades against profiteering, the same papers' news columns did not. Bent denounced the fact that the press was experiencing "grave encroachments on freedom of opinion and of speech" from both the business and political worlds.[103] While revealing the financial dimension of the journalistic profession, he noted that the massive revenue increase derived from years' worth of advertising made it "preposterous" to suppose that the news business could ignore its best customers. At work, in his view, was not just news distortion but a more sinister change in news making and news consumption that turned the reader from recipient of objective reporting into a "ready victim of the advertiser's exploitation."[104]

For Bent, the two key strategies were the deployment of "stereotypes," or "stories which appealed to primary passions and unconscious hungers," and the use of celebrities, evident in the press's penchant "to ballyhoo night club hostesses, bathing beauties, pugilists, baseball players, channel swimmers, stunt aviators and tennis stars, solely for the aggrandizement of its own pocketbook."[105] With a polemic tone suggestive of Lippmann, he concluded that in America "the manufacture of public opinion [. . .] is in the hands of private enterprise which thinks only of its own treasury and very seldom of the public good."[106]

The idealized distinction between private business and public good, between private and public profit, had been the basis of Progressive politicians' rhetoric. But the outcome of their actions, by an ironic heterogony of ends, intertwined private and public domains in creative new ways. In his dated but still useful study of business and public relations in early twentieth-century America, Alan Raucher questioned the conventional wisdom that opposed Progressivism to unfettered business. On the surface, Theodore Roosevelt and muckraking journalism had punctured the sacred inviolability of American business giants. In truth, however, Progressivism had provided a "rationalization of business through government regulation" which, in conjunction with the development of new methods of communication, had reformulated the role of American business in the country's polity.[107] American businesses may have acted in self-defense against Progressivist attacks. But in a move that appropriated a Progressive argument, they also developed a new public morality—or corporate social responsibility, as we might say today. In contrast to William Henry Vanderbilt's "the public be damned," uttered in 1882 in response to a reporter's question about railway routes and fares, the development of the public relations profession responded to modern corporations' new public-centered stance. It signaled the rejection of a model of unrestricted competition and laissez-faire in favor of one ostensibly based on the widest possible benefit and thus constantly engaged in the use of mass communication.

In this light, the heritage of Progressivism lasted beyond its usual chronological boundaries. By 1917, in fact, corporations that had faced public hostility and the threat of regulations were using publicity agents not just to counter attacks but also to publicize proto-welfare programs and new safety measures, as well as to promote management's close relationship with civic leaders.[108] News publicity was the preferred medium to "make a private cause look like a public cause and [. . .] to create of a public cause a public duty."[109] Some, like journalist and editor Harper Leech went beyond the straightforward assertion that public relations activities were the legitimate function of business and argued that they were none other than the guarantors of the right to free speech. In a 1927 polemical contribution, "Is American Business Entitled to the Rights of Free Speech?," Leech made a vehement case in the affirmative. In his presidentially appointed role as public relations director of the Railroad Labor Board, Leech stressed that American civilization had conferred "upon the masses benefits never before possible to them" and denied that business's "scientific civilization" had any "conscious social policy." Against the development and obvious benefits of capitalist enterprise, he denounced as "intellectual perversity" the positions of "radical college professors, kept liberals, [and] pink journals of opinion" who denied businesses "the right of free speech." Theirs was an "anti-capitalist" stance that, Leech happily noted, did not pervade mainstream media, which was becoming "a vast industry itself."[110]

We have come full circle. In 1915 cinema was regarded by the Supreme Court as simply a business and thus not as "organ of opinion" entitled to free speech. By 1927, it was not simply that the motion picture industry qua national industry was recognized as an organ of opinion but also that large corporations, and particularly public utility companies, had to operate as both businesses and organs of opinion. The Great War had played a role. Before 1917, public utility businesses had established a few practices that grew to national and international scale during the European conflict. As Raucher concedes, the Creel Committee introduced a "scope of its operations" on the national and international level that in 1917–1918 was unprecedented, and the government's involvement uniquely helped the publicity business gain the legitimacy of a professional vocation.[111] During the war years, the public status of American business was changing: private profit and public good were not in opposition any more, as the Progressive rhetoric had always intimated, but were running on seemingly parallel tracks. In the arena of public opinion, the regimentation of an old profession, variously renamed publicity agent, public relations counsel, and so on, discernably intertwined business and public interest.

Cinema did not remain impervious to these dynamics. During and immediately after the war, through a massive use of public relations activities pervading the press and public spaces, cinema emerged as America's most influential mass entertainment and, as such, a public utility of sort. At its center was a key public relations device, the authority of celebrities. As special pleaders, celebrities were deployed to manage the rise of American film spectators' attendance in lavish new movie theaters and to broadcast modes of behavior centered on the values of individualism, leadership, and success. The next chapter will show how the motion picture industry, just as it was acquiring the financial and managerial fundamentals of more established corporate entities, gained unprecedented commercial and cultural hegemony as an American industry both domestically and in the world. Eventually, as we shall see in parts 2 and 3, in synch with its ambitions for *transnational* appeal, Hollywood's celebrity culture found itself inevitably crowded with foreign figures and infused with international cultural models.

3

Wartime Film Stardom and Global Leadership

Charlie Chaplin and Mary Pickford led Pershing's Crusaders *and* America's Answer *into the enemy's territory and smashed another Hindenburg line.*
GEORGE CREEL, 1920[1]

PREPAREDNESS, WAR, AND CONSUMERISM

In the first chapter I discussed how U.S. government agencies set into motion a range of propaganda initiatives that relied on an unprecedentedly close collaboration with Hollywood. In this chapter I focus on the same wartime relationship from the standpoint of the film industry. Specifically, I am interested in exploring Hollywood's response to the heightened patriotic climate of the war years—before and during America's actual intervention—not in terms of individual films but in terms of the industry's pursuit of national significance. The war granted a novel political authority to some of Hollywood's greatest celebrities, particularly Mary Pickford and Douglas Fairbanks, turning them from icons of lowbrow amusements into recognized representatives of American patriotism. This dynamic occurred just as Hollywood sought to gain economic and cultural legitimacy through financial consolidation and international expansion. To support the war effort, the industry had to make sensitive decisions in terms of pleasing both patrons and exhibitors. If films with overtly patriotic themes helped advance the argument that filmgoing was not an irresponsible wartime amusement, they still needed to walk a fine line between patriotism and entertainment value. Taking her cue from an expression of the time, Leslie Midkiff DeBauche describes such a combination as "practical patriotism."[2]

In the years prior to America's entry into the First World War, the protection of the country was central to the debates surrounding so-called war preparedness. Men and women were featured in numerous films fighting to protect their home soil, including Sigmund Lubin's *The Nation's Peril* (1915), J. Stuart Blackton's *Battle Cry of Peace* (1915), and the Public Service Film Company's *Defense or Tribute?* (1916). Narratives and mode of address were not indifferent to gender. Elizabeth Clarke has showed that when the narrative action was about domestic defense, heroic women appeared regularly as daring defenders of the home or the nation.[3] The serials *Pearl of the Army* (1916) and *Patria* (1917), for instance, introduced the very possibility of foreign invasion but cast strong and independent heroines as the first line of defense. Played by star actresses Pearl White and Irene Castle respectively, these serialized adventure tales turned the political issue of preparedness into entertaining narratives aimed at the industry's largest segment—interclass and multiethnic female audiences. Released in conjunction with print versions in the Sunday papers, these serials popularized their elegant queens as fashionable models of vigorous Americanness, thereby contributing to a commodification of patriotism. As White's and Castle's politicization fully capitalized on their gendered identity, consumerism was inscribed in the logic of war necessity and thus not at odds with patriotic obligations to frugality and sacrifice.[4] Once the war began and narratives started focusing on military expansion and not defense, violent actions appeared as a "man's game."[5] Female heroine figure did not disappear, Clarke argues, but their stunning on-screen accomplishments were narrowed to a more polarizingly gendered necessity: military recruitment. Even in films released before the declaration of war, including *Womanhood, the Glory of the Nation* (April 1917), the promotional discourse shifted from celebrating the image of its star, Alice Joyce, to campaigns for male enlistment—despite the film's title.[6] But Alice Joyce was no Pickford.[7]

In her systematic assessment of Hollywood's film production during America's actual war engagement between April 1917 and December 1918, DeBauche has argued that "in proportion to the number of films [released], the number of films bearing any relation to the events of the war was small," amounting to 14 percent of a total of 568 titles. Half of those were newsreels or documentaries. Mainstream film producers did not exploit the war themes of preparedness or even full engagement and began releasing war-related films in larger numbers only around "September 1918, two months before the signing of the Armistice."[8] The limited number of war-related productions, however, did not imply that they were insignificant in terms of trade or public discourse. War-related films constituted half the industry's output of prestigious "specials," longer and more expensive productions, released between April 1917 and December 1918. Furthermore, the entire film industry, including producers, exhibitors, reviewers, stars, and spectators, were debating "the appropriate function of popular culture, especially during a period of national crisis."[9] Hollywood's response to the declaration of war was remarkable not just for what it did for the patriotic cause, but also for what it enabled the film industry to achieve culturally and commercially in the short and long terms.

In DeBauche's analysis, Hollywood's practical patriotism took two main narrative directions: an antagonist one, featuring ruthless German enemies, and a celebratory one, stressing American heroes' resistance and ultimate victory. Among the productions falling into the first category were "hate the Hun" propaganda films, which included *The Kaiser, the Beast of Berlin* (1918) and Raoul Walsh's *The Prussian Cur* (1918). Of the films in the second group, the most famous were Cecil B. DeMille's *The Little American* (1917), shot just days after the United States declared war and starring Mary Pickford, and D. W. Griffith's *Hearts of the World* (May 1918), starring Lillian Gish. Set in France, the latter repurposed the moralistic message of *Intolerance* (1916) with the urgent agenda of American patriotism, but its dated Manichean melodrama turned Griffith "from being the father of the cinema to being its grandfather."[10] His quintessential leading lady, Gish, seemed to be an outmoded "picture personality" that Pickford, with her multidimensional and extracinematic fame, was fast replacing.

LITTLE 100-PERCENT WHITE AMERICAN

By the time Pickford made *The Little American,* she had already become a paragon of film popularity and publicity. During the first days of block booking, Pickford's steady production of six or eight features a year, compared with Chaplin's two-reel shorts, had made her a distribution force for whatever company with which she was working.[11] More than any other star, she was uniquely capable of driving "the marketing of movie fan magazines, postcards, posters, trading cards, buttons, and photographs."[12] A savvy businesswoman, she managed her fame through control of her print visibility. Between late 1915 and late 1916, she signed a syndicated newspaper column, "Daily Talks," ghostwritten by her close friend and scenarist, Frances Marion.[13] The column offered "helpful beauty secrets, advice on friendships, and memories of her 'happy girlhood,'" and answered her readers' questions.[14] In one June 1916 column, Pickford/Marion enthusiastically praised the Citizens' Preparedness Parade that had taken place a month earlier in New York City. It was a daring move since, as Wilson was campaigning for reelection on an isolationist platform, military preparedness did not yet constitute a mainstream position. Still, the procession represented a call to arms because it awakened a patriotic spirit that Pickford's later involvement with the war bond drives would fully unleash.[15]

Of the eight films that Pickford released during America's involvement in the war, halfway into her career as Hollywood superstar, only *The Little American* (July 1917) and *Johanna Enlists* (September 1918) dealt with the conflict. The former was a blockbuster; the latter wasn't. Production for *The Little American,* under the direction of Cecil B. DeMille, began a week *after* the war declaration, on the same day the CPI was established, on April 13, 1917. Shooting continued during the national mobilization and was released on July 2, 1917, as the nation was preparing its armies to go overseas. Back in March, a month before production had started, Jesse L. Lasky had told DeMille that he wanted the film to arouse "the spirit of preparedness [. . .] in American girlhood and womanhood." Lasky wrote to DeMille that he intended to create a character that "typifies the spirit of the American Girl in War times, something that would portray a girl in the sort of role that the feminists in the country are now interested in—the kind of girl that dominates[, . . .] who jumps in and does a man's work when men are at the front."[16] Pickford's persona on and off screen conveyed an iron-willed patriotism without running the risk of destabilizing gender roles. *The Little American* inaugurated such charming and unthreatening political commitment in a way that ultimately shaped her later screen characterizations.

In the film, Pickford plays the role of Angela Moore, a young and naïve American woman from Washington, DC. Her first name and her birthday (July 4) make her a symbol of goodwill and American innocence. Angela is in love with Karl Von Austreim, a German American living in the United States. When the war breaks out, Karl is asked to return to his native land and join the fight as a German officer. Shortly afterward, Angela sails for Europe to assist her dying French aunt, and she survives a torpedo attack before finally reaching her destination. Her aunt has died, but Angela decides to stay and aid wounded French soldiers. When the German forces occupy and pillage the village, she becomes their prisoner and is almost raped by a drunken Karl, who stops himself only after recognizing her. After Angela persuades him to switch sides out of his love for her, he helps her smuggle information to the French army. Eventually caught, they are brought before a firing squad but are liberated by a timely bomb blast. One of the film's key dynamics is Angela's transformation from victim to a patriot who is unwilling to stand idle in the face of German atrocities. The intertitles that express her reaction eloquently capture and repeat Wilson's public stance with a timely and perfect rhetorical pitch:

> *I was neutral—'till I saw your soldiers destroying women and shooting old men! Then I stopped being "neutral" and became a human being! [. . .]*
> *I am done with you and your Emperor! I'd rather die free than live in the grip of your damnable "system."*

While her character's change of opinion is critical to the film's plot, it also encapsulates the different ideological positions of the time—from idealistic pacifism to practical preparedness to staunch military support. *The Little American* was one the most successful films of the entire war period, and Pickford's dramatic patriotic performance "cast the shadow of the war on all her films."[17] For instance, in June 1917 the *Duluth News-Tribune* hailed the film as an extension of her "moral, mental, and physical support of the flag."[18] Under the spell of the conflict, Vachel Lindsay later mused that "to repudiate this girl in haste is high treason to the national heart," since "democracy crowns those it loves."[19] It should not be surprising then that *The Little American*'s release coincided with the first circulation of Pickford's promotional tag lines "America's Sweetheart" and "Our Mary."[20] What is certain that the film served the Toronto-born Pickford as a springboard for her new patriotic reputation.

From the spring of 1917 and throughout 1918, the press extensively praised Pickford's support for the war effort: fundraising, giving speeches at benefits, and

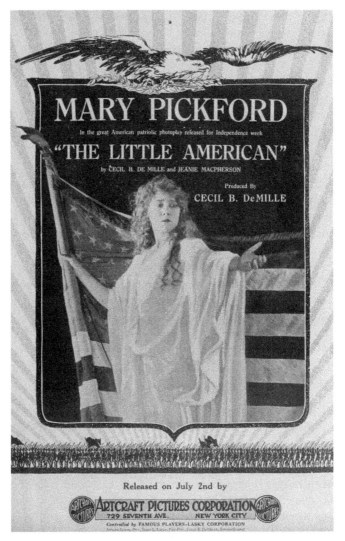

FIGURE 6. Advertisement for *The Little American* (Mary Pickford Co., 1917). *Motion Picture News*, June 23, 1917, 3833.

releasing the short, lighthearted comedy *100% American* (1918) to publicize war bonds. The most visible result of all this activity was the Third and Fourth Liberty Loan campaigns, held in both Washington, DC, and New York City in the spring of 1918 and featuring Pickford, Fairbanks, and Charlie Chaplin, among others.[21] After the New York drive, the stars brought the campaign to the rest of America along with their films: Pickford covered the West Coast, Fairbanks the Midwest, and Chaplin the South.[22]

The press described Pickford as a "modern Joan of Arc" and stressed that the actress had done more for the cause than "soldier, king, pot or prophet."[23] Throughout the latter part of 1917 and into 1918, Pickford enhanced her cinematic persona to the level of national cultural icon and opinion leader. Her growth as a public figure did not mean abandoning her long-standing association with roles of very young women characters. Almost exactly bookending *The Little American* were two productions that cast Pickford as an eleven-year-old girl: *The Poor Little Rich Girl* (March 1917) and *Rebecca of Sunnybrook Farm* (September 1917).[24] Nonetheless, something else had changed since 1916.

Until that year, Pickford had played many characters of non-European descent. These included a Native American in *Ramona* (Biograph, 1910) and *A Pueblo Legend* (1912), a Mexican in *Two Brothers* (1910), and a Filipina in *A Manly Man* (1911). Pickford played the majority of her nonwhite roles from 1909 to 1912 and, after a short hiatus, resumed playing them in 1915, by interpreting a Native Alaskan woman in *Little Pal* and a Japanese one in *Madame Butterfly*.[25] Yet, a year later, as Elizabeth Binggeli has shown, "these nonwhite characters abruptly disappeared from her repertoire."[26] After 1916, looking like Pickford meant looking indisputably white. This was not the case for other popular stars, including Norma Talmadge and Colleen Moore, who continued to be exoticized with dark makeup.[27] While it is true that Pickford's film impersonations in this period included frequent roles as little girls and even as unattractive women, as in *Stella Maris* (January 1918), these changes revealed her growth more in acting virtuosity than in racial adaptability. She could cast aside her maturity, her femininity, or her charisma, but "after 1916, Pickford did not cast aside her whiteness." Whiteness came at a dramaturgic cost. While in general an idealized white masculinity meant a "noble mastery over base bodily desires, including lust, greed, and violence," the idealized white femininity rested on the embodiment of virtue.[28] Yet, the mere display of virtue itself posed a challenge to narrative developments since generally it is desire, and not virtue, that provides dramatic intensity. The solution for Pickford's characters was to situate their whiteness in a preadolescent youth.

Critics and biographers have often discussed Mary Pickford's career in terms of the resilience of her roles as a child or a young girl against the frequency of more mature ones. In contrast to her amazingly savvy "creative authority over her silent film career," as Gaylyn Studlar has rightly noted, "many of her most important and popular films present her in the role of a child."[29] Still, if we look at her career in the context of the nation's preparation for and experience of the war, something else becomes clear. Out of the fifty-two feature films in which Pickford acted, she plays a little girl in only seven of them, and in only three does she remain a child throughout the story. Significantly, these three films are from 1917, the first year of America's war involvement: *The Poor Little Rich Girl, Little Princess,* and *Rebecca of Sunnybrook Farm.* Further, her post-1917 collaboration with the former combat correspondent Frances Marion, whose contribution to Pickford films at least from *The Poor Little Rich Girl* on was particularly evident in the pungent humor of the intertitles, helped consolidate Pickford's association with the playful and vital stubbornness of her young characters.

By relying on "juvenescence, virginity, righteousness, feistiness" and embodying a "hyperbolic white femininity," Pickford could embrace a virtuous and resourceful screen persona capable of "tragedy with innate feistiness."[30] Rather than facing immutable bodily and social limits, her character could achieve final victory through "her indomitable white spirit."[31] It was the victory of a young white person's free spirit that overcame either the narrative stasis associated with traditional female roles or the doom linked to an apparently insurmountable inferior identity.[32] Her screen persona, in other words, embodied the combative and energized possibility of growth and self-improvement rather than that of resignation and invariable destiny. The comedy effects of some of her films derive from the relief, as Binggeli has noted, "that her backwardness is merely a product of acculturation and dirt, not a problem of blood."[33]

By largely impersonating white characters and by being Anglo-Saxon herself, Pickford had it both ways: she could effortlessly display racial privilege while aligning herself with the early-twentieth-century framework of "personality," which identifies an individual not on the basis of an inner core or unchanging character, as was typical in the nineteenth-century epistemology of personhood, but from acts of self-improvement and performance.[34] During the war years, in other words, Pickford's film characterization coherently intertwined youth and whiteness into a celebrity who, beyond her innocent impersonations and wholesome acting style, exuded racialized patriotism and success from every pore.

Her prewar and wartime screen presence and her visibility on magazine covers, in product advertisements, and on postcards had stressed a coherent image of a down-to-earth everywoman, sporting long, dangling, golden locks but also capable of saucy banter and heroism. On screen and off, Pickford projected ideas of indomitable courage and moral righteousness into her films' domestic and foreign markets. After having stopped playing nonwhite roles and after years of impersonating white working-class or immigrant figures, her American charm became synonymous with white people's resilience and resourcefulness. Her characters' actions amounted to a "hunt for happiness and beauty in the face of misery and ugliness," which embodied two prewar American attitudes: "the 'practical idealism' of Herbert Spencer's Social Darwinism, and the advocacy of social change of Lester Frank Ward's Reform Darwinism."[35]

In the 1920s Pickford's political import and recognizable style, made of classically simple tastes in fashion and couture, turned out to be somewhat at odds with the growing popularity and appeal of transnational actors of less immaculate whiteness. To best frame our understanding of this shift, I shall first address the war's impact on the stardom of the other all-American superstar of the time, Pickford's soon-to-be husband, Douglas Fairbanks. Secondly, I shall discuss the postwar reorganization of the industry in terms of financial consolidation and cultural institutionalization that increasingly led Hollywood to appreciate its public relations clout abroad as well as domestically.

FAIRBANKS, DEMOCRATIC AND ELITIST

Publicity at any price has become the predominant passion of the American people.
ANITA LOOS, OPENING TITLE, *HIS PICTURES IN THE PAPERS* (1916)

A star of the New York stage, in the spring of 1915 Douglas Fairbanks transitioned from light stage comedies to light film comedies that revealed an appealing "masculinity that danced a national optimism through speed, agility, and aggressiveness."[36] In late 1916, George Creel, soon to head the CPI, wrote his admiration of Fairbanks's "dynamic individuality,"[37] and a few months later *Photoplay* foresaw his career as "not only a triumph of acting but a *national expression*."[38] Starting with his film debut and throughout the second half of the teens, Fairbanks's Americanness emerged in spirited, resourceful, and optimistic characterizations that turned gangster and Western narratives as well as comic melodramas into social satires and energy-filled sermons. His comic adventures addressed widespread anxieties about office life, corporate hierarchy, and careerism and their combined threat to virile American manhood. His films often combined a romantic narrative with a free-spirited display of masculine instincts juxtaposed to the danger of overcivilization, usually represented by a corporate office job. As Michael Kimmel and others have shown, the regeneration of American masculinity was inherently contrary to the pervasiveness of corporate desk jobs with their modern sites (i.e., office buildings), technologies of interaction (i.e., typewriters and memos), and social encounters, particularly between individuals of different gender and national backgrounds.[39] In a modern workplace that had finally allowed women, though mainly as typists and stenographers, exclusively white male homosociality was a thing of the past. Fairbanks's leading roles provided two recurring types of masculine self-affirmation and adaptation to these new environments, neither of which were particularly open to interactions with novel types of female characters.

One quality unifying his films is the light, satirical tone of his characters' actions and viewpoints. As Alistair Cooke remarked back in 1940, titles like *His Picture in the Papers* (February 1916), *Reaching for the Moon* (November 1917), and *A Modern Musketeer* (December 1917) "parodied, with no discernable time-lag, the pattern of a rapidly changing social scene."[40] With a very American and at times very populist taste that Fairbanks himself helped fashion, his characters "briskly demolished" several affectations of his day, including "the Eastern clubman, pacifists, blue-bloods, ouija boards, slumming parties, pictorial journalism, nervous breakdowns, bobbed hair, and Couéism."[41] This playful and humorous disapproval confirmed Fairbanks as the same jovial star underneath the clothes of whichever character he was playing. Mostly set in present-day America, his satirical films were also self-reflexive regarding the nature of Hollywood fame. At the end of *His Picture in the Paper*, after Fairbanks's character has secured enough press coverage to prove his manhood and marry his beloved, the final winking intertitle, "Ain't he the REEL hero?," teasingly associates the story's narrative arc with the made-up nature of film celebrity. In his volume on Fairbanks, Richard Schickel has aptly argued that the post–World War I novelty of celebrity status pertained to "the realms of play" rather than to the traditional notion of worthy achievement.[42]

Still, satire did not exhaust his characters' approach to the issue of masculinity in a corporatized world. Fairbanks's more practiced solution was the revitalizing adventure set in the West or in faraway lands. This had already been apparent in *The Lamb*, his first film. As the weakling son of a wealthy New York family, his character undergoes a transformation through time spent in the wilderness. Given the fame of Theodore Roosevelt as the most prototypical masculine hero of such transformative narratives, Fairbanks's audiences could appreciate both the "farcical excesses" of his performances and the familiar "stereotype of the westernized Easterner."[43] "In this West," Studlar has noted, "even a mollycoddle could attain a manhood in which natural primitive urges found expression because such experience recapitulated the past."[44] While these transformations were generally interlaced with a good dose of comedic and athletic antics, in times of war the regenerative power of the "wilderness cult" maintained a vigorous cogency.[45]

Most of his screen roles did not explicitly address the European conflict or America's subsequent involvement. Still, Fairbanks's public contribution to the Liberty Bonds campaigns, through public appearances and promotional films, allowed his persona to become an all-American icon.[46] In a remarkable photograph from one of his public appeals, taken on April 8, 1918, Fairbanks is seen campaigning for the Third Liberty Drive at the Sub-Treasury Building in New York City, now the Federal Hall National Memorial, transfixing a large crowd beneath American flags and sharing the platform with an imposing statue of George Washington (figure 7).

Despite his intense visibility at these rallies, his only film to address war mobilization explicitly was the antipacifist *In Again–Out Again* (April 30, 1917), released three weeks after the U.S. declaration of war against Germany and following months of division between promoters of preparedness and pacifism. In the film Fairbanks is Teddy Rutherford, a properly named advocate of preparedness, engaged to a dull and pale girl named Pacifica Jennings—named after the former antiwar secretary of state, William Jennings Bryan. In addition to scenes meant to deride peacemakers, the display of Teddy's athletic energy and vigorous handshake aligns the film's ideological stance with one of the war's most familiar proponents. Written by Anita Loos and directed by her husband, John Emerson, the film was

FIGURE 7. Douglas Fairbanks speaking about Liberty Loans in front of the Subtreasury building. Photograph from the Douglas Fairbanks Collection, General Publicity, Academy of Motion Pictures Arts and Sciences. Courtesy of AMPAS.

the first one to be released by Artcraft Pictures Corporation, a distributor for Paramount. Artcraft marketed it by flooding newspapers with "full-page ads stating that Uncle Sam congratulated Fairbanks on 'his great patriotic picture [, . . .] the most timely feature in months, teeming with action, patriotism, thrills and laughs.'"[47] The film and its campaign burnished Fairbanks with a novel patina of patriotic pride. Other Rooseveltian references would soon follow in his works.

A few Fairbanks films from 1917 juxtaposed country and urban lifestyles by making explicit references to the personality of his lifelong idol, President Roosevelt, and his known fondness for the strenuous life. In the comedy-Western *Wild and Woolly* (June 1917), Fairbanks played the son of an eastern railroad tycoon, sophisticated and fond of dime novels but unaccustomed to life on the frontier. Once he is sent to the West to investigate the feasibility of a new railroad route, he proves himself to be a pugnacious leader and is rewarded with success and romantic love. The same Rooseveltian contrast between corrupting city life and regenerative country life was also at the center of *The Down to Earth* (August 1917), which a critic dubbed as "a five-reel Fairbanksian sermon for Teddy Roosevelt."[48]

Along with Roosevelt, another of Fairbanks's heroes and a close friend, at least for a while, was the religious preacher Billy Sunday, a "baseball evangelist" who shared his athleticism, goodwill, and sense of tough-minded brotherhood.[49] Between 1908 and 1918, roughly corresponding to the emergence of Fairbanks's career, Sunday delivered his popular sermons in week-long road shows, filled with tricks, speeches, and athletic entertainments.[50] In 1918, Fairbanks and this "gymnast for Jesus," as Sunday was often dubbed, appeared in baseball uniforms at a benefit to raise funds for American soldiers in France. To many the two figures seem to have congenially similar personalities. The friendship did not last. Although Americanism had a positive ring for domestic audiences, it could easily turn into aggressive nationalism. When Sunday's post-1918 sermons favored the extermination of the German race, Fairbanks was nowhere to be seen.

Fairbanks's religious vocation, which consisted of preaching the optimistic sermon of physical fitness against social ills, pretensions, and fears, made him akin to what Cooke described as a "popular philosopher."[51] This was not just an effect of the films on which a loyal group of collaborators routinely worked—from the aforementioned Loos and Emerson to writer-directors Allan Dwan and Joseph Henabery. It was part of the Fairbanks brand, which promoted character building through physical fitness and was broadcast in interviews, fan magazine columns, and biographical profiles, as well as several ghostwritten volumes, including the bestselling *Laugh and Live* (1917) and *Making Life Worthwhile* (1918).[52] "He was a muscular itinerant preacher," Cooke pointedly observed, "sailing gaily into the social novelties and the occupational neuroses of a new era dizzy with growing pains."[53]

During the war years, a new facet in Fairbanks's screen characterizations began to appear, though it would fully develop only in the 1920s: an elitist tendency suffused his persona in a few films made between 1917 and 1919. Fairbanks's characters were increasingly transformed from outsiders, who were quick to deride the rituals and pretensions of Old World nobility, to American aristocrats. Joining the familiar routines of social mockery and derision was a novel endorsement of personal ambition and entitled leadership. As an explicitly American outcome, such celebration solved the apparent contradiction between social and national predestination and individual merit.

America has always had its elites. In the preindustrial period, elites marked their difference from the nouveaux riches through an emphasis on ancestry, education, and taste. Any individual achievement had to be balanced and filtered by membership in clubs, Blue Books, and private schools. A few Fairbanks films from this period foreground these tensions between aristocracy and merit-based individualism. In *American Aristocracy* (November 1916), he plays Cassius, a preindustrial "natural" aristocrat and scion of one of America's first families. Although he is named after the Roman senator who conspired with Brutus to kill Caesar, this historical figure's repute in contemporary America was that of honorable patriot, capable of killing a dictator for the creation of a republic.[54] Cassius-Fairbanks operates in a world that looks down on "upstarts," "climbers," and trade in general. While Cassius is virile and daring, his romantic rival is a fearful malted-milk manufacturer. Cassius invents a new hatpin that makes him rich: in combination with his prestigious lineage, such an outcome represents the perfect American amalgam of earned success and aristocratic predestination. This conjunction of a sense of special distinction with the notion of American exceptionalism recurs in *The Americano* (January 1917), *Reaching for the Moon* (November 1917), and *His Majesty the American* (August 1919)—all set in imaginary republics and kingdoms.[55] In these films Fairbanks is no longer the gymnastic evangelist but a new American aristocrat who sports the Hamiltonian mantle of autocratic leadership and who, due to his inherent superiority, is able to bring democracy to Europe and Latin America.[56] Fairbanks's works, even in their comedic tempo, exuded a Rooseveltian temperament that bestowed upon his protagonists a cogent ethic of personal and global leadership.[57] For instance, *His Majesty the American,* released a few months after the signing of the Treaty of Versailles in June 1919, provides an example of *"imperial reach"* that powerfully appropriates Old World traditions and Americanizes them by sheer force.[58] The costume adventures of the 1920s, set in distant times and exotic locations, showcase a more aggressive American aristocratic character without losing the familiar ironic touch. From *The Mark of Zorro* (1920) and *Robin Hood* (1922) to *The Iron Mask* (1929), Fairbanks would often become the champion of the oppressed in distant countries or centuries—a neat conjoining of Rooseveltian masculinity with Wilsonian idealism.

Pickford's and Fairbanks's respective wartime cultivation of an all-American identity would expand after the war. The two stars took part in the post-Armistice Fifth Liberty Bond drive (April 1919), known as the Victory Loan, during which they continued to publicize their good relationship with the president (figure 4). They also continued to position themselves as dignitaries at home and in the international scene. Before returning to discuss their postwar careers, we need to examine the financial and commercial infrastructural context that made postwar American cinema dominant domestically and internationally and enabled this couple to remain a paragon of all-Americanness in 1920s film and public culture.

HOLLYWOOD POWER AND PERSUASION

The war provided a jolt to the challenges that the film industry had been facing since well before the U.S. military went to Europe. These included films' standardized length, commercial incorporation and financing, studios' publicity hype vis-à-vis promotion of screen personalities, and threat of censorship vis-à-vis the industry's aspiration to cultural relevance. The war helped to reframe such challenges by repositioning American cinema nationally and internationally. For instance, the recasting of the geopolitical and financial relationships between the United States and European countries significantly affected Hollywood's commercial reach, institutional role, and ideological import. Stars turned out to be privileged vectors for film companies' balance sheets and domestic market shares, as well as for Hollywood's emerging public profile as a main driver of national and international public opinion.

The drive toward cultural institutionalization and financial incorporation had started even before the studios were set up in Hollywood. By the mid-1910s, producers had begun to adapt to the new feature-length format and reduce the number of pictures. The trend escalated during the war. Although the conflict and the Spanish influenza diminished foreign distribution, the overall decrease in the number of titles and reels was also part of a deliberate "fewer and better" strategy.[59] Out with the cheaper pictures, in with "specials," which, while often associated with stars, secured higher rental costs, longer runs, and higher admission prices. Even independent productions featured celebrities as several stars sought to acquire independence from mainstream studios, avoid paying income war tax, and produce works of higher artistic merit.

During the war, Famous Players–Lasky and the First National Exchange Circuit began acting like integrated corporations that competed over stars' salaries and credits. The company led by Adolph Zukor was originally a studio that entered the distribution business after it acquired Paramount. First National followed the opposite path: from distribution to production. Established three weeks after the U.S. declaration of war, it brought together independently owned theaters and state rights franchisees to consolidate exhibitors' interests against Paramount's controlling distribution practices. Most prominent among such practices was block booking, wherein the major studios forced exhibitors to rent packages of minor films in order to secure stars' pictures. First National's strategy was to corner the exhibition business by creating alliances among the country's most prominent movie theaters and forcing scores of small, independent, and rural movie houses out of business. In a system of flat rental fees, theater chains had gained much clout over distributors. Competition between Zukor and First National raised the need for outside financing to acquire, control, or build movie theaters and produce films featuring ever more expensive stars: "the single most important factor determining a film's box office success."[60] Pickford and other screen icons found themselves in the middle of this war and sought to benefit from the practice of star-series distribution.[61] Between 1917 and 1918, First National began to hire away Zukor's precious commodities: Pickford, Chaplin, and Lillian Gish, as well as Constance and Norma Talmadge. Zukor's response provided the second act of his ongoing battle with First National.

After 1919, emboldened by a fresh infusion of stock financing, Zukor began building and acquiring controlling interest in numerous first-class movie theaters (more than three hundred theaters by mid-1921), which had been First National's initial key asset.[62] In response, through mergers and Wall Street financing, First National entered directly into the field of production by building its first studios in California. Meanwhile, taking advantage of the ongoing duel between Zukor and First National, film exhibitor Marcus Loew created MGM in 1924 by merging Metro Pictures Corporation with Goldwyn Pictures Corporation.[63] By the mid-1920s, a few vertically integrated corporations came to dominate the industry through their control of theaters and the employment of a variety of "monopolistic trade practices such as block booking, blind bidding, price fixing, and a system of unfair clearances and runs."[64] If these could be seen as the unredeemable features of a shady business, the regularity of profits, the secure financial return of stars' contracts, and the acquisition of prime real estate (or "fixed assets in the balance sheet" in accountants' parlance) reassured Wall Street that the film industry was a solid business.

Financing film production, directly or through securities, had already been attempted before the war, but after Triangle Film Corporation's 1917 financial debacle, the industry underwent a number of structural changes, particularly in terms of partnerships among exhibition outlets or between production and distribution firms.[65] Broader conditions had also changed. Film stardom had grown into a giant national and international cultural phenomenon; Hollywood exercised a novel hegemony in international distribution; and Wall Street firms had amassed tremendous liquidity in conjunction with massive credit extended to European banks and companies. This last point deserves closer examination in light of its larger geopolitical implications.

Even during America's neutrality, the war had offered new commercial and financial opportunities to American companies that maintained relations with all belligerents in the conflict. According to historian Mary Nolan, "U.S. exports increased from $2 billion in 1913 to $6 billion in 1916," and several banks, most prominently J. P. Morgan and Company, were the beneficiaries of these international transactions.[66] To pay for these war goods, Britain sold its foreign investments, sent gold to America, and borrowed billions from U.S. banks. The consequences of Europe's massive dependency on the United States were significant: the Old World lost its prominence in the world's financial and commercial traffic, America "moved from being a debtor nation to being the world's number one creditor," and "New York replaced London as the center of world finance."[67] It was a momentous change in the "character of transatlantic and global capitalism and consumer culture."[68] A new global geofinancial nexus would also soon shape Hollywood and American film culture.

To conduct its foreign policy, the U.S. government began to engage private financial interests in projects of unprecedented scale and reach. Wall Street firms started conducting financial rehabilitation of foreign countries in the service of the U.S. national interest. While masking the projects as civilizing missions, these firms became "financial missionaries to the world."[69] The internationalization of the American film business was part and parcel of a geoeconomic policy that aimed to secure the political stability of countries identified as important to U.S. governmental and business elites. War propaganda made it easy to appreciate that a successful policy of American economic intervention would turn foreign countries into investment sites and markets for American goods and lifestyles.[70] The Wilson administration had been active on this front early on. The Webb-Pomerene Act of 1918 granted immunity from antitrust regulation to companies that, once organized into exporting cartels, operated in a trade deemed to be essential to the war effort.

Geopolitical strategies brought structural changes to the home front. With the strengthening of the U.S. commercial and financial sectors, as Wasko has noted, "more money became available for industries that were proven according to the investment community's standards." By the end of the war, the film business had begun to meet those requirements by developing basic industrial methods and establishing both a national distribution system and an international one that extended to the Far East and South America.[71] Quite importantly, as the film industry began to oversee its international reach from New York City and no longer from its London offices, it came to center both global film distribution and finance in the United States.[72]

Beginning in 1919, a new era of movie financing began. Studios turned to investment banks to raise funds by selling stocks and bonds or turned to commercial banks to secure loans. A February 1920 article in *Variety*, while inaccurately prophesying the imminent involvement of J. P. Morgan, described the unprecedented incursion of Wall Street's financing power into Hollywood's commercial sovereignty as an "invasion."[73] While there is no evidence that J. P. Morgan considered entering the film business before the 1930s, other bankers did, including Otto and Felix Kahn of the investment bank Kuhn, Loeb and

Company and Amadeo Peter "A. P." Giannini and his brother Attilio Henry Giannini of Bank of America.[74] After establishing itself as a rival to J. P. Morgan through considerable financial involvement in the railway business, during the war Kuhn, Loeb and Company managed to establish a credit relationship with France and with the city of Paris. In 1919, flush with financial resources, the firm underwrote a $10 million stock issue to Zukor's Lasky Corporation/Paramount, the most important film company in America and thus in the world.

Kuhn, Loeb and Company's financial decision was based on domestic and international considerations. Before proceeding, the company had commissioned H. D. H Connick, vice president of the Morgan-controlled financial firm American International Corporation, to do a complete study of Famous Players–Lasky.[75] Filled with statistics and financial data related to imported and exported films, box office receipts, and numbers of foreign movie theaters, the study concluded that the largest returns were in exhibition, not production. Addressing the widespread concern that stars' salaries were a major industry problem, the report described compensation as a matter of supply and demand and identified performers as the key to a film's exhibition and financial prospects.[76] The report praised Famous Players–Lasky's stars and directors, who gave tangible value to the company's films, but also suggested, in an overt recognition of the role of publicity, "a more aggressive sales campaign" to increase domestic and foreign rental returns.[77]

Though the report was undated, its emphasis on publicity coincided with the publication of a special section on film publicity in the July 1918 issue of *Moving Picture World*.[78] The section ran thirty-five pages and included a snapshot history of publicity and short articles "by the leading motion picture publicity men," some thirty department heads and press agents. One of the contributors, James L. Hoff, defined publicity in opposition to advertising. While advertising consisted of "display announcements written by an ad writer," Hoff argued, publicity consisted of "text matter that is written by a press agent." The key difference pertained to cost: "the display is paid for and the publicity is not."[79] For many other contributors, the value of free publicity depended on press agents' ability to tailor a message to a specific newspaper's needs. "The newspapers want short stuff, snappy and to the point, and so written that it does not have to be rewritten," maintained one of them.[80] Publicity could effectively migrate from a studio's press office or the desk of a star's agent onto a newspaper page if it could masquerade itself as news and secure the widest possible attention as such.

Possibly more openly than any other banker, Otto Kahn showed great appreciation for the ways the film business could mold public opinion through news publicity. In an address entitled "The Motion Picture," delivered at the Paramount sales convention banquet on May 2, 1928, in Washington, DC, he spoke as an industry advocate. He intertwined praise for motion pictures' soundness as both a business and a vector of public sentiment with the recognition of their

American, democratic, and even idealistic value.[81] To explain how motion pictures took hold of "the emotional impulses of the people" and represented the most effective democratic factor in American life, even ahead of the automobile and the radio, he told of a curious historical coincidence. He recounted the public response to the deaths of former Harvard University president Charles William Eliot and, of all people, Rudolph Valentino, which in his account occurred on the same day, August 23, 1926.[82] Both deaths made news, but the reactions of the American media and people were dramatically different. For the Harvard president, Kahn remarked, "public opinion rendered respectful and reverential tribute."[83] News of Valentino's death, in contrast, "brought forth a veritable flood of popular grief, expressing itself in almost hysterical demonstrations as his body was transported across the country." As a response to those who had denounced the disparity of merits and reactions, not to mention the questionable taste of public demonstrations, Kahn pointed out what today might seem obvious: cinema's unique capacity to arouse mass responses.

Rather than being a cheap or morbid fad, Kahn continued, for many millions, Valentino represented "the very embodiment and symbol [of] romance, beauty, grace, chivalry, and youth" because "his art and personality on the screen had endowed, enriched, and beautified their lives."[84] News of his death revealed motion pictures' triumph as a most appealing modern phenomenon worthy of most serious cultural consideration—and thus beyond the fact that "the credit facilities [. . .] are ample [and] their securities have a ready market." Kahn invited his audience of investors and businessmen not to linger on high-minded objections but to appreciate the distinctively American features of motion pictures' popularity and to consider the commercial and geopolitical advantages of American cinema's world success.[85] As both art and popular entertainment, Kahn posited, motion pictures "present a striking parallel to that dualism of the spiritual and material which I consider as one of the most notable and distinguishing characteristics of America." For Kahn, cinema constituted that most American combination "in fifty-fifty proportion" of "hard-headed business capacity and deep-seated idealism" that could secure major geopolitical returns.[86] As a wartime practitioner of coupling financial returns with propaganda, Kahn was a most credible postwar advocate of aligning Hollywood's international commercial success with American cultural influence. His speech ultimately sought to persuade his listeners to divorce cinema from mere entertainment and appreciate it instead as "an advertising medium of remarkable effectiveness in making known all kinds of American products throughout the world" and thus in shaping world's public opinion about the United States.[87] Kahn's reference to film stars as Hollywood's prime commodity showcases his understanding of their role as the nation's ambassadors in advertising testimonials. It is now time to turn to this dimension of the motion picture business—that is, the enormous role of international film distribution and its key publicity vehicle: the stars.

GLOBAL REACH

American film manufacturers need a world-trade, not merely a local fetch-and-carry.

PHOTOPLAY, 1921[88]

One of the most important dynamics affecting postwar American cinema was Hollywood's growing worldwide hegemony. The war favored U.S. companies in the competitive European markets by, for instance, cutting off France from Central and East European markets and the Germans from the Allied film circuits.[89] According to a 1930 *Harvard Business Review* article, by 1925 American films made up to 95 percent of the total shown in Great Britain, 70 percent in France, 65 percent in Italy, and 60 percent in Germany. "Few American industries," the business periodical concluded, "are more dependent on foreign markets than the motion picture industry."[90] By the late 1920s, foreign markets amounted to about 35 percent of Hollywood's total income.[91] Together with Wall Street financing, the income from foreign distribution helped studios seek control or ownership of the best domestic theaters, raise their films' production values, and compete for and develop top global stars. In turn, these additional commercial and entertainment advantages helped sustain Hollywood's success abroad.

This outcome resulted from several concomitant factors but also stemmed from a sustained collaboration between Hollywood and the U.S. government that went back to the First World War. The American film industry received key logistical and publicity help from the CPI during the war. By virtue of the U.S. government's control of the wireless, cable, and postal services across the Atlantic, the CPI was able to place said services at the disposal of the film industry, particularly through the Foreign Film Division. All told, "some 24 nations were sent 6,200 reels of American pictures."[92] In return, the CPI received the authority from the War Trade Board to issue licenses to Hollywood films destined for the world's markets, which Creel used to distribute CPI works. The same licensing clause applied to foreign exhibitors, who, if found exhibiting German films, were prohibited from receiving Hollywood fare. Distribution of the latest Signal Corps and American commercial films to Allied populations brought together the government and the film industry's respective goals: war propaganda and commercial profitability.[93] To paraphrase Creel's famous sentence, Chaplin and Pickford led *Pershing's Crusaders* and *America's Answer* across territories where they would have otherwise remained unseen and unwanted.[94]

While Creel's intention was to exercise a good measure of control over foreign film markets, the resulting CPI policies achieved unexpected long-term results. As the U.S. government broadcast American values and lifestyles through printed and visual media, Hollywood stars nurtured habits, expectations, and the international appetite for even more American culture. "The advertising that America obtained [. . .] by the CPI," Larson and Mock recognized, "played no small part in the great commercial expansion enjoyed in the 1920s."[95] The industry took advantage of this partnership. In the summer of 1917, the National Association of the Motion Picture Industry (NAMPI) "was elected to membership in the U.S. Chamber of Commerce," which signaled its "recognition within the wider business and financial community."[96] In 1918, during negotiations over foreign film distribution, Hollywood obtained recognition of its distinct patriotic and educational role, which extended not just to "news weeklies, screen magazines, [and] American travelogues" but also, as a NAMPI-CPI agreement reads, to "films purely entertaining in nature, but which clearly portray some idea of American life and purpose."[97]

The combined effects of the weakening European film industry and American cinema's growing hegemony over Europe mainly through block booking and direct control of major movie theaters were long lasting. The trade expressions of the time, "Film America" (for Hollywood) and "Film Europe" (for a pan-European film industry devoted to Continental coproductions), informed a wave of press coverage that characterized their relationship as nothing short of an "undeclared war." "In a ridiculously short time span," wrote a German trade paper in 1926, "Film Europe has become a colony of Film America."[98]

The conventional view about the 1922 establishment of the Motion Picture Producers and Distributors of America (MPPDA), replacing NAMPI, is that the latter found itself to be ineffectual in protecting the film industry's public stance from the many scandals that had tarnished it in the late 1910s and early 1920s.[99] Wall Street investments had to continue and the alliance with the government had to be reinforced against the censorship calls made by religious and moral constituencies. While historically valid, this argument tends to overlook that the MPPDA's newly appointed head, Will H. Hays (formerly Republican National Committee chairman, manager of Warren G. Harding's successful presidential campaign, and U.S. postmaster general), had two main goals: to ward off censorship legislation and to enhance Hollywood's international domination. The order of priorities might even be reversed. "The MPPDA's original bylaws," notes Kristin Thompson, "charged it to represent the industry's interest abroad."[100] In Hays's hands the MPPDA ultimately operated as a public relations machine that changed Hollywood's actual import, not just its image, in the country and the world.

To quash calls for federal censorship, Hays stressed an approach that relied on industrial organization and an idealization of "self-government."[101] To represent the film industry's international interests, Hays relied on a Wilsonian rhetoric of universalism that was clearly accented with notions of exceptionalism. He promoted cinema as enhancing "the international understanding by the peoples of the world" but maintained that only "America in the very literal sense is truly the world state. All races, all creeds, all men are to be found here."[102] But he also publicized and practiced the Wilsonian principle that "western ideas go in with the western goods" and the selling of American goods will "convert the people of the world to the principles of America."[103] In a 1923 speech delivered in London,

Hays outlined the international aims of the film industry: "we are going to sell America to the world with American motion pictures."[104] "Trade follows the films" became a trope in film and business periodicals.[105]

While embedding his defense of the film business into a universalistic and suggestive rhetoric of republican ideals of democracy and self-determination, it is not surprising that Hays viewed the MPPDA "almost as adjunct of our State Department."[106] After developing a strong collaboration with the U.S. Department of Commerce, whose Bureau of Foreign and Domestic Commerce offered key assistance in gathering information on foreign markets and critical advice for negotiating foreign countries' protectionist policies, Hays fostered an even closer alliance with the State Department.[107] He understood that an alliance with the government departments responsible for negotiating with foreign governments would be instrumental in expanding the film industry's global presence. While the United States may not have had a clearly defined domestic or a foreign film policy, Hays did. In his view, Hollywood facilitated America's global economic and political preeminence within a new global cultural perspective. By the same token, the recognition of America's place in the world impacted the nation's self-understanding and appreciation of what cinema could be as powerful global vernacular.

At a time when, in Victoria De Grazia's words, "hard-bound lines [. . .] still divided the high and academic from popular and mass cultures" in Europe, American cinema's popularity made Europeans question "whether old-world states still exercised sovereignty over their citizens' leisure."[108] Was American culture so powerful and pervasive because of the country's decisive role in winning the war, superior industrial and commercial organization, and ensuing economic occupation of foreign film industries? Or was it because it uniquely appealed to European audiences of all classes through its dynamically acted and appealingly shot stories of optimism, resilience, and final justice? In other words, was Hollywood success the result of power or persuasion? De Grazia notes that European commentators touched upon both explanations but, she maintains, "arguably, American movies were more responsive to consumer desires than European films," particularly in conveying new, attractive "social identities" that exuded glamour and individual achievement.[109] Although they had emerged out of a distinctively multinational Pacific Coast outpost and displayed a sort of "Norman Rockwell preciousness," these figures—Hollywood stars, that is—appeared to Europeans unmistakably American.[110]

To spectators at large, no matter their national, class, or ethnic background, Hollywood stars appeared as models of individual distinction, enviable lifestyles, and universal desires. To the studios, stars represented loyal brands, vectors of high and standardized quality, sold to both exhibitors and audiences and publicized to the point of saturation in tabloids, film periodicals, and even the daily press. If the war had helped to sell America, the celebrities of the 1920s were doing the heavy lifting at a time when the advertising industry was relying on their mass appeal to design its pitch and reach. Referring to a 1917 *Vogue* article entitled

"Great Actors, as Other Great Men, Are More Alive Than the Herd," Jackson Lears notes that the great actor was exploited as cheerleader, "rousing inert masses into disciplined enthusiasm." As "redemptive celebrity figures" and "demigods on the field," Hollywood stars "became standard features in the testimonial advertising that blossomed after the war."[111]

What was there to sell? The narrative and stylistic appeal of American cinema relied on the aestheticization of an ideological cosmos at once American and universal, animated by such values as freedom, youth, optimism, and leadership.[112] During the war and immediately after, Pickford and Fairbanks were two of the most authoritative—and marketable—representatives of this etiological universe whose aura reverberated far outside movie theaters. As democratic leaders of public opinion, at least for a few years, they did not seem to have many rivals. And yet, in the 1920s, their all-too-American allure left a wide-open space for different kinds of marketable characterizations.

PICKFAIR'S OLD DIGNITARIES

Beginning in the early 1920s, despite her continuous success, Mary Pickford's much-praised image of innocence and virtue became increasingly at odds with the new national mood and with her own real age. "America's Sweetheart" sought to move away from her traditional roles as young girl, but the results were mixed. In the ten reels of *Little Lord Fauntleroy* (1921), she gave an unprecedentedly bravura performance as both a boy and his mother, but her role as Spanish street singer in Ernst Lubitsch's *Rosita* (1923) was too much of a radical departure from her public image. Her 1920 marriage to her boy-man did not mean the end of her conventional childish roles, made of curls and long skirts. But the conservative image was a paradox for her career. While the aestheticized nostalgia she continued to exude in film after film, from *Through the Back Door* (1921) to *Sparrows* (1926), was particularly successful in small-town America, it condemned her to being an anachronism.

Opposing her curls was the bobbed hair of the flapper, who became synonymous with the modern, worldly woman, who was American in youth and sexual daring but cosmopolitan in manners and fashion. Between 1919 and 1920 Alla Nazimova, Constance Talmadge, and Gloria Swanson adopted the new hairstyle just as the passage of the Nineteenth Amendment had begun to have a special significance for younger generations of fans who viewed new grooming and dress codes as evidence of expected emancipation. Unlike Pickford's characters, real and fictional flappers were young women comfortable with their overt sensuality, as Clara Bow, Louise Brooks, and Joan Crawford were to reveal. By the middle of the decade, gossip columnists were publishing career obituaries about Mary Pickford. Her "reign is over," the former unofficial Valentino publicist Herbert Howe noted in 1925: "she has outlived the popularity of her type." In her place, he wrote, "We now have with us the flapper generation that rolls both its socks and its cigs, and even hips a flask now and then."[113] The flapper's worldliness did not just signify her loss of innocence and a bold assertion of sensuality; it also signaled a cosmopolitan that reproduced the "infinitively more attractive [. . .] sophistication of old Europe."[114] After describing the flapper as "the most authoritative and intelligent movie reviewer," Howe elected her as the true "representative public" vector of the new Hollywood taste, since "it doesn't matter much what men like; the women lead to the box office."[115]

Throughout the 1920s, the domestic authority Pickford had gained as a cultural icon during the war kept declining. America was elsewhere, and Pickford, now in her late thirties, had overextended her youth. When Pickford had her hair bobbed after her mother's death in June 1928, the event made the front page of the *New York Times*.[116] Grief, rage, and disappointment were some of the sentiments expressed by her nostalgic fans. Even though her first talking picture, *Coquette* (1929), became her biggest box-office success and secured her an Academy Award for Best Actress, the career of "the Bank of America's sweetheart," as Zukor once called her, was ending.[117] Her popularity remained strong abroad, where her enduring American appeal was always connected to the figure of her dashing, energetic, but also aging husband.

In the 1920s, Fairbanks's popularity and characterizations were changing too. In longer and ever more expensive productions, set in past fictional worlds without flapper-like female coprotagonists, his roles became less and less about social satire. Instead they promoted a proud, often juvenile display of all-American male leadership—even if the character was not American. Regularly set in a familiar literary past, his 1920s films cast him as a hero-leader whose ironic take on distant settings and cultures showed him off as morally and physically superior. In truth, his characters did not exactly emerge as champions of democratic and egalitarian values and were not really revolutionary figures. Instead they appeared to support a strong and legitimate authority, often in the name of a noble personal background fueling his courage, chivalry, and leadership. They may have been outlaws and rebels, but they were often aristocrats by heritage (Don Diego in *Zorro* and Robin of Huntingdon in *Robin Hood*) or had earned royal attachment (d'Artagnan). In other words, his screen persona held an elitist allure, one that insisted on the nobility of birthright, character, and deeds. At the same time, while operating in distant lands and remote times, his characters turned a certain primitivism of manners into a primary, almost nostalgic, scene of governance. No matter the character or century, the larger-than-life Anglo-Saxon Fairbanks was always a leader to his socially inferior followers, including women. The commoners and citizens who inhabited his films' exotic worlds appeared grateful to submit to his aristocratic and starlike authority and functioned as social décor in narratives in which justice was ultimately served and conflicts were neatly resolved—as in *The Mark of Zorro, Robin Hood,* and *The Black Pirate.*

Fairbanks's characterization had also a Wilsonian dimension that idealized fair governance against usurpers, illegitimate rulers, and just plain cruel tyrants. He was the recognizably American hero "working on behalf of 'the people' to support and restore the people's regimes of Spanish governors in the two *Zorro* films [1920, 1925], King Richard the Lion-Heart in *Robin Hood* [1922], and Louis XIII and XIV, respectively, in *The Three Musketeers* [1921] and *The Iron Mask* [1929]." With admirable leadership skills, "Fairbanks did similar deeds while deposing a wicked Mongol usurper in *The Thief of Bagdad* [1924] and a totalitarian South American dictator in *The Gaucho* [1928]."[118]

His characters did not intend to take over the world, only to return it to its rightful leaders. Their toppling of authoritarian and cruel regimes was set in a mythical and easily romanticized past, not in the present. For Siegfried Kracauer, that was a telling sign. "Douglas Fairbanks, the gallant champion of the oppressed," the German critic remarked, "goes to battle in a previous century against a despotic power whose survival is of no consequences to any American today."[119]

Rather than subvert unfriendly contemporary forms of governance, these nostalgic pageantries articulated a different kind of liberation. Fairbank's celebrity on-screen and off appeared to address a widely felt need for the revitalization of American masculinity. By virtue of his characters' superior moral vigor and athletic skills, his costume adventures sought to restore and perpetuate the wholesome virtues of the ideal American male. It is not surprising, then, that in film after film Fairbanks's characters remained juvenile figures, both diegetically and iconically, and were shielded from emotional and narrative involvement with the new feminine types. In this regard, Fairbanks's 1920s swashbucklers also paid peculiar homage to boys' literary favorites of the time, from Dumas's *The Three Musketeers* to *Robin Hood* and the *Arabian Nights,* or featured a son eager to please a father figure (i.e., *The Mark of Zorro, Don Q, Son of Zorro,* and *The Black Pirate*). In contrast to his films from the teens, his character- and leadership-building narratives showcased protagonists who walk a fine line between comedic playfulness and a marked desire for justice and paternal approval.[120] In *The Mark of Zorro,* Don Diego Vega is both the effeminate young man, or mollycoddle, and the fearless and righteous hero who confronts and defeats the local despot and realizes his father's most unlikely expectations. As such, Fairbanks's 1920s films indulged in a patriarchal past that, set in faraway places, oppose a virile, active masculinity against a passive femininity. "The star's retreat into a fictional past," as Studlar has acutely noted, "secured a place where his protagonists could continue their heroics without confronting those adult prerogatives and impurities made synonymous with the Roaring Twenties."[121] His characters' exuberant male energy was thus safely reinscribed in reassuring narratives of male heroism and unambiguous sexual roles. Neither flappers, competent and erotically powerful women, nor deviant effeminate males were anywhere to be seen in his films. His all-too-insulated film roles deflected any tension between his characters' diegetic youth and his biographical age.[122] Instead, they joyfully took children and nostalgic adult spectators into a world "when life was life, and men were men," as one of the intertitles of *The Three Musketeers* reads.

When Douglas Fairbanks and Mary Pickford were married in 1920, their love story had the whiff of a scandal, since both had divorced to be together, but also the enduring quality of a fairy tale. They were America's royals after all.[123] At the height of their fame, they were known as humble royalty, old-fashioned trend-setters, and politically conservative. Their magnificent and exclusive residence of Pickfair, the "Buckingham Palace of Hollywood," was the site of official indus-try functions and entertainments, regularly covered by the press as a matter of course.[124] Pickfair "became the nation's second White House and the crossroads of the world for boldface names," from Albert Einstein and Amelia Earhart to King Alfonso VIII of Spain and Babe Ruth, to name a few. The two royals "were, in all but name, unelected officials of the U.S. government, and they shirked none of it."[125] As iconic embodiments of health, sobriety, and good humor, they also became national and industry spokespeople, especially outside the United States. During their trips abroad, they were regarded, as Pickford herself acknowledged, as "ambassadors, not only of the motion picture industry, but of our own country."[126] For a while, at least.

As the 1920s went on, the heroes of the Liberty Bond campaigns found them-selves restricted to typecast roles that, though still popular at the box office, were increasingly seen as passé. The nation that had catapulted them to world fame and turned them into models of physical activity and innocent youth was grateful to the couple but was also intrigued by not-so-all-American ambassadors and public opinion leaders. The two stars' meeting with Mussolini in Rome in 1926 seems to exemplify this delayed passing of the baton to a different kind of celebrity—surprisingly, a foreign one.

In theory, several phenomena should have countered Valentino and Mussolini's degree of nationwide popularity in the political and cinematic affairs of 1920s America. The Great War's aftermath led to the rise of isolationist and nativist sentiments. Politicians and intellectuals urged the end of what they deemed to be messy political entanglements in international affairs, and their articulation of hyperbolic nativist positions and eugenic hierarchies led Congress to pass unprece-dented immigration restrictions.[127] How then could two racially othered foreigners become leading figures in America? Further, how to explain their popularity vis-à-vis the nationalizing trajectory of wartime film stardom that had anointed Pickford and Fairbanks as the most popular icons of an all-American national spirit? And finally, how could two icons of chauvinist Latin masculinity become pub-lic opinion leaders in a nation that was undergoing a major democratic expansion in terms of gender equality, social mobility, and political representation? In part 2, I address these questions with respect to Valentino's career trajectory and reveal the critical role of mediators—namely, unofficial publicity agents and various kinds of promoters—in the development and consolidation of his popularity. In part 3, I focus on Mussolini's heavily mediated popularity in America during the same period. Both sections focus on two interrelated postwar dynamics pertaining to the *internationalization* of American film narratives and characters and the rising *transnational* appeal of foreign, racialized masculinities.

PART TWO

The Divo, or the Governance of Romance

4

The Divo, New-Style Heavy

*You know producers can't make stars. The public makes stars. You can't make
a star by writing the name on a lot of advertising. [. . .] Nobody can make
stars of nothing.*

ADELA ROGERS ST. JOHNS, *PHOTOPLAY*, 1922[1]

TRANSNATIONAL AMERICA

During the first years of the twentieth century, the American film industry was
compelled to produce films of clear national significance capable of prevailing
over foreign films' competition. Richard Abel has described this process as the
"Americanization of American cinema."[2] The outbreak of World War I furthered
this phenomenon but also introduced, at least in highbrow intellectual circles, an
opposing, post-melting-pot formulation of Americanism. As we saw in chapter 2,
from the mid-1910s onward, progressive intellectuals like Kallen, Bourne, and
James came to acknowledge America's constitutive openness to transnational
influences. This notion eventually moved from the lofty pages of highbrow
periodicals to more popular ones. By the war's end, film journals had begun to
recognize the critical role that America's national diversity played in U.S. films'
propaganda effectiveness. In 1918 Louella Parsons argued that America's "cosmopolitan population of mixed races" was what enabled Hollywood to "reach the
very people Germany is struggling to get into its clutches."[3] Similarly, film periodicals praised both the seamlessness with which foreign immigrants become
American film spectators and American film culture's inclusion of foreign characters and representations. In a 1921 *Photoplay* article entitled "Making Americans
by Movies," Max Watson argued that the Americanizing process did not start at
Ellis Island, where educational films were shown, but abroad where would-be
immigrants first learned about America before embarking on their long journey.
"Wherever one goes the world over," he wrote, "[the traveler] finds the American
movie, for ninety per cent of the motion pictures of the world are American."[4]
The flip side of Watson's proud statement was something that his own periodical
had been covering for some time: the multinational openness of film culture. In
an illustrated, full-page editorial in 1918 entitled "The Melting Pot" and devoted to

Isaac Zangwill's famous play from a decade earlier, *Photoplay* published a remarkable polemical plea:

> Zangwill's vision is to today's actuality as an assayer's flame to a blast furnace. In the roaring converter of war more than nations are fusing. [. . .] The Iowa lad is learning that the French aren't frog-eaters, nor are the Italians "Ginnies."[5]

Five years later, *Motion Picture Classic* identified American cinema's fondness for foreign settings and characters, particularly European ones, as an index of a widespread inclination unknown a few years earlier. The article compared the phenomenon to nothing less than a psychological fixation:

> Hollywood is undergoing a European complex. Nearly every production now filming, or in immediate prospect, has a foreign setting. Witness: "Ben Hur," [. . .] "The Hunchback of Notre Dame," "Scaramouche." [. . .] The scene of every one of these plays is laid abroad.[6]

While the discursive emergence of a transnational and cosmopolitan America did not defeat anti-immigration policies in Congress, it contributed to spreading a notion of *cultural pluralism* that permitted popular appreciation of foreign personalities. Still, how could two foreigners be made into national celebrities? How could any embrace of foreign masculinity be made not just possible but also desirable?

COSMOPOLITAN MASCULINITY AND ITALIANNESS

In *Manliness and Civilization: A Cultural History of Gender and Race in the United States, 1880–1917,* Gail Bederman offers one of the most articulate contributions to the history of turn-of-the-century American manhood. First, she clarifies the terms of the question. She names manliness as the idealized notion of male identity that since the early nineteenth century had pervaded American society. Its chief traits were "moral character, high-minded self-restraint, and virtuous self-mastery." For over a century, she argues, manliness represented *the* source of middle-class men's authority over women and the lower classes.[7] By the 1890s, however, manliness and middle-class identity were noticeably faltering. The causes were diverse: economic crisis and a prolonged post-1893 depression, related to large-scale capitalist competition; greater demand for urban clerical jobs in large, anonymous corporations; increased gender and racial diversity in the labor force; movements for women's suffrage; immigrants' left-leaning political engagement; and the expanded role of consumer culture in shaping class and gender identities.[8] Different causes but, in Bederman's analysis, a convergent result: ideas and practices of racial distinction were used to recast ideas and practices of manhood. "As white middle-class men actively worked to reinforce male power," she argues, "their race became a factor which was crucial to their gender."[9] A novel attention to corporeal features, particularly regarding race, became pivotal to middle-class white men's attempt to remake manhood in order to sustain their cultural and political power. European immigrants and working-class men provided useful examples. The popularity of saloons and music halls, with their displays of plebeian muscular virility, led to a reformulation of Victorian manliness through the adoption of a cult of strenuous life that translated into physical prowess, pugnacity, and sexuality. Taking decades to unfold, this trajectory from idealized to corporeal manhood, or *masculinity*, produced several iconic characters, popular practices, and institutions, including the widely admired Prussian muscleman Eugene Sandow, Theodore Roosevelt's Rough Riders, and the growing popularity of college football and YMCA. According to Bederman, this complex recasting was rooted in the invocation of a notion of civilization that while seeking to balance nature and culture, served to relegitimize hierarchies of race, gender, and class.

The broad tension between civilization and primitivism resulted in two different outcomes. The first relied on opposition: imperialists and nativists maintained that only civilized white men possessed the racial genius for self-government, a status that implied the subjugation of primitive races—both at home and abroad. The second was one of appropriation. Against the risks of overcivilization and "neurasthenia," to use a contemporary term,[10] the other option was to embrace the racially impure and plebeian notion of muscular physicality while simultaneously gentrifying it. Popular culture fostered this safe transformation and developed it on a grand scale.

Several major cultural events can be read in this light. The exceptional popularity of the 1910 fight between Jim Jeffries and Jack Johnson, which opposed "Protestant virtue" (and whiteness) against "uncivilized [black] savagery," managed to lift boxing to a defining arena of white men's male identity. Not despite but because of Jeffries's loss, the event signaled the embrace of physical force as a marker of new masculinity. Likewise, Edgar Rice Burroughs's widely successful *Tarzan of the Apes*, serialized in 1912 and published as a book in 1914, combined the best of two worlds: as the scion of British aristocracy who was lost and raised by apes, Tarzan effortlessly masters the laws of the jungle and displays a double primacy: a noble and civilized morality in an exuberant, primitive body. The inclusion of forceful (and sexual) physicality into the definition of gender identity was not to be an exclusively male affair, however. In 1913 Burroughs also serialized the adventures of a sensual "cavegirl," and the same cultural tenet reemerged in the 1922 best seller *Caveman within Us*. Primitivism came to hold a wide appeal for "civilized" white audiences.

Unleashing primal instincts could also be done with style. Growing attention to the body, in the context of the growing consumer culture, enhanced other forms of gendered identity that were rooted in physical strength or athletic ability as well as elegance, sexuality, and youth. This was a dynamic that brought together white men and women—the flapper and her lesser known boyfriend, the bachelor— around insistent consumer fantasies that challenged Victorian ideals of diligence, thrift, and self-control (for him), domesticity (for her), and selflessness (for both).[11] If the flapper represented a new urban female figure, the bachelor had precedents in the "dude" of the nineteenth century (who was marginal and often ridiculed), as well as in the iconic British dandy and the Continental flâneur. At a time of soaring college enrollment, greater job opportunities in the cities, and a flourishing consumerism geared toward younger people with disposable income, unattached bachelors and uncommitted flappers fostered a peer-based, sensualized, and hedonistic youth culture. It centered on fashion and seduction strategies visible at dance halls, billiard parlors, and movie palaces. Even advertisements for men's clothing contributed to broadcast a "sporty and virile image in ordinary life that guaranteed stylishness but not at the cost of effeminacy."[12]

The heterosocial culture of this "flaming youth" came with new rules prompted by the development of exotic music and dances that were associated with different races and geographies. In nightclubs and public dance halls, jazz, the fox-trot, and especially the tango allowed for new casual rituals of courtship in an elegant atmosphere of risqué displays of youthful desire and exotic sex appeal.[13] While soon to be accepted in America, one need only think of the flaunting sexual primitivism of Josephine Baker's famous banana dance that debuted in Paris in 1925. Not all primitivisms and not all alleged primitives, however, were acceptable. How would the new masculinity of the Divo and the Duce fare in relation to American racial dynamics of the 1920s? Their Italianness, after all, could have hindered as much as fostered their acceptance as American role models.

In American silent films, Italians had come to occupy a varied but not unlimited range of characterizations. Through the aesthetic and centuries-old prism of the picturesque, Italians' cultural foreignness and alleged anthropological dissonance had unfolded into two main types of appealing but othering representations. The first one insisted on their backwardness and domesticated primitivism, mostly through love melodramas of passionate jealousy and heartbreaking loss. The second one relied on a notion of innate criminality, unfolding in stories of impossible-to-romanticize violence. From 1915 on, however, the American stage and film actor George Beban had become the master impersonator of tragic but *sympathetic* Italian subjects capable of undergoing moral domestication amidst heartbreaking circumstances. In such feature-length immigrant dramas as *The Italian* (1915) and *The Sign of the Rose* (1915 and 1922), his performances enabled American audiences to develop an intense emotional solidarity—although not necessarily an identification—with heavily racialized white, foreign characters.[14]

Meanwhile, other narratives about Italian immigrants had begun to appear after Behan's rise to fame. Written by female screenwriters such as Sonya Levien, Anita Loos, Jeanie Macpherson, June Mathis, and Frances Marion, these dramas of transoceanic migration and tenement life did not reproduce Beban's safe trajectory of adaptation. They featured female protagonists, not male characters, engaged in passionate and controversial love stories that questioned conventional ideas of American morality and propriety. While presenting the departure from the Old World as a journey that severed oppressive traditional ties, titles like

A Woman's Honor (1916), *The Ordeal of Rosetta* (1918), and *Who Will Marry Me?* (1919) explored questions of social freedom and personal sexual expression without any of Beban's noted moralism.[15] Such daring narratives can be viewed as symptomatic of broader changes in American culture. At a minimum, though, they tell us about Hollywood as a powerful dynamo that created new character types and ideas of personal fulfillment that were not evident in the country's social and cultural landscape. As film periodicals boasted, "Motion-Picture Land" was an ideal living space filled with independence-seeking women of different backgrounds and uncommon talents. If the West had represented a virile space for many of Fairbanks's Rooseveltian characters, "the modern West's possession of Hollywood," as Hilary Hallett showed, "created perhaps the most powerful generator and lure for a New Western Woman in full flight from feminine norms."[16] The trope of democratic access, informed by a new sense of self-reinvention, identified Hollywood as not just a center of national and world film production but also a capital capable of modeling spectatorial experience and consumption.[17] It may have been a dream factory, but "women's remarkable record of influence inside the movie colony of this era was no fantasy."[18]

Against the stereotype of the "movie-struck girl," the growth of women's presence in early 1910s Hollywood corresponded to the film industry's efforts to turn the boisterous and plebeian films into a profitable family-friendly entertainment. It was a move that enabled and then capitalized on the post–World War I emergence of American film and fan culture as women-oriented, given the prevailing gender of both moviegoers and screen magazine readers. The results were, however, not just conventional morality tales of family reunion and romantic love but also stories that pushed the boundaries of traditional female roles.[19] Consider the film heroines of such serials as *The Adventures of Kathlyn* (1914), *The Perils of Pauline* (1914), and *The Exploits of Elaine* (1914). Centered on plucky female characters who prefer harrowing adventures to conventional family roles, the serial queen melodramas represented one of the first attempts by the film industry to cater to female patrons on a national scale.[20] The culture of these films challenged the notion that increasing female film patronage went hand in hand with the industry's efforts to attain a higher moral respectability. "Serial content was anything but tame," Shelley Stamp argues, "and reports of audience behavior suggest that fans conducted themselves in anything but a 'respectable' manner."[21]

In the same period, women began to enter many areas of the film industry itself under the shared, though not enduring, assumption that women knew best how to cater to the female spectators.[22] Even though women occupied several critical positions at the creative and management level, in no other field were women as powerful as in screenwriting.[23] Women wrote "at least half of all silent films," were among the highest-paid and most-recognized screenwriters, and "were responsible for crafting many of the era's landmark screen personalities (Mary Pickford, Rudolph Valentino, Douglas Fairbanks, Clara Bow, and Gloria

Swanson)."[24] Women screenwriters made an impact on a number of genres, including the social-problem film and the historical epic, but they left their most recognizable mark in the creation of modern narratives about romance and marriage.

During and especially after the war, the expansion of work and consumption possibilities for young women created the material conditions that allowed many to envision equality in marriage and in romantic relationships. These changes did not exactly correspond to the aspirations of generations of suffragists culminating in the passing of the Nineteenth Amendment. As Frederick Lewis Allen perhaps too dismissively noted in his iconic *Only Yesterday,* "few of the younger women could rouse themselves to even a passing interest in politics."[25] Still, Hollywood screenwriters embraced the novel civic arrangements and wrote scripts that explored new secularized forms of gender relationships that distanced themselves from traditional religious prescriptions. In the postwar context of an expanded suffrage and corporatizing Hollywood, the film industry turned women's search for emotional and sexual expression into a management strategy for consumer and ideological choices through, once again, the mediating power of the actor testimonial. Only this time, the daring reimagination of marriage and romance unfolded within a much tighter framework of promotion and consumption. Cecil B. DeMille's films in the late 1910s and early 1920s starring Gloria Swanson and largely written by Jeanie Macpherson walked a fine line between the new demands for equality, self-expression, and the appeal of consumerism.[26] While mostly adopting a female perspective, *Old Wives for New* (1918), *Don't Change Your Husband* (1919), and *Why Change Your Wife?* (1920) commodified marriage by stressing the intrusion of trendsetting fashion and consumer taste into romantic relationships. In these star-centered films, to quote Lary May, "leisure became an egalitarian arena."[27] Through the exemplary mediation of the star, Hollywood studios sought to bypass film audiences' segmentation by gender, class, and race (and their respective subcultures) by appealing to a broader, more democratic fascination for consumer goods. More accessible and less elitist, the democratization of aspirational luxury turned Los Angeles into a daring and flashy adversary of Paris as the new arbiter of national and international fashion.

Multitudes of female (and male) spectators were made to see stars as models for the commodified democratization of their lives. The pervasiveness of the star system, particularly through the promotional input of fan magazines, accompanied the same massive education and influence pursued by the advertising agencies. At the same time, the industry's rhetorical positioning of moviegoing as a democratic practice cast audiences' choice of favorite films or stars as a free and *spontaneous* exercise. Spectators' preferences rewarded personalities who appeared to possess character, charm, and sex appeal. Nothing allegedly was supposed to stand between stars and audience according to a logic of unfiltered access, reception, and pleasure. In reality, the process by which audiences identified their favorite stars was hardly as spontaneous and democratic as film magazines made it out to be.

Populist and star-centered explanations helped to conceal the role of a whole host of intertextual mediators, including fan magazines, and public relations specialists who molded audiences' reactions and directed their preferences to this or that figure according to both traditional, tried-and-true tactics and new tricks.

The case study of Valentino helps us understand that, by enabling the commodified democratization of American women spectators' lives, stars did not have to be female themselves and did not have to be American. Still, they were required to be white. The Divo's association with the celebrated, century-old myth of the romantic and sensual Latin lover not only shielded him from association with the vulgar hordes of Southern Italian immigrants but also made his performances function as an exploration of female desire that his all-American male peers could not themselves replicate.[28] This may explain why Valentino, particularly after achieving nationwide notoriety in 1921, was never cast in the role of a contemporary immigrant landing and striving in America.[29] He was a *Hollywood* Italian, after all, not a New York one.

NEW-STYLE HEAVY

Because *The Four Horsemen of the Apocalypse* is customarily identified as the first relevant item of Valentino filmography, scholars have paid scant attention to what he did or what was known about him before March 1921. On closer inspection, this may not be prudent. The reputation Valentino developed in New York, particularly during a sensational high-society scandal, arguably functioned as a primacy intertext for the publicity discourse that informed both the design and reception of his early film characterizations. Usually mentioned only in passing, Valentino's pre-*Four Horsemen* career allows us to reconstruct his trajectory toward mainstream acceptability from his early characterizations as a slick, evil foreign deuteragonist, or "a new style heavy"—the category he used to describe himself under the name of Rodolfo Di Valentina in the 1918 *Motion Picture Studio Directory* (figure 8).[30] Pre-1921 titles may help explain how the perception of a foreign actor who often impersonated charmingly exotic villains provided screenwriters the basis to design characters' possible moral conversion and allowed publicists to harness his scandalous charm.

In fact, scandal is where we ought to start. After arriving in New York from Italy in December 1913, Valentino sought to make use of his background in agronomic sciences, but his first serious job as gardener on a Long Island estate did not last. Following Italy's entry into the First World War in 1915, he even sought to enlist in the Italian army—an event that would appear in several of his (auto)biographical profiles—but was turned down for poor vision by the Italian Recruitment Bureau. Finally, he found a semblance of financial stability as a dancer for hire in New York's musical clubs, where he was known by his given name, Rodolfo Guglielmi. Starting a career as a "taxi dancer" did not immediately translate into film roles,

RODOLFO DI VALENTINA
Playing a New Style Heavy
in
Joe Maxwell's First Feature
" THE MARRIED VIRGIN "
Address: 7369 Sunset Boulevard
HOLLYWOOD, CAL.

FIGURE 8. Rodolfo Di Valentina playing a "new style heavy." *Motion Picture Studio Directory and Trade Annual* (New York: Motion Picture News, 1918), 193.

save as a movie "dress extra" in New York film productions, but it gave him an opportunity to flaunt his talent as gifted dancer and seducer.[31] Taxi dancing, in fact, was available for unchaperoned, well-off married women in search of a Continental-looking, fashionable young companion. Among the society women who gathered at the so-called tango temples, "dreading that they were going to be shocked, and fearing they were not," Valentino built a reputation as a typical "tango pirate."[32] Yet, his life was not restricted to this potentially lurid trade. Hired by Broadway musical dancer Joan Sawyer in 1916 and touring with her on the Keith circuit, he even danced at a New York roadhouse for President Wilson. These gigs enabled him to meet actors who would later become friends and supporters, including Mae Murray and Norman Kerry.

In 1917, however, he hurriedly left New York following his turbulent involvement in legal proceedings that had dominated the gossip press throughout the previous year. He had agreed to serve as witness in the divorce case of a New York socialite, Bianca de Saulles, with whom he had been allegedly involved. His testimony attracted the vindictive ire of her powerful and soon-to-be former husband, Jack de Saulles. A friend of Wilson and cousin of a recent New York City mayor, Jack de Saulles was known to have strayed from the marriage much more often than his wife ever did. He arranged for Valentino to be arrested on the pretext of a white-slavery investigation in the home of a notorious madam who had been accused of blackmailing wealthy New Yorkers. The vice charges were ultimately dropped, and Valentino was released. Still, what has recently been described with retrospective hyperbole as the "Valentino affair" and the "Jazz Age murder scandal that shocked New York society and gripped the world" was not a minor public event.[33] As many commentators later recounted, the press published disturbing (but inaccurate) accounts of his confession. For instance, the *New York Tribune* reported that he admitted being "a bogus count or marquis" but also added District Attorney Swann's description of Valentino as "a handsome man" who "wears corsets and a wristwatch" and "was often seen dancing in well-known hotels and tango parlors."[34] As a homophobic insinuation about his masculinity, this coverage constituted a prolepsis of the infamous *Chicago Tribune* "Pink Powder Puffs" editorial that a few years later would provoke Valentino's fiery reaction. At the time Valentino did not yet have access to the powerful publicity enablers or friends who could have responded in kind to allegations against his masculinity or spun public opinion to his advantage. A minor figure on the fringes of polite society and mired in scandal, his best option was to leave town. Later that summer, Bianca de Saulles, unhappy about the custody agreement following her divorce, shot and killed her husband. The name Rodolfo Guglielmi resurfaced in the press. By then, he had fled to California.

The scandal followed him in ways that both threatened and shaped his career. His presumed association with white slavery, blackmail, and homosexuality left a persistent and unsavory mark on his reputation. Yet, even though several newspapers eventually issued retractions, the initial coverage's long-term impact was not entirely negative.[35] Although it appears that the court records have remained sealed since 1917 and his arrest record mysteriously disappeared in the early 1920s, Valentino did not forget the infamy that the charges had brought him. "At the height of his fame, the world kissing his hand," publicist Herbert Howe wrote in a posthumous article, "he could not forget the three days he spent at the Tombs prison of New York on a false charge. [. . .] The retraction was small compared to the headlines that had damned him."[36] If Valentino could not forget, neither did the publicity machine that ultimately surrounded him.

Initially, in order to escape from the coverage of the de Saulles scandal, Valentino moved to San Francisco. Mary Pickford was there for the production of *The Little American,* which had cast his friend Norman Kerry for a minor role. Encouraged by Kerry, Valentino made a few trips to Los Angeles to look for employment both in and out of the film business.[37] His first Hollywood bit role was in *Alimony* (First National, 1917), written by Hayden Talbot, where he met another extra, Alice Terry, who would be his partner four years later in *The Four Horsemen of the Apocalypse.*

One of his earliest roles was that of a somewhat sympathetic character in *The Married Virgin* (Maxwell Productions, 1918), which was distributed only in 1920, both with its original title and the alternate one, *Frivolous Wives.*[38] Directed by Joe Maxwell, the film was adapted for the screen by Hayden Talbot, the screenwriter of *Alimony,* from one of his own stories. While the original 1918 credits identify Valentino as "Rodolfo di Valentini" (with promotional material using "di Valentina" instead), later prints, including the restored one I examined, report his name as "Rudolph Valentino" in capital letters. *The Married Virgin* is a minor film, but the names of the conventional lovers, Doug and Mary, whose romance Valentino's character briefly but successfully threatens, are an obvious reference to Mary Pickford and Douglas Fairbanks. In 1918, while married to other spouses, they collaborated on several Liberty Bond drives, which fueled speculations of a destined affair. Valentino's hard-to-resist and intrusive erotic appeal in the lives of the fictional Doug and Mary is an emblematic prolepsis of his soon-to-be much publicized threat to conventional romantic scripts.

In *The Married Virgin,* Valentino plays the role of Count Roberto di San Fraccini, "an Italian nobleman and soldier of fortune," as one intertitle notes, who dresses impeccably in black, rides a black horse, and appears ambitious and morally unencumbered. His main occupation is as the illicit lover of a married woman, Mrs. Ethel McMillan. Obsessed with fashion, Count Roberto is a master of manners and seduction, as revealed by a lingering close-up of him gallantly kissing his older lover's hand (figure 9).

Upon learning from Ethel that a man is blackmailing her husband, a wealthy political operator, Roberto plots a criminal and financial scheme. The blackmailer claims that he can produce a revolver that Mr. McMillan had used to kill an enemy many years back. The count first plans to interject himself in the deal by also blackmailing Ethel's husband in exchange for the infamous gun (which he does not possess) and eloping with her. After the plan fails, he proposes an alternative to Ethel: he will marry her stepdaughter, Mary, to secure her dowry before escaping with Ethel to South America. The problem is that Mary is engaged to Douglas, a young lawyer, and the two of them form an apparently inseparable all-American couple. Roberto disrupts their idyllic love of romantic rides on their white horses with his sinister and opportunistic charm. He pays Mary a visit while she is spending time at a seaside resort without her fiancé. While the film should depict his scheming attempts at seducing Mary as utterly disagreeable, it instead lingers on his Old World gallantry and athletic skills. The unexpected intimacy between Roberto and Mary, evident in intense conversations and playful morning swims, grows intense, while his professional ambitions keep Douglas busy and distant. Although in her letters Mary reassures him about her loyalty, her prose notably does not hide her admiration for the mischievous Italian nobleman ("the most wonderful athlete I ever saw"). But soon Roberto reveals his calculating nature. He proposes marriage to a shocked Mary "with all the confidence a hundred conquests inspire" and later self-assuredly explains to her father that the "wedding is self-protection" and that "there *shall* be—a marriage settlement" (emphasis in the

FIGURE 9. Valentino's appealing gallantry in *The Married Virgin* (1918), frame enlargement. Courtesy of CINEMATEK, Brussels.

intertitle). Mary succumbs to the plan only after learning from Ethel that unless she weds the "fortune hunter," as Ethel describes him, her father will go to prison.

While the moral compass of the film's overall narrative appears unambiguous, the depiction of the charming Roberto does not invite complete condemnation. Shortly after the wedding, Roberto reveals a surprisingly sympathetic side. After being reassured about the post-wedding check in exchange for the infamous revolver, he appears respectful of Mary's body and emotions. He suggests the marital arrangement of two sleeping quarters: "We are a house divided. Your half is there—mine here." But his charming and seductive temperament leaves the door open to change: the arrangement, he suggests, "shall continue so—until you come to me of your own free will." These are not the suggestions of a wholly disagreeable character, and they are what allows Mary to remain the "married virgin" of the film's title, even if precariously so. Insisting on his (partially) evil and scheming nature, the film sympathetically displays Roberto's visible pain for this chaste arrangement that he has forced upon himself. Only after witnessing Ethel's car accident and drinking himself into a stupor does he abandon all respectful manners, invade Mary's space, and attempt to rape her. The maid's successful display of a cross as a last resort to protect a horrified Mary prevents the inebriated Roberto from pursuing the vile action. The final scene, in which he confesses his love for Ethel, his indifference to Mary, and desire to return to South America sounds more like a convenient ideological closure. It excludes future interference in the happy life reserved for Mary, whose unconsummated marriage is quickly annulled, and her less-than-exciting Doug.

The few moments in which Roberto manages to charm Mary may have been a novelty for a motion picture but did not constitute a novelty *tout court*. American women's fascination for the elegant and noble foreigner was a common cautionary tale, popular in newspaper accounts about tango teas. Such narratives had to convey the attractiveness of the refined and exotic "tango pirate," while also showing foreigners' moral threat to the Anglo-Saxon race. Still, the role of the "slick foreigner, treacherous gangster, foul blackmailer, and disreputable gigolo" may have been hard to accept for an actor who had been branded with similarly infamous charges in real life.[39] His hunger for the admiration and praise he had usually received on the dance floor, however, might have matched the recognition—his own and that of those casting him—that these film roles embodied a widespread fantasy of fear and desire that the film's fictional diegesis made safe for actors and spectators alike. It was the fantasy of surrendering to the expert seduction of a Latin foreigner, without sexual consummation, but with plentiful display of erotic desire.[40] The Paramount promotion that appeared that year courted exactly such a salacious imaginary. It described Valentino as "the handsomest lounge lizard that ever infested a tea dansant," while referring to Mary as "the girl who deliberately marries a man who she feared."[41]

During this period, not every film that availed itself of Valentino's presence cast him in this kind of role, and their publicity rarely exploited or enhanced his dangerous appeal. It probably did not help that, after dropping his last name, Guglielmi, as too hard to pronounce and too easy to associate with the de Saulles scandal, he kept changing his moniker. Initially, Valentino used variations that evoked or replicated the name of the saint associated with courtly love or Cesare Borgia's noble title (Duca Valentino). This resulted in either a noble-sounding double name (De Valentino, di Valentino, De Valentina, di Valentini) or a single one (Valentine, Volantino, Valentino).[42] Several unremarkable films typecast his Latin mannerisms into morally devious roles. Either alien or just exotic looking, he appeared prone to exploit either his attractiveness or brutality, or both. In 1919, he was cast as a thug from the Bowery in *Virtuous Sinners*, an accomplice in a gang of thieves in *The Homebreaker*, a fatuous and cheating boyfriend in *The Big Little Person*, and a tough Montmartre apache dancer in *A Rogue's Romance*. He was also a sinister figure bound to ruin the life of the female protagonist in *Nobody Home / Out of Luck* (August 1919), a scheming Frenchman in *An Adventuress* (1920), and a notorious criminal in *The Wonderful Chance* (1920).

While these films translated his exotic Mediterranean appearance into morally disagreeable roles, they did not systematically cast him as a foreigner. Consider *The*

Delicious Little Devil (Universal, 1919), in which he played the role of a wealthy and hypocritical young man named Jimmy Calhoun, who is afraid to propose marriage to a young dancer, played by Valentino's friend and early advocate, Mae Murray. Sporting heavy makeup but no sign of racial otherness, his dancing skills are rarely exploited even though several scenes take place in a cabaret. His most common emotional state is one of shyness and demure restraint, interrupted only once by a sudden outburst of anger: the charming and passionate temperament that would characterize his early popular films is missing (figure 10). These roles indicate that studios and filmmakers did not yet know how best to cast him for productions designed for mass audiences. What was clear, however, was that Valentino's charming appearance could not be confused with the kind of Beban-like characters that would have associated him with Italian immigrants. Even in the films in which he appeared more a victim than a creator of circumstances, his most constant characteristics were his personal elegance, proud bearing, and high social status.[43]

A turning point apparently occurred with *Eyes of Youth* (Garson Productions, October 1919). Adapted from the popular eponymous 1917 play by Max Marcin and Charles Guernon, the film explores the choice between true love and financial convenience faced by a young American opera singer, played by popular screen personality Clara Kimball Young. Valentino is cast not as an Italian but as "Clarence Morgan, a cabaret parasite," as one intertitle introduces him. The protagonist, Gina Ashling, is married to a rich man who, after growing tired of her, has hired the young seducer Clarence to discredit her reputation so that he can get a divorce and remarry. Clarence invites Gina to his place and assaults her just before her husband and his lawyers burst into the apartment and pretend to witness a conjugal betrayal (figure 11). A married woman in the company of a young and dashing Latin-looking man played by Valentino was a familiar scene. At the trial, she describes Clarence as "a man without honor—and without conscience." The outcome of the legal proceedings matters greatly to Gina, but what is also at stake, as the film emphasizes, is her public reputation. An intriguingly animated intertitle first juxtaposes the court of law with that of public opinion: "Guiltless! Condemned by the merciless judge, Public Opinion—'To hell for life and no parole!'" The same title card then shows a folded newspaper intruding into the printed text, revealing an article bearing the unforgiving headline "Financier Goring Charges Wife with Infidelity" placed above a close-up photo of her. The film was a success. *Variety* greeted it as "a knockout" and even avoided summarizing it, for "the story of the play is too well known."[44] In its twisted plot, in fact, the film's insistence on newspaper coverage of an adultery trial featuring a once-respectable couple and a slick and charming young gigolo likely evoked the de Saulles scandal and other similar ones. But not many people could have known that the film's Rudolfo Valentino was Rodolpho Guglielmi. Taking part in a fictionalization of events reminiscent of the heavily reported New York affair could have been a career-killer move. Instead, it turned out to be the opportunity of a lifetime.

FIGURE 10. Valentino as the sad and restrained Jimmy Calhoun in
The Delicious Little Devil (1919), frame enlargement. Courtesy of EYE
Filmmuseum, Amsterdam.

According to several accounts, among the attentive spectators of *Eyes of Youth*
was Metro's top screenwriter and executive, June Mathis, who would later play a
key role in casting Valentino in *The Four Horsemen*. It is fair to assume, however,
that the links between Mathis and Valentino were less serendipitous than what this
single film viewing might suggest. Mathis was commercially as well as artistically
ambitious and had many connections in the world of the stage and motion pictures. Some of those connections knew the Italian actor. Certainly, in the wake of
his interpretation in *Eyes of Youth,* Mathis might have remembered his talent as a
dancer, including his reputation as tango pirate, his physical traits, and perhaps his
temperament on and off screen. It is also likely that Mathis, based in New York at
the time, had become familiar with the scandal of the de Saulles family. Could she
have connected the Rodolpho Guglielmi of the de Saulles scandal with the Rudolfo
Valentino of *Eyes of Youth*?

The degrees of separation between the two were few and revolved around the
Russian actress Alla Nazimova and Metro Pictures. In the late 1910s, Mathis had
scripted a few pictures at Metro starring Nazimova, including *Eye for Eye* (1918)
and *Out of the Fog* (1919), and possibly knew of her friends, famous parties, and
occasional lovers.[45] One of them was actress Jean Acker. In November 1919, a
month after the release of *Eyes of Youth*, the fairly established Acker suddenly wed
the less-known Valentino in what quickly turned out to be an ill-fated marriage.

FIGURE 11. Valentino stifling the cries of an innocent wife (Clara Kimball Young) to stage their consensual rendezvous in *Eyes of Youth* (1919), frame enlargement. Reproduced from the collections of the Library of Congress, Moving Image Section.

The wedding received a singular, rarely discussed imprimatur from Mathis's own company, Metro Pictures. The couple's best man was Metro's general manager, Maxwell Karger, and the wedding celebration took place at the home of the company's treasurer and in the presence of the company's president, Richard Rowland.[46] It is unlikely Mathis was absent; it is impossible that she was not aware of the ceremony and of who was Acker's groom. More than just an actor who caught her eye in a screening of *Eyes of Youth*, Valentino was certainly an acquaintance connected to Mathis's close circle of friends and coworkers and an individual whose liaisons with married women had made headlines in the press and had been used twice on film. Mathis might have recognized something original in his film performances, but her casting of Valentino in *The Four Horsemen* also depended on her personal and professional identity—gender, talent, and ambition—and on the film's promising international appeal and resulting promotional campaign.

A WOMAN'S (COMMERCIAL) VIEWPOINT

Mathis was much more than a scenario writer. She was a writing supervisor, an editorial director, and a film producer—a combination that "allowed her to control the writing ideas she guided onto the screen" and to be voted in 1926 the third most influential woman in the history of motion pictures.[47] She wrote countless scripts, first as one of Metro Pictures' scenarists then as its editor-in-chief. Between 1921 and 1922 Mathis completed five scenarios for Valentino, beginning with *The Four Horsemen, Camille, The Conquering Power* and, in 1922, *Blood and Sand* and *The Young Rajah*. Her later writing credits included other major accomplishments such as Eric von Stroheim's *Greed* (1924) and *Ben Hur* (1925). No matter how much recognition her work received, her name remained closely associated to that of the Italian actor whom she had allegedly discovered and launched to superstar fame. When she suddenly died in 1927, less than a year after Valentino's passing, her *New York Times* front-page obituary read: "June Mathis, world-famous motion picture scenarist, who adapted 'The Four Horsemen of the Apocalypse' for the movies and discovered Rudolph Valentino, died last night."[48]

In recent years, the critical discourse about Mathis has tended to pair her superb talent with an artistic and (proto)feminist poetics. "Mathis was committed to 'artistic' filmmaking as opposed to the formulaic films turned out by many women writers in Hollywood," Donna Casella has argued, and she explored "sexual, racial and national themes in her films, with particular attention to woman as a social force."[49] Her personal approach, critics agreed, was already visible in the subversive female roles she had designed during the war as well as in the scouting of her unconventional leading men against the background of the patriarchal and nativist ethos of both Hollywood and America.[50] Regarding her scripts for Valentino and in dialogue with Gaylyn Studlar and Miriam Hansen's insights into his ambivalent masculinity, Thomas H. Slater has also argued that Mathis's scripts construct a fragile, fatherless man who has to rely on the figure of a strong, spiritually sound and sexually mature woman to test his masculinity and either find himself or fail.[51] In the wake of "the world war's desecration of masculinity," Mathis's Valentinos "were not athletic action heroes unencumbered by family and social concerns as were Fairbanks's characters" but "'wounded' figures who required an alternative to violence and adventure as a basis for identity." In Slater's view, Valentino "did not become as wildly popular among men and boys" because he was not attuned to the "boy culture" that Studlar has recognized in Fairbanks's celebration of rugged masculinity.[52] Instead, he argues, Mathis's scripts designed Valentino as a character who views the future "with dread (*Blood and Sand*), hopefulness (*The Conquering Power*), or uncertainty (*The Four Horsemen, Camille*)," and for whom death is the ultimate horizon of personal actualization or failure. The danger of war (or of bullfighting) served as the grounding moment of patriarchal failure and personal crisis. The risk of personal bereavement did not just imply the deconstruction of traditional masculinity, but also anticipated its novel reconstruction (or "becoming," in Slater's analysis) in ways that were more agreeable to women's imagination.[53]

Slater's critical perspective is centered on an equation of personal expression with a feminist one, and an American one at that. In his analysis, Mathis's scripts are a woman's work in the sense that they express a feminist take on narratives and characters—as if other dimensions played little or no role in her work. Slater's approach appears to downplay two significant professional dynamics: one pertaining to authorship and one to promotion. The first involves the delicate balance in Mathis's screenwriting poetics between the aforementioned ethics of gendered expression and her well-recognized domestic *and* international commercial aspirations. The second dynamic, which I will explain in the next section, involves the role of publicity in linking Mathis's name to Valentino and in constructing a commercial exploratory space for his novel masculinity in ways not necessarily anticipated by her scripts.

Regarding the first issue, early 1920s profiles, as well as her own pronouncements, were at pains to reconcile the apparent contradiction between her gender identity and her professional shrewdness. For instance, in *The First One Hundred Noted Men and Women of the Screen* (1920), author Carolyn Lowrey sought to reassure her readers that the author of the script of *To Hell with the Kaiser,* which *Variety* had praised as a "wonderfully effective propaganda film," had not lost her femininity, despite her professional drive and success.[54] In an effort that we may find trivial, Lowrey noted the presence of flowers in Mathis's book-lined office and described the décor as "original [and] in many respects delightfully feminine."[55] Here the reference to her femininity worked to correct and thus downplay her exceptional talent and dogged determination. Lowrey, however, added a critical qualification to her success that had great resonance at the time: she praised the *professional* quality of Mathis's work by commending her ability to register a prevalent temperament and draw popular characters, rather than regarding her work as a form of mere artistic expression. To Lowrey, if scenarios constitute "the base from which the cinema makes its public appeal," Mathis's ones were what stood "behind the popularity of many stars."[56]

Mathis herself had stressed her sensibility for public opinion in a *New York Times* article from the spring of 1923. "Quite often I have picked out something that appealed to me as being wonderfully dramatic, but which has not made the same impression upon other readers," she wrote about her process of adapting famous novels. To modulate and expand her positive first impressions into developed screen treatments, Mathis had a careful two-step method that first involved "noting down each point and the number of persons in favor of it" before deciding on the dramatic points of the scenario on the basis of at least seven favorable opinions out of ten.[57] Two years later, in a contribution to the *Film Daily,* she summarized this approach by linking a "female perspective" in moving pictures to questions not just of gendered expression but also of commercial viability and success—which may not have been any less subversive. After noting that scenarios had to appeal to millions of specta-tors and that women played a huge role in reaching that goal ("of those millions the hand that rocks the cradle is the ruling spirit"), she celebrated the significance of having female scenario writers, art directors and set dressers, for "they understand the decoration of the home, the setting of tables, the arrangement of flowers."[58] The most difficult thing for men to acknowledge is that "there is such a thing as a woman's viewpoint that is possibly commercial" and that a "magic something" impos-sible to ignore had "made American films supreme in the world's market.[59] As her promotion of Valentino would show, women spectators could be won much more easily by an exotic leading man than through floral arrangements.

THE TANGO DANCER BECOMES A STAR

The available evidence on the production of Valentino's breakout film raises important questions about June Mathis's actual contribution and specifically about the difference between the protagonist of her script and the lead character that the studio ended up promoting after the film's release.

In early 1919, Metro had purchased the screen rights to the best-selling novel *Four Horsemen of the Apocalypse.* First published in 1916, the book by the Spanish writer Vicente Blasco Ibáñez (1867–1928) had reached about 170 editions world-wide, including as a *Photoplay* movie tie-in edition (1918). An established version of the facts suggests that Mathis chose to adapt it against the opinion of the film industry's top leaders. As the story goes, Hollywood producers mistakenly believed that the novel had a complicated plot and would require an expensive produc-tion. Moreover, by the end of the 1910s war subjects were believed to be no longer appealing to an American public eager for lighter fare.[60] Yet, the truth appears to be somewhat different: Mathis played a remarkable role, but the selection of the novel may not have been her idea.

In March 1919, the first coverage of Metro's purchase of the rights does men-tion her name in conjunction with the planned adaptation but also indicates that Metro president Rowland had secured the filming rights to the novel after per-sonally meeting Ibáñez during the author's brief stay in New York City.[61] Only then, Rowland communicated his actions to Mathis and "hurriedly summoned" her to New York to meet the novelist and "undertake at once the screen adaptation and scenarioization of the novel."[62] As newly promoted head of Metro's Scenario Department, she took full charge of the project. Together with the studio's key figures, Loew, Rowland, and Maxwell Karger, Mathis met again with Ibáñez during his late February 1920 visit to Hollywood to discuss the project. Their meet-ings were made part of the film's promotion (figure 12).[63]

Coverage of the months leading up to the film's shooting sheds some light on its commercial raison d'être. Right before the cameras rolled, a late December 1919 issue of *Moving Picture World (MPW)* summarized a speech given by Rowland in

FIGURE 12. Key figures at Metro Studios. From left: June Mathis, Marcus Loew, Vicente Blasco Ibáñez, Metro president Richard A. Rowland, and Metro treasurer Maxwell Karger. *Moving Picture World*, March 6, 1920, 1657.

New York in which he described what he considered two incontrovertible facts. The first was "that American producers must make concessions to foreign distributors because of the present disparity in money exchange." The second one was "the entry of so-called big business into the motion picture industry," which he viewed as "an inevitable step which need cause no alarm especially to the independent exhibitor."[64] Rowland was quite familiar with the European market after a two-month trip to Europe, where he had interviewed prominent film manufacturers and distributors. In the wake of the growth of the film business, which had finally turned into a "legitimate field for investment" and was becoming ever "stronger in the popular affections," he reflected on the surge of "high-grade pictures." It was in this very context of business corporatization and secured international appeal that Rowland mentioned in the *MPW* article Metro's "latest coup": the acquisition of "the sensational novel by Vicente Blasco Ibanez."[65]

If Rowland was quick to stress the commercial prospects associated with the popular novel's film adaptation, Mathis may have sensed a unique opportunity to combine high professional aspirations with her own poetics. "The bigger the subject, the bigger the inspiration," she declared in an interview orchestrated to appear in the same issue.[66] In order to grasp how Mathis set out to adapt the almost five-hundred-page book into a film script, cast protagonists, and aim for the widest possible success, we must turn briefly to Ibáñez who, already in his early fifties, had authored very different kinds of novels and was an established figure in world literary circles.

The critical canon about his output tends to differentiate between the naturalism of the early works and the controversial psychological sensationalism of his subsequent output, of which *Blood and Sand* (1908) is the most famous work. Established Spanish critics viewed his later attention to the slum dwellers and lower classes in general as an attack against the church, the monarchy, and the army.[67] *Los cuatro jinetes del Apocalipsis* belonged to a third phase, comprising war novels that feature a cosmopolitan sensibility that found great success in Hollywood.[68] *Los cuatro jinetes* tells the story of an aging authoritarian Argentinian landowner whose grandsons, fathered by his French and German sons-in-law, return to Europe at the outbreak of the First World War and find themselves fighting on opposite sides. For Ibáñez, who was living in Southern France at the time and had befriended French political leaders, the novel was an opportunity to make a broad geopolitical statement. The nation's president, Raymond Poincaré, had invited him to visit the site of the Battle of the Marne with the hope that Ibáñez would use it in one of his novels and thus support the French cause. In *Los cuatro jinetes,* the novelist gave a remarkably realistic account of the battle, together with an exposé of one of the most controversial aspects of German Kultur: its militarism. The resulting novel, as critics later noted, was "an impressive feat of propaganda."[69]

History provided help. The book's translator, Charlotte Brewster Jordan, bought the book's U.S. publishing rights for only $300 shortly after its 1916 publication. Yet, few could imagine the impact of America's April 1917 declaration of war on the book's release nearly a year later. In the first ninety days after its publication, the volume sold about ninety thousand copies and, within a few more months, it reached twenty editions for a total of more than two hundred thousand copies. What is rarely acknowledged is that Ibáñez was a master self-promoter who did not hesitate to merge conventional literary promotion with mass commercial advertisement. "There are silks, cigarettes, soaps, toys, whose brands include the same image of *The Four Horsemen* that is on the cover of my novel," he told the Spanish press in 1919.[70] A year later he traveled to North America for a series of conferences in New York, Chicago, and Toronto, among other cities.[71] In late 1921, in the wake of the novel's tremendous success, Ibáñez proudly described himself as a "universal film novelist" (*novelista universal cinematográfico*).[72] It is reasonable to assume that Mathis (and Rowland before her) found Ibáñez's wartime fame and notorious ability to connect to a mass readership quite appealing. Mathis likely met with him several times, and, while she must have had great respect for his literary inventiveness and popularity, she also had clear ideas about his novel's cinematic adaptation.[73]

As an efficient manager, Mathis was to take control of cast and crew. Her choice for director fell on Rex Ingram, who had a notoriously difficult temperament but with whom she had collaborated quite well a year before on the now-lost *Hearts Are Trumps*.[74] For her leading man, she needed an exotic actor flexible enough to play a privileged young Argentine, a Montmartre artist and poseur, a gifted tango dancer, and a fantastic lover who ends up sacrificing his life to win the approval of the woman he loves. Some commentators at the time and later critics have described Valentino as "raw material" who could be transformed from a "thick-set young Italian peasant into an elegant Argentinian nobleman." One may argue instead that his scandalous previous roles in life and on film as slick tango dancer and seducer of married women, in addition to being part of Mathis's circle, made him more a sound choice than a long shot.[75]

While the extent to which Mathis expected that Valentino would become a runaway star after the film's release is unclear, her changes to the ways Julio enters and exits the story reveal her ideas about his role. In the novel, Julio is neither the protagonist nor the main hero. Those roles are reserved for Julio's father, the old Desnoyers, and the Russian mystic, Tchernoff, who promotes Christianity as true revolution and whose centrality explains the novel's title. In Mathis's surviving script, title sheet, and the finished film, which she closely supervised, however, Julio Desnoyers is a leading figure, deserving a grand introduction and undergoing a sympathy-inducing transformation, indeed a conversion, from spoiled womanizer to romantic and patriotic martyr.[76] In the film, Mathis introduces Julio as a leading man with the famous tango scene set in Buenos Aires (figure 13) and thus *early* in the narrative and not, as the novel does, later in Paris after the beginning of the war (figure 14). Secondly, she purifies Julio's reasons for his transformation by linking them to a noble search for romantic approval. In the novel, Julio's motivations for his apparent change are merely utilitarian, linked to a selfish desire to maintain admiration from his beloved and the world around him. Finally, Mathis's construction of the character of Julio did not exactly coincide with how the studio set up the film's promotion, which followed the novel's plot, not Mathis's own rewriting.

Thus, the film's most memorable scene, set in a working-class Buenos Aires café with Valentino leading a tango dance before a variety of admiring characters, is, strictly speaking, absent from the novel. A comparable scene is set in Paris and thus unfolds much later in the story. Moving the tango scene to the Argentinian capital was apparently Mathis's idea and helped to establish Julio as leading man and set up his development and transformation from early on. In Buenos Aires, Julio can appear in full gaucho regalia and can display an exotic authenticity that the film spectators can project onto the Parisian tango when, wearing a splendid tuxedo, he can impress his married companion with the dance learned in his boyhood. But by then he is already undergoing a personal transformation. The initial publicity did not distinguish between the two tango scenes; instead it confused them. It advertised illustrations from the Buenos Aires film sequence, with Julio

FIGURES 13 and 14. Pure exoticism versus charming elegance in *The Four Horsemen of the Apocalypse* (1921): the tango scenes in Buenos Aires and in Paris. Courtesy of Museum of Modern Art Film Stills Archive.

in Argentinian costumes, by attributing it to a Paris setting and thus following readers' expectations.

Still, the famous scene was not entirely Mathis's invention. She had reworked information from Ibáñez's novel that conveyed, about seventy pages in, Julio's dissipated lifestyle, made of "imprudent borrowings" that the patriarchal Madariaga had encouraged.[77] Ibáñez had also stressed Julio's leadership by depicting him as "ringleader of a band of toughs in the Capital" who liked to recount his "nightly escapades" of "gay, wild life" to his eager grandfather.[78]

In both texts, Julio's life of vice, debauchery, and vulgar romance—and their representation—does not last long, but the difference is that in the film, he displays signs of authentic change *before* moving to Europe. In Mathis's film treatment, for instance, when Madariaga gives unmistakable signs of failing health, Julio's self-confidence diminishes dramatically. Further, the film scene showing Julio's desperate reaction to the reading of Madariaga's will, in which the old man did not single him out as a special heir, constitutes an original addition; it is absent from the novel. In Ibáñez's work, Julio apparently undergoes some change between Argentina and Paris, but it is more a superficial makeover than a conversion. In Paris, Ibáñez's Julio continues to attract and enjoy public admiration as a tango dancer, displaying a thirst for attention and praise that grows subdued and almost disappears in Mathis's character. Since the novel casts Julio as a remarkable character but not as protagonist, its author can delay the description of the tango's tantalizing appeal until well into the story. When Ibáñez writes that the Argentinian dance was "in full swing in Paris" and that it had become "a new pleasure for the delight of humanity," he is detailing the exotic appeal with which Mathis charged her new leading man from the film's opening and which in her script set the stage for his conversion.[79] Ibáñez's description of the tango unfolds in pure physical, caveman-like terms, and centers on the Euro-American's co-optation of subversive and racially different scripts of romance.

> The tango had taken possession of the world. It was the heroic hymn of a humanity that was suddenly concentrating its aspirations on the harmonious rhythm of the thigh joints, measuring its intelligence by the agility of its feet. An incoherent and monotonous music of African inspiration was satisfying the artistic ideals of a society that required nothing better. The world was dancing . . . dancing . . . dancing.[80]

The tango fever crowned Ibáñez's Julio as the ruler over the Parisian tango teas and champion in the art of romance. While "appraising his slender elegance, medium stature, and muscular springs," ladies hoped to be seen being held "in the arms of the master."[81] In the film, by contrast, the Parisian Julio is bound to differ from his earlier, frivolous days. While he seems to remain dependent on his mother for financial support, he regains some measure of control over his destiny and his identity as a painter—a *picture-maker,* that is. Further, his falling in love with a married woman, Marguerite Laurier (Alice Terry), challenges his emotional immaturity: she is wiser and more sensitive than he is, particularly regarding the tragedy of war.

While she is initially delighted that the mandatory conscription of all able-bodied French men has spared her Argentine lover, she is soon overwhelmed by feelings of guilt and remorse for her adulterous affair. Deciding to nurse her husband, who has just returned blind and disabled from the front, Marguerite separates herself from Julio. In a combination of admiration for her sacrifice and desire to please his father, who many years earlier had escaped conscription by moving to Argentina, Mathis's Julio undergoes a spiritual transformation (figure 15). He volunteers for the French army and becomes a selfless man driven by romantic abnegation and ultimately patriotic self-sacrifice.

In the novel, his motivation is less honorable. Julio is drawn to Marguerite because her combination of "confident advances" and "capricious outbursts of modesty" represents "a new type for him."[82] After the war starts, Marguerite's complex new emotions divide them. Revealingly, her inconsolable reaction to her brother's death in battle "did not please his amorous egoism."[83] Julio notices that the times are changing, as admiration for selfish individuality is giving away to "a new love— a love for the man who is suffering, desire for abnegation, for sacrifice." Rather than being inspired by the new idealism, he cynically registers the change as a new form of popular taste and not as a spiritual transformation.[84] When his female fans ask him why he is not wearing a uniform or going to the front, Julio realizes that he is "no longer fashionable" and that the age of the "tango is dead."[85] Similarly, when toward the end of the novel Julio reaches Bordeaux, where Marguerite is caring for her wounded husband, he realizes that she considers her older spouse to be a man far superior to her younger lover. This realization provokes his decision to enlist immediately, out of a "hasty heroism" though not out of a spiritual or patriotic élan. Even the ensuing internal dialogue, in which he imagines himself a soldier, reveals a fatuous and narcissistic nature still driven to attain personal glory: "Soon she would hear him well spoken of," for he would either die right away or "astound the world by his bravery."[86] Once enlisted, however, Ibáñez's Julio practically disappears. He dies in battle, but no details are given regarding the circumstances. When his father visits his "rustic grave" in a vast burial site, he considers building a mausoleum for his son before realizing the uselessness of it all. Likewise, Julio's sister cannot even keep him in her mind for more than few moments. And there the book ends.[87]

The Spanish writer bestowed upon the young man the ability to act differently, to take new actions, but not to feel differently and grow intimately. By contrast, the film's narrative division between Argentina and France is startling not just because the tango's wild otherness is confined to Buenos Aires and downplayed in Paris, but also because it showcases Julio's transformation from self-centered playboy to spiritual lover, sensitive to the call of duty and to Tchernoff's teaching.[88] Mathis's presumed interest in constructing a more sympathetic male character, one whose virile leadership eventually gives way to selfless sacrifice, bestowed upon the role of Julio more narrative and emotional weight and found fertile ground in the film's

FIGURE 15. Valentino's spiritual conversion in *The Four Horsemen of the Apocalypse* (1921), leading to voluntary military service and, ultimately, personal sacrifice. Courtesy of Museum of Modern Art Film Stills Archive.

attendant promotion. Still, what *The Four Horsemen*'s publicity achieved was to launch Valentino as a Latin-lover star who was rather different from the sensitive Julio with which Mathis had ended her script and much closer to the tango dancer of the film's beginning. The primacy effect of the tango scene prevailed over the film's narrative trajectory and resolution.

LAUNCHING THE *APOCALYPSE*

In line with the epic status of the production, the publicity for *The Four Horsemen* was most effective. During the film's production, *Moving Picture World* publicized the historical accuracy of the war scenes, for which "army officers, war correspondents and other experts have been consulted," as well as their scale—an "entire French village had been built to be destroyed."[89] The company also created pseudo-events, including a "poster drawing contest,"[90] and filled the pages of trade journals with images of Valentino in a tango outfit and of gauchos riding through Argentina's open spaces.[91] The film's New York premiere, held on March 6, 1921, was a public celebration of cinema's geopolitical relevance. The film's link to

World War I brought together a heterogeneous assemblage of film celebrities, politicians, and powerful individuals. In attendance were the Spanish and Argentine ambassadors from Washington in addition to Nicholas Murray Butler, president of Columbia University, Winston Churchill, Adolph Zukor, Anita Loos, John Emerson, Lee Shubert, and David Belasco, among others.[92]

The initial publicity around the premiere reveals an element that the critical discourse on the film has often overlooked: the massive community of the novel's readers. MPW insisted that the novel "had passed its 161st edition" and "its legion of readers throughout the United States alone [was] estimated at more than 10,000,000 persons."[93] A month later, when the film opened at the Astor Theatre, MPW boasted that the number of readers had doubled.[94] By then, Metro had pulled off what MPW labeled "an outstanding achievement in the publicity for this film." Armed with posters that promoted both the book and the film, it had gained virtual possession of the biggest store windows in New York, from booksellers (McDewitt & Wilson) to department stores (Lord & Taylor, Gimbel Brothers, Macy's, Abraham & Straus). The trade press described it as "one the best window campaigns ever worked anywhere."[95]

After the film's launch, reactions shifted from the celebrated links with the novel and the memory of the war (which the novel had powerfully reignited) to the picture's multiclass appeal. In a Motion Picture News issue that appeared the day before the film's premiere, an anonymous reviewer argued that Ingram's film could not "be called a war picture," since it was "more a study in racial traits with adventure, romance and the effects of war used to give it color."[96] The same reviewer then detailed the features he admired the most: Valentino, "the Argentine," and with him "the natives and their national dance, the primitive white heat of passion [...] all caught and presented in kaleidoscopic proportions."[97] What years earlier would have been reason for racial and cultural separation became a motif for aesthetic delectation in this most charming of film characters. The studio's publicity material helped a great deal.

A thirty-two-page booklet containing advertising and publicity suggestions for the film, edited by J. E. D. Meader, Metro's New York–based director of advertising and publicity, aided the effort. In addition to information about the costly filming, the booklet included suggestions for several catchphrases ("In which a youthful libertine, useless as a drone and as dangerous, finds that he owes God a death") and two kinds of printed lobby displays—all centered on Valentino's presence. The first suggested display, called "The Argentine," "represents one of the most flashing scenes in the preliminary part of the story: the tango scene where Julio, the spoiled young South American, takes away the dancing partner of another man." The second one, "Paris by Night," depicted "the revels of the hero, Julio, in the days after he went to Paris."[98]

For months following its release, The Four Horsemen remained a blockbuster. MPW reported than more than one hundred road companies were exhibiting it—a practice that was reserved for special or uniquely successful productions.[99] At the same time Metro began receiving "unsolicited tributes" from numerous cities and "from all classes of people."[100] Further, the public discourse about the film began to insist less on the merits of the adaptation itself and more on what the industry valued the most: stardom. A few contemporary reviews, from the *New York World* to the *Literary Digest,* began to single out Valentino. "The characters used primarily to give color to the picture—South-American natives, Spanish, French, and German specimens," wrote the *Literary Digest* reviewer, "are all strikingly individualized, and those who have the more extensive roles not only look their parts, but act them intelligibly, especially Rudolph Valentino as the young Julio."[101] Even *Motion Picture Play* critic Frederick James Smith, who loudly criticized Mathis's script and Ingram's direction for missing Ibáñez's antiwar message, identified the "early episode of the Argentine café" as the film's "highest point." There, he noted, "Julio flashed with life, passion, vibrated across the screen, and the atmosphere radiated with reality."[102]

Mathis may have not necessarily recognized the charming and exotic Valentino that pervaded the emerging publicity discourse, but that image was there to stay. Between *The Four Horsemen* and his next blockbuster, *The Sheik,* released in November, a distinct fan discourse began to emerge. In June, for instance, in an article entitled "A Latin Lover," *Photoplay* boasted the unexpected and fortunate discovery of a star: "Rudolph Valentino played Julio in *The Four Horsemen*—and immediately the film world knew it had the continental hero, the polished foreigner, the modern Don Juan in its unsuspecting midst."[103] The trope of exceptional and exotic sensuality soon dominated his highly individualized early reception and found expression in a classic publicity vehicle, the biographical profile—part personal story, part publicity device. Already established for Pickford and Fairbanks and for a wide range of actors who never became big stars, this journalistic genre boosted Valentino's fame and generated a fascination that it would be erroneous to describe as unmediated or spontaneous.

PROFILING

One of the earliest of a long list of biographical profiles that would not stop even after his death appeared in *Motion Picture Magazine.* Penned by film critic Gordon Gassaway and entitled the "The Erstwhile Landscape Gardener," the profile sought to legitimize Valentino's status as a star. It portrays him as a talented Italian actor whose life and manners defy the negative stereotypes associated with Italian immigrants and appeal to American and world audiences alike. Accompanied by two photographs, where Valentino appears in modern clothes and in the typical Argentinian outfit, the profile walks a fine line between immigrant story and narrative of an effortless Americanization. It begins by reminding readers that Valentino had tried his luck as uninspired landscape gardener and as dancing partner for the famous Bonnie Glass and Joan Sawyer. But in this account even his setbacks acquire a mantle of heroism. During World War I, as Gassaway recounts, Valentino "was trying frantically to enlist in the Italian service," but his rejection due to a serious eye defect "was a hard blow for the young Italian, son of a cavalry captain and offspring of generations of military leaders."[104] To further stress his difference from the average Italian immigrant, Gassaway aestheticizes Valentino's real-life appearance as noble, timelessly Italian. His appearance could easily remind one of "little peak-eared marble satyrs you see in Italian gardens" and even though, in preparation for the interview, a studio's makeup artists had thickly covered with pink paint "Rudy's olive complexion" and applied blue-black penciled shadows to further emphasize "the blackness of his eyes," "the finely-chiseled lines of his patrician nose and mouth were au naturel."[105] In Gassaway's prose, Valentino's racial and national otherness, including his accent, are transmuted into a noble and purely exotic charm.

In his responses to Gassaway's questions, the Italian actor himself took pains to make his diversity appear acceptable by distinguishing it from that of African Americans. He refers to the danger of spending too much time in the sun at the beach since he is "very dark in complexion" and "the sun it burn me too black for pictures. I become like a neegroe [sic]."[106] Such a demeaning kind of racial distancing proved useful for casting Valentino as an ultimately acceptable Arab-looking lover in *The Sheik*. Another way in which Gassaway seeks to tame, without erasing, Valentino's otherness is to combine it with several recognizably American traits that Valentino had quickly learned to showcase—including self-control, reserve, and constant physical activity. The sustained references to his new habits and controlled manners makes Gassaway predict that "the stars seem very favorable toward this young, very Americanized foreigner."[107] Ultimately, and in conjunction with shorter reviews and biographical pieces, this profile was the first to suggest that the *Four Horsemen*'s impressive success was due to Valentino's emergent stardom. In 1926 Terry Ramsaye voiced this opinion quite explicitly when he reported that although "the gross earnings up to the end of 1925 on the picture were about $4,000,000 [. . .] it was not, after all, a triumph of a war picture." Instead, he insisted, "it was a triumph of a new Don Juan of the screen, a victory for Latin love and suppressed desire among the movie millions."[108]

The rhetorical emphasis of these profiles was spontaneity, as if Valentino's stardom was effortless and inevitable. Gassaway's 1921 profile, however, attached a distinct name to the prediction of Valentino's rise to fame—that of Herbert Howe. In praising the Italian actor's talent and describing his bright future, Gassaway felt he was usurping "Howe's prerogative [. . .] in predicting that [Valentino] will achieve his most notable successes in manly, bandolined roles."[109] Howe was an influential contributor to fan periodicals, as well as a publicist, often a secretive one, yet known for his ability to manage stars' public reputations. The frequency of his editorials and range of his collaborations amount to a significant contribution to the emergence of Hollywood star discourse. He was possibly one of the first of a list of ballyhoo experts who shaped Valentino's career and reception in America. Like many other early film writers and journalists, he has remained marginalized in traditional film histories.

Information about Howe is limited. Born Herbert Riley Howe in South Dakota in 1893, Howe "began working as a film publicist in New York in the early 1910s," served in the U.S. Tank Corps during World War I, returned to New York as a *New York Telegraph* reporter and started writing for fan magazines, including *Photo-Play Journal, Motion Picture Classic,* and *Photoplay.*[110] Under contract as a publicist in 1921 with both Brewster Publications and the Vitagraph Company, he was by then a recognized star scout, effective interviewer, and so-called ethnographer of the Hollywood colony's peculiar mores. Due to his sophistication and intellectual preparation, he was known as a "Hollywood boulevardier," which was also the name of his column, first for *Motion Picture Classic* and later for the *New Movie Magazine.* He was also a most consummate publicist, unabashedly willing to use his columns and reputation to launch and support stars' career. At the time of the *Four Horsemen*'s success, Howe was writing a popular column for *Picture Play Magazine,* entitled "Right Off the Grill," which was devoted to "unrestrained comment on picture players, and correspondents." In August 1921, four and a half months after Valentino appeared on screen as Julio, Howe devoted a remarkable profile to the Italian actor not to celebrate his "screen glamour," but to study him "as a subject for success."[111] It was the first of many publicity pieces. Arguably, Howe's overall contribution to Valentino's fame was as significant as Mathis's. The Metro chief screenwriter capitalized on the public interest that Valentino had spurred first as a private citizen and then as a minor actor and translated his appeal into a daring but sympathetic role that brought him an unprecedented level of fame. Howe also took advantage of her creative work and translated Valentino's notable screen performance into an alleged real-life personality that fueled other performances and a lifetime of coverage.[112]

Howe's 1921 profile articulates the acceptability of Valentino's otherness for the film industry—censors and spectators alike. Against the intentions and plans of the "fanatical evangels," Howe notes, Valentino's screen presence "suggests *a devil within the law,* liable to break through without notice. That's why the ladies are going to like him." By depicting him as a romantic creature from another time, Howe had clear ideas about the new space that Valentino came to occupy in America's film imagery. "Most of us still have a sort of moonshine love for the outlawry," he argues, pointing to Valentino as someone who "suggests romance with a crimson thrill."[113] Howe predicates the actor's acceptable otherness as a mixture of successful immigrant narrative—from rags to riches, elitist personal background, and Orientalist racial traits.

While Valentino had migrated to America like millions of immigrants, his alleged social background separated him from them. Because of his personal ancestry (a "cavalry officer" for a father and "a lady of gentility and lineage" for a mother), Howe argues, the economic hardship and the solitude initially experienced in New York were harder on him than on other, lower-class migrants. "The peasant of Europe can get work digging in the sewers," Valentino observes. "I had nothing to offer, and even if I had I couldn't tell them about it." What Valentino had, however, were "all the forms of gallantry known to the Continental cavalier." As a result, "Women were enamored of his manner, his beauty, his grace, his low-murmuring Latin tones."[114] Still, his humbling experience of landing in New York with the other immigrants was a healthy antidote against arrogance. When success came, Howe remarks, he was not "reshaped by the arch-sycophant, Mademoiselle Fame." Instead he remained grounded and always mindful of "those days in New York when I didn't know where I could get food." Howe's interview does not shy away from the actor's scandalous past ("People thought of me only as a dancer—a lounge lizard") but uses it to attract sympathy for an idol profoundly misunderstood, terribly lonely, but much wiser for all that. And yet national difference ("A jug of wine, a plate of spaghetti, a pack of cigarettes, and Valentino is a success most anywhere") had to be combined with an appealing exoticism. In Howe's article Valentino explains his "wanderlust" in terms of his possibly Orientalist physicality ("His narrow, lotus-lidded eyes are enigmatic. Another reason for the interest of the curious sex. They are the eyes of the Orient") and outlook on life ("The Orient fascinates me. There seems to be some secret wisdom in it").[115] Ultimately, the actor emerges from the profile as "an introspective Bedouin, a youthful Omar searching the Mystery, a pagan lover of the spirit," who admirers intimately related to as "Rudie."

Between *The Four Horsemen* and his next blockbuster, *The Sheik*, three productions failed to catalyze a comparable fan discourse. For instance, *Uncharted Seas* (April 1921) and *The Conquering Power* (July 1921), also produced by Metro, did not contribute to Valentino's stardom as exotic Latin Lover—whether unapologetically daring or contritely sensitive. In the former, he played the role of a courageous ship commander Frank Underwood, active in the Arctic Seas. But as *Variety* noted, the film's plot appeared "unconvincing and conventional," and all the characters, including his, were "so unnaturally drawn" that it was "impossible to associate them with ordinary human beings."[116] In the latter, he was a wealthy young dandy named Charles Grandet, and his interpretation was singled out as charming for its "youthful appeal, vivacity and cleverness" but nothing more.[117] The same can be said for *Camille* (September 1921), an Alla Nazimova vehicle, also produced by Metro, adapted by Mathis from *La Dame aux camélias* by Alexandre Dumas fils and featuring art direction by Valentino's second wife, film costume and set designer Natacha Rambova.[118] Valentino played the role of Armand Duval, a young and unsophisticated law student, who falls in love with the Nazimova character, but at no point in the film, which critics labeled artificial and unrelatable, did he appear as other than a victim of passion and circumstances.[119]

The publicity leading up to the film placed him in the "supporting company" even though the role in *The Four Horsemen* had "won him celebrity."[120]

Unsurprisingly, these films do not figure prominently in the established discourse about Valentino's different masculinity because the fan discourse still looked at his interpretation in *The Four Horsemen* as his primary role. By the fall of 1921, months after its release, critics and editorialists still described its freshness and originality in terms of the racial and cultural novelty of its leading man, for whom *Photoplay* eventually abandoned its long-standing front-page policy. "If we ever decide to have men on the covers," the editors wrote in October, "[Valentino] will be the first man."[121] The plan came to fruition with the February 1922 issue of *Photoplay*, which sported an image of the Italian actor in attire suitable to the sheik craze. And it is to *The Sheik* and the publicity the film generated that we should now turn.

5

The Ballyhooed Art of Governing Romance

Interest in The Sheik *continued to build and a studio press agent was assigned as a buffer between Valentino and the press.*

IRVING SHULMAN, *VALENTINO*, 1967[1]

One of the striking characteristics of the era of Coolidge Prosperity was the unparalleled rapidity and unanimity with which millions of men and women turned their attention, their talk, and their emotional interests upon a series of tremendous trifles—a heavyweight boxing-match, a murder trial, a new automobile model, a transatlantic flight.

FREDERICK LEWIS ALLEN, *ONLY YESTERDAY*, 1931[2]

A "POISONOUSLY SALACIOUS" BESTSELLER

The year 1921 turned out to be magical for Valentino even though the aftermath of the success of *The Four Horsemen* was anything but rosy. After *Camille*, he and Mathis left Metro Pictures to join Famous Players–Lasky. It was an ambitious move for both of them, but Valentino was also motivated by his frustrations with Metro's unwillingness to raise his salary and public profile substantially despite the success of *The Four Horsemen*. Upon learning that Metro underappreciated Valentino's star potential, Jesse Lasky hired him and then paired him with Mathis, whom he had just lured away from the same company, to work on *The Sheik*. Before their move, Lasky had acquired the filming rights to the eponymous British best-selling novel and for a while remained unsure whether to turn it into a film. *The Sheik* had first become a smashing success in the United Kingdom, eventually going through 108 printings between its release in 1919 and 1923, but as overwhelming as the novel's British popularity was, it "could not compare with its bedazzling success in the United States."[3]

The novel had something mysterious about it: the gender of the unknown author, E. M. [Edith Maude] Hull, remained long unclear until it was revealed that she was a first-time female writer. The book was also quite controversial in America not just because it described the repeated rape of a white Englishwoman by a man who for much of the novel seems to be an Arab, but also and most signifi-cantly because it portrayed the result as a passionate love affair. Although the *Liter-ary Review* described it as "poisonously salacious in conception" and the *New York Times* found its story "preposterous," the novel struck a chord among thousands of female readers—which greatly intrigued Lasky.[4] Still, publishing the book and adapting it for the screen were obviously two different commercial enterprises. At the height of nativist propaganda and a Ku Klux Klan revival in America, the fear of *showing* and thereby endorsing miscegenation was real and profound.[5]

Hull's *The Sheik* could circulate freely because it had successful precedents: it belonged to a tradition of romantic novels that had become popular since the beginning of the century and that included Robert Hitchens's *Garden of Allah* (1904) and Kathlyn Rhodes's *The Lure of the Desert* (1916).[6] After her most famous novel, Hull went on to publish other works in the same vein, including *The Shadow of the East* (1921) and *Son of the Sheik* (1925), which was adapted into Valentino's last film. Critically speaking, the film and its surrounding literary tradition raises questions about historical female readers' (and spectators') attraction for "desert Arabs, portrayed as barbaric, sensual, dangerous and unpredictable."[7] At issue is the ostensible discrepancy between the early-twentieth-century scripted "fanta-sies of opulence, barbarism and sensuality," centered on the notion of the Orient as the West's feminized other, and new postwar discourses about gender equal-ity and female identities.[8] The discrepancy was only superficial. Because of read-ers' familiarity with the genre, the sheik's dangerous demeanor as kidnapper and sexual predator is never purely shocking. It is mitigated by the narrative tradition within which he operates and which relies on a number of recognizable motifs—the abduction, the sandstorm, the desert ride, and the heroine's futile attempt to escape. This distant but familiar universe ensures that apparently alien characters are "carefully pre-packaged into familiar narrative parcels, which can be enjoyed without undue anxiety."[9] The exciting barbarism of the story's othered, yet highly aestheticized protagonist operates on familiar terrain. At the level of narrative, the stereotypical ideological rivalry between East and West could be both excitingly and safely projected onto Western women's attraction to the sensual and barbaric Oriental man not only because it was a familiar script, but also because its characters engage in masquerades. In both the novel and the film, as we shall see, the two protagonists undergo and display significant transformations that grant ideological legitimacy to their romantic entanglement and enable spectatorial pleasure without erasing the story's racy and dangerous atmosphere.

Famous Players–Lasky purchased the film rights because it apparently appreci-ated the novel's success among female readers, who constituted cinema's most loyal patrons. Still, visualizing a white woman's dangerous and illicit romance with a racially othered man posed challenges that had to be addressed at the levels of casting, narrative, and promotion. As Lasky recounted in his memoir, he remained uncertain about whom to choose for the leading part of the passionate desert savage. He had excluded Wallace Reid because he "was too much the good-natured, big-brother type" and Thomas Meighan for being "too wholesome and casual." After watching *Four Horsemen,* he was struck by its unknown male lead who displayed "the lithe grace of a panther" and whose "sheer animal magnetism" made women go to the movie theaters "to swoon."[10] Because he believed that the newly popular Italian actor could play Ahmed Ben Hassan's performative racial otherness and turn it into a subject of sensual desire, Lasky signed him away from Metro. Although Valentino was quickly on board, June Mathis refused to work on the script because, according to Joan Vale, she "disapproved [of] the sexist theme which focused on physical humiliation, in part desired by the helpless female captive of the desert warrior."[11] By contrast, American producers feared that Diana Mayo's falling in love with an Arab and being indifferent about the consequences— "she did not care what he was, he was the man she loved," says the novel—would have led to major problems with the censors and a sure commercial disaster.[12]

Mathis's refusal to reprise her collaboration with Valentino tells us about the challenge that the adaptation posed (as well as about the opportunities it opened). First, Ibáñez had an artistic reputation that Hull lacked. Second, as the story was written, Ahmed did not appear to be as credibly capable of the kind of conversion that Julio underwent from spoiled young heir to sensitive and irresistible lover. Given how talented Mathis had been in responding to public taste, the film's success vis-à-vis her refusal to collaborate on the project calls attention not just to the differences between novel and film but also to the continuity of the Valentino type first noticed in the promotion of *Four Horsemen.* Directed by the established George Melford and written by the company's screenwriter Monte M. Katterjohn, *The Sheik* ended up solidifying the Divo's popular image for years to come.

The film's adaptation was far from a literal adherence to the book. It presented narrative additions and reworkings that affected the construction of the characters and the film's overall ideological register. Since the novel had received wide recognition in America, the film's production, distribution, and publicity largely, although not exclusively relied on audience familiarity with Hull's work. By January 1922 the fan magazines frequently referred to the novel's racy appeal to publicize the film. "Here is romance. Red-hot," promised *Photoplay.* "If you read the story you will go to see the filmization. If you haven't, you will go anyway." Even though highbrow critics had scoffed at the novel for its sensationalist style and sexually provocative content, the article insisted that it was "read and re-read by two-thirds of the women in this country."[13] While stressing that the film amounted to sure entertainment, however, the most important fan magazine of its time went on to describe the movie with two apparently contradictory terms: "a very exciting, very old-fashioned photoplay."[14]

The coexistence of these attributes should be surprising. Less than two years after the passage and ratification of the Nineteenth Amendment (June 4, 1919, and August 18, 1920), how could a film that celebrated its dependence on a novel that contains rapes and the most controversial form of interracial romance (featuring a white woman, that is) be deemed both "exciting" and "old-fashioned"? Had not years of campaigning for gender equality pushed storytelling to more equitable forms that made sexual violence toward women utterly unacceptable, even as fantasy? Let us consider the circumstances of the film's production and specifically the narrative changes wrought in the novel's story line to assess how the studio released a film that despite its source's controversial plot defied censorship restrictions and was marketed to female fans as most alluring.

(SAFE) DESERT LOVE

Largely dependent on Hull's narrative arc, the film tells the story of a rich tribal prince, Sheik Ahmed Ben Hassan, who meets a British tourist, the independent Lady Diana Mayo, visiting the Saharan town of Biskra. When she ventures into the desert, Ahmed kidnaps her, takes her to his tent, and tries to seduce her. To his dismay, she rejects him and tries to shame him. Captive and forced to wear traditional Arab garb, Diana is embarrassed to meet one of Ahmed's closest friends, a French novelist named Raoul, who assumes the worst. Fortunately, the novelist and Diana become friends, and Raoul encourages Ahmed to release her. The proud Ahmed keeps her prisoner but, moved by her prayers, no longer tries to assault her. Meanwhile, during an escorted horseback ride outside the camp, Diana scribbles "Ahmed, I love you" on the sand before falling into the hands of Omair the bandit, a character who sports a much darker complexion than Ahmed does and who does not have any of the hero's style and eventual restraint. Ultimately, Ahmed saves her from captivity, but he is injured during the battle. While attending his wounds, Diana learns from Raoul that Ahmed is the orphaned son of an English father and a Spanish mother. As she prays for his recovery, Ahmed awakens and the two lovers finally recognize each other.

In contrast to the novel, Melford's *The Sheik* developed new ways to turn Ahmed and Diana into acceptable characters and legitimate lovers and subjects of desire and identification for film audiences. Notwithstanding its debts to the novel, the film includes two complementary sequences that reveal Ahmed and Diana as *masquerading characters*. The scenes show that, despite the exoticism of settings, costumes, and story, Ahmed and Diana are much more conventional, or "old-fashioned," than they first appear to be. The two sequences strengthen the protagonists' characterizations as individuals devoted to romantic love, and both additions resonate with scenes that were in the novel—particularly one from the beginning that depicts Ahmed's repeated singing and Diana's reactions to it.

The film opens with a set piece, the "bride market" scene in which Ahmed takes part in the "ancient custom by which wives are secured for the wealthy sons of Allah," as one intertitle reads. After noticing how the traditional custom would end up separating two true lovers, he exercises his authority in favor of authentic romance. The importance of the scene is proleptic: "It makes clear that his erotic imagination," observes Stephen Caton, "can warm to the concept of romantic love, by means of which he is subsequently subdued and won over by Diana."[15] Ahmed appears to be an Arab sheik, a creature who is allegedly foreign to Western notions of romance. In truth, he is only masquerading as an Arab sheik and the coupling of the scene with audiences' knowledge of his true diegetic (and extradiegetic) identity as a European man introduces a double layer in his reception. We may see him as an Arab male chauvinist, but the story constitutes a safe fantasy with a conventional outcome—a foreseeable and familiar romance ending in marriage.

This initial scene frames the film's narrative and the spectatorial experience on two interrelated levels. It provides the original sign of Ahmed's inner nature and as such anticipates his transformation into a character devoted to romance—a change that will also extend to Diana. The scene also trains the spectator in appreciating the visual and dramaturgic solution of the self-exoticizing masquerade that enables the two protagonists to engage in the practices of racial cross-dressing that are consequential for their romance. While this may seem obvious for Ahmed, it is truer for Diana. Initially, she "is a prototypical desert romance heroine," who "flaunts her independence," has a penchant for "boyish clothing," and appears "uninterested in traditionally feminine pursuits."[16] Despite these characteristics, Diana is not exactly equivalent to the American flapper, who was known for being sexually active and appreciative of constant courtship. Diana has never kissed a man, does not understand the attraction of physical contact, and lacks the contentment with her femininity that Arab women seem to display. Being in the desert and knowing Ahmed will change that.

Their first direct encounter is an exchange of gazes that reveals his impenitent desire and her fear. But the next morning, Ahmed's passionate singing from afar of "The Kashmiri Song" ("Pale hands I loved beside the Shalimar. Where are you now? Who lies beneath your spell?") stirs a profoundly sensual feeling in Diana.[17] She remains utterly enchanted, ignoring that her captor is the performer. While describing her reaction, the novel defines his charming and passionate baritone as "strangely un-English." By contrast, the romanticism of the film's first scene of the bride market compels the spectator to register her listening enthrallment as an aural sign of the two protagonists' inevitable romance. His singing reveals a romantic passion that is utterly absent in her brother and her peers. Diana recognizes the song, names it, and is pleasurably reminded of India, and thus of a context of both racial difference and interracial attraction.[18]

Along the same lines, the filmmakers added another scene not included in the novel that fits with Diana's transformation from self-righteous interloper to caring wonderer and finally lover. While in Biskra, Diana intentionally practices racial cross-dressing. She persuades an Arab woman to lend her clothes so that she can masquerade as an Arab wife-to-be and access the casino's inner chambers where local chieftains gamble for brides. Once there, she becomes both a horrified *witness* to the barbaric ritual she so despises and a *participant* in it, while briefly hidden in plain sight as a native woman willing to accept a sexual sacrifice. Yet, in "her disapproval of these Eastern injustices, she sets up criteria against which the sheik is measured."[19] The film's initial scene, in which Ahmed authoritatively rejects the Arab custom in favor of true love, sets up Valentino as capable of shifting from primitive sheik to fully acceptable romantic partner. It is a transformation that has both moral and racial implications: its unfolding exposes the civilized nobility of Ahmed's whiteness. Similarly, once Diana's masquerade is revealed by her different skin color, she can escape the primitive ritual for exactly the same reason, thanks to her race. But the cross-dressing has touched her. Only after wearing the costumes of a culture that she judges as primitive can she attain the power to immerse herself in what she considers one of its most barbaric rituals and eventually exit it. Karen Chow notes that female spectators "who identified with her participated, by proxy, in the crossing of gender and racial boundaries as Diana's changes of clothing give her the power of transgression through masquerade."[20] It is an exciting but safe journey. The scene reveals that racial masquerading is not just an opportunity for Diana to trespass in an alien culture but also a chance to "try on" an alien dimension of her own life, that of wife-to-be, ready for the kind of full sexual experience in which she had long expressed no interest.

At the center of these racial masquerades, at once exoticizing and domesticating, is the Arab desert. More than a geographic location, the desert was the projection of rich and long-standing Orientalist visual and literary imageries that had turned it into a site of daring sexual license.[21] Since the beginning of the century, the so-called desert romance contributed to such imagery in a remarkable way: it "proved a particularly rich genre for popular engagement with fantasies of sexual identity."[22] Specifically, in the imaginary desert, women could find freedom from the ideological boundaries of prescribed gender roles through their identification with the sensual Orientalist fantasy that featured unprecedented degrees of explicitness and even violence. In both novel and film, the character of the desert sheik Ahmed animates these fantasies of sexual license. He daringly sexualizes Diana's persona by recognizing her masquerade as a modern woman who refuses to acknowledge her true womanhood. Immediately after kidnapping her, he recognizes her desert clothes as deceptively manly ("You make a very charming boy, but it was not a boy I saw two nights ago in Biskra") and forces her to display her full figure by commanding her to wear Arab garments which accentuate bodily contours.[23] Even more strikingly, he interpellates her sexual knowledge in an all too explicit fashion, but he does so by advancing a very modern notion of womanhood. After a scared and horrified Diana asks him, "Why have you brought me here?" Ahmed replies with the famous line "Are you not woman enough to know?" which addresses her as a woman who is familiar with erotic desire and is not just drawn to romantic entanglements.

These exchanges invite a consideration of the film's mysogyny in a broader diegetic and cultural context. On the one hand, it is striking to note that through

Ahmed's brutal conquest (and in the novel through explicit and repeated rape), Diana attains a degree of sexual maturity and emotional self-knowledge that she had lacked. On the other hand, as Karen Chow maintains, the shift from initial asexuality to full-bodied erotic knowledge gave both her and women in general "a new sexual freedom as desiring subjects."[24] In other words, both novel and film must train their consumers to look *past* the sexual violence toward its transformative effects—diegetic and extradiegetic. The challenge is to develop strategies to dedramatize Ahmed's barbaric violence and highlight Diana's power to affect change in his heart. Both his racial and gender masquerades must be obvious in order to ensure the feasibility and authenticity of his later conversion. By displaying both the appearance of an outward racial difference and its own performative quality, the film, much more than the novel, enhances the acceptability of its star actor's diegetic conversion. Caton has noted that "the sheik, not Diana, is at the heart of the cinematic melodrama," and he appears "much more 'feminine' to begin with than his novelistic counterpart."[25] His long flowing robes, his fastidious sophistication, and his visible makeup undermine the threat of his darker, racialized masculinity by revealing a sort of refined and androgynous character. Valentino-as-Ahmed is always impeccably dressed, appears clean and urbane, even in his display of primitive desire. Overdetermined as a seeker of scopic pleasure, he also lends himself to erotic contemplation on the part of other characters and, of course, the film's spectators. He is also quite learned and fluent in many languages, has studied in Paris, and is acquainted with established writers, including Raoul de Saint Hubert. What sets him apart from all the Arabs around him is that he is at home both in the desert and among cosmopolitan (Western) individuals. The true villains, as the film makes clear in the second part, are the "real" and much darker Arabs, who cannot cross-dress culturally, let alone racially, in the way he can. To return to Bederman's framework, an apparent display of racial and national otherness was needed to rework conventional manhood into a romantic and passionate masculinity capable of taming Diana's novel and independent female type. At the same time, the film also uses Ahmed's feminizing features as indexes of personal sensibility and probity to tame his alleged racial otherness and to signal his covert racial nobility.[26]

The person who catalyzes Ahmed's rediscovery of his personal moral sensibility is Diana. Her personal faith enhances and validates his transformation from abusive kidnapper to conflicted, melancholic, and respectful companion. If we ask what keeps Ahmed from further violating Diana after the kidnapping—at least to the degree that the film reveals—we find the repeated scene of Diana praying, which awakens his compassion and remorse.[27] "It is she [. . .] who tames and redeems *him*," Caton has noted, "largely through her Christian faith."[28] Even before the unveiling of the racial/national masquerade, it is his respect for her Christian devotion and thus to Western civilization that informs his change of behavior and ultimately abates the horror of miscegenation. That horror is instead conveniently displaced onto the darker and morally unrepentant Sheik Omair, representative of Christianity's "arch adversary, Islam."[29]

As the spectator may surmise at the end of the film, Ahmed's inner whiteness and Christian nobility justify Diana's attraction to him. It is not a total discovery, of course, on either fictional or biographical grounds. Having read the novel, film spectators recognized the film adaptation's narrative twists. Further, while Hull simply invented the fictional Ahmed, Lasky's casting of Valentino made filmgoers unfailingly aware of the character's underlying whiteness. Thus, the realization that Ahmed is not really an Arab but a European, with English and Spanish blue blood in his veins, provides a much more surprising and ultimately reassuring closure in the novel than in the film. Readers of the novel were also exposed to a much more daring and unconventional version of Diana's desire than viewers of the film. Without the aforementioned added scenes, the novel's racial distance between Ahmed and Diana remained far more deep-rooted than in the film. What remains true for both novel and film is that "for the desert romance heroine, marriage with the sheik provides the best of both worlds: a domestic life and [. . .] exotic presence in her life."[30] The thrill of a dangerous relationship had found a most reassuring last-minute resolution.

Famous Players–Lasky knew very well that the success of *The Sheik* depended on shrewd and glamorous publicity. In October 1921, a month before the film's release, the director of Paramount publicity, Jerome Beatty, asked his London representative to interview Mrs. Hull. The assembled information was incorporated in a publicity campaign that Paramount described as "one of the biggest ever put behind a motion picture."[31] The studio and Chalmers Publishing Company played what we may call the audience-pleasing game by linking the book and film. Book editions carried a special jacket designed to tie "directly with the picture through the printed line, 'A Paramount Picture with Agnes Ayres and Rudolph Valentino—a George Melford Production.'" That jacket sported a color reproduction of a painting by popular illustrator Marshall Frantz that had been used in the twenty-four-sheet posters and other advertising illustrations (figure 16).[32] The publisher meanwhile was "20,000 volumes behind in orders" and had "planned to use the twenty-fifth edition simultaneously with the release of the Paramount picture [. . .] to advertise the double event in a manner befitting the occasion."[33] The studio's promotional tie-in squarely stressed the theme of interracial love on and off screen and offered a titillating homage to an Oriental style of courtship that was unapologetically passionate and even despotic. What is more, the promotion justified itself as merely an attempt "to satisfy the public's expectations," Lasky boasted to *Moving Picture World*.[34] "A photoplay of tempestuous love between a madcap English Beauty and a bronzed Arab chief" read a double-spread advertisement in *MPW*. It included a line from the novel that was used in the film: "When an Arab sees a woman he wants, he takes her" (figure 17).[35]

The star-centered promotion worked. The film was a box-office success. On November 10, a *Wid's* news item reported that the picture, with almost 54,000

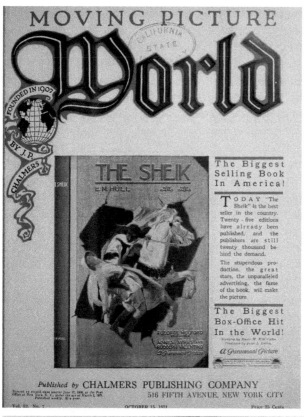

FIGURES 16 and 17. Advertisements for *The Sheik* (1921). *Moving Picture World*, October 15, 1921, 713; and *Moving Picture World*, October 22, 1921, 830–31.

paying spectators, had "smashed all attendance records at the Rivoli and Rialto theatres" in New York during the first three days and was on track to establish "a new record in Broadway entertainment history".[36] After its release, a number of articles sought to brand the film as a Valentino-style romance. With pages filled with images and only a few lines of text, *Motion Picture Classic,* for instance, promoted the film as a unique opportunity to learn about the type of romance that Diana experienced—"desert love."[37] But another dimension emerged as linked to Valentino's diegetic and extradiegetic public authority, one pertaining to a novel model of leadership. It was still intertwined with notions of romantic entanglement, but it was also easily readable in political terms. After all, *The Sheik* had started as a story about the whims and desire of a charming Oriental despot.

WHITE LEADERSHIP AND THE ART OF PLEBISCITE

The Sheik, Ahmed Ben Hassan, upon whose shoulders has fallen the heritage of leadership.

Growing to manhood as an Arab, he was sent to Paris to be educated and [. . .] returned to the desert to assume leadership of the tribe.

THE SHEIK (1921), INTERTITLES FROM THE OPENING AND CLOSING SCENES

With Bederman, we learned that in the early twentieth century, the older formulation of manhood as moral character was eclipsed by an understanding of masculinity that relied on the bodily traits of prowess and sensual appeal and not solely on the moral values of probity and self-control. The legitimation of such elementary traits, often romantically narrativized through racial masquerade, went hand in hand with praise for leadership. Consider the Argentinian tango: in general, it provides a sanctioned acting out of a primitive form of male dominance that relies on the collaboration of a subjugated partner. The recognition of Valentino's tango expertise signified both the actor's embodiment of a primeval appeal and his partner's devoted consent. Similarly, consider Edgar Rice Burroughs's *Tarzan of the Apes,* featuring an aristocratic British child, John Clayton, raised by apes who call him "Tarzan" (White Skin); he is at once at home in the jungle and instinctively noble. Or consider the British diplomat and officer T. E. Lawrence who, dressed as a Bedouin, managed to *lead* an Arab revolt against the Ottoman Empire in the context of Britain's African front in World War I.[38] Tarzan, Lawrence of Arabia, and *The Sheik* (both novel and film) relied on the expedient of racial masquerade to exhibit a new form of white masculinity that exercised effective leadership over nonwhite crowds—or apes.

Since what keeps these figures from going fully primitive are the sensibility and restraint that allegedly are proper to the white Anglo-Saxon man, the problem with this racial profile is that the Italian Valentino is not one. How was it possible that, given his racial status, he was placed in a position usually occupied by eugenics' top-ranked individuals? Ahmed's progressive acceptability and the revelation of what lies beneath his racial masquerade, in fact, calls attention not just to the racial status of the *character* but also to that of the *actor* playing it. Thus, for Valentino, there were questions regarding his adequacy not just as a romantic partner for a white woman but also as a leading subject of American audiences' appreciation and desire on and off screen. Taming the feminization of his character and persona and recuperating his otherness as acceptable leadership relied on three dynamics: his differentiation from other characters within *The Sheik,* his juxtaposition to Italian immigrants' cultural and racial makeup, and a talent to secure plebiscitarian consensus.

Diegetically, *The Sheik* juxtaposes Valentino against characters who appear to be chromatically and thus racially different. Valentino's leadership is exercised over figures who are clearly darker, including, close to him, a Nubian house servant played by an uncredited African American actor. By the same token, the rival sheik is an unmistakably darker Arab (a white man in blackface), whose even darker bodyguard safeguards Valentino's racial otherness from any possible diegetic or ideological confusion with nonwhite characters or darker-appearing crowds.

In the racial framework of the period, Italians as Europeans enjoyed legal, political, socioeconomic, and social advantages of whiteness that were unavailable to Latino, Native, Asian, and African Americans.[39] Still, Italians were not exempt from charges of radical racial difference and anthropological inadequacy. Racialization was thus the terrain on which narratives of adaptation could be denied or allowed. As a native Italian, Valentino was heavily racialized, but his status had to be differentiated from that of his fellow Southern Italian immigrants. It is within this framework that one can understand the strategy at work in the phrenological profile that appeared in a March 1922 issue of *Photoplay.* In it, Valentino emerged as "the Physical-Romantic type," who "is fond of romantic and dangerous action." It was a characterization that, both in its nomenclature and explanations, sought to turn the inevitable identification of racial difference into a set of appealing features, the most remarkable of which were unapologetic individualism, sexual desire, and leadership:

> His strong, heavy chin and jaw indicate aggressiveness combined with an accentuated ego and a marked self-esteem. His features (especially his eyes and mouth) show that he is strongly attracted by the opposite sex [. . . .] The vertical structure of his back-head does not permit of his being influenced or taking on impressions easily.[40]

As an exceptional migrant of semiaristocratic background, Valentino had to be positioned above the fray, as a leading man capable of eliciting reactions that were stronger than mere acceptability. Beyond his screen presence, publicity coverage translated the distinct, original, and un-American novelty of the Italian divo into captivating, anticonformist individuality. At the center of editorial-like articles, interviews, and promotional news was the columnist and secret publicity agent

Herbert Howe. Possibly more than anybody in the 1920s, Howe displayed a peculiar fondness for writing about film stardom through the language of institutional
politics and by comparing Hollywood stars to celebrated political leaders—from
Napoleon to Mussolini. During the brief but productive collaboration between
Howe and Valentino, which lasted until early 1923, the Divo signed off on rare
but studied pronouncements that merged film stardom with politics. Howe likely
ghostwrote these and inserted them in his profiles of the Italian actor. In these,
Howe walked a fine line between highlighting Valentino's charming and sophisticated foreignness and underscoring the agreeable character of his forceful ideas.
Recent criticism, while productively engaged in reading Valentino's ambivalent
gender image and mode of address, has largely overlooked this political dimension, which first surfaced in coincidence with *The Sheik*'s release.

In the December 1921 issue of *Motion Picture Classic,* Howe published an extensive profile-interview of Valentino entitled "Hitting the Hookah with Rudie." The
actor contributed to it with a wealth of biographical details.[41] As a way of introducing his subject, Howe first sought to overcome the obstacle of national prejudice.
While showing intimate knowledge of his subject, Howe depicts Valentino's arrival
in the United States as the result of glamorous, cosmopolitan meandering. "His life
has been tempestuous melodrama," he writes admiringly, "commencing in a noble
family of Taranto, Italy, passing thru escapades in Paris, curious and sensational
adventures in New York, on up to the present moment of screen idolatry."[42] Then
Howe makes sure that the actor's temperament, and not just his life circumstances,
can in no way be associated with the culture of the familiar "alien-intruders"—Italian
immigrants. For Howe, Valentino displays only good Italian qualities, such as
"emotional warmth," but "none of the volubility that we have come to expect as
an Italian characteristic thru commerce with push-cart financiers." Instead, the
actor has the "dreamy melancholy of the stoic" and although "he has more the
facial appearance of the Bedouin than the Roman," he displays "the sturdy muscled
physique of the Roman gladiator." The celebration of Valentino's membership in
European aristocracy on his mother's side was utterly fictitious: she was not aristocratic, only French. But it resonated well with the appreciation of his cosmopolitan
sophistication that further separated him from Italian immigrants.[43]

In the same profile-interview, Valentino effortlessly combines discussions of
marriage and women's rights with his take on democracy and the meaning of
leadership in both political and romantic affairs. First, he blames divorce on what
Howe calls the "democratic delusion," then he moves "from the dangerous subject
of woman's rights to the theories of government." For Valentino, democracy was as
bad a word as anarchy, whether in a person's private or public affairs:

> In America democracy has been carried even to the home and you see the con-
> sequences. There must be a leader for a nation, for a state, for a home. There is no
> such thing as equality. The woman is not the equal of the man, intellectually or any
> other way.[44]

Valentino's celebration of male authority did not actually match some key events in his personal life that had become public knowledge. Shortly after the success of *The Four Horsemen,* in fact, his life had began publicly unraveling. In May 1921, his first wife, Jean Acker, with whom he did not spend a single night, had accused him of desertion. Shortly after, his domestic affairs were "aired in a Los Angeles courtroom," as *Photoplay* noted.[45] The public coverage of his marital fiasco in 1921 and subsequent divorce from Acker (January 1922) shaped a public perception of Valentino as weak, dependent, and exploitable by strong women.

It was this context that gave Valentino and Howe's public celebration of male authority more than a whiff of overcompensation. It was meant to recast Valentino's image and position him as an idealized romantic partner with the personal standing to display effective self-governance and forceful authority over women. Vocally against women's right to vote, he critiques the self-repressive and excessively compliant male American temperament. He takes pride in his Italian origin, but he does so in a recognizably American manner. Valentino stresses the key tenet of individualism a short ten months before Mussolini's March on Rome (October 1922) made the Duce an admirable model of effective autocracy. He thus presents the old-fashioned (yet never passé) Italian *individualistic* ethos as traditionally American, as if twentieth-century progress had brought decadence and corruption to the New World. He repeatedly praises personal freedom and authority as values lost in the American political system but alive and well in the Italian monarchy:

> Not because I am Italian do I say it, but I do believe the Italian form of government— and the English—gives more individual freedom than the republic [. . .]. Here in America they attempt to dictate what you shall see on the screen, what you shall put in your mouth—even what you shall do on the day the Lord gave you. Bolshevism is just another democratic theory and it will fail.[46]

In Howe's striking prose, Valentino conflates types of political governance with forms of individual freedom. He judges the modern phenomena of mass consensus and persuasion as conformist perversions and, as such, most un-American. Within a rhetorical framework constantly centered on gender difference, he recognizes the most glaring effects of what he describes as a Bolshevik democratization at the intimate level of romantic relationships. American women's sense of independence and initiative, in his view, result from men's failure to exercise close supervision and authority over their partners. When he returns to the issue a few months later in a comparable article-interview, he advances a familiar autocratic solution: "There must be a leader, one sex or the other, and women in America have found that the men are not leading them. Commercially, the initiative of the American man is supreme on earth. Socially, domestically, he is subordinate."[47] Beyond gender differences, Valentino also comments on the issue of individuals' sovereignty or control over their lives. Despite the "finest educational system in the world," Americans puzzle him. "You do not think, except in masses," he charges,

"You hide your individuality. You accept. That is the sum of it. The newspapers propound and you accept." In Europe, he claims, even without a comparable level of mass literacy, "the so-called reforms established here" would never be accepted. There, "education or no education, each person is an individual."[48]

As Valentino's criticism of the limits of American manhood bled beyond the domain of romantic relationships into the political domain of forms of government and responsible citizenship, Howe too deployed political references—electoral ones, specifically—to read the phenomenon of stars' popular consensus. His columns presented a wealth of political metaphors that equated spectators to "electoral constituents." His views about who is a film star, who makes stars, and who approves them relied on an apparently obvious analogy between stardom and the electoral process and depended on two poles: a star's personality and the public's ability to celebrate it.[49] Conveniently, he ignored the idea that a studio's publicity efforts played any determining role in the process. The notion of audiences' *spontaneous* consensus was obviously a trope the industry cultivated in its continuous aspiration to bypass censorship restrictions. It was also an argument that gossip writers like Adela Rogers St. Johns presented somewhat ironically to their readers with such slogans as "Nobody can make stars of nothing."[50] Free choice helped frame Hollywood as an industry that catered to the desires of the audiences and thus ultimately served American democracy, against the arbitrary actions of state and local censorship boards. This was also the very serviceable rationale deployed by fan magazines, directors, and individual critics.[51]

Officially, Howe's ideal model was that of a direct democracy that celebrated fans' unprompted agency in the choice of their favorite stars. In truth, he knew that such a democratic model was a fiction. After Valentino's fame emerged, Howe contended, "the critics and the public pronounced him a 'find,' but of course the critics and the public know nothing about pictures. They only patronize 'em; they don't make 'em."[52] In other words, the public expresses a free and direct opinion about a candidate only by way of accepting or refusing a proposal that it did not frame or articulate in the first place. Howe also believed in the inevitability of a star when endowed with a novel, appealing personality. Valentino easily embodied an exoticism of manners that young Americans could appreciate as a relief from the "cleanliness [that] makes them believe in their godliness."[53] Howe's favorite way to reconcile these two positions—the public's mere power of ratification and the star's inevitability—was to make a comparison with the plebiscite. The fan community, just like an entire electorate, is simply invited to ratify or reject an appointment that, in case of a successful outcome, allows stars to behave according to unconventional rules and exercise a unique authority over their base. In politics, plebiscites or decrees by the people turn elected leaders into imperial figures who are virtually unaccountable except during new elections or impeachment. It is not difficult to understand why such plebiscitary logic soon encouraged Howe to associate film stars with authoritarian political leaders—particularly Mussolini. Even more importantly, it is also possible to recognize arguments in Howe's political views that do not necessarily involve dictatorships or antidemocratic leaders. As a reference point, I would suggest returning to Woodrow Wilson's pre-twentieth-century writings on political sovereignty.

In his 1893 volume *An Old Master, and Other Political Essays,* Wilson called for an expansion of executive power in light of his diagnosis about the "nature and lodgment of sovereignty." Distinguishing between government and the *process* of governing, Wilson questioned the rhetorical and routine identification of sovereignty with the will of the people. He first defined sovereignty "as the highest political power in the state, lodged in active organs, for the purpose of governing." Then he distinguished between sovereignty and control: if "sovereign power is a positive thing; control [is] a negative thing." He concluded that if "power belongs to government[, . . .] control belongs to the community," and if power "is lodged in organs of initiative," control "is lodged with the voters."[54] To read Howe through the lens of Wilson's political writings, one may restate the former's argument by positing that film audiences, like regular voters, may think they are exercising their consecrated sovereignty when casting their ballots for their favorite stars. In reality, their preferences are, to quote Wilson, "exercised by way of approval or disapproval, acquiescence or resistance; they are not agencies of initial choice,"[55] or, to quote Howe again, spectators "only patronize [stars]; they don't make 'em." Wilson's argument in that volume may further illuminate Howe's less-than-forthcoming position regarding the "true organs of initiative." Decades before establishing the CPI, Wilson had expressed his deep concern about the arbitrary and aggressive power of the press, which he recognized as uniquely capable of "assuming the leadership in opinion."[56] Unlike Wilson, Howe was in convenient denial about the power that he, film periodicals, and studios' promotional campaigns exerted on whom to celebrate as a star—or, to put it differently, on whom to include on voters' ballots.

Howe wrote repeatedly on the *unmediated* relationship between a star's personality and voters' preferences. In a contribution to *Photoplay* entitled "They Can't Fool the Public," he praised American spectators for recognizing the novelty of Valentino's exotic personality and casting their votes accordingly, for "the regular motion picture public is infallible in its election of stellar favorites."[57] In response to the widespread view that the studios' promotional activities played an important role, Howe described filmgoing as the only model of actual popular sovereignty:

> Fortunes have been expended in publicity and in lavish production to force a player into favor—but to no avail. You can stuff a ballot box, but you can't stuff a box office. Here is one democratic institution where the public will prevails.[58]

Finally, the collaboration between Howe and Valentino was also evident in the actor's serialized autobiography, which Howe likely ghostwrote.[59] Entitled "My Life Story," it ran in three *Photoplay* issues from February to April 1923. Earlier that year, a one-page announcement in *Photoplay* repeated the familiar notion of a direct, semiconfessional autobiographical tale: "This is his story. Not his press agent's; he hasn't a press agent. It is the first authentic record of his life, related by himself."[60] This was also the register allegedly adopted by Valentino himself in an "open letter to the American Public" that appeared in the same January 1923 issue right as the actor was engaged in a legal battle with Famous Players over his salary. In it, Valentino sought to explain his refusal to make "cut-and-dried program features" in favor of more artistic projects. His motivation for writing the letter in appeal to the American public was the familiar tenet that the audience holds all the cards. "You discovered me and created me," he wrote with rhetorical gratitude. "You made theater managers know me and you caused film magazines and newspapers to be conscious of me."[61]

The appeal to unmediated democratic consensus allowed Howe to draw comparisons between film stars and Prime Minister Benito Mussolini. Like that of a film star, Mussolini's personality, Americans understood, engendered a direct rapport with the Italian public. After the March on Rome, references to Valentino's autocratic public persona began to assume new political attributes. Writing from Europe in early 1923, Howe commented on the two celebrities in terms of the undivided enthusiasm each received. "The most applauded men in the current world are Valentino and Mussolini," Howe proclaimed. He went on to equate the establishment of a new form of government with the release of a film: "In Rome we witnessed the Fascisti revolution and cheered for Mussolini and Vittorio Emanuele. In London we witnessed *Blood and Sand* and cheered for Valentino."[62] In the same issue, he also wrote an article entitled "What Europe Thinks of American Stars." In it Howe wondered "what reception Italy [would] give to [Valentino]" since his films had not yet been released there, and he sought to compare Italian and American audiences on the basis of their shared attraction to exotic figures.[63] However, the cartoon that *Photoplay*'s editors paired with Howe's piece made a much more interesting comparison (figure 18). Drawn by the renowned illustrator Herb Roth, the cartoon and its accompanying caption imagined the Roman social and architectural landscape for a hero's welcome. Tied across the columns of ancient ruins is a giant poster carrying Valentino's name (in its latest form) above an image of the star attacking a bull—clearly an homage to *Blood and Sand* (1922)—amidst colorful individuals of all classes happily dancing, greeting their hero, and congratulating each other. Even a *carabiniere,* or police officer, visible in the lower right corner, cannot help but join what appears to be a harmony of passions, a communion of interests that the celebrity has catalyzed. Given the historical moment, the caption alerts the reader: "This is not the Fascisti revolution celebrating the victory of Mussolini, but merely the Roman welcome to the all-conquering Valentino."[64] It is a legitimate, albeit ironic, notification. The sight of a crowd of excited Italian supporters gathered under the same banner amidst architectural ruins may point more to a spirited plebiscite for the Duce than to the gathering of a throng of film fans.

FIGURE 18. Herb Roth's illustration for Herbert Howe's "What Europe Thinks of American Stars," *Photoplay*, February 1923, 97.

Howe's comparisons to Mussolini centered on overt admiration of the Italian prime minister's forceful manners and his mastery of public performances and promotional strategies. Howe felt that comparisons to the Italian dictator constituted an appropriate reference not just for Valentino but also for another major Hollywood star of the time, Mary Pickford. In a 1924 *Photoplay* interview with America's sweetheart about her favorite stars and her own career, Howe first reported how Pickford sympathized with Valentino's decision to quit Famous Players in opposition to the commercial demands put on him. When talking about her own future and expressing her willingness to become a producer if she was ever asked to retire, Pickford assumed a tone that Howe compared to an "ultimatum hurled with the force and the curtness of a Mussolini from under a flowery girlish hat." Further, while praising her talent as a strong-willed business leader, Howe labeled her "Premier Pickford" and insisted on the comparison with the Italian politician despite obvious physical differences: "She hasn't as big a jaw as Benito, but it's just as firm and determined."[65]

Howe viewed a comparison between a Hollywood star and an iconic authoritarian figure as perfectly legitimate because of his competence "as a critic of screen personalities."[66] Unsurprisingly, he used this very self-description to justify his prediction about the front-runner of the 1924 U.S. presidential elections. He may have been facetious and self-deprecating when he observed, "As a critic of high integrity, who heralded the discovery of Valentino[, . . .] I realize what I say is going to carry considerable weight at the presidential election." But his ironic judg-ment calls about the effectiveness of media *and* political communication relied on readers' immediate understanding of their equivalence. "As everyone knows," he remarked, "the chief duty of our executive today is to film and radio well. Mr. Coolidge does not."[67] A successful model instead was the Duce, whose role as himself in the newly released Hollywood production *The Eternal City* (1924) provided an enviable alternative.

> This month I give three vivas for George Fitzmaurice, who made "The Eternal City" with Barbara La Marr and Benito Mussolini. With Babbie and Benito in the cast the picture certainly should not be lacking in action.[68]

When in 1923 Howe moved on to work as publicity agent for Ramon Novarro, his name remained associated with those of Valentino and Mussolini, both through reports commenting on his activities and through his own writing. Fan magazines knew quite well of Howe's "masquerading" as Valentino. Reporting on Howe's presence as Novarro's lover and publicity agent on the Tunisian set of Rex Ingram's *The Arabian, Photoplay* sarcastically hinted at the extent to which the writer-pro-moter had been involved in manufacturing Valentino's public image. An imagi-nary cable inquiry from the "Lost and Found Department" had located "Mr. Howe in Tunis operating under the name of Rudolph Valentino. He had opened a cor-respondence school of sheiking and was coining money."[69] Howe never denied his demiurgic contribution. Instead he took pride in his prescience as a talent scout and agent. In early 1925, in one of his regular *Photoplay* columns, he sought to single out those stars who had shown the "sterner" requirements of stardom over the years.[70] Howe recognized that the early craze about Valentino, in particular, had to abate eventually, but because of his talent and ambition, he would reemerge a better star. After fighting a "Napoleonic battle" against the studios, he was destined to find a "more stable popularity [. . .] as a creator of pictures, thus evading the fate that lurked like a serpent amid the roses on the path of sex attraction."[71] It was the same combination of personal charisma and show business acumen that had made Howe a vocal admirer of Mussolini. His appreciation only increased after an alleged personal meeting with the Duce in Rome, where Howe had gone to visit Novarro on the set of *Ben Hur*. Following the meeting, Howe described Mussolini as his "favorite star in the current world movie," governing over "the most courteous, ingratiating and genuinely democratic of peoples."[72]

In mid-1925 Howe continued identifying himself with both Valentino and Mussolini. In a tongue-in-cheek article that he prefaced and possibly also wrote about the lives of *Photoplay*'s staff writers, including James R. Quirk, Adela Rogers St. Johns, and himself, he claimed that his real name was "Romeo Galahad Mussolini Leadpipe Howe, Duc de Jambon et des Oeufs" and "in private life" he was "Natacha Rambova's husband."[73] As these facetious sketches reveal, Howe was identifying himself with the publicity strategies that had enabled Valentino and

The box office—the one and only un-
sentimental ballot of motion picture
favorites

This, likewise, will give you an insight as to the difference
between stars and personalities, or featured players. Some
players who are starred in the billing cannot draw any greater
attendance than pictures of equal merit without stars. They
are simply personalities who are being forced into stardom
or in whom producers have the hope of developing
star attraction.

The relative value of stars is gauged by
comparing the average attendance records of their respective pictures.
*How can you gauge the
value of the star versus
the story?*
— The Song

GROUP III

The quality of their pic-
tures will most quickly
change the rating of the
names in this group

According to Mr.
Schenck they are:
1. Acting ability.
2. Appearance.
3. Individuality, i.e., personality of appearance that is so
distinctive as to differentiate them
from all others in marked degree.
No one of these qualities is enough
to make a star. We have fine actors
who are not star attractions because
they haven't youth and beauty, and
we have players with beauty and personality who cannot hold because
they are poor actors.
Mr. Schenck does not believe in
character actors as stars, though they
may rate high as featured players and

Pola
Negri

of Love," star-
ing Norma Tal-
madge, earned eight
hundred thousand dollars.
Without Miss Talmadge it
would have earned less than three
hundred thousand, because it was a
poor story and on a par with pictures earn-
ing from two hundred to three hundred thou-

FIGURE 19. Box office as ballot box. Herbert Howe, "Here Are the Real Box Office Stars,"
Photoplay, June 1926, 29.

Mussolini to become extraordinary stars. In the case of Valentino, Howe's identification was confessional and self-congratulatory. In the case of the Duce, it was a
form of distant admiration for the efficiency of the Fascist public relations machine.
Howe's decision to place a politician and a film star side by side attests to his understanding of moviegoing as a form of democratic voting, and thus of star appeal
(or film fandom, as we might say today) as a form of plebiscitary consensus (figure 19).[74]

When the close relationship between Howe and Valentino came to an end,
other figures came to legitimate Valentino's public rapport with the press—and
ultimately with the studios. In the 1922–1924 period, two figures in particular had
an impact on his career: writer and publicity expert Elinor Glyn, very publicly
albeit quite briefly, and Natacha Rambova, Valentino's second wife. In both cases,
Valentino's image on and off screen underwent changes that were not, commercially speaking, fruitful. The ensuing crisis, however, sheds light on the resilience
of popular appreciation, and over time even nostalgia, for the daring, unapologetic sheik as attempts to tame that original publicity imprint ran into problems.

THE TAMING OF THE SHEIK

The Four Horsemen and *The Sheik* represented twin peaks in Valentino's popularity
because of the films' narratives, which informed the actor's characterizations and

their postrelease publicity. The two productions showcased the same dramaturgic trajectory: Julio and Ahmed initially exhibit a raw, primitive, and even dangerous erotic passion before metamorphosing into heroically caring lovers. At the conclusion of the two films, Valentino's characters are either dead or physically wounded, but their personal destinies signal the triumph of romance. Yet, the Divo's press promotion (and self-promotion) mainly insisted on his forceful erotic prowess. Rather than touching equally on the two poles of erotic charge and tenderness, and specifically as a fictional conversion *from one to the other,* the initial publicity insisted on the dominance of the first, aggressive trait, which imprinted his key mainstream appeal. Still some corrections were needed.

Many in the industry, in fact, felt that the promotion of Valentino's decadent and unremorseful erotic desire had to be balanced by traits and habits that American male spectators could recognize as familiar: professional ambition and physical fitness. That women adored him was as obvious as the fact that men had suspicions about his exotic and threatening foreignness. Men could be brought on board if only they could recognize something conventional in him. That's why Valentino himself, through ghostwritten interviews and direct appeals, took part in a novel publicity discourse that stressed both his suitability for romantic involvement and a distinct, but relatable masculinity. At the same time, the more balanced combination of European and American personal traits had to emerge as a direct, unmediated expression and not as the result of calculated publicity pitches and adjustments. The risk was that his sheik characterizations could appear passé, performative, and inauthentic, and, as such, subject to sarcastic critique and lampooning.

Enter fifty-year-old Elinor Glyn, a consummate expert in selling the glamour and sexual daring of Continental artistry. Her appeal, as her employer Jesse Lasky admitted, derived from her keen understanding of publicity.[75] Glyn already had used editorials, lectures, advice manuals, and even novels to position herself as a champion of female sensual appeal and a shrewd promoter of exotic encounters, primitive desires, and personal fulfillment. Lasky's decision to invite Glyn to Hollywood to script the next Valentino vehicle, *Beyond the Rocks* (May 1922), from her own 1906 novel speaks to his desire to exploit the Orientalist glamour that had in both Glyn and the Italian actor two widely recognized testimonials. Beyond the eccentric taste that led her to redecorate her hotel room like a "Persian tent,"[76] Glyn had creative and efficient ideas about how to promote herself, her films, and cosmopolitan romance in general.

Today Glyn is mostly linked to a famous publicity stunt, the identification of the erotically charged "It" girl that informed the 1927 film of that title starring Clara Bow. Before that episode, however, Glyn had articulated her own "philosophy of love" centered on women's physical and emotional satisfaction. "Glyn's touch" was virtually antithetical to the ways the *It* phenomenon linked economic and sexual freedom with consumer culture. Fond of sensationalism more than cultural daring, Glyn endorsed women's physical and imaginary gratification through "role plays of dominance and submission" and *not* through "the cheapening of sexual relations under commodity capitalism."[77] She claimed that American men "could simply not make love" since they treated their leading ladies like "aunts or sisters."[78] Generally advocating "eugenic progress through racial hybridity," Glyn was known for her statements that Latin men's glamorous and Continental model respected, nurtured, and sparked women's different desires more effectively than their Anglo-Saxon rivals did. At the same time, this apparent openness to racial diversity was always conjugated with social elitism and persistent promotion of herself as a master of posh erotic ceremonies. Ultimately, Glyn's infatuation with men of exotic and aristocratic extraction well suited Valentino's public image, including his consistent distance from fellow Italian Americans.

On the surface, Lasky's casting of Valentino in Glyn's *Beyond the Rocks* appeared most promising. And so did the actor's pairing with Gloria Swanson, who had become a star in her own right as a pioneer of new forms of relationships in the so-called marriage and divorce pictures directed by Cecil B. DeMille between 1919 and 1921. Her lavish personal life and erotically alluring roles could appear cosmopolitan rather than damningly decadent and sinful. Together, Valentino and Swanson could normalize new gender and sexual norms through a strategy of consumer capitalism centered on glamour that made them international fashion trendsetters. As Hilary Hallett rightly points out, "As promise of fulfillment, glamour *naturalized,* for certain subjects, their sensuality not as a perversion, but a natural, and positive, expression."[79] In theory, Valentino and Swanson's transnational glitz added a cosmopolitan cachet to their stardom that deprovincialized both American film culture and its aura in international film markets.

The promotional work showcases the collaboration between Glyn and Valentino as media synergy—from page to screen and back to page. In 1922, Glyn's novel *Beyond the Rocks: A Love Story* appeared "with illustrations from the Paramount photo-play." One of its pages featured a photograph of Glyn and Valentino, presumably taken on the film's set (figure 20). Two months prior to the film's release, Glyn allegedly ghostwrote Valentino's first extensive contribution to *Photoplay*. Published in March 1922, it squarely addressed the issue of male leadership in romantic affairs. Entitled "Woman and Love," the article was meant to draw attention to Valentino's style of romance and show that it was fully compatible with that of Swanson ahead of the release of their (and Glyn's) film.[80] It was not a reprise of the swaggering leadership that Howe had written into Valentino's pronouncements. It was much closer to the narrative trajectory of his earlier successful films, which had portrayed him as an earnest romantic lover, but that contrasted with those films' publicity, which instead had celebrated him as a daring, primitive seducer. In the article, Valentino spoke about passionate romance and openly abhorred the use of sheer physical force. In place of what he termed "the caveman method," he endorsed the more effective "mental caveman" strategy, which would

Rodolph Valentino, as Lord Bracondale and Elinor Glyn,
the author.

FIGURE 20. Valentino and Elinor Glyn as
collaborators. Elinor Glyn, *Beyond the Rocks:
A Love Story* (New York: Macaulay, 1922), 3.

still produce the kind of highly physical romance that he described as "caveman love." "By cleverness, by diplomacy, by superior mental force, by skill," he contended, "that is the way to win a woman."[81] For the Valentino that Glyn scripted, effective romantic leadership had to be combined with "tenderness," which the actor described as "absolutely the strongest, most lasting, most trustworthy emotion that a woman can arouse in a man."[82] The two heart-shaped images—one from *The Sheik* (1921), the other from *Beyond the Rocks* (May 1922)—introducing "Woman and Love" exemplify this double strategy, which is summarized in their caption (figure 21). This approach advocated none of the indomitable erotic governance that Howe had woven into Valentino's earlier statements. Unsurprisingly, the public response to the film did not meet expectations.

The move away from Howe's autocratic characterization of Valentino to Glyn's softer version continued in *Blood and Sand,* which brought the Divo and June Mathis together again. Released in September 1922, the film was based on Ibáñez's best-selling novel and featured Valentino's old daring and primitive characterization for only a few scenes. In its place was a different character, one who is utterly at the mercy of a Spanish vamp, played by Nita Naldi, even though the promotional illustrations stressed the Divo's power of romantic subjugation.[83] Paramount

FIGURE 21. Valentino as "caveman" and as tender lover. "Woman and Love," *Photoplay*, March 1922, 41.

believed that the film was "destined to eclipse the sensational success" of *The Sheik* because of the volume of its prerelease engagements in New York, Los Angeles, and Chicago.[84] Directed by the Lasky-appointed Fred Niblo, *Blood and Sand* initially broke "all records for attendance and receipts at the New York Rivoli during the first week of its runs in the metropolis."[85] Some reviewers, aware of Mathis's role in once again adapting an Ibáñez work, saw admirable continuity in Valentino's acting as well. They claimed he had "never shown such facility and variety of expression since his work in 'The Four Horsemen.'" Still, they found uniquely praiseworthy "the delightful episodes of romance and the fiery scenes of passion, smouldering and flaming."[86] Other critics however, found a fatal flaw in *Blood and Sand*, as they had in *Beyond the Rocks*. These productions continued the restrained characterization of much of *Four Horsemen* but disrupted the continuity with the more original and daring sheik character. Commenting on spectators' reactions to *Blood of Sand*, *Variety* noted: "It was the struggles of the hero to resist the temptation of the siren widow that made them chuckle. The spectacle of the erstwhile sheik holding a beautiful woman at arm's length was too much." While getting Hull's name wrong, the review had it right when it explained audiences' disappointment:

> Valentino's performance of Mrs. Hutchinson's [sic] "Sheik" fixed his status among the fans as a super-heated love maker and the sudden switch to a St. Anthony type comes as a shock.[87]

Mathis and Glyn were not the only enablers who sought to distance Valentino from earlier publicity strategies. An even more daring taming of the Sheik came from his wife, the ambitious Natacha Rambova. As Glyn had done, she too sought to advise Valentino on his artistic and professional decisions. Over the years Rambova had grown discontented with Valentino's popular role as the sensual Oriental despot. She deemed it a form of surrender to commercial exploitation and contrary to the artistic ambitions she projected onto his star persona. She wanted him to be her "ultimate work of art"; thinking of herself as the new Sergei Diaghilev, she hoped Rudy "would be her Nijinsky."[88] When she became costume designer for the mystical drama *The Young Rajah* (November 1922), which Mathis had written for Valentino, Rambova drew on Nijinsky's choreography for Debussy's *L'Après-midi d'une faune*. Wearing the costume his wife had designed and posing as a languid Hindu prince dressed as a fawn, Valentino was unrecognizable to many. The film's story, together with his costumes and poses, contributed to its abysmal commercial failure. They conveyed a disturbing version of masculinity, ambivalent and heterodependent (even on Rambova's elitist artistic ambitions), that proved too much a departure from his daring Sheik heroings.[89]

The last film Valentino made before the breakup with Famous Players and his self-inflicted hiatus presents a narrative trajectory diametrically opposed to that of *The Sheik*. Released as *Moran of the Lady Letty* (December 1922), the film was adapted for the screen by Mathis from Frank Norris's eponymous novel. The story's starting point is comparable to that of *The Sheik*: Moran, the tomboy female protagonist, is a superb sailor who "has never been in love" and who despises men's penchant to command.[90] Her coprotagonist, played by Valentino, is the San Francisco socialite Ramon Laredo, who is bored with his life until he gets shanghaied onto a pirate ship and finally experiences "reality, savage reality."[91] Derided and forced to work, he reveals an unexpected strength and dexterity, which gains him respect and a leading role on the ship.[92] When the crew captures another ship, Laredo rescues the only surviving sailor, Moran. Upon learning Moran is a woman, the captain wants her for himself. Defending her means that Laredo has to kill, but nothing deters him from doing just that because "the blood of the primeval tiger man leaped through him."[93] Laredo's heroism saves Moran and transforms both. Before his newfound combination of physical violence and tenderness, an awakening Moran acquiesces to love: "You win, mate," Moran said, "And I love you for it."

Unsurprisingly, critics very much appreciated this combination of eroticism and sheer violence. "The handsome Rodolph Valentino showed he could wield a wicked fist with as much art as he can make love," wrote Maude Cheatham of *Motion Picture Classic*.[94] But the trajectory of his character was more a *conciliation* of "caveman love and tenderness" (actually, tenderness and caveman love) than a daring display of Sheik-like desire. It once again confirmed the importance of the Sheik's first imprint which, like a picture in everybody's head, could even lend itself to lampooning. For instance, a month after the "Woman and Love" article, in an April 1922 contribution to *Photoplay,* writer-cartoonist Richard W. "Dick"

Dorgan satirized the Italian actor's most famous film role. Dorgan described Valentino's gazing at Diana as the "'I gotcha look' à la Ben Turpin" (anticipating by a year Turpin's own lampooning of the actor's role in the short *The Shriek of Araby*).[95] In what Emily Leider described as Dorgan's "slang review" of *The Sheik*, in which he never mentions Valentino by name, Dorgan questions the actor's contribution to the construction of his own character. He even "outs" Valentino's close publicity collaboration with Glyn, although Glyn had not exactly endorsed the Sheik performative style.[96] "He must have been reading Elinor Glyn closely or else be stealing Theda Bara's stuff," Dorgan wrote before ironically alluding to the rigid prescriptions that Wilson had prepared for the Versailles Peace Conference, "'cause he had all the fourteen points down great, with a couple of the amendments tacked on."[97] Similarly, in 1923 and 1924, populist and politically vocal vaudeville star Will Rogers caricatured several stars, including Valentino's stylized and histrionic acting style, first in the two-reel *Uncensored Movies* and later in *Big Moments from Little Pictures*, both produced by Hal Roach.[98]

Others took the primary scene of the Sheik-like unrepentant lover seriously, often by insisting on a theme that the industry held as essential: a star's personal, direct, and extraordinary appeal to American audiences. A most indicative example of these contributions appeared with the title "The Vogue of Valentino" in *Motion Picture Magazine* in February 1923. Months into Valentino's self-induced exile from the screen due to his refusal to abide by Famous Players' contract, "one of American's most eminent psychologists" sought to explain "the sex psychology underlying the tremendous popularity of Rodolph Valentino."[99] The actor successfully inflamed "the feminine imagination of an entire country," the anonymous psychologist claimed, because he "epitomizes the lure of romantic passion[, . . .] the brigand of love."[100] To make sense of his popularity, this expert argued that Valentino was "at once graceful and aggressively masculine" and that his expression suggested "a suspicion of cruelty" even though "he appears capable of salving whatever cardiac wounds he might inflict."[101] The psychologist described the actor's exotic charm as more Latin than Italian, saying he was accustomed to clothing himself "with spectacular elegance," which did not threaten his masculinity, "for the modern feminine sense of beauty contains that heritage from ancient times which delighted in the gorgeousness of male attire." Finally, the unnamed psychologist asked the critical question: "What condition of affairs in America has brought about Valentino's present status?" He answered with an indictment echoing Valentino's 1921 self-promotion and Glyn's ghostwritten contribution. According to the expert, the Divo's success revealed that "American men are not lovers! [. . .] The American business man has little or no imagination for aesthetic activities and sentimental pastimes. All his imagination has been focused and expended on commercial enterprise. [. . .] The result is, the American woman is starving for romantic love."[102]

A year later, Adela Rogers St. Johns adopted the same perspective of a direct relationship between star and film audiences by seeking to explain both what had made

Valentino so attractive and why men despised him. She deemed it "manifestly silly" that most women "will deny flatly that they are ever attracted by anything in men but grand and noble character." In reality, she argued, "the first essential element of love being flattery, a woman's vanity is most vitally touched by a man's desire for her." Valentino is women's idol, she wrote, because his lure "is wholly, entirely, obviously the lure of the flesh."[103] Along with women's favorable reactions, St. Johns also explained that men "resented Rudolph's popularity [. . .] because they believe he appeals to the worst side of women."[104] What St. Johns clearly had in mind was Dorgan's notorious 1922 "A Song of Hate," in which the famous writer-illustrator expressed his distaste for Valentino's physical appearance, acting style, and success and presumed he was speaking on behalf of all American men. Dorgan used such explicitly racist tones that one might even assume an ironic hyperbole:

> I hate Valentino! All men hate Valentino. I hate his oriental optics; I hate his classic nose; I hate his Roman face [. . .] . I hate him because he dances too well; I hate him because he's a slicker; I hate him because he's the great lover of the screen; I hate him because he's an embezzler of hearts [. . .] . What! Me jealous?—Oh, no—I just Hate Him.[105]

What Dorgan's piece, St. Johns's comments, and the anonymous psychologist's praises all point to is the novelty of Valentino's dominating style of governance of romance that had inaugurated his popularity in late 1921 and had framed women's expectations and men's frustrations ever since. Yet, given the dominance of female spectators among American film audiences, what tamed the Sheik was not the displeasure he provoked in male moviegoers, but the abandonment of roles and publicity coverage that rested on such "celluloid naughtiness."[106] During the next four years, he either chose roles that, like the pre-Sheik *Camille,* presented him more as a romantic follower or victim of a woman's love, or he just disappeared from the screen, as he did throughout 1923 until early 1924 due to his rift with Famous Players. During this hiatus, *Photoplay* even wondered "whether or not Rudolph Valentino's long absence from the screen would affect his drawing power on his return." The answer was often in the negative.[107] If coverage of his divorce from Famous Players–Lasky did not abate, neither did his screen presence diminish. But it was now a nostalgic visibility. Film distributors started rereleasing and retitling his older films, including *The Married Virgin* (1918) as *Frivolous Wives,* and gave him new prominence in the credits.

Meanwhile, Valentino and a coterie of promoters launched a series of publicity initiatives that were meant to keep his name in the press during his diminished screen visibility. The unintended consequence, however, was that they muted the excitement of his most daring characterizations. For instance, Valentino contributed to his own publicity by collaborating with the publisher Bernarr Macfadden on several projects aimed at smoothing his rougher edges and Americanizing his masculinity.[108] In 1922, Macfadden published a two-part autobiography of the actor, entitled "The Romance of Rudolf Valentino's Adventurous Life (By Himself)," and in 1923 he increased the Italian actor's print exposure.[109] First came a book of poetry, entitled *Day Dreams*. Next was a series of articles on Valentino's bodybuilding habits that appeared in *Physical Culture* and *Movie Weekly* and were aimed at showcasing how fully attuned the actor was to the American male values of sportsmanship and endurance. These were followed by a manual of physical culture, *How You Can Keep Fit*, allegedly authored by Valentino himself. This eighty-page volume featured dozens of photographs of the bare-chested Hollywood star engaged in physical exercises (figure 22).[110] In 1925, after he had resumed his acting career, Valentino also multiplied his written contributions to *Photoplay*.

Perhaps the most peculiar initiative was the lucrative, but also unflattering, decision to accept the business proposal of an unknown lawyer, George Ullman, when Valentino was not receiving a salary from Hollywood and needed money to support his lavish lifestyle. Ullman, who would play a key role in the last years of Valentino's life and beyond, devised this publicity stunt for his employer, the beauty firm Mineralava.[111] The idea was a well-promoted national tour in which Valentino and his wife, clad in Argentinian costumes, would repeat the tango routines of the *Four Horsemen*, praise Mineralava beauty products, and judge dancing and beauty contests (figure 23). While a Famous Players' injunction prevented him from appearing on a legitimate stage as an actor, nothing prevented him from dancing with his wife in public in other locations. The three-month tour, from mid-March to mid-June 1923, touched eighty-eight cities in the United States and Canada. Valentino and his wife earned $7,000 a week. The winners of the local beauty contests participated in a highly publicized event in New York City, where Valentino was crowned the winner of the national competition.[112] The final Mineralava performances took place just as bookstores began selling Valentino's volume of poetry.

The tableau of the Divo and his wife inspired affectionate mockery, but it was also the subject of serious discussion about the commercial appeal of an actor who had followed his wife's career advice to his ruin.[113] When Valentino reappeared on screen in *Monsieur Beaucaire* (August 1924) and then in *A Sainted Devil* (November 1924), the reviews anticipated a familiar argument. *Monsieur Beaucaire* exhibited a lavish and artistic quality, but "something has happened to the Valentino of 'The Sheik,'" wrote *Photoplay* editor James R. Quirk. "Rudy," he explained, "is trying to be an actor at the expense of the personality that made him a sensation." Even though he played the part of a French prince, "he doesn't look a bit dangerous to women." Quirk opined. "The fact of the matter is that they like their Rudy a little wicked. He had what is known in pictures as 'menace' to a higher degree than any actor on the screen."[114] A few pages earlier, the editors made the same point with regard to *A Sainted Devil*. A caption for one of the photographs depicting an all-too-romantic love scene referred to the film as "The Taming of the Sheik."[115]

Quirk explicitly linked the flops of Valentino's films to his wife. He blamed her for the professional breakup between Valentino and J. D. Williams of Ritz-Carlton Pictures apparently over commercial results and future plans. "Mrs. Valentino's

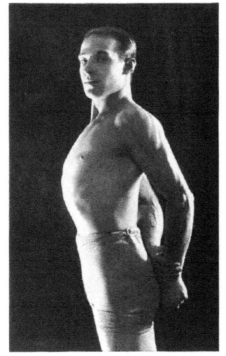

Yours for Health and Vigor

FIGURE 22. Frontispiece in Valentino's *How You
Can Keep Fit* (New York: Macfadden, 1923).

strict management of her husband is not consistent with the career of a screen sheik,"
Quirk noted, and "the picture of a devil-may-care Latin lover with a wife-manager
is rather inconsistent." Referring to whether Valentino had control over his career,
he concluded: "The illusion must be maintained."[116] The cartoon accompanying
his article made the same point about Valentino's ill-advised commercial path.
The syndicated artist-humorist and cartoonist Reuben Lucius Goldberg, widely
known as the inventor Rube Goldberg, created the two-page cartoon (figure 24).
On the left, it features a crowd of thousands of spectators in line to enter a movie
theater to watch films starring Ramon Novarro and Antonio Moreno, as the two
posters indicate. On the right, it features Valentino and Rambova on a pedestal
inscribed with "The Valentinos." While uttering slogans associated with their
anti-studio stance, they find themselves without an audience, except for a single
disheveled spectator, whose cry "Atta boy, Rudy!" captures ironically the actor's
disastrous dependency on his wife's beliefs.

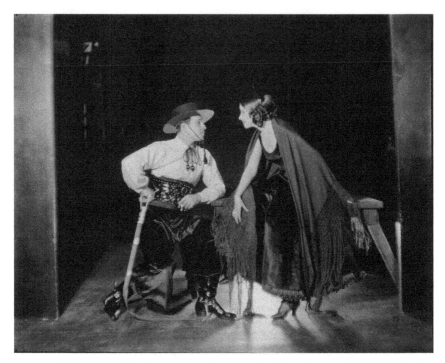

FIGURE 23. Valentino and Rambova as tango dancers on the Mineralava tour. Rudolph Valentino, no. 49, Core Collection Biography Photos, Academy of Motion Pictures Arts and Sciences. By permission of AMPAS.

While Rambova was advising Valentino on his professional choices and intervening directly on scripts and art direction, the newly hired George Ullman was taking care of the actor's finances, contractual obligations, and publicity. Ultimately Rambova and Ullman came to have very different views about Valentino's post-Mineralava-tour film career. Initially, as Evelyn Zumaya has argued, Ullman "crafted his press releases with the intention of transforming the public's perception of Rudy from that of marauding, sex-obsessed Sheik to the courtly *Monsieur Beaucaire*."[117] He successfully negotiated Valentino's contractual closure with Famous Players–Lasky, resulting in *Monsieur Beaucaire* and *A Sainted Devil*, and began shepherding a collaboration with J. D. Williams. Rambova meanwhile began working on the screenplay for a film entitled *The Hooded Falcon*, adapting it from the story of El Cid, but her dismissal of June Mathis, initially co-opted for the script, confirmed Hollywood's perception of her disastrous understanding of the film business. When Williams realized that the Valentinos had no sense of budgetary limits, he walked back from promises and agreements and made Ullman inform them that the project was shelved. Eventually, unbeknownst to the Valentinos (but not to Ullman), Williams sold the distribution rights of *The*

FIGURE 24. Rube Goldberg's cartoons about Valentino. James R. Quirk, "Presto Chango Valentino!" *Photoplay*, May 1925, 36–37.

Hooded Falcon to Paramount, which later also distributed *Cobra* (Ritz-Carlton; November 30, 1925)—a contemporary drama featuring Valentino in the role of a rather un-Sheik-like Italian count. When Ullman informed the Valentinos that he had started negotiations with United Artists on possible future productions, Rambova was quite happy about the prospect until she read the contract. There was no executive or creative role for her. The Italian actor signed it anyway on March 30, 1925.[118]

Valentino's signature on the contract led to an insurmountable rift between the pair and eventually led to the end of their relationship. They were divorced by mid-January 1926, although news of the split did not leak until much later.[119] United Artists had clear ideas about what to do with Valentino. It was sufficient to pay attention to how editorials and letters to the editors, public commentators, and private individuals alike had long argued that Valentino's popularity waned the moment he stopped being a ruthless and fascinating leader in love affairs. A letter published in *Photoplay* in June 1926 and written by a lady fan in California made the best case. In *The Four Horsemen* and *The Sheik*, she wrote, "Rudolph showed us the gay, passionate Latin lover—a juggler of women's hearts. A bit ruthless, perhaps, but oh, how fascinating!" Since then, she claimed, nothing had ever been the same:

> Now, only Rudolph's perfect manners save him from being completely Americanized. [. . .] We do not want to see Rudolph enslaved by Dagmar Gogowsky or even Nita Naldi [both had played opposite Valentino in *The Sainted Devil*]: we want to see Nita and Dagmar enslaved by Rudolph.[120]

By early 1926, fan magazines were covering his "marriage suspension" from Rambova, his affairs with Pola Negri and Vilma Banky, and the shooting of *The Son of the Sheik* with Agnes Ayres and Banky. The industry had been welcoming Valentino's return to the fold of expert playmakers with open arms.[121] Already in late 1925, the *New York World* had anticipated the shift in an article eloquently subtitled "Advisers of the Film Star Would Make Him a Real He-Man," which insisted that "the pastels will go [and] virile oil paintings [would] take their place."[122] The exploitation agents knew how to shape his image back to an exciting one, on and off screen, and even took advantage of his unexpected hospitalization and surprising death occurring just a few months later.

6

Stunts and Plebiscites

A VALENTINE TO VALENTINO

The promotional work that Howe, Glyn, and Ullman performed for Valentino in fan magazines and trade journals expectedly informed how the country's syndicated press covered the actor's success and tribulations. The least chronicled promotional initiatives about Valentino were the publicity stunts, which critically accompanied the final months of his short professional life. One of Hollywood's most inventive and best-paid publicity men, Harry Reichenbach, had pulled off an earlier and rather small-scale one, which nonetheless anticipated more significant tricks. In the fall of 1924, Reichenbach was working for Famous Players–Lasky, which was about to release *A Sainted Devil*. He asked Valentino to grow a goatee for his forthcoming role during the ill-fated European preproduction of *The Hooded Falcon*. Upon returning to the United States in mid-November 1924, Valentino surprised everybody by sporting never-before-seen whiskers. Shortly afterward, Reichenbach went to the annual convention of the Associated Master Barbers of America in Chicago where he found a way to address the convention. Once on stage, he announced in alarm that Valentino had returned from Europe with unwelcome new facial hair: if it were to become popular in America, it would threaten the members' livelihood. Reichenbach then lobbied for a resolution "that called for nothing less than a boycott on all Valentino pictures until Rudy shaved off his beard."[1]

In its coverage of Valentino's sudden change of appearance, *Photoplay* also published a sonnet and a drawing condemning the Divo's decision and insisting that he return to his old image. Its author, Margaret Caroline Wells, first revealed her shock before wishing for a complete return to normalcy: "He'd better see a barber and be the same old sheik. [. . .] We want our Valentino just as he used to be."[2] The accompanying drawing illustrated the whiskers' unnatural appearance by showing how Fairbanks, Chaplin, Keaton, Harold Lloyd, William S. Hart, and an unspecified flapper would look with them (figure 25). While news of his beard continued to be printed for months in American newspapers, by December 21, 1924, Valentino had shaved it off.[3] This stunt did not remain a well-kept secret. As a *Photoplay* profile revealed a year later, Reichenbach had persuaded Valentino to grow a beard "to cause a bad reaction that was followed by a good one when he 'agreed' to shave it."[4]

145

What!!! Valentino???

FIGURE 25. Illustration inspired by Valentino's new goatee. Margaret Caroline Wells, "What!!! Valentino???," *Photoplay*, February 1925, 72.

The most important stunt, however, occurred, during the days preceding the premiere of *The Son of the Sheik*. United Artists chairman Joseph M. Schenck faced a marketing challenge. For Valentino to regain his unique popularity, the actor had to appear different from other Latin lovers, including Ramon Novarro and Antonio Moreno. Schenck viewed the adaptation of Hull's sequel, *The Son of the Sheik* (1925), as a great opportunity to do just that. In the film, Valentino played both father and son, and the cast included Agnes Ayres, who returned in the role of Diana, Ahmed's wife. The figure of the son, described "Young Chief" and "displaying a firm, obstinate chin and a straight, somewhat cruel mouth," brought back the untamed wildness of the original *Sheik*.[5] Beyond the promotional opportunities of the narrative, the film had to be sold to distributors who were skeptical of the Divo's enduring commercial appeal.

Before the mid-1920s, Valentino's sophisticated manners, not to mention his history of dependence on strong women, had met with some criticism, even indignation, but always with a good dose of irony—as if these reactions were a ruse. Miriam Hansen recognized the performative dimension of these denunciations of deviance and suggested that they "were part of the ritual," perhaps "self-ironic," certainly "performing a rhetorical role" in a discourse "presumed to speak for all men."[6] At the time, however, there had been serious reactions to printed rumors aimed at minimizing the actor's difference from mainstream American masculinity. "There is nothing repellent, nothing unmasculine about Valentino," Willis Goldbeck of *Motion Picture Magazine* had written in the spring of 1922, "merely a heavy exoticism, compelling, fascinating, perhaps a little disturbing, as might be asphalt to the average cobbler."[7] Still, as Mark Lynn Anderson has compellingly discussed, "Valentino's star presentation and his appearance within a mass cultural context [. . .] helped establish a queer space for the reception of mass culture."[8] For Anderson, it was not just that his diversity encouraged "investigating the relations between sexuality and gender," but also that "stardom provided a rather startling number of points of similarity with the visible aspects of contemporary gay male culture in America's largest cities."

Anderson is quite right in positing that "the question of Valentino's queerness considered within the context of America mass culture is not [. . .] about his individual sexual identity, but about the types of sexualities his stardom made possible, gratified, or otherwise indulged."[9] However, his argument that the actor's queerness ("radically queer star") was akin to the prebourgeois sexual culture of working-class New York—especially its immigrant quarters—deserves close scrutiny. In his attempt to show how it was possible that Valentino's indeterminate sexuality stood out for "its utter *indifference* to American middle-class culture," Anderson appears to reify both bourgeois and immigrant working-class cultures and project contemporary critical tropes of heteronormative sexuality onto the latter.[10] While he is careful to point out that he is not idealizing working-class neighborhoods as if they were "immune from homophobia," he relies on George Chauncey's work on middle-class homosexuals' social and sexual interactions with the less prudish immigrants of the Lower East Side to posit that in New York's ethnic neighborhoods, there was a "relative lack of stigma" for a " 'masculine' man who had sex with fairies or accompanied them on dates."[11]

This argument should be measured against two counterfacts: first, New York's urban working-class culture in the 1920s was not homogeneous but consisted of many immigrant subcultures with different views of sexuality and individual conduct. Secondly, Valentino and the promotional discourse about him, particularly regarding his alleged nobility and timeless Italianness, had consistently endeavored to distance the actor from Italian immigrants' largely unappealing bodies and culture. Unsurprisingly, his reception in Italian neighborhoods largely depended on generational differences. Young men were attracted to him not necessarily because their culture gravitated to a "queer space," but because he presented an admirable Italian path to Americanization that radically differed from Enrico Caruso's—who was the idol of the old guard. In his 1924 urban travelogue *Around the World in New York*, Konrad Bercovici noted:

Since the advent of Valentino all the youth of Little Italy try to look as much as possible like the moving-picture hero, and to haunt the moving-picture studios of the city, having in their Americanization somewhat abandoned the desire to become grand opera singers.[12]

The older generations, particularly those who controlled the ethnic press, pushed back against the untraditional masculinity of the Italian star. Only after his death did they express pride in his Horatio Alger trajectory—a narrative that was barely mentioned by that press during his lifetime.[13]

It is in a framework nonetheless imbued with often-veiled references to queerness that historians have largely read the famous *Chicago Tribune* editorial published on July 18, 1926, as an index of both the actor's sexually ambivalent image and the anxieties he produced in 1920s America.[14] One of the most-repeated passages blamed Valentino for the installation of a face-powder dispenser in one of the city's new public men's room:

A powder vending machine! In a men's washroom! Homo Americanus! Why didn't someone quietly drown Rudolph Guglielmo *[sic]*, alias Valentino, years ago? [. . .] Do women like the type of "man" who pats pink powder on his face in a public washroom and arranges his coiffure in a public elevator? . . . Hollywood is the national school of masculinity. Rudy, the beautiful gardener's boy, is the prototype of the American male. Hell's bells. Oh, sugar.

Valentino responded twice to the editorial, both times from the pages of the *Tribune*'s rival, *The Chicago Herald-Examiner*. The day after the "Pink Powder Puffs" editorial came out, he called the anonymous author "a contemptible coward" and challenged him to a boxing match:

You slur my Italian ancestry; you cast ridicule upon my Italian name; you cast doubt upon my masculinity. I call you, in return, a contemptible coward and to prove which of us is a better man, I challenge you [. . .] to meet me in the boxing or wrestling arena to prove, in typically American fashion (for I am an American citizen), which of us is more a man. [. . .] I do not know who you are or how big you are, but this challenge stands if you are as big as Jack Dempsey.[15]

In his second response, after his return to the Windy City from New York, he shamed the anonymous editorialist again and declared victory because the slanderer dared not reveal his or her identity. The fact that Valentino immediately issued "a public challenge to the cowardly writer to reveal himself," as Anderson acutely points out, has prompted "the public to understand the nature of the editorial in precisely this manner"—as a personal assault on the actor's virility and national origin.[16]

The identity of the editorial's writer has never been determined with any measure of certainty, and this authorial mystery has seemingly encouraged the same, recurring kind of culturalist interpretation, either as a display of homophobic hate or, in Anderson's analysis, as an index of an emerging queer space in American culture.[17] Anderson in fact has perceptively rejected a reading of the editorial as a straightforward homophobic and racist attack and has instead identified in it a "playful sarcasm" and a certain "self-consciousness about its own overstatements." Namely, in a climate that was already pervaded by rhetorics of public scandal, Anderson has questioned whether the piece, despite its pretense of aversion, was actually scorning "those who were threatened by the actor's deviant masculinity." Or whether it was "a public 'outing' of Valentino by and for those who identified themselves as queers, or by and for those who participated in and were supportive of gay culture generally."[18] While the editorial's tone certainly exudes a feigned sense of scandal and not clear-cut hatred, the contemporary critical principle that reads "gossip [as] often an act of resistance" does not completely explain its raison d'être.[19] The archival record, in fact, tells a different story—the story of a successful stunt that exploited the scandalous queerness of Valentino's popular image to pretend to scandalize Valentino himself, his fans, and, most importantly, those who found him effeminate and indecent.

At the story's center is one of the industry's most talented publicity men, Victor Mansfield Shapiro, who, in 1916, had founded the Associated Motion Picture Advertisers (also known as the Association of Motion Picture Advertisers).[20] Shapiro's papers, held in the UCLA Library's Special Collections, consist of public relations and promotional materials relating to the motion picture industry and include questionnaires, his own biography, scrapbooks, photographs, and tapes and transcripts of interviews. Shapiro had a major career as an independent publicity man for the Hollywood film industry and even met Valentino on the set of *The Eagle* (1925). In May 1926, he was hired by United Artists (UA) managing director Hiram Abrams to work on publicity for *The Son of the Sheik*.[21] As UA's publicity man for Valentino, he seemingly ghostwrote many of the actor's articles published during his final months.

In his transcribed recollections, Shapiro at first expressed the sort of conventional thinking that emerged out of brainstorming sessions in UA's Publicity and Still Photography Departments. The sessions centered on "how to make Rudolph Valentino more acceptable to the men customers." Predictable tactics included the use of photographs of Valentino "sparring with Jack Dempsey," "horseback riding," and "playing polo with Doug Fairbanks." A more daring publicity idea was to "photograph him nude from the waist up" and then "invite lady reporters to interview him thusly during his athletic diversions."[22] The punch line of these play-the-Sheik-card strategies was quite straightforward: "Use the catch line 'Men, why be jealous of Rudy Valentino?' You too can make love like he does. See 'Son of the Sheik.'" The obvious question, however, was whether these ideas would have garnered the "front page splash" that was needed to revive Valentino's career.[23]

As expected of a loyal Hollywood professional, Shapiro underplays the role of publicity. In several instances, he claims that publicity could not manufacture a star out of nothing. "The dramatic impact Rudolph Valentino had on woman-hood was not created by a press agent. [. . .] Press agentry did not manufacture Valentino's extraordinary attributes. Publicity merely called attention to them."[24] Notwithstanding these disclaimers, Valentino offered inventive publicity poten-tial. Still, Shapiro recalls that at first he followed conventional methods. From his New York base, he began collecting biographic profiles, which insisted on Valentino as "sensual with animal grace," requested photographic poses, and planned "also to make a film trailer of these activities with the title, quote, 'The Physique of the Sheik.' "[25] He sent all this material to the press, first-run theaters, and pictorial outlets. "They only caused a ripple with the males."[26] Then he recounted the episode of the "Pink Powder Puffs" article, which fell outside the scope of conventional thinking and achieved the ultimate goal of any publicity campaign: "get the opening."[27] He called it "a Valentine to Valentino."[28]

The impetus came from his boss, Abrams, who had started negotiating the dis-tribution of *The Son of the Sheik* with Balaban and Katz, the largest theater chain in Chicago. It had rebuffed his offer of exhibiting rights, bargaining down the price since, it claimed, "Valentino didn't mean a thing in Chicago." This response prompted Abrams to ask Shapiro to devise a "publicity campaign unmatched in [Valentino's] career."[29] "On July 10th, 1926," Shapiro recounted, "Abrams suggest-ed I send him the livest wire on my staff to do something about Valentino when he stopped over between trains in Chicago." Shapiro chose Jimmy Ashcroft, "a veteran skilled in necromancy of press relations and exhibitor convolutions," who was charged to leave New York for Chicago within two days and secure "something on the front page, something—anything, provocative and entertain-ing." On July 12, at Grand Central Station, Shapiro met Ashcroft for last-minute instructions. The two veteran publicists, Shapiro later noted, thought alike.

On July 19, when Valentino arrived in Chicago from Los Angeles, the *Chicago Tribune* had just published the infamous "Pink Powder Puffs" piece—which in Shapiro's papers is identified as "A," as in Exhibit A.[30] Ashcroft showed it to the actor and began "stoking up [his] indignation." Then he handed Valentino's pre-written reply, (or "B," as in Exhibit B) to Hearst's *Herald Examiner,* the *Tribune's* archrival.[31] Anderson has noted that the quickness of the response helped others take the editorial seriously and thus effaced its ironic tone. Within a few hours, Hearst was putting Valentino's prepared response "over the wires, the wire service, to all twenty-six [of his] papers and his other outlets."[32] Shapiro recounts that Ash-croft then wired him copies of both the editorial and Valentino's response. Shapiro responded by asking Ashcroft to "keep [Valentino] fired up" on the way to New York since Shapiro's assistant, Warren Knowland, was about to hop on the train in Harlem and brief him on what to do next before arriving at Grand Central Station.

> Give him some printable catch lines, have him carry a copy of the novel Cellini, his next picture. We'll have, we'll have photos at the station, press conference at the hotel,

with Prohibition's best handing out copies of, of Chicago editorial and Rudy's answer. Then it's up to ye gods, and ye gods it was [laughter].[33]

Part of Shapiro's choreography was a dramatic police escort for Valentino from Grand Central to the Ambassador Hotel on Park Avenue and 51st Street, inevitably followed by dozens of journalists. On the morning of July 20, Shapiro updated his friend Lloyd "Red" Stratton of the Associated Press on the latest news and told him where Valentino was staying—a veiled promise of first, if not exclusive, access. At the station "the crowd surged but the station guards managed to wedge Rudy to his auto without having his clothes ripped off." Everything was prepared in advance. The police motorcycle escort "was arranged through Frank Sennett," a college pal. In the car, Shapiro finally met Ullman, and while they seemed to agree as to who was handling what (Shapiro, the "picture end of the publicity"; Ullman, "the personal matters"), in reality Shapiro was handling it all. At least that's how he tells it. It was his idea that "Rudy was to receive the press in his blue and green silk robe and purple pajama, for the benefit of the lady reporters [laughter]."[34] By early afternoon the Associated Press and the Hearst syndicated newspapers were carrying the story. "From that moment the telephone rang incessantly. Every news outlet in town, fan and general magazines, foreign press, film critics, males and females, sport writers, called for and received personal interviews. More than a hundred correspondents by actual count paraded in and out of Rudy's hotel suite."[35]

Shapiro has recounted the circumstances of Valentino fighting the sportswriter and boxing expert Franck "Buck" O'Neal on the hotel's terrace in front of a Pathé News cameraman. It was the promotional equivalent, as staged event, of Valentino's prepared response to the press. The 167-pound Rudy fought the 200-pound, six-foot-one former fullback O'Neal and won. But if that was not enough, the news was what O'Neal repeated to the press: "Make no mistake. That guy throws a punch like a mule's back." "Why not print that," said Shapiro to his 1966 interviewer. That very line was included in an article, "Powder Puff? Wham!," that recounted the match.[36] The news that Valentino wanted to challenge the anonymous editorial writer in staged fights that were nothing other than public relations stunts was the subject of satirical cartoons (figure 26). To close the circle, when Shapiro's man in Chicago, John Ashcroft, called him again, he reported that "stories were breaking front page there, that the Balaban and Katz crowd never, never again would say Valentino doesn't mean a thing there."[37] Ashcroft also told Shapiro that Valentino, upon his imminent return to Chicago, would issue another statement to the anonymous "editor" of the *Chicago Tribune*.

In his reminiscences, Shapiro notes that eventually Ashcroft told him that "the writer who penned the Pink Powderpuff [sic] editorial was named John Glasscock"—a name that may well have been fictitious.[38] What is certain is that the whole initiative amounted, in Shapiro's words, to "the most extensive and intensive publicity break in Rudy's short life."[39] Shapiro's description of himself and

FIGURE 26. Cartoon depicting the prospect of a boxing match featuring Valentino as a major public relations event. Harry Haenigsen, "Isn't Life Complicated," *Evening World*, July 21, 1926, 16.

Valentino as "more than passable actors" and his admission that Rudy indeed had a sense of humor and "was acting his resentment" appear to support the notion that the actor was a willing participant in the scheme.[40]

The result was an artful scandal. Mobs of spectators filled the Strand on Broadway for the film's opening. A few days later the same occurred in Chicago, where Valentino had returned as promised after presiding at the New York premiere. In front of a "cheering crowd swirling around the station," the actor, who was clearly on board with the stunt, exclaimed what Shapiro defined as his "Lafayette, I am here" statement. Before the crowd, he addressed the author of the offensive editorial, shouting: "Mr. Editor, I am here. I am ready. Where are you?" Thanks to the wires, his challenge went national in a few hours.[41] At this point, Shapiro refers to "C" (as in Exhibit C), which was Valentino's second prepared statement to the press.

> The heroic silence of the writer who chose to attack me without any provocation in the *Chicago Tribune* leaves no doubt as to the total absence of manliness in his whole makeup. I feel that I have been vindicated.[42]

In Chicago, Valentino also posed with several boxers while renewing his challenge, surrounded by a new kind of fan. The "continuous pink Powderpuff imbroglio," as Shapiro described it, "brought out what one writer said was 'a sporting audience known for its literary, dramatic, social and artistic distinction, a cross-section of Chicago's most cosmopolitan.'"[43] After recounting similar triumphant processions occurring in Atlantic City, Shapiro mentioned that "leading trade papers publishers" Martin Quigley of *Exhibitors Herald* and Sam (a transcription error for "Sime," short for Simon) Silverman of *Variety* calculated the financial impact of this scheme. They allegedly told Shapiro that the Valentino campaign "must have garnered millions of lines of free space all over the world, which if purchased at regular advertising rates would exceed millions of dollars," not to mention adding a million dollars "to the box office gross on *The Son of the Sheik*."[44]

After almost two weeks of front-page coverage, the "sensational Pink Powderpuff hullabaloo" had gained a strength of its own that even affected its architects. When on August 16 Shapiro, out of town, read in the papers of the actor's sudden hospitalization in New York, he thought it another ploy. "As a press agent somewhat immune to shock," he recalled, "I didn't believe it. Nonsense!" So he called his assistant, Knowland, fearing that he had been "pulling a stunt without [his] knowledge."[45] Valentino's sickness, however, was no stunt. Although Shapiro, Ullman, and UA hoped it would quickly pass, in the meantime they saw it as another publicity opportunity. Shapiro and Knowland went to the "press room at the hospital" and, even though Ullman was in charge of "personal publicity," the crisis called once again for a breach of contractual protocol: "Biographies and pictures of Valentino were passed out by Knowland." United Artists sought to install a press room in the hospital.[46] Instead of recuperating, Valentino's condition only

worsened after developing peritonitis and septic endocarditis following an operation for perforated ulcers. He died on August 23, 1926, to the apparent surprise of
everyone—his fans, the studio, and his publicists. The latter group was the quickest
to react to it in ways that would frame both his passing and afterlife.

DEATH AND BALLYHOO

Ullman and Shapiro and his men were not the only publicity people who followed
Valentino's deteriorating health and sought to construct posthumous narratives
that would exploit his story. Their efforts challenge the conventional opening of
countless volumes and articles about Valentino, which regularly insist on fans'
spontaneous and authentic display of mass grief, visible in some newsreel footage, following the actor's unexpected death.[47] To contemporary Italian papers such
popular displays amounted to a *plebiscito di dolore* (plebiscite of pain). In truth,
the coverage of the actor's hospitalization, infirmity, and death was infused with
publicity ploys aimed to spur fans to emotional displays, apparently out of control
yet well choreographed, and present their affection for the Divo as unprompted.

Valentino's hospitalization, death, and New York funeral were a bonanza for all
the city's papers from the *Journal* to the *Evening World* and *The Telegram*. During
this time, the publicity stunts became also photographic. At the center of these
efforts was the *New York Evening Graphic*, commonly known as the *Graphic*, a
tabloid newspaper published from 1924 to 1932 by Bernarr Macfadden, which specialized in scandals and made-up news about celebrities. Beyond its mendacious
stories, the *Graphic* managed to outsell competitors through a "brazen staging and
manipulation of photographs" known as a "composograph."[48] In late August, the
Graphic published a composograph, made from twelve photographs, of Valentino
being lovingly assisted by nurses while in the operating room that caused the
Graphic's circulation to soar. It was just the beginning.

The *Graphic*'s picture editor Frank Mallen recounts in his celebratory and often
imaginative memoir, *Sauce for the Gander*, that when Wallace Reid and Olive
Thomas died, "their pictures died with them" as "there was strong public sentiment and general disapproval of the exhibition of pictures after death."[49] Not so for
Valentino. "[Frank E.] Campbell had made a deal with officials of United Artists,"
Mallen reports, referring to the prominent New York funeral director. "He told
them that if they would let him handle the funeral, in the event of death, he would
make Valentino's pictures more popular and profitable than ever." After United
Artists accepted, Campbell solicited the *Graphic*'s help. While Valentino's body
was still at the Polyclinic Hospital, a composograph was being made of it as if it
had already arrived at Campbell's funeral home.[50] To the surprise of its editors, the
Graphic was breaking records.

According to Mallen, the tabloid had negotiated a special relationship with
Campbell's publicity aide, former reporter Harry C. Klemfuss. A "pioneer in the

field of public relations and a master of the publicity stunt," Klemfuss assisted the press "by advance distribution of photographs and material regarding the chamber where the screen star's body would lie."[51] The role of this New York publicity man is confirmed by Silas Bent in a chapter on free publicity in his 1927 book *Ballyhoo.* Bent notes that "around the undertaker's place of business were rioting mobs" and "the crowd stretched through eleven blocks of streets."[52] Mallen recounts that Campbell and Klemfuss, "old hands at handling crowds," had a system in place to make sure that the crowds were kept at mob size and agitated: "The funeral church doors would be locked for twenty minutes out of the hour. This gave time for replacements to arrive at the rate of twelve for each one permitted to view the remains."[53] Although a plate-glass window was smashed and several were injured, generally speaking the "mobs were photogenic and obliging, whether in formation or as individuals" (figure 27). They gladly became part of the show and "would turn in any direction and strike any pose as long as a camera lens was in front of them."[54] As Bent saw it, Klemfuss viewed the result as "a minor triumph. The name of his client appeared four days successively on the first page of one newspaper, in addition to many tabloids, in 'fourteen-point type,' and when he had noted a million lines of free publicity he quit counting."[55] Both Bent and Mallen reported that, during the procession of Valentino from the funeral home to St. Malachy's Church on 49th Street, the *Graphic* managed to sell thousands of copies of a special edition featuring a front-page photograph of the very same procession! Mallen quoted Paul Gallico, from *True* magazine, describing the photograph as "the journalistic miracle of the ages." It was instead a composite photograph prepared a day ahead with mock pallbearers, a rose-bedecked coffin, and hired mobs.[56]

In the months following the funeral, the *Graphic* wanted to match its outstanding August 1926 circulation. When its editors heard of spiritual mediums contacting Valentino, who told them that he was "happy 'up there with the angels,'" the periodical resumed the Valentino composographs. Two, in particular, are worth mentioning. One shows Valentino upon his arrival in heaven; the other in the company of Enrico Caruso, who had passed away in 1921 (figure 28). They were constructed from, respectively, five and eight photographs.[57] The latter scene had allegedly been described by a psychic, and the resultant *Graphic* story was sold for serial publication in early 1927 to the Doubleday Page Syndicate. It appeared on the frontispiece of Silas Bent's *Ballyhoo.* These two images solidified the perception of a close association between Valentino and the spiritualist tradition of séances that the actor frequently engaged in with his second wife.[58] More significantly, the miraculous new images prolonged his exploitation posthumously.[59]

Shapiro does not mention these publicity feats. Instead, to safeguard the star's direct appeal, he contended that Valentino's popularity needed "little propulsion or fanfare." After all, the actor's "screen portrayals, so real to so many, were his most potent press agent" and, Shapiro argued, "no press agent, no front-page publicity gave Valentino this indefinable something. He had what no other screen star ever

FIGURE 27. Crowd gathered outside the Frank E. Campbell Funeral Chapel, August 1926. Photograph by International News Photos, a division of W. R. Hearst's International News Service.

had."[60] One could argue that in light of the aforementioned queer overtones in the actor's public image, which the powder puff stunt had so effectively exploited, Shapiro's rhetoric conveniently divested studios and publicity agents from any moral responsibility over Valentino's reception. Following the many damaging scandals that characterized 1920s Hollywood, the studios had every interest in insisting that their stars' private lives constituted a domain over which they had no control. That way they could allege that Valentino's public image simply mirrored the alchemy of who he was and what his fans expected and desired.

Still, the "indefinable something" was more than just fame; it was also a form of authority over the masses, which in Shapiro's recounting justified the use of political attributes: "the newspapers covered the proceedings," he noted, "as they would in obsequies of president, prime minister or potentate." "No king in any realm was more revered or honored," Shapiro concluded rather bombastically.[61] In doing so, he placed Valentino's widely publicized wake and memorial in relationship with another celebrated Italian figure in America, Benito Mussolini. Specifically, he referred to the clash outside Campbell's between New York–based Italian Blackshirts and Valentino's friends, who knew of his anti-Mussolini stance. The former claimed that they were paying homage to the actor by standing guard around his bier, allegedly on the Duce's orders. This incident requires a brief explanation.

FIGURE 28. Valentino and Caruso in heaven. *New York Evening Graphic*,
March 17, 1927, composograph.

After becoming a star, Valentino attracted little interest on the part of Fascist
and anti-Fascist groups in both the United States and in Italy. In America, he had
little contact with Italian American groups even after Mussolini's March on Rome
in October 1922, about eighteen months after his breakout film, *The Four Horsemen*. In the old country, his films were for years invisible except in major cities.
For a while, the Divo and the Duce coexisted peacefully in mutual indifference.
In 1923, during Valentino's first trip back home, he stopped in Rome but he and
Mussolini failed to meet. Mario Quargnolo has suggested that Valentino was close
to collaborating with producer Arturo Ambrosio in 1924 on the film adaptation of
Mussolini's 1909 novel *L'amante del cardinale* (The Cardinal's Lover). It would have
been a publicity dream to sell a film written by the Duce and starring the Divo.[62]

But in late 1925, a public rift occurred. On November 10, while in New York for
the opening of *The Eagle,* Valentino applied for U.S. citizenship, which the *New York*

Times reported.[63] At the time double citizenship was not an option: acquiring U.S. citizenship meant the relinquishing of Italian citizenship. The response of the Fascist regime was quick and negative. Castigated as a traitor, Valentino saw his films first boycotted and then banned in Italy between late November and early December 1925.[64] Pressured by Paramount and United Artists, he wrote (or simply signed) a letter directed to his Italian critics, and thus Mussolini, in which he sought to explain his reasons. Entitled "Una lettera di Rodolfo Valentino, attore italianissimo," the letter was published on February 15, 1926, in the pro-Fascist Italian American newspaper *Il Corriere d'America*. A month later it also appeared in Italy in the Fascist newspaper *L'Impero* (March 12, 1926). His letter conveyed his gratitude to the United States for the outstanding personal and professional opportunities that he enjoyed but also vehemently maintained that *"no one has felt and continues to feel more than I do the sacrosanct pride and privilege of being born Italian."*[65] In the summer of 1926, news of the Italian ban kept making headlines in America where, possibly because it was a repeated initiative, it was promoted as "persecution."[66] The controversy was still in many people's minds when, after news of his death, newspapers began reporting that his films were being exhibited again in Rome following the Duce's decision to end the boycott after reading Valentino's public letter.[67]

In America, Valentino's sudden death had an even more radical impact, particularly among Fascist authorities and in the patriotic Italian American press. From the very day of his passing, nationalist newspapers such as *Il Progresso Italo Americano* and *Il Corriere d'America* emphatically praised the Italian actor.[68] The most patriotic of the ethnic press filled its front pages with daily reports on the number of people crowding outside Campbell's or on the Hollywood personalities paying homage to the Italian divo and participating in his funeral.[69] Ex post facto patriotism was to be expected, but the quick about-face of the New York–based Fascists was also impressive. Had Mussolini actually ordered his loyal Blackshirts to pay homage to Valentino and do so publicly?

First the facts: In the evening of August 23, a group of Italian American Fascists set out to post an honor guard around the film star's flowered bier at Campbell's funeral home. They gained access to the funeral home by declaring that Mussolini himself had given such instructions—a claim that the Italian authorities soon denied. Italian American members of the Anti-Fascist League, who claimed to know the thirty-one-year-old Divo's personal opposition to the regime, tried to prevent the Blackshirts' physical and ideological appropriation of his body and fame.[70] A fight erupted. Eventually, Fascist representatives were able to stand guard in an official, military fashion over his corpse and lay a wreath at his side with the inscription "From Benito Mussolini," thus saluting Valentino as one of them (figure 29). At midnight they were asked to leave. The morning papers spread images of the startling display.[71]

The archival evidence sheds evidence on this issue.[72] On August 26, 1926, three days after Valentino's death, several things happened. In the morning, the

Le camicie nere di New York posano i fiori del Duce sulla bara di Rodolfo Valentino

FIGURE 29. New York Blackshirts pose with the Duce's wreath for Rodolfo Valentino's coffin. *Il Grido della Stirpe* [The Roar of the Race], August 28, 1926, 1.

front page of the *New York Times* reported on the clash between Fascists and anti-Fascists at Campbell's. Quite alarmingly for Italian government officials, the *New York Times* quoted Pietro Allegra, secretary of the Anti-Fascist Alliance, denying the Fascists the right to post guard at the actor's bier. The article included a long excerpt of Allegra's telegram to Ullman in which he denounced the behavior of the American Fascists as an "insult to the memory of the great artist, who in life manifested his opposition to the anti-democratic policies of Mussolini."[73] Possibly even more distressing was the contradiction captured by the *New York Times* between the American Fascists' claim that they were operating "on instructions from Mussolini" and an Associated Press dispatch from Rome that suggested that Mussolini had not given any such order.

Then the Italian embassy got involved. In a letter to Ambassador Giacomo De Martino on the same day, the consul informed him that he had just sent a telegram to Mussolini upon the request of Count Paolo Ignazio Maria Thaon di Revel, a noble figure and naval commander who in the fall 1924 had been sent to New York on a difficult mission. His job was to organize the politically dangerous Fasci Italiani all'estero, or Fascists abroad, into the more disciplined and reliable Fascist League of North America (FLNA). Thaon di Revel had told the consul that *he* was the person responsible for the Fascist guard at Valentino's funeral home. He had taken the initiative of asking a few individuals to wear their Blackshirt uniforms and place a wreath by Valentino's casket with the inscription, "From Benito Mussolini." His intention was to highlight the "nationality and Italian sentiment" of the fallen actor. In his communication to the consul, Count Revel acknowledged that he had not received any authorization by or on behalf of Mussolini. Since the anti-Fascists were accusing him of having acted alone, Revel feared that the issue was becoming a political one and that, if Mussolini were to deny that he had ever given the order, the count's own authority and that of the regime would be discredited. Revel asked that his action not be retracted.[74] Two days later, the consul informed the ambassador that Mussolini had responded. "Please inform Count Revel that I approve gesture of sympathy toward Rodolfo Valentino. It is appropriate," Mussolini wrote in a telegraph, but added, "in the future my name ought not be used without my prior authorization."[75]

PLEBISCITE OF PAIN

Such postmortem reconciliatory gestures, including the end of any boycott of Valentino films, should not obscure the Divo's and the Duce's ideological differences. In Italy, the dictator's antiegalitarian manliness and ideological virilization—molded on the political and discursive repression of the feminine—was hardly compatible with Valentino's sexually transgressive and ambiguous masculinity. The latter resembled the androgynous decadence of another contemporary male political icon, the by-then-passé poet and writer Gabriele D'Annunzio. Still, in the American context, the two figures presented striking affinities. Emphasizing their differences should not discourage our efforts to identify the function of their commonalities within American culture. To look at Valentino as a celebrity, for instance, his impact on the movie public and fan culture turned out to be one of regimentation, the opposite of the conventional narrative of out-of-control crowds of young women attending his funeral. As such, his untimely death dovetailed with the earlier promotion of his mesmerizing romantic power as well as with his overt antidemocratic stance. For years, Valentino made young American women (and men) stand in line at the box office, buy movie magazines, and return to the movie houses for comparable romantic stories. The coverage of his death and the allegedly spontaneous hysteria it provoked does not reveal the well-regimented political economy and publicity of his cinematic celebrity. Instead, it conceals it. When examined closely, we discover that the hysteria was manipulated and the coverage of the funeral often aimed to produce an interclass universality of response—ranging from grief to mere curiosity—evident in images of continuous orderly lines of visitors outside Campbell's. *Il Progresso Italo-Americano* and *Il Corriere d'America* captured this (staged) unanimity in terms of a "plebiscite of pain" (plebiscito di dolore) or "universal plebiscite of grief for Valentino" (plebiscito universale di cordoglio per Valentino).[76]

Even in the end, the transnational star Valentino, through his exotic screen image and the rational and affective activities of publicity men, was capable of turning America's threatening masses into discreet and generally well-behaved film audiences. The public record does not include reports of out-of-control mobs invading the movie theaters that throughout his career exhibited his films; and if they elbowed their way in, once inside, "for one hour and a half they sat spellbound applauding" him.[77] His spectators were actually identifiable and reliable targets for consumer and political agendas during his life and after.[78]

If the plot of *The Sheik* and *The Son of the Sheik* is any indication of his reception, the final destiny of the devoted female protagonist, Diana Majo, is not that of an independent flapper but of the loyal, domesticated partner destined for marriage. With "cave-man love and tenderness," Valentino may have empowered flappers or new women sexually and romantically. American film audiences' unprecedented display of sensual attraction to a foreigner became a familiar trope of reviews and reports. Yet, his iconic popularity did not open up radically subversive possibilities for gender equality (or democracy), on or off screen. Conforming to Hollywood's business and cultural prerogatives, instead, his groundbreaking stardom had a very familiar and conservative ring to it. It remains to be seen whether, when positioned side by side with Mussolini's celebrity, what emerges in both cases is the fungibility of a foreign individual for the growth of domestic institutions of crowd management.

PART THREE

The Duce, or the Romance of Undemocratic Governing

7

Promoting a Romantic Biography

The public man is born "public"—he bears the stigma from his birth. [. . .] He can never escape it. [. . .] I am perfectly resigned to my lot as a public man. In fact, I am enthusiastic about it.

MUSSOLINI, 1925[1]

The rise of Benito Mussolini on the world stage is conventionally associated with the March on Rome of late October 1922, which forced the Italian king to appoint the Fascist leader to the post of prime minister. The American media coverage of the events was extensive: interest in his striking rise to power, original personality, and leadership pervaded daily reports and editorials. Soon periodicals devoted commentary and illustrations to the iconic Fascist leader, and within a few short years newsreels began to feature him as an alluring celebrity. Economic and geopolitical factors explain the interest that American financial and political centers had in his anti-Communist leadership but do not clarify his status as an iconic public personality, which resulted from a host of public relations efforts informing an intense media coverage.

In truth, Mussolini had already attracted the attention of a very limited but not inconsequential group of individuals years before the March on Rome. After the United States joined the hostilities, American officials found themselves benefitting from this pro-war socialist's remarkable ability of stirring public opinion to accept Italy's participation in the conflict and alliance with the United States. In the late 1910s and early 1920s, he positioned himself as an invaluable anti-Bolshevik interlocutor and a loyal ally to financial centers seeking to invest in a strike-free nation. In this section, I tell the story of how mainstream media support for the Duce consistently intertwined geopolitical rationales and alleged individual traits according to a personalizing strategy that Mussolini himself, a longtime journalist, skillfully exploited. Even though several reporters, editors, and writers of leftist and liberal bents condemned what they recognized as a coup d'état, a number of American and Italian mediators enabled his rise to fame by fostering a personality cult that largely deterred any serious questioning of his antidemocratic regime.

They did so at least until the mid-1930s, when his American fortunes shifted for worse following the Duce's decision to emulate other colonial powers and start his imperialistic campaign in Africa.

WARTIME PUBLIC INFORMATION

As discussed in chapter 1, the Committee for Public Information had branches all over Western Europe, including in Rome. Between April and October 1918, the head of the Italian CPI was the eminent political science professor Charles Edward Merriam, whom many regarded as "the most important political scientist of the interwar years."[2] As the American high commissioner for public information in Italy, Merriam's mission was to encourage the Italian public to have faith in the country's military alliance with the United States, support pro-war socialist leaders, and undermine anti-war socialist and communist groups.[3] Despite his short tenure, Merriam was perhaps one of the truest interpreters of Wilson's propaganda-based diplomacy. In his role, he came into contact with the most important men influencing Italian public opinion. Possibly among them was Mussolini who, after being expelled from the Socialist Party in late 1914 due to his sudden pro-war stance, embraced a rhetoric of militaristic nationalism and broadcast it through his new interventionist newspaper *Il Popolo d'Italia*.[4] Diplomatic historian Louis John Nigro Jr. has suggested that it was quite likely that in 1918 Merriam offered financial support to Mussolini's newspaper to increase its circulation and subsidize a Rome edition. Funneled through the Rockefeller Foundation, Merriam's support compensated the future Duce for his influential support of the American war intervention and contributed to his public ascendancy.[5] This occurred just as the CPI was endeavoring to advertise President Wilson in Italy as the personification of a nonpartisan moral authority and idealistic champion of democracy and world peace. Merriam was in Italy when Mussolini celebrated Wilson's popular authority with a six-column front-page headline in *Il Popolo d'Italia* that hailed the American president as "the supreme *duce* of the free peoples" (figure 30). Mussolini would soon adopt for himself the same rhetoric (and lexicon).

Upon his return to the United States in late 1918, Merriam wrote an official account of his Italian experience for the *American Political Science Review*. It read like a manifesto of realpolitik, pleading for better-funded and -organized propaganda efforts not just to strengthen patriotic idealism but to serve geopolitical interests. "International misunderstandings," Merriam noted, "menace our industrial, political, social and national ideals and progress."[6] The selling of Wilson's America—and with it, American interests—to Italy was premised on the notion that, as he wrote to George Creel in June 1918, "Italy needs the influence of some great international personality."[7]

Merriam did not name anyone in particular, but his close office colleague in Rome, Gino Speranza, used the same argument to identify an Italian, not a

FIGURE 30. Woodrow Wilson headlined as "the supreme *duce* of the free peoples." *Il Popolo d'Italia*, October 10, 1918, 1. Courtesy of Biblioteca Nazionale, Rome.

foreign, figure. Speranza was an Italian American lawyer who was serving as personal aide and advisor to the American ambassador to Italy. On July 1918, he reported to Washington about "a man of vision," whom he identified as "the fighting leader of the Reform Socialists," whose popularity was winning approval among "members of all parties."[8] Given his public profile, this person could only have been Mussolini. Against the fear that Italy could have been next after Russia to succumb to a communist revolution, Speranza's reassuring reports provided indications of a possible and very welcome counter-strategy. Beyond the political influence of any "great international personality," what was needed for Italy was the emergence of a strong, anti-Bolshevik *Italian* leader. This remained the American view for years to come.

After the war, President Wilson experienced a dramatic drop in popularity in Italy because of his intransigence regarding the destiny of the Adriatic city of Fiume. Concomitantly, Mussolini replaced the dogmatic "poet-soldier" Gabriele D'Annunzio, the defeated leader of the occupation of Fiume, as Italy's nationalist icon.[9] The Duce's early-1920s rise to domestic and international fame was part of a script that unfolded against an ideological landscape of growing misgivings about the stability of Italian democracy and fears of a Bolshevik drift. In this context, Mussolini became of great geopolitical interest to the United States because of his relationship to America's immediate economic and political goals. The novelty of his authoritarian style also mattered to American political scientists and observers because of what it could teach about future governmental arrangements in America. In Merriam's 1931 analysis, Italy represented a "striking experiment," one "full of meaning for the student of civic training."[10] It was an experiment that had started at least officially and certainly with great promotional efficacy with the March on Rome, to which I now turn.

NEWS OF THE MARCH ON ROME

Almost a century later, the abrupt and dramatic effectiveness of Fascism's power seizure is still compelling, but it also has the whiff of a colorfully choreographed performance that was taken all too seriously. As a combination of a staged *threat* of insurrection and actual violence between Blackshirts and Communist activists throughout the country during the week of October 22–29, the March on Rome succeeded in forcing the king to give Mussolini the reins of the country. In theory it was a perfectly constitutional and legal power transition. In practice, as several observers recognized, it was a usurpation by an autocrat who had plotted the whole initiative away from Rome. Few expected it to be followed by even more dramatic moves. Twenty-six months later, Mussolini erased the authority of the Parliament and inaugurated a full-fledged dictatorship.

Italy's most politically gifted minds did not necessarily see it coming. Initially, notable anti-Fascists like Gaetano Salvemini deemed Mussolini a "clown [. . .] surrounded by young thugs," who was bound to "defeat himself."[11] Eventually, Salvemini explained the march as a "coup d'état, staged as a spontaneous rising of 'Blackshirts,' but in reality carried out by a military 'Black Hand.'"[12] While the confrontations between the Fascist militia and socialist groups resulted in dozens of deaths and hundreds of injuries, the human cost of the march went largely unreported. Journalists regularly insisted that there had been virtually no clashes between the police or the army on the one side and Mussolini's Blackshirts on the other. For instance, on October 31, 1922, the *St. Paul Pioneer Press* described the March as a coup d'état "accomplished with extraordinary skill," and a few months later the *Wall Street Journal* was still praising Mussolini for taking "Italy without shedding a drop of blood."[13] To outsiders, the march was a coup d'état sans coup. Several commentators read this as a sign of widespread consensus. Others diagnosed it in a bleaker fashion, as an undemocratic abuse of power resulting in unreported violent acts.

Over the decades, historians of Italian fascism have studied the March on Rome by seeking to move past reductive and ritualistic celebrations or condemnations. Despite marked methodological differences, they have shared the view that the name March on Rome is misleading on multiple levels because it refers to a single event unfolding in a single geographic site.[14] What they have agreed upon is that the atmosphere of confusion and the collapse of state power led to the choreographically effective Roman scene as the watershed moment for Mussolini's political stature.

Though it has enlarged its focus from the city of Rome to an Italian theater, mainstream scholarship on the early days of the Fascist government has largely operated within an intranational framework. The context and theater of the March on Rome consisted of a broader, international scene that prominently featured the geographically distant United States.[15] The mediating role of American journalists and, especially, governmental officials reveals that they quickly recognized the

importance of the events of late October 1922, before, during, and immediately
after their unfolding: America's key political and financial players were not passive
spectators of Mussolini's rise to power. While they did not aid Mussolini's ascendancy in situ, they fostered American public opinion's positive reaction to, and
thus legitimatization of, his quick seizure of power.

Despite a few cautious responses (and fewer denunciations) to the Blackshirts'
violent methods, several first responses to the march were celebratory, in fact.
It was not just that notable individuals and organizations that expressed high
expectations for Mussolini's appointment as Italian leader. What was remarkable
was the swiftness with which the American press published positive responses to
the Duce, within days or just a few weeks of his ascent to power. The tempting
explanation for this rapid approval is that Mussolini met American aspirations for
a leader who could not only counter the strikes and disorder that was disrupting
the country's political and economic life, but who could do so with wide popular
support. The lack of substantial reports about the human costs of the March on
Rome provided the much-desired proof of Mussolini's popularity. Still, more precise questions ought to be asked. Where did these papers get their news?

Beyond the power interests at stake in the published stories, of notable historical importance was the infrastructure of the coverage—that is, the network
of journalists working for wire services and major newspapers. In the early 1920s,
120 members of the foreign press worked in Rome, and "of these, perhaps 40 to 50
were genuine correspondents, the rest were police spies or hacks in the pay of the
regime." Most American newspapers received their foreign dispatches from the
few Rome-based news bureaus (i.e., Associated Press, United Press, and International News Service), which were largely friendly to the regime.[16] There were also
newspapers that could afford direct reports from Italy, including the *New York
Times* and the *Christian Science Monitor,* as well as the *Chicago Daily News* and
the *Chicago Tribune.* They too, with notable exceptions, were not inimical to the
regime. The *New York Times* counted on several correspondents who generally
tended to report favorably or with measured distance on Mussolini, as did the
Christian Science Monitor. The coverage from Chicago was polarized. For most of
the initial Fascist period, the *Chicago Daily News* correspondent was the Fascist
sympathizer Hiram K. Motherwell, who in 1928 would even translate Mussolini's
1908 novel, *The Cardinal's Mistress.*[17] The *Tribune's* George Seldes, instead, wrote
such extremely critical articles about the regime that they eventually cost him his
job.[18] Another fierce critic was the South African British writer William Bolitho,
who wrote for both Walter Lippmann's *World* and the *Manchester Guardian.* His
1926 volume *Italy under Mussolini* called Mussolini's rule "tyranny" and labeled it
a "slave state."[19] Other outlets debated whether Fascism truly represented the will
of the Italian masses or whether Mussolini was just the leader of a violent mob.

The coverage of the events in Rome did not always focus on Mussolini. A few isolated articles focused more on Fascism as a novel ideology and a mode of governance.

In early October 1922, *Current Opinion* described the Fascist movement as fundamentally a "challenge," not aristocratic but highly popular, to the weakness of traditional governments.[20] The *New Republic* included articles by journalist and writer Giuseppe Prezzolini, an old friend of the Duce. In November 1922 he praised Fascism as an "utterly new movement" that "had become particularly 'popular.'"[21] The same month, the former military attaché of the U.S. embassy in Italy, Gino Speranza, argued that, despite its violence, the Fascist movement was the revolt of the middle class against the "sinister spell of an exotic Marxism."[22] A few months later, he described Fascism in *Outlook* as a "spiritual national reconstruction."[23] In a few rare instances, publications that primarily focused on the Blackshirts took a more worried stance due to these Fascist adherents' overt use of violence. Newspapers and periodicals like the *New York Tribune* and *Literary Digest* published dystopian descriptions and cartoons that painted the Blackshirts as a backward and violent movement, comparable and related to America's Ku Klux Klan (figure 31). Other outlets instead openly defended the authoritarian modus operandi of the Blackshirts, arguing that their youthful antidemocratic force was the right medicine for Italian democracy's sick and aging body. They appeared to rehash the forgiving rhetoric that in 1921, Anne O'Hare McCormick, then a young freelance contributor to the *Book Review and Magazine* of the *New York Times,* had deployed when covering the Fascists' violence in Rome. Through her romantic view of Italy as a land of artworks, she hailed the socialists' riotous protests and staining walls of medieval churches with Soviet slogans as the very epitome of brazen disorder and demagogic tyranny. Fascism, instead, was for her the middle class's "healthy and necessary reaction," perhaps "a ruthless movement, as youth is ruthless," but capable of substituting "swift and decisive action for the slow processes of legislation and experiment."[24]

By and large, however, Fascism and the Blackshirts were intertwined with the figure of the Duce and consequently deserving positive consideration as a worthy political movement and method. Just a few days after the March on Rome, the *New York Tribune* described Mussolini as "A Black-Shirted Garibaldi," referring to the celebrated military commander that led the 1860–1861 state formation. With Mussolini, the paper continued, Fascism was "rough in its methods," but it had "tonic" aims "against degeneration through Socialist internationalism." Ultimately, if "Garibaldi won freedom in a red shirt, Mussolini is fighting for normalcy and Italianism in a black one."[25] The *New York Times* intertwined its description of Mussolini as a de facto "dictator of Italy" with a celebration of the Fascist revolution as a "relatively harmless Italian type" of political upheaval.[26] On November 3, the *New York Herald* praised the forty-year-old Mussolini as the "regenerator of the Italian nation."[27] It was a flattering compliment, though one still within the domain of conventional political rhetoric. On the same day, however, the *Birmingham Age-Herald* wrote that Mussolini looked "like a movie star," which was clearly a move away from traditional political assessments and even from the most enthusiastic forms of praise.[28] Instead, this comparison signaled unprecedented attention to

FIGURE 31. The Blackshirts compared to the KKK. *Literary Digest*,
November 11, 1922, 13.

and celebration of a new, personalizing set of characteristics for a contemporary
leader: political power, physical presence, and personal appeal. As other similar
comments reveal, the Duce's masculinity exuded an old-fashioned charm, but it
also expressed the irrepressible energy of modern youth.

As the newly appointed *New York Times* Rome correspondent, McCormick contributed to a view of Fascism as a governmental style that matched its histrionic and
hypermasculine leader. She celebrated the new premier as "swashbuckling
Mussolini," using a term usually applied to Fairbanks.[29] McCormick repeatedly
deployed a pragmatic rhetoric and medical metaphors in defense of Mussolini's
antidemocratic methods. Assuming "one-man power to be less dangerous than
the powerlessness of many men," she wondered whether he was not the remedy to
"the disease of politics that infects civilization." Most interestingly, she argued that
Mussolini's autocratic methods were justified by his popularity. "The people were
already yearning for a dictatorship when Mussolini appointed himself a dictator,"
she charged. "His march on Rome was like an answer to a prayer."[30] What fueled
his popularity was not necessarily an ideology, about which McCormick never had

much to say, but governance through the crowd-pleasing showmanship that dominated the press coverage at home and abroad. Nobody had ever seen anything like
it in Italy before—or elsewhere, for that matter. "The new government cultivates the
spectacular," she observed before claiming that "one of the reasons for its popularity
among a people" that was usually undervalued was that Mussolini gave "them at
last a leader who is a headliner, so to speak, able to command public attention and
keep Italy on the front page." More than a politician, he was a celebrity, even though
McCormick never used this term: "He makes politics a kind of noble show and
keeps enlivened and interested the audience, so bored by his predecessors."[31]

As a political celebrity, Mussolini could be compared to non-Italian political
superstars, which heralded the recognition of a fame that stretched beyond the
limited domain of politics—as he well knew. In mid-1923, in the pages of the *New
York Times Book Review and Magazine*, McCormick compared Mussolini to Theodore Roosevelt: "A nation that thrilled to the Vigilantes and Rough Riders rises to
Mussolini and his Black Shirt Army."[32] By 1923, books in English about Fascism
and Mussolini were regularly featured on the shelves of American bookstores,
sold as comparable to the celebratory profiles of American business and political heroes. This literature was often characterized by a description of Mussolini's
authoritarian stewardship as a reaction to inanity and incompetence, with some
reservations about his use of violence.[33]

His leadership and popular consensus thrilled the business community, which
had been discontented with the feebleness of postwar Italian governments. Writing
in the pages of the *Nation's Business,* Basil Miles, the Paris-based American representative of the International Chamber of Commerce, praised "Mussolini's Blackshirts
as a potent factor for better business" and deemed their actions a "bloodless revolution against a wasteful government." Miles's article included a detailed account of
Mussolini's economic program, based on the "abolition of the law compelling the
registration of all securities," which had discouraged investors and delayed the "flow
of capital into industry." The program also included radical tax reform, privatization
of telephone services and railways, reduction of state expenses, and balancing the
national budget.[34] Unsurprisingly, the U.S. business press (i.e., *Barron's Commerce
and Finance,* the *Nation's Business,* and the *Wall Street Journal*) was overall quite
optimistic about Italy's economic prospects under Mussolini.[35]

Praise of the Duce's undemocratic authority often impinged upon a misogynist
rhetoric. As a self-made patriarch, the son of a blacksmith, and someone tirelessly
engaged in continuous self-improvement, Mussolini was the virile new leader
domesticating a stereotypically unruly nation gendered as feminine. In 1923, *Time*
magazine put him on its cover for the first time with a caption that referred to
castor oil, which Fascists forced their opponents to drink and which became,
together with the bludgeon, a symbol of Fascist discipline and obedience. A few
years later, another *Time* magazine cover showed him courageously behind bars
with a lioness that he had tamed. Her name was Italia.[36]

Even critical reports, such as those that often appeared in *Literary Digest,* referred to and popularized Mussolini's Caesarism, especially when granting him space in direct or indirect quotes from interviews. The Duce's political novelty, in fact, came with an outspoken rejection of democracy ("mass cannot govern mass") and liberty ("civilization is the inversion of personal liberty").[37] The same articles also popularized his direct, acclamatory definition of Fascism as the change "from parliamentary government [. . .] to a government in which the prime minister is directly bound to the multitude."[38] Emboldened by the space granted to it in the press, Mussolini used his celebrity status to justify his regime's methods. When rumors spread regarding fascism's antidemocratic policies, the *Saturday Evening Post* adopted medical metaphors to argue that "desperate diseases need desperate remedies. Italy was a surgical case that called for a major operation."[39] In her 1924 overview of world's dictators, McCormick praised Fascism as "the triumphant example of popular and successful dictatorship" and found the Duce's style of plebiscitarian governance ("Mussolini glories in autocracy") utterly acceptable and even better than the American system. "The people may not be freer than they were under a weaker and more representative government, but they are certainly freer from trouble," she opined. She went on to claim that "under Mussolini [Italy] has changed from an enfeebled and divided kingdom into one of the most [. . .] prospering powers of Europe," where Italians enjoy "a personal liberty unknown in an indefatigably regulated commonwealth like ours."[40]

In the early years after taking power, Mussolini sought to exercise a measure of control over the promotion of his leadership. While keen on nurturing personal relationships, he soon benefitted from more institutional forms of publicity mediation that would articulate and sustain his positive reception in America for years, through the near fatal delegitimization of his regime in the aftermath of the 1924 Fascist murder of Socialist congressman Giacomo Matteotti.[41] Mussolini's assumption of personal responsibility in a January 3, 1925, speech to the Parliament is often regarded as the official beginning of Mussolini's dictatorship. Before, during, and after the Matteotti crisis, Mussolini, as both prime minister and minister of foreign affairs, relied on a network of mediators, consisting of the entire Italian diplomatic corps in the United States, beginning with the embassy and the consul general of New York. The diplomatic force made a critical alliance with the Italy America Society (IAS), a key lobbying association with links to the State Department and Wall Street, as well as to powerful individuals such as U.S. ambassador William Washburn Child and the chief executive at J. P. Morgan & Co., banker-diplomat Thomas W. Lamont. Often advised by IAS's president, corporate lawyer Paul Cravath (who had ties to J. P. Morgan), the Italian embassy put American journalists and editors in direct contact with Mussolini. Through a system of patronage that guaranteed access and sumptuous receptions in Italy, the Duce befriended a whole host of journalists and writers, including Isaac F. Marcosson of the *Saturday Evening Post;* public relations experts and periodical contributors, including Ivy Lee;

and bankers and businessmen, including John Morron, a director of the First National Bank of New York, and financier Charles Torrey. These relationships proved quite effective. Even when periodicals sought to publish critical reports—as, for instance, the *Atlantic Monthly, Harper's Magazine,* and *Literary Digest* did—their coverage still amounted to publicity. It is to these most formidable mediators that we shall now turn.

A CLOSED SOCIETY: THE JOURNALIST, THE BANKER, THE AMBASSADOR

Dear Dad, we are having a fine revolution here. No danger. Plenty of enthu-siasm and color. We all enjoy it.

RICHARD WASHBURN CHILD, U.S. AMBASSADOR TO ITALY, TO HIS FA-THER, THE DAY AFTER THE MARCH ON ROME[42]

The most reliable network of publicity mediators that Mussolini depended on for his swift and favorable emergence in American public opinion was the Italy American Society (IAS). Since its establishment in March 1918, IAS had the goal of fostering "between the United States and Italy an international friendship based upon mutual understanding of their national ideals," which essentially meant, as the masthead of its *News Bulletin* boasted, a "co-operative effort to develop international trade."[43] To accomplish this, IAS intertwined the interests of both the State Department and Wall Street on the American side with those of the Italian embassy on the Italian side.

With some pretense of cultural engagement with a nation that was rich in art but poor in infrastructure and foreign investments, IAS sought to open up a political space for new financial and economic relations between the two countries. Although nominally private, the IAS relied on a broad network of powerful interests: the American and Italian American financial community, the Italian and U.S. governments, and Italian American leaders.[44] Through the press influence of these interests in the two countries, IAS contributed—directly and indirectly—to manage Mussolini's reputation within the broader U.S. financial, governmental, and popular spheres.[45]

On the economic side, IAS's reach was ambitious. Like the bankers and corporate lawyers who constituted its membership, the most prominent of whom were linked to J. P. Morgan & Co., IAS was favorably disposed toward Italy, whoever its leader, even before the March on Rome.[46] Morgan's "purchasing organization had executed large orders on behalf of the Italian military during the war" and, after the end of the conflict, sought to do "a substantial underwriting business in Italian securities."[47] In many respects, IAS considered Mussolini just the next leader, the one it had to deal with after the failure of the previous liberal governments. In other respects, Mussolini was such a peculiar politician that arguments for promoting investments in Italy could not be merely economic. In this regard,

IAS provided a highly placed public relations platform for Mussolini's political legitimacy, which was a key condition for American investments in Italy. A quick rebuttal against the argument that his government was *autocratic*—a word that the war propaganda had taught Americans to condemn—was a priority. In its first *Trade Bulletin* (October 1922), published after the March on Rome, Irene di Robilant, an Italian aristocrat living in New York who was to become IAS's organizing factotum, quenched any anxiety about the Blackshirts' quick and seemingly authoritarian rise to power. In a three-page editorial, she described the Fascisti as the heirs of Garibaldi's Red Shirts and "the power and the law of ancient Rome" and referred to Mussolini as a genius organizer who "personifies their power in action."[48]

On the political side, the IAS's reach was equally impressive. Reproducing Wall Street's financial giants' intertwined approach to finance and world politics, IAS cultivated powerful ties with many parts of the U.S. government, particularly the State Department. In the spring of 1920, Thomas Nelson Page, who had been ambassador to Italy from 1913 to mid-1919, was elected an honorary vice president of IAS.[49] The same annual elections appointed a forty-year-old Harvard-educated lawyer, writer, journalist named Richard Washburn Child to the IAS executive committee.[50] A year later President Harding nominated him U.S. ambassador to Italy (figure 32). Child represents one of the most interesting contributors to the convergence of political and cultural characterization that informed Mussolini's public image.

Unlike Page, whose clashes with Merriam revealed his opposition to overt propaganda tactics, Child had no diplomatic background.[51] Instead, in the 1910s while working in a New York law office, he had started his public career as a writer, publishing short stories and a few novels.[52] A lifelong Roosevelt supporter, he had also written a few influential political pieces for *Century Magazine* and *McClure's Magazine* that consistently stressed vigorous citizenry and strong leadership.[53] His horizons widened when, before the U.S. involvement in the European war, he took up assignments first as a foreign correspondent in Europe and Russia and then as a publicity man for the U.S. Treasury. In 1916 he published *Potential Russia*, a book that called for U.S. investments in the tsarist nation.[54] The Soviet Revolution scrapped any such plan. Still, known as a writer conversant in foreign affairs and a policy promoter, he worked during the war for the CPI's Division of Features, "which enlisted the volunteer services of the leading novelists, essayists and short-story writers of America."[55] Writing in 1919 about Wilson's centralization of war powers, he justified the president's "one-man leadership" as "the only emergency action we know" despite his long-standing opposition to the former New Jersey governor.[56] At war's end, Child worked briefly as the editor of *Collier's Weekly*, covered the Paris Peace Conference, and attacked Wilson's League of Nations for what he feared was America's unnecessary involvement with foreign nations. He promoted a Progressive social politics and a pragmatic isolationism that supported economic interests with minimum political involvement. He continued to denounce the demise of representative democracy

FIGURE 32. Richard Washburn Child in Washington, DC, 1924.
Photograph (digital file from original). Library of Congress, Prints &
Photographs Division, LC-DIG-npcc-10526.

and leadership that perniciously advantaged financial and industrial elites. In 1920, possibly thanks to his connections among the New York City's lawyers, he joined IAS's executive committee, which, as Child had viewed Russia in 1916, looked at postwar Italy as a favorable investment destination.[57] In the same year, he wrote effective speeches for Warren G. Harding, contributing to his election. On May 26, 1921, the president awarded Child the ambassadorship to Italy. Child probably did not know the first thing about being a diplomat. Rather than limiting his role, however, his background in creative writing and political advocacy was going to provide the skills he needed to promote Mussolini in America. The *New York Times* reported that Child was "the first of the 'younger generation' of American writers to achieve ambassadorial distinction."[58]

During Child's first months in Rome, the context of the relationship between the United States and Italy was dominated by two intertwining elements: the threat of Bolshevism and the question of war reparations. Italy had experienced two years of massive disorder and strikes that had revealed the government's inability to control the violent clashes between Socialist forces and a rising Fascist militia, and, in the process, weakened the national economy. The U.S. government's fears about the instability of the Italian administration, subject to continuous reshuffling and changes of coalitions, prevented any long-term American political and economic commitment.[59] The American embassy and consulates in Italy kept the State Department well-informed on the country's climate of violence and instability.[60] For instance, Child informed Secretary of State Charles Evans Hughes that Mussolini was emerging as a leader firmly in control of the most violent elements of the Fascist political movement. In early October, Child apprised Hughes that Mussolini was willing to start a revolution and become Italy's dictator. "People like the Italians hunger for strong leadership," he wrote, seemingly with approval, "and enjoy [. . .] being dramatically governed."[61]

Child's communications were not merely the result of an impersonal political assessment. Apparently Mussolini, who had a profound appreciation for America's political support, had befriended him. A few days before the March on Rome, in fact, the Duce visited the American embassy and informed Child of his plan! The ambassador immediately notified Hughes. "A few days ago," Child wrote on October 26, "Mussolini came to see me and addressed to me inquiries as to the attitude of the American public toward Fascisti."[62] There is no record of Hughes's answer, but it is not difficult to guess what it was. Given Child's previous cables and given any lack of an agitated response from the State Department, the response must have been cautious but positive.[63] Even with the intense domestic negotiations about Mussolini's seizure of power, he apparently remained quite attuned to the American response. A few hours after being nominated prime minister, one of his first public acts was to cable Secretary of State Charles Evans Hughes cordial good wishes and "express confidence in the friendly, economic and spiritual collaboration of our two countries."[64] Hughes duly responded shortly afterward, congratulating Mussolini on his new position and assuring him that the collaboration between Italy and the United States would continue to promote their mutual interests.[65]

Mussolini went out of his way to show that his relationship with American officials was quite special and unique. In early November, Child approached the premier's office to ask for the customary meeting with the new head of government. The opposite happened. Child made this report to the State Department:

> In response to my request to be received by the new minister [. . .] Mussolini instead of making an appointment called upon me this morning for an extended interview explaining his departure from the usual custom on the basis of personal friendship and his desire to emphasize his belief that while Italy should maintain friendly relations with all nations, an understanding of the new Italy and its young and

progressive spirit by the American government and particularly by the American people was of primary importance. He said that American cooperation was vital for the plans he had in mind.[66]

What Mussolini had in mind was the opening up, through the State Department, of special channels of communication with the business and financial world and, in turn, with American public opinion. The terrain of such possible future economic cooperation—and the bait—was economic progress, which all parties understood to be vital for reparations payments. This promoted policy amounted to privatizing public utilities, especially railways, and opening them up to U.S. investments. "Americans would be given all the opportunities this policy might yield," Child reported Mussolini telling him. As for the public image of Fascism, Mussolini insisted on a politics of alliance between capital and labor, as opposed to the "false hopes and vaporous expectations" that had been instilled previously by the Socialists upon the population.[67] Child registered all these arguments and ended his communication in formal diplomatic terms: "Mussolini indicates that he would appreciate it if the Department were to inform the American press that he had made to me 'hearty expression of friendship for America and of faith in mutual frankness in all exchange of views [between] the two nations.'" Finally, he summarized Mussolini's plan: "In brief, I believe he hopes that the Department will find a way to give him a little American publicity."[68] Child would take Mussolini's request to heart.

For the American government, the dramatic, but apparently orderly regime change in Italy was good news: there would not be any further risk of a Bolshevik revolution in Italy and reparations repayments would have been made on a regular basis. Still, from the American perspective, how could the country that had justified its war participation as a battle of democracy against autocracy now go on supporting Mussolini's authoritarian and overtly antidemocratic regime? The best way Washington and, with it, Wall Street could justify support of Fascism to American public opinion was by broadcasting the new Italian regime's unwavering commitment to a capitalist economy and openness to foreign investments. Such important preconditions, however, could not sufficiently build Mussolini's celebrity status in the United States. His full American acceptance depended on narratives that could script his personal and political biography in more relatable ways. What diplomatic communications, press briefings, and newspaper editorials seemed to share was a focus on his widespread attractiveness and recognition—at home and abroad. In his dispatches from Rome, Child was quick to characterize Mussolini as widely popular and uniquely capable of bringing the country to normalcy. And, in the post-Wilson era, normalcy was the precondition for international alliances.[69] Against "weak and halting ministers, who for four years have been unable to lead," Child wrote, "Italians prefer a determined Mussolini," who has a "magnetic character" and a "stern deportment and convincing oratory."[70]

In these colorful descriptions, Child-the-diplomat was handing the baton to Child-the-fiction-writer, a practice he was keen on repeating.

A little more than a year after the March on Rome, for instance, Child was the guest of honor at an IAS dinner held in New York on November 27, 1923. Child's speech had nothing of diplomatic reportage. Instead, it combined political advocacy (or partisanship) with a heavily personalized rhetoric that, to the ears of the businessmen in the room, helped legitimize investment opportunities in Italy. Child spoke about Italy and U.S. foreign policy and announced the dawning of a new political season, not solely for Italy but for America and world politics in general. The rhetorical impetus for his argument centered on the figure of the Duce:

> The tide has turned. The word democracy attached to drifting mobs no longer deceives us. We have come back to the realization that often the great hunger in the human heart is for strong leadership. We have come back to a decent appreciation that no matter how much we may desire to pat the heads of the weak and the wailing, no matter how great our pity and our charity, the hands worthy of our clasp of friendship are the strong and honest hands.[71]

In other writings and public speeches, while holding office and afterward, Child consistently articulated the same narrative about Mussolini, one centered on his daring and iconic leadership vis-à-vis the lack of efficacy of democratic governments.[72]

In assessing Child's effectiveness as a public relations operative, or as "Mussolini's mouthpiece in America," it is important to recognize the long-standing role of banker-ambassador Thomas W. Lamont, J. P. Morgan's exceptionally gifted and influential executive. During and after World War I, J. P. Morgan & Co. had already played a key role in financing the Italian military effort and postwar reconstruction. After the March on Rome, the American firm led by Lamont was ready to endorse Mussolini as Italy's preferred banking agent for all international financial institutions interested in investing in the peninsula.[73] Further, the Morgan firm eventually turned out to be the regime's U.S. bank, capable of extending loans to Mussolini's regime.[74] The banking giant was a fairly constant presence in Child's Italian affairs, having been for a while a close observer of the nation's financial health.[75] If Child was an activist and perhaps heterodox ambassador, so too was Lamont.

Lamont's active relationship with European affairs started after the end of World War I. Invited by Wilson to attend the 1919 Paris Peace Conference, Lamont was aptly named the "Ambassador from Wall Street" due to his ability to intertwine Morgan's financial plans with U.S. policy. An inveterate Italophile, he was interested in extending his financial skills to a nation he viewed as uniquely "touched with poetry and romance."[76] To this end, in Paris Lamont networked heavily with members of the Italian delegation. In particular, he befriended Giovanni Fummi, a former stockbroker who was to become Morgan's Rome agent and enable Lamont to enter Italy's top financial and political circles. Back in New York, Lamont's involvement with IAS, first as a trustee and treasurer (and in 1925 as president), was widely advertised and often reported in the press. After the March on Rome, Lamont kept up a close relationship with the Italian ambassador Gelasio Caetani by often reporting on criticisms of and negative rumors about Mussolini. At times, he even sought advice on how best to respond to criticism against the Duce.[77] Six months after the premier had taken office, Lamont met Mussolini to discuss restoring Italy's financial credit, and their relationship would only strengthen in both direct and indirect ways over the next few years.[78] In the summer of 1924, in the critical aftermath of the Fascist murder of Congressman Giacomo Matteotti, Lamont's reaction was steadfast. He managed to organize a lunch with the editors of all the major New York papers in order to give Ambassador Caetani a platform "for explaining his version of events to the editors and commentators."[79]

In post–World War I America, references to international leaders were becoming more common to newspaper readers than ever before. Fascism could be sold to Americans, but it all depended on how it was presented. The regime's violent nature had to be masked through national and racial distancing—that is, by stressing that different countries had different political cultures. One of the most direct examples of this rhetoric appears in a letter sent by Lamont to J. P. Morgan's Rome agent, Fummi. The context was the very delicate one of late 1925. Lamont was "considering a loan request for $100 million" from Italy, but knew that Secretary of State Frank Kellogg would have vetoed it unless the question of Italy's $2-billion debt was settled.[80] Lamont played the role of the skillful mediator. It helped that earlier that year, he had been elected, by unanimous vote, IAS president.[81] Champion of a style of "relationship banking" in which banker-client rapport went beyond shared financial interests, Lamont, through his Roman representative, offered remarkable advice to Mussolini on how to market his regime in America:

> If Mr. Mussolini declares that parliamentary government is at an end in Italy, such a declaration comes as a shock to Anglo-Saxons. If, on the contrary, Mr. Mussolini had explained that the old forms of parliamentary government in Italy had proved futile and had led to inefficient government and chaos, therefore they had to be temporarily suspended and generally reformed, then Anglo-Saxons would understand.[82]

The Morgan executive was relying on a familiar argument. Carleton Beals had written in *Current History* a few months earlier that historically, Italy was much more familiar with forms of "enlightened despotism," insisting that "the cloak of popular democracy and representative government does not fit comfortably or gracefully upon the body politic."[83] In the end, Lamont was successful both in advancing the negotiations over Italy's war debt with the United States and securing the loan to the regime. These successes "proved to be a catalyst for further American investment."[84] Lamont's mediating lesson went on to be applied to other public contexts. It would, for instance, find a profitable application in the unexpected collaboration and personal amity between Mussolini and William Randolph Hearst, whose syndicated newspapers and newsreel services would feature the Duce's weekly columns and speeches from October 1927 to May 1935. Overall, Lamont's reputation never suffered from his closeness to Mussolini. In the days after the crash of 1929, he even earned the cover of *Time* magazine as the "right hand of John Pierpont Morgan [. . .] who steered the ship of U.S. prosperity through the storm."[85]

Another prominent financial operator like Lamont who helped legitimize Mussolini in America and was also a member of the IAS executive committee was the aforementioned banker Otto Kahn. In the mid-1920s, Kahn publicly endorsed Mussolini as a reliable business partner and a guarantor of public order. His eloquent speeches were widely appreciated in the city's financial world and, at times, were even published. One in particular stood out. Kahn gave it to the Foreign Policy Association on January 3, 1926, at the Hotel Astor in New York. The Italian American Fascist periodical *Il Carroccio* published it in Italian as "Otto Kahn e il Fascismo." In the speech, Kahn defended Italians' political self-determination, but he also argued that in contexts other than the American, democracy and freedom were not necessarily overlapping notions, particularly when the popularity of a leader could productively disentangle them. It is worth reporting the speech's critical passages:

> To judge Fascism with fairness we must remember two things. Italy belongs to the Italians, not to the British or the Americans. [. . .] Secondly, and this is true for every nation, before freedom [. . .] is the public order and the protection of the idea and life of the nation. True freedom is impossible where there is no order and where a government does not work properly. [. . .] [Mussolini] is not a dictator in the usual meaning of the word, because he exercises his power with the explicit and overwhelming consensus of the people and by will of the King, the State's constitutional ruler.[86]

Lamont, Kahn, and the New York press could support a favorable reception for Mussolini, but what they all needed was a direct contact with the premier. Such contact was guaranteed by the very gifted Italian ambassador to the United States, Gelasio Caetani (figure 33). For about four years, between 1922 and 1925, and in collaboration with the Italian consuls in America, Caetani mediated between the Duce and American power centers by maintaining direct, personal relationships with Lamont, the U.S. State Department, the Italy American Society, and even Will H. Hays, the chairman of the Motion Picture Association of America. Of noble background, Caetani was a war hero and fervent nationalist. He had taken part in the March on Rome, at the end of which, in November 1922, he was named Italian ambassador to the United States directly by Mussolini. Personally and ideologically loyal to the Duce, he was also right for the job: a prince, a decorated officer, and an engineer trained in Italy and the United States, Caetani was already familiar with American cultural and economic life, and he had a mediating temperament.[87]

Celebrated by the *New York Times* at the time of his nomination, Caetani exuded the charm of old and new Italy.[88] In early 1923, IAS organized a banquet in his honor as the newly appointed Italian ambassador. The event, which was also under Morgan's patronage, put him in contact with the city and the country's political and financial elite.[89] In his address, Caetani defended Mussolini's authoritarian actions as both urgent and audacious. "It is not a dictatorial government," he insisted, "but one of unflinching determination to put through those reforms that everybody had been advocating for years but nobody so far had had the courage of applying for fear of unpopularity."[90]

Even though the embassy had already engaged in publicity initiatives before Mussolini took power, under Caetani's leadership it came to operate like a public relations agency for the Duce. In early November 1922, just a few days after the March on Rome, the ambassador solicited press clippings about the Duce or Fascism from all consular authorities, made summaries, and sent them to the Duce. In one of these cables, the embassy clarified its institutional role: to shed light on the aspects of recent events that Americans might have found otherwise confusing. The government change, for instance, deserved to be explained as resulting from constitutional rules and as being "nothing other than the effect of Italian popular will."[91] As we saw earlier, this was a message that effectively informed much of the coverage of the March on Rome.

In his dual role as prime minister and minister of foreign affairs, Mussolini used Caetani to relay and publicize his new Italian policies through the "diplomatic, political, financial, and journalistic circles," as Mussolini's short cables insisted.[92] Caetani's ability to get things done was impressive, whether it meant promoting a new institutional accord between the Fascist Government and the unions (August 1923);[93] or arranging for a personal meeting between Mussolini and Ivy Lee following Lee's *Time Magazine* article appreciative of Mussolini's communicative style.[94] Caetani also introduced Isaac Frederick Marcosson, the European correspondent of the *Saturday Evening Post,* to the Duce: the relationship with the most important U.S. periodical was to last more than a decade.[95] Caetani seems to have known or met everybody in Washington, New York, and even Rome. It was in Rome in mid-1923 that he met with Ambassador Child.[96] Caetani was there overseeing the production of a film featuring Mussolini that he had promoted, as we shall see in the next chapter.

Officially, the embassy's political agenda had to address two main questions: the negotiations of the war debt between Italy and the United States, for which favorable economic news about Italy was always helpful, and the dangerous issue of the American Fascists' loyalty to Italy. Their activism was an issue for Rome because their unrestrained violence represented a dangerous form of interference in American affairs and affected the American reputation of Fascism in general.[97] Despite the importance of these political matters, a significant portion of the communications between the embassy and consuls related to Mussolini's reputation

FIGURE 33. Prince Gelasio Caetani, December
12, 1922. Photograph (digital file from original).
Library of Congress, Prints & Photographs
Division, LC-DIG-npcc-07583.

and image in America. The term *image* included not just Mussolini's general public reception, but also his very likeness. "Every time American newspapers publish
a portrait of Mussolini," Caetani wrote to the Italian consuls in the United States,
"they mostly rely on an awful photograph that represents him with a menacing
expression and often a wild one. That gives American readers a bad impression."
To address this problem, in Rome Caetani acquired a large number of photographs that in his view more faithfully and attractively presented the Duce. He
then invited all the consuls to submit said photographs to the newspapers. But
he prudently advised the consuls that their distribution "was not to appear as an
institutional gesture, but as a special gift to a friend." Obviously, the photographs
were to find their place in the newspapers' archives, ready to be used.[98]

Caetani left office in 1925 following the positive public relations resolution of
the Matteotti assassination: a few commentators believed that the crisis could
have meant the end of Fascism but were sure it would not have meant the end
of Mussolini. Comparing the Duce to Roosevelt in terms of leadership skills,
Frederick Collins of *Collier's* rationalized this outcome as follows: "Fascism is not a
world factor. Mussolini is."[99] While certain sectors of the American press launched
a full attack against Mussolini,[100] Child's articles for the *Saturday Evening Post,*
which began to appear a few months after he had left his Italian post on February
1924, greatly helped the Duce.[101] Caetani acknowledged the former ambassador's
positive impact on American public opinion toward both Mussolini and Child

himself.[102] Since they came from an independent voice, Child's counternarratives were even more effective than Caetani's efforts during the crisis. These had included an interview granted to the Associated Press and a well-publicized and reassuring meeting with President Harding.[103]

In both his diplomatic memoir and published essays, Child returned often to Mussolini's personal stature as a kind of *Übermensch*.[104] By the mid-1920s, the Duce's reputation in American public culture was of someone who was more than a forceful foreign politician. To many, his unconventional approach to governance appeared to transcend Italy's borders and traditions and, as such, to produce results both exceptional and exemplary. Fascism was an experimental political system that could inspire other nations, including democratic America. For instance, anti-immigration novelist Kenneth L. Roberts viewed Mussolini's Fascism as a welcome antidote to the radical demagogy and corruption endemic to mass democracy.[105] Through but also beyond his noteworthy accomplishments, Mussolini became a public personality whose entire life was worth telling and retelling to U.S. readers, particularly if writers knew how to combine exotic Italian elements with recognizably American features. As a former journalist and novelist, Child knew that. After leaving the ambassadorship, he continued to write for years about and on behalf of Mussolini. In his work, he began to weave together narratives about the Duce as both a foreign leader and an American one. His contribution paralleled other hagiographic endeavors.

HAGIOGRAPHIES

The graduating class [. . .] at Yale selected Kipling as the favorite poet. Will Rogers was the favorite world figure, with Al Capone and Mussolini tied for second honors.

CHICAGO DAILY TRIBUNE, 1931[106]

The key genre for the promotion of the Duce was the celebratory biography, whether in short or long format. Since the March on Rome, the American public had become used to reading short biographical profiles of the Duce. *Forum, Literary Digest,* and *Living Age* had published them as early as 1923.[107] By the mid-1920s, the literature on Fascism and Mussolini began to include serialized autobiographies, such as those published by the very influential United Press news agency (UP) and the popular *Saturday Evening Post.* Consisting of ten installments each, they bore the name of Mussolini as their sole author but actually depended on the ghostwriting of Child and other remarkable mediators.[108] As we saw with Valentino, the serialized autobiography enabled promotional agents to play a very effective role, particularly when revealing previously unknown personal details about their subject's life. Overtly or covertly, Mussolini's biographers sought to position the Duce as a most likeable figure who had effortlessly adopted American traits, especially love of order and efficiency, but who had also maintained defining Italian ones, including authoritarian leadership.[109]

Child adopted this approach to Mussolini's composite character in his memoir *A Diplomat Looks at Europe*. Three of the memoir's eleven chapters reworked, with only minor changes, Child's *SEP* articles on Mussolini.[110] In this volume, he unabashedly praised the Italian dictator as the architect of a new, postdemocratic nation. Child touched upon the familiar picturesque imagery of Naples before announcing the dawn of a new nation. "When I sailed up the magnificent Bay of Naples in July 1921," he wrote, "I was the American ambassador to old Italy. When, after nearly three years, I looked back at the Italian Alps on my way home, I was still the ambassador to Italy, but it was a new Italy."[111] Child's account then intertwined personal and political considerations, Italy's alleged desperate need for a radical change, even a dictatorial one, and the unique fitness of Mussolini's temperament for the job:

> When a people faces an intolerable situation, the real ravenous hunger is not for a program, but for a man. In modern Italy they have the tradition that when a man is really needed he will rise up from the crowd. [. . .] Benito Mussolini was the strong leader of the expression of national spirit.[112]

For Child, the Italian situation was not at all a foreign one. Even though Italians' recent strike-ridden history required the intervention of a strong hand, Mussolini's rise could teach something to America. In this vein, he argued:

> The real story, from which Americans and our own statesmen can draw useful lessons for the future, is a story not of an armed attack upon a flabby democracy which was wheedling and coddling everyone, but a story of leadership and discipline and national unity in the labor of erecting a new government.[113]

The former ambassador also maintained that Fascism constituted a model antidote to the political impasse he associated with the excesses of democratic machinery, including the demands for minority rights, which in his view had led to the decline of patriotic spirit. Fascism could reverse this worldwide political and constitutional gridlock by insisting on individual responsibility and civic obligations.

> *Fascismo* is a philosophy and an emotion running counter to the recent stream of thought, which centers mankind's attention on rights. Mussolini, without distinguishing between classes, is the first conspicuous leader since Roosevelt that has organized political unity not around rights but around duties.[114]

In other words, when approaching Fascism in terms of a *disciplined regime,* Child stressed what he considered Mussolini's exhibition of the very American (albeit traditional) traits of self-control, order, and governmental effectiveness. As a result, comparisons with American presidents were easily conceivable. "The two preeminent rulers of the world today are not difficult to name," he wrote in 1926.

"They are Mussolini and Coolidge. Each represents in his particular power of personality the revolt of peoples against unreality and their weariness of parliamentary government—government by talk."[115]

In addition to Child's hagiographic work, Mussolini's American fame was also indebted to the work of a cultured Venetian woman of Jewish background, the writer and art critic Margherita Sarfatti. A publicly loyal supporter, the polyglot Sarfatti remained one of the Duce's closer advisors and nonexclusive lovers from late 1912 until the mid-1930s. She greatly influenced his theorization of the Fascist mission, particularly regarding the relationships between the Italian state and the country's artistic culture.[116] Before her ghostwriting work on the serialized UP autobiography and her uncredited collaboration on what became Mussolini's *My Autobiography* (1928), Sarfatti wrote, under her own name, the authorized biography *The Life of Benito Mussolini* (1925). With a preface by Mussolini himself, published both in English and in a handwritten facsimile Italian version meant to convey authenticity, the volume appeared both in the United Kingdom and the United States with said title (preferred by the publisher) and in Italy a year later with the title Sarfatti had wanted for all editions, *Dux*.[117] Between 1926 and 1928, the American edition went through eighteen printings (five in 1926 alone). In the same two-year period, the book was translated into eighteen languages.[118]

Unlike Child's political approach in his profile of the Duce, Sarfatti's booklength portrait focused more on Mussolini as a great man, specifically drawing out his character and personality as a young "Italian [. . .] par excellence."[119] In describing Mussolini as an exceptional individual and a predestined leader who achieved greatness by virtue of his own willpower, Sarfatti made it clear that she refused to follow "a pedantic chronological unity." Instead, she adopted a "more genuine unity which is inherent in the character" of her hero, proceeding "as life has done with him and he with life—by leaps and bounds, by rapid advances and sudden retreats."[120] Sarfatti's book intended to show how Mussolini's charismatic leadership and attractive personality, not just his politics, would appeal to the Anglo-American reader. Possibly following the lead of established biographies of the giants of the American financial and industrial world, from Andrew Carnegie to Henry Ford, she told a story that most readers must have found familiar. Mussolini was a self-made man who had managed to rise from the anonymity of the crowd, effect change in the world of politics and journalism, and modernize Italy. His remarkable character and modern personality were his weapons. He combined the very traditional trait of exceptional personal discipline with the modern traits of charming personality, determined self-improvement, and committed self-care. Unsurprisingly, a significant section of *The Life of Benito Mussolini* was devoted to the Duce's bodily activities and healthy diet.

Sarfatti showcased the Duce's character by summarizing his life's trajectory as a movement from humble origins to powerful positions that skillfully deployed such personal qualities as bravery and determination. In her tale, several episodes attested that even in his early years he had displayed the qualities of "the true leader he already was."[121] Sarfatti presented the young man's uncompromising stance against his old party and in favor of Italy's intervention in the war, broadcast from the newspaper he had founded, as the mark of a true national hero and leader. Following what was already a hagiographic cliché, Sarfatti stressed how his participation in World War I and his injury were the turning points of his life. He overcame his painful near-death experience, during which he bore pain without medications, with superhuman willpower. In Sarfatti's estimate, the Italian dictator, just like Oliver Cromwell, George Washington, and Napoleon before him, had found his heroic calling during dramatic battlefield events.[122] Beyond personal courage, what further launched him toward the country's modern leadership was his political vision and communicative talent.

The volume, in fact, ended with a chapter titled "Mussolini the Man" in which Sarfatti insisted on not just the strength of his personal temperament but also on his talent as a successful journalist and communicator. In passages that were reminiscent of Anne O'Hare McCormick and Ivy Lee's characterizations, Sarfatti singled out Mussolini's exceptional oratorical skills, whose "frank, sensible, brusque" methods resulted in a directness unprecedented in Italian politics.[123]

> His eloquence, resembling the bulletins of Napoleon, is not that of a man of letters, accustomed to seek at his writing-table the nuances of expression. He is a true man of action, living through in his own experience the experiences of history and touching the heart of a people through its imagination.[124]

Illustrated with eleven never-before-seen photographs of the Duce (Child's volume had only two), *The Life of Benito Mussolini* paraded the special intimacy between author and subject. Instead of familiar poses of the Duce giving speeches or utterly still, the volume included two rarely seen photographs, one of Mussolini riding his horse and one in the company of his lioness, named Italia, which *Time* magazine used a year later on its second cover dedicated to the Italian leader.

The reviews of Sarfatti's account were enthusiastic. The *Illustrated London News* greeted it as "likely to rank with the classic biographies." It also admiringly marveled at Mussolini's preface, in which the Italian dictator did not necessarily articulate an ultimate political goal beyond his desire to "make a mark on [his] era with [his] will, like a lion with the claws." The British paper found the way Mussolini described himself vis-à-vis his fame astonishing. Rather than defining himself as a political visionary, his self-assessment focused on his transformation under the media spotlight. The dramatic expansion of Mussolini's public self through an intense and incessant degree of interest had produced a sort of anthropological change in his persona that went far beyond political merits and goals. Mussolini wrote:

> The public man is born "public." [. . .] The public man, like the poet, is born to his doom. He can never escape it. [. . .] I am perfectly resigned to my lot as a public

man. In fact, I am enthusiastic about it. Not just on account of my publicity which it entails. [. . .] No, it is the thought, the realization, that I no longer belong merely to myself, that I belong to all—loved by all, hated by all—that I am an essential element in the lives of theirs: this feeling has on me a kind of intoxicating effect.[125]

Quite similarly, in his review of the Italian dictator's first authorized biography, John Carter of the *New York Times* wrote that "its principal interest lies in the currency it gives to the Mussolinic Legend." In other words, the degree of public interest—his celebrity quota, so to speak—was for the reviewers the true and only criterion on which to assess him politically. "Sarfatti's book," Carter added, "is important for making us realize that it is impossible to appraise a statesman on any other basis than mythopoeia."[126] Carter attributed the Duce's proud leadership to his Latin masculinity by sexualizing his relationship with Italians and with Italy as a whole:

> Latin races appreciate virility in a statesman far more than do the Anglo-Saxon, whose politicians are expected to have distinguished themselves by their conspicuous chastity at least before seeking office. Mussolini's grasp on Italy is susceptible to the analysis of the psychology of sex.[127]

Possibly because written by someone who many knew to have been, and who perhaps still was, intimate with the Duce, Sarfatti's *The Life of Benito Mussolini* appeared to reviewers open to consideration about the Duce's virility. At the same time, however, Sarfatti's work also represented a very modern way to read the personal dimension of political leaders. The virtues of public men—as the Venetian author implied and as her reviewers recognized—could not be limited to questions of morality, policy, and political talent but had to include insights into a person's physical traits and inclinations.

In the following years, Sarfatti continued to weave biographical narratives about the Duce, but this time not under her own name. She apparently contributed to two serialized biographies of Mussolini, published by the UP news agency and the *Saturday Evening Post*. They exhibited her daring stylistic approach but were also in tune with the modern American notion of personality as "mastery and development of the self," which entailed an explicit discussion of bodily talents and dispositions. These biographies focused on such celebrated and uplifting traits as work efficiency but also gave large space in praise of Mussolini's magnetic voice, rhetorical ability, and physical self-care. The first of these serialized biographies, entitled *Mussolini's Own Story of His Busy Life,* was syndicated between January 5 and January 15, 1927, by UP, which at the time served over a thousand newspapers across the United States and in another thirty-five countries.[128] Apparently, the authors of this series were Sarfatti and UP's Rome manager, Thomas B. Morgan.[129] In "one of the outstanding newspaper exploits of recent years," boasted the promotional material as if it were referring to a film celebrity, "Mussolini tells the intimate, personal story of his daily life."[130]

Over ten articles, the series deploys the theme of efficiency to an exceptional degree, as its title's use of the word *busy* foreshadows. In the introduction to the first article, the editor presents the dictator as someone who "works intensively fourteen to sixteen hours a day" and who regards "personal efficiency [as] his fetish" to the point that "every minute of each day is scheduled in advance."[131] Mussolini's opening words read like a Macfadden self-help manual of personal productivity: "It has been my rule of life to employ the body and mind to render the maximum output." To guarantee such efficiency, Mussolini notes, he has to follow a series of strict rules and personal daily routines, including eating and drinking habits (i.e., milk instead of alcohol).[132] The link between control of his own body and that of his country was an obvious rhetorical isomorphism linking body politics with body economics. It also held a proud nationalist dimension. By transferring the concept of efficiency from American business culture to himself and his own administration, Mussolini sought to contrast the stigmatizing characteristics usually attributed to Italians—such as disorganization, ineptitude, and sentimentalism—with the image of a new Italian man who was efficient, pragmatic, and, most importantly, disciplined.[133] At the same time, he acknowledges the American imprint of the vaunted notion of work efficiency. "The United States [. . .] created smooth-running organizations of human units," he writes in the fourth article of the series. "It is just such business efficiency on a larger scale we have tried to work into the government machine of Italy. We are succeeding."[134] Ultimately, Mussolini's work efficiency was associated with his effort to change, renew, and improve Italy and the Italians effectively, but it was also well attuned to the businesslike American attitude that emphasized achieving results no matter the personal costs.

Shortly after, another series much richer in tone and content appeared in the *Saturday Evening Post*. Published from May 5 to October 27, 1928, in one of America's most popular periodicals, this series did not have single, overarching title and was later republished in a volume under the title of *My Autobiography*.[135] Allegedly written by Mussolini himself, both the *SEP* installments and the resulting volume in fact had multiple authors. Mussolini's brother Arnaldo, possibly with Sarfatti, wrote the Italian text. Child translated this into English in collaboration with the *Corriere della Sera* correspondent Luigi Barzini Jr.[136] Child also wrote the volume's eight-page foreword, finalizing it probably during a late 1927 trip to Rome.[137]

In the foreword, Child described Mussolini's political leadership as "celebrity" and adopted a cinematic term of comparison ("his own size on the *screen* of history") to emphasize the modernity of his public image. As in other accounts, Mussolini emerges in *My Autobiography* as a leader who was born in a great nation but personally came from nothing. Even though he had a strong father figure, in his early life he was often aimless. The Great War marked his path and made him see the "the death struggle of a worn-out democracy," to quote one of the chapters, found Fascism, and take Rome. The book also includes chapters on the "five years of government," the future of the Fascist state, and the "political and social doctrine of fascism." But Child's foreword provides the lens with which all the narrative can profitably be read as the profile of a larger-than-life politician.

The virilized physical newness of Mussolini's energetic political leadership, visible to Child in the dictator's "firm jaws" or audible in "a sentence suddenly ejaculated," glorified rather than tamed any reference to the dictatorial nature of his regime.[138] In an American context that could safely imagine from afar what it would be like to witness the demise of democratic institutions, Child did not see any reason to downplay the autocratic measures that Fascist government had taken:

> In our time it may be shrewdly forecast that no man will exhibit dimensions of permanent greatness equal to those of Mussolini. [. . .] It is one thing to administer a state. The one who does this well is called statesman. It is quite another thing to make a state. Mussolini has made a state. That is superstatemanship.[139]

As he did in his IAS speech and elsewhere, in the foreword Child transitions from an emphasis on Mussolini's domestic political leadership, which had resulted in an infusion of vigor into Italy's new generations ("youth itself, appears as if born with a new spirit, a new virility bred in the bones"), to comparisons with his political idol. "Mussolini, like Roosevelt," he notes, "gives the impression of an energy which cannot be bottled, which bubbles up and over like an eternally effervescent, irrepressible fluid."[140]

My Autobiography, like other biographical profiles of the Duce, also seeks to stress the extent to which Mussolini's Latin masculinity made him quite different from his American counterparts. While describing his work discipline and political aspirations, for instance, Mussolini often advised against the presence of women in the workplace. "I have given imperative orders that [. . .] where I work [. . .] no woman shall be admitted," he noted in an installment of the UP autobiographical series, since women "interfere with the efficient procedure of the work."[141] He did not hesitate repeating such misogynist and backward views on other occasions, even when a woman was interviewing him. Still, his prejudice did not prevent women journalists from expressing admiration for his charming Latin personality—a contradictory phenomenon that paralleled Valentino's potentially damaging, but regularly forgiven, public statements against gender equality.

"MUSSOLINI A SHEIK"

I began all over again to meditate upon this extraordinary man whose attitude toward women is so disdainful and yet who has so undeniable a charm. Psychoanalysis cast aside, I found myself reflecting before the Chigi Palace entrance was reached: "No wonder women are crazy about him."

ALICE ROHE, *LIBERTY MAGAZINE*, 1927[142]

In different ways, Child and Lamont emphasized Mussolini's leadership and political ingeniousness as well as the regime's suitability to the Italian people. A few American female journalists stressed the same political angle in their reports. Yet the mere fact of their gender seems to have pushed them, either by their own will or by the insistence of their editors, to combine political analysis with insights into Mussolini's personal temperament.[143] If the emphasis on leadership constituted the shared *political* domain between the Divo and the Duce, personal charisma and Latin sensuality provided the *erotic* one. A few women writers performed this double public relations service. In addition to the already mentioned Anne O'Hare McCormick, we should also include UP writer and photojournalist Alice Rohe, who translated the Fascist regime's political novelty into a masculine model and for more than ten years penned a positive account of the chauvinist Mussolini.

As already discussed, the Great War was a seismic event for communication and journalism. More female reporters than ever before joined male colleagues on European soil to cover the war. Kansas-born Alice Rohe was one of them. A few jobs as a reporter for newspapers in Kansas and Colorado enabled her to cross paths with George Creel. After she joined the CPI, she soon became a national figure.[144] Already in Rome in 1914 as a correspondent for UP and the *Exchange Telegraph* of London, she remained in the Italian capital until 1919. By then she had become the first woman to manage the Rome office of UP's international bureau.[145]

A few days after the March on Rome, Rohe interviewed Mussolini for the *New York Times*. At the end of the long, four-column piece, after offering praise for his youth, outstanding culture, and visionary leadership talent, Rohe focused on what today we might refer to as his gender politics. A committed defender of women's equal rights, Rohe asked Mussolini whether he thought that "the mind of a woman, given the same opportunity for development, the same education, doesn't function as well as that of a man." "Certainly not—it is impossible," he replied.[146] Rohe voiced her disappointment at the Duce's unapologetic display of male chauvinism but was not wholly discouraged. She gently reprimanded him, but closed the piece with a surprisingly affectionate tone: Mussolini "laughed good-naturedly, but with that fine superiority with which the Latin male regards woman."[147] An article Rohe published five years later in *Liberty Magazine* on the Duce as "idol of women" best captured this contradictory reaction in its subtitle—"He Pours Contempt on the Softer Sex—And It Adores Him!" (figure 34).[148]

That article begins by reporting how the women of Rome, "titled beauties of ancient Italian lineage, look upon the Fascist Dictator."[149] They adore *what* he has done for Italy, but most surprisingly they adore *him*. Rohe describes one of them as behaving "like a schoolgirl over her favorite movie hero." By her own admission, the comparison with the film world led her to a recently published article in the search for a successor to Valentino in Italy. Rohe then combines the two domains, film and political stardom, in a way that surprises even her:

FIGURE 34. Mussolini's perplexing appeal. Alice Rohe, "Mussolini: Idol of Women," *Liberty Magazine*, September 17, 1927, 9.

Suddenly I began to think of Mussolini in a new light. Why search further? I struggled to suppress the boldly intrusive idea. *Mussolini a sheik*—perish the thought! Yet this dominant, indomitable Dictator, whose contempt for women is proverbial, not only has Italy in the hollow of his hand, but he has Italy's women at his feet.[150]

The equation of the real Mussolini with a Hollywood archetype require articulation: on what grounds is it based? The author's visits to Mussolini's rallies reveal to her the outstanding appeal he enjoyed among Italian women, to the point that she herself does not feel immune from it. "Everywhere adoration illuminated the faces of the women," she observes. "Young and old, they kept creeping nearer and nearer to where he was speaking. Before I realized it, I, too, was among them, drawn forward by the magnetism of the black-shirted premier." While the general enthusiasm of the masses for the Duce may find an explanation in a broad discussion about leaders' power over mobs and masses ("To see Mussolini before his cohorts is to understand the power of the individual over the mass mind"), for Rohe, there is something else worth exploring. Given the Duce's public disdain for any role for women beyond biological service to the nation, Rohe wonders how to explain "this feminine phenomenon" and whether it proves "conclusively that women prefer the dominant, patronizing, arrogantly indifferent male." At first, Rohe attributes such a self-defeating attitude to an Italian cultural trait. "Italian women worship a dominant male. They revel in submission to super contempt," she charges, and she identifies such misplaced "feminine idolatry" for a man who mainly regards women as servants as evidence of "a somewhat primal force in modern, Fascist Italy." And yet, she notices, "I have seen too many of my own countrywomen completely enthralled [by him]." They are a diverse lot: "sophisticated cosmopolites, 'hard-boiled flappers,' placid wives of prominent U.S. citizens, skeptical newspaper women, 100-percent feminists." But no matter their backgrounds, when they have the chance to meet "Italy's man of destiny," they reemerge "as utter vassals."[151]

How could Rohe explain women's tolerance for the Duce's misogynist attitude, which had not changed over the years? To her dismay, the explanation lies in their experience of his irresistible personal appeal, a "great magnetism" which she herself has experienced. In a combination of psychoanalytic reading and cinematic reviewing, Rohe states, "The plain answer is sex appeal," and "Dr. Freud could give the most illuminating explanation [by suggesting that] this element is at all times extremely vital in Italy."[152] Rather than describing sex appeal as resulting from a direct relationship between the Duce and his admirers, her exploration of this cinematic quality leads her identify a photographic mediation that is close to her reporting practice: the close-up view. "The very strength of the face, with its uncompromising, sensual mouth, the compelling domination of the prominent eyes, the brutal tenacity of the head," she admits, "radiated sex appeal" because a photographic camera captured it at close range before countless reproductions multiplied it ad infinitum. "When you study a personal close-up of this dominant, domineering, imperial, and imperious face, the spell which he exerts over women is not surprising."[153] Ultimately, his mass-reproduced captivating charm easily lends itself to comparisons with stars' appeal. A few months earlier Elinor Glyn had even included Mussolini (and the Prince of Wales) among those who "have IT."[154]

Rohe did not change her view or tone over the years. In 1937 she could still write: "There are certain types of women who are even attracted by his contempt."[155] This time she provides a fresh insight: "I have known Mussolini for fifteen years. I have watched his power over the mass mind, but more significant *because of the publicity given him in the Great Lover role*, I have witnessed his power over women."[156] It was not just "that he has 'It' and 'Sex Appeal.'" More cogently, it was the fact that something of the private dimension of this Italian political leader had been made to become his defining trait.

> The sudden introduction of the love element into the macabre drama which Mussolini is enacting on the world stage calls attention to an important phase of Il Duce's life. This is his power over women, a power which has played no small part in his success.[157]

The public exposure of a person's private personality, unprecedented for someone playing such a demiurgic political role, was for Rohe part and parcel of his cinematic allure. A few articles that appeared in *Liberty Magazine* were even more explicit with cinematic metaphors and terms of comparison. In a spring 1927 piece on screen tests, the method of determining actors' cinematic suitability and appeal beyond mere physical appearance, the staff writer and editor Brenda Ueland points out that passing a screen test is just a first step toward success. "To become a star you must have something else. Some call it 'charm;' some 'personality;' some, 'sex appeal.'" She inevitably quotes Elinor Glyn, "who calls it 'it.'" The rest of the article constitutes a series of insights on the subject shared by a Hollywood filmmaker, A. Edward "Eddie" Sutherland. After referring to famous actors, Sutherland argues that history's greatest statesmen had cinematic magnetism:

> When Napoleon walked toward a squad of men whose rifles were pointed at him, they couldn't fire. [. . .] Now, Napoleon and Caesar, if they had gone into the movies, would have become great stars. So would Mussolini, Bernard Shaw, Nell Gwyn, Henry IV, Abélard and Héloïse, Lord Nelson, Diane de Poitiers, and many others. And that is about the best way I can explain it.[158]

The ease with which the Hollywood director moved from discussing stars' successful screen tests to the charm of great statesmen impinges upon two intersecting domains. Film culture does not just pertain to leisure time; political leadership does not just pertain to policy positions, ideological convictions, or (traditional) personal character. True, political adversaries deployed a combination of alarm and sarcasm in their emphasis on Mussolini's performative talent. Anti-Fascist historian Gaetano Salvemini labeled him a "clown," while expatriate anarchist Camillo Bernieri went so far in 1934 as to call the Duce "the Rodolfo Valentino of politics."[159] But the intersection of the two domains produced comparisons between the Divo and the Duce, in a speech or a cartoon, that were not motivated solely by political antagonism. In an interview, the Hollywood actress Nita Naldi, who had played the femme fatale in Valentino's *Blood and Sand* (1923) and was a close friend of the actor, confessed her preferred type of male companion. "I like very dark handsome men with slick hair who wear evening clothes like ambassadors," Naldi confessed to the reporter that she liked men who look like Rudolph Valentino. But she went on: "Also I like them to be fierce and quarrelsome. Soldiers I adore! Mussolini! Cave men!"[160] In her terms, "Valentino" was a person, whereas "Mussolini" was an attribute, a *popular, and thus mass-mediated, type of masculinity* that was "fierce and quarrelsome"—and as such akin to a "sheik." For the Duce's masculinity to become "typical," it had to be publicly associated with the *personal style* of his political governance rather than with its substance. And it could achieve this level of cultural amplification mainly through references to motion pictures. Cinema, in fact, provided the terrain of comparison as well as of competition with Valentino.

An illustration that appeared in the January 1926 *Liberty Magazine* captures exactly that (figure 35).[161] Created by the famous *New Yorker* cartoonist Ralph Barton, the drawing pairs the Divo and the Duce under the fresh, personalized terms of a public confrontation that obviously stresses both their differences and similarities.[162] Graphically, the two figures are in parallel positions, with the back and top of their heads radiating the same white reflections out of well-oiled hair or a formal hat (or topper).[163] Calvino would have recognized in the image the "first Mussolini," the emblem of respectability and restored order who at official ceremonies habitually sported a morning coat and a tie.[164] The cartoon's implied context is Valentino and Mussolini's widely publicized rift over the former's decision to acquire U.S. citizenship and the latter's response of having his films banned in Italy. In the drawing, however, the actual terrain of their confrontation is not legal citizenship but cinematic visibility. Underneath the cartoon is a long caption that begins in capital letters. It goes on to explain the drawing in terms that certainly refer to the issue of citizenship but qualify the two figures in cinematic terms:

> Benito Mussolini, Italy's Premier and leading news-reel actor, caught off his guard by our camera man as he views a poster announcing Rudolph Valentino in a motion picture. A boycott was shortly afterwards proclaimed on Valentino pictures.[165]

The cartoon's raison d'être (and its design) was the fact that Mussolini and Valentino were both public popular figures, subjects of countless publicity initiatives. While in the mid-1920s this may have appeared obvious for a film star, it was still a novelty for a politician. In a 1928 *NYT* article, UP publicity director Warren Nolan, who had handled publicity for Chaplin, Pickford, Fairbanks, and even for Valentino's funeral, praised Mussolini as a masterful "space-grabber."

> Benito Mussolini is the world's champion space-getter, because in five years he has press-agented Italy into a front-line position as a world power and himself into Julius Caesar's mighty sandals. Il Duce is even more famous than that countryman of his, Rudolph Valentino, whose illness and death sent more verbiage over press wires than did the illness and death of an ex-president.[166]

Further, the basis for the cartoon's comparison between Valentino and Mussolini was the fact that they were both film stars—one of fiction films, the other of newsreels. The recognition that Mussolini, too, was a film celebrity had been made explicit and literal by the news and by the release of films starring the Italian leader. These began with *The Eternal City* (1924) and continued with *The Man of the Hour* (1927) and several hard-to-find American newsreels, as we shall see in the next chapter.[167] Yet, as we saw at the beginning of this chapter, the identification

PROFESSIONAL JEALOUSY BETWEEN FAMOUS ITALIAN SHEIKS? Benito Mussolini, Italy's Premier and leading news-reel actor, caught off his guard by our camera man as he views a poster announcing Rudolph Valentino in a motion picture. A boycott was shortly afterwards proclaimed on Valentino pictures.

FIGURE 35. Mussolini versus Valentino. Ralph Barton, "News of the World," *Liberty Magazine*, January 16, 1926, 53.

of Mussolini as "movie star" had inaugurated his popular hagiography in early November 1922, when no films about him were known to be in the making.[168] The fact that Mussolini was considered "cinematic" in American press discourse before being screened in the New World supports the methodological postulate of this work that the cinema effect extended beyond the domain of movie theaters.[169] It is time now to look closely at how American and Italian films exhibited in the United States sought to tell stories about Mussolini as Fascist leader by showcasing his role as political leader through romanticized transfigurations.

8

National Leader, International Actor

I have a picture of Mussolini in a scene in which I am directing him how to act.

GEORGE FITZMAURICE, DIRECTOR OF *THE ETERNAL CITY*, 1924[1]

Italy's pet fire eater is the star of the newsreel sections.

PICTURE-PLAY MAGAZINE, 1924[2]

The literature on Mussolini's relationship to motion pictures within the Italian context has been extremely rich, particularly since the late 1970s. It has generally focused on the extent to which the Fascist government, through various ministers, programs, and talented individuals, sought to exercise an effective control over film production, distribution, and exhibition. The creation of the newsreel agency Istituto LUCE (L'Unione per la Cinematografia Educativa) in 1924, the sponsor of the Venice Film Festival in 1931, the creation of the ENIC (Ente Nazionale dell'Industria Cinematografica [General Directorate of Cinematography]) in 1935, and the building of Cinecittà Studios in 1937 are just some of the milestones of the regime's efforts to control most aspects of Italian film culture.[3] A growing literature has focused on the ways in which Mussolini's actions and images came to dominate several aspects of this culture—from newsreels to film stardom.[4] Finally, more recent scholarly attention has been given to the cult of Mussolini within Italian film culture and in other forms of mass communications.[5]

The Fascist government, however, could only indirectly control Mussolini's screen presence and circulation in the United States, in terms of both Italian and American productions. The regime had to enter into partnerships with Hollywood studios, newsreel companies, and distribution firms; to negotiate directly with the MPPDA to ensure what it deemed a fair national representation; and sometimes to establish agreements with private distributors and individual theaters (which often ended in disappointment). What kind of stories about itself could the regime sell to Americans? The conventional distinction between Fascism as movement and as regime, articulated by Renzo De Felice in his monumental biography of the Duce and his study of Fascism's institutionalization, does not apply to its American representation.[6] Fascism as either a violent movement, a complex historical

phenomenon, or an autocratic ideology was not commercially viable in democratic America. Instead, Fascism could be sold as a triumphant administrative
solution to the challenges that every government faces. Yet even a well-organized
regime could not easily be translated into a popular narrative: a national arrangement centered on a single public personality, bigger than any movement or
regime, was preferable. This possibility rested on a caveat that concerned Mussolini's
American middlemen. Casting the Duce as the Fascist regime's celebrity-performer
meant inserting him in fictional or nonfictional narratives that were familiar to
the American public but that were not of his own making or under his control.[7]
Early fictional productions from Italy, especially when set in Roman times and
thus aligned with the regime's celebration of Rome's political history, were no longer appealing to American audiences. The case of *Messalina* (1924), a passé historical epic by Enrico Guazzoni, who ten years earlier had directed *Quo Vadis?* (1913),
is symptomatic. American trade papers maintained that costly Italian historical
productions relied on financial backing from Mussolini's regime and served his
interests.[8] The film struggled to find distributors who did not prefer the superior
production values of Fox's colossal *Dante's Inferno* (1924).[9]

The distinction between productions from Italy and from the United States is
a productive one, but it is also complicated by the fact that several key American
productions were shot in Italy and as such were not divorced from the regime's
tentative reach. The case of *The Eternal City* (1924), a modern political melodrama
produced by a Hollywood studio and filmed in Rome, is extremely illuminating
of the kind of intense negotiations that Hollywood and the regime's middlemen
engaged in not long after the March on Rome.

THE ETERNAL CITY

*As we have all come to realize, even the most important of "international
relations" have to be carried on by individuals.*
WILL H. HAYS, 1955[10]

With the possible exception of a few brief newsreel sequences, the first opportunity for Mussolini to be screened across America was through the Goldwyn production *The Eternal City*. Besides granting cinematic visibility to a dictator that
some in the press had been raving about for almost two years, the film is important
for two other reasons. On a production level, it identifies the various institutional
and commercial parties interested in the propagation of Fascism and its leader in
America. On the level of reception, it shows what Mussolini and his American
representatives came to learn about political propaganda.

Directed by George Fitzmaurice and written by his wife, Ouida Bergère,
The Eternal City was filmed in Rome in the summer of 1923 just a few months
after the March on Rome.[11] Italy was not an uncommon destination for several

FIGURE 36. Fascist leader David Rossi (Bert Lytell) rallying his supporters inside the Coliseum, before clashes with Socialist adversaries in *The Eternal City* (1924). Courtesy of Museum of Modern Art Film Stills Archive.

Hollywood companies at the time. Fitzmaurice, who would direct *The Son of the Sheik* in 1926, had already filmed *The Man from Home* (Famous Players–Lasky, May 1922) in Sorrento.[12] According to Goldwyn's biographer A. Scott Berg, it was Fitzmaurice who had "recommended a play Paramount had filmed in 1915, Sir Hall Caine's 'The Eternal City'" and it was Ouida Bergère who had "suggested updating this love story, set against post-Risorgimento Rome, to Mussolini's Italy."[13] At the turn of the century, the British writer Hall Caine (1853–1931) was extraordinarily popular. He had originally conceived *The Eternal City* as a play but published it as a novel in 1901. It became his most successful work. It would be translated into thirteen languages and sold more than a million copies in English alone. The stage version was also a success in both the United Kingdom and the United States.[14]

The story is a political romance in which the hero, David Rossi (Bert Lytell), is accused of plotting to murder the Italian king. The screen adaptation changed the story's political color from a celebration of socialist heroism to one of Fascist victory. In this updated film version, the hero is now Mussolini's right-hand man, whose beloved Donna Roma (Barbara La Marr) first appears to be on the wrong political side due to her close rapport with a Communist villain, Baron Bonelli (Lionel Barrymore), before she reveals her loyalty to her man. After scenes of mass gatherings of Fascist sympathizers at the Coliseum and clashes with the Communist rivals, the film climaxes in an actual view of a victorious Mussolini on the balcony of the royal palace, beside the Italian king, and David and Donna's romantic reunion (figures 36 and 37).

FIGURE 37. *The Eternal City* (1924), full-page advertisement, *Photoplay*, January 1924, 3.

The extent to which the Fascists contributed financially and logistically to the filming of *The Eternal City* has long remained unclear. Berg suggests that "when the Fascists caught wind of the film and demanded its confiscation, Fitzmaurice and his crew quickly left the country," and the cinematographer "smuggled the negative safely out of Italy."[15] The archival evidence tells a slightly different story. The embassy's press clipping service and the correspondence of the Italian ambassador Gelasio Caetani with several individuals, from Fitzmaurice and MPPDA head Will H. Hays to various Italian ministers and even Mussolini himself, shed light on the circumstances of the film's production, final version, and commercial distribution. They also reveal *how* American producers and Italian authorities sought to work together to promote the film.

This is not a story of a well-planned and direct public relations campaign in favor of Mussolini but of a series of collaborative attempts between Hollywood filmmakers and Italian authorities to enable the production and distribution of a supportive and profitable film. *The Eternal City* also constituted a learning curve for the Italian officials involved: while they quickly regarded it as a unique opportunity for effective propaganda, they were initially unaware of the commercial imperatives of American film culture. The archival record does not include documents that reveal who approached whom, but they suggest that upon Goldwyn's request, Hays first contacted Ambassador Caetani to assess whether the Italian government was in favor of the production and was willing to support it.

Caetani's initial support of the film was likely due to the Fascist regime's new directive about the importance of motion pictures for political communication. That directive had come down as a ministerial circular (no. 16) from Mussolini himself in his role as minister of foreign affairs and was widely distributed on March 1, 1923. Devoted to propaganda abroad, the Duce's directive centered on the cinematic medium. For Mussolini, films were to illustrate "in an attracting and interesting way the wealth and power of our industries, the unmatched natural and artistic beauty of Italy [. . .] while always culminating with glorifying visions of our army and military forces." The circular informed all interested parties—mostly diplomats, ambassadors, and consuls—that Mussolini had created a commission of experts who were to curate the publication of literary works that would faithfully reproduce in words what films showed on screen.[16] Considering how carefully Caetani would always approach the issue of Fascist propaganda in America, being aware of the obvious risks of meddling with American politics, the opportunity to support an American production by established Hollywood filmmakers that featured the Duce must have seemed more than intriguing.

Before Mussolini's circular reached his desk, Caetani had already understood the importance of motion pictures for broadcasting a positive image of Italy in America. Earlier that year, he had contacted the MPPDA about past and recent anti-Italian productions. On January 26, 1923, the vice president and secretary of the MPPDA, Courtland Smith, reassured Caetani that "Mr. Hays again desires to assure you that it is our most sacred duty and greatest pleasure to assist in developing international good will and friendly relations with each country, and that our members would not do consciously that which in a broad sense would give offense to any nation."[17] Caetani immediately copied the letter and conveyed its content to both Mussolini and to the head of the League for the Protection of National Interest, Oscar Sinigaglia. The ambassador added that he had notified the consular offices to collect and submit to him information about anti-Italian productions in order to pressure the MPPDA to secure appropriate measures according to its own promises.[18] Yet, this rather defensive approach soon gave way to a more assertive one.

One day in April 1923 Caetani phoned Hays, asking for a meeting. He knew that the first American fiction film about Fascism could be, as he wrote to a high Fascist

official, "most important for our American propaganda."[19] But he needed assur-
ances that the production and the final result would turn out to be in accordance
with what he considered the story and essence of Fascism.[20] Hays scheduled
the meeting for May 4 and informed Caetani that Sam Goldwyn and George
Fitzmaurice, *The Eternal City*'s producer and director, would also be present.[21]
Further, Hays confirmed to the Italian ambassador the MPPDA's policy regarding
representations of foreign nations that in terms of diplomatic strategy aligned with
the U.S. State Department.

> As [Undersecretary of State William] Phillips explained to you[, . . .] it is the earnest
> purpose of the producer and the Association that the production may square exactly
> with all of the proprieties and that the picture may be a definite contribution to the
> progress of international amity.[22]

The meeting took place and apparently went well. Still, as Mussolini's key representative in America, Caetani wanted *written* assurance about the film's treatment
of Fascism. In a letter to Hays, he used the MPPDA chief's own words: "I shall
highly appreciate if, as you suggested, this production will give a correct picture
of my country and will be a definite contribution to the progress of *international
amity.*" Only upon receipt of such written confirmation could Caetani offer all
possible help in the form of "letters recommending to the authorities in Italy that
all possible facilities be given."[23] To reassure the ambassador, Hays sent him letters
that the MPPDA chief had received from Sam Goldwyn, whose prose was so formal that it was likely written with the explicit goal of sounding like "a very definite
commitment," as Hays later described them to Caetani.[24] The ambassador found
these exchanges "quite definite and satisfactory."[25] He was further reassured following meetings with the director, Fitzmaurice, and his wife, Ouida Bergère, who was
working on adapting Caine's novel to the Fascist context.

Through these exchanges, the practice of a Fascist official mediating between
Hollywood and the Italian government started to take hold. In his letter to Hays,
Caetani suggested that it was Mrs. Fitzmaurice who had come up with the idea of
securing a trusted representative of the ambassador (and the Fascist government)
assist them in Rome and correct any historical inaccuracies to avoid subsequent
embarrassment. In a June cable to Mussolini, however, Caetani claimed that he was
the one who had the idea of inserting a trusted representative to assist, advise, and
report about the filming in Rome. That person turned out to be none other than
Countess Irene di Robilant, IAS's factotum secretary and Caetani's close collaborator on this and other propaganda initiatives. Both the studio and Hays himself were
enthusiastic about her presence, whose power in Italian government circles and
knowledge of American and Italian cultures would well serve all the parties involved.

On June 8 Caetani informed Mussolini about *The Eternal City*'s production,
mentioning Hays as "the chief of American cinematography," and describing the
film as a grandiose $600,000 production destined to circulate widely throughout

the United States.[26] Caetani told the Duce that he "immediately saw the importance of such an instrument of propaganda." Still, in order to avoid any misunderstanding about "the nature and the spirit of the fascist movement," he informed the Duce that he had managed to secure the presence of di Robilant, whom he described as "secretary and soul of the Italy American Society," to serve as chief location adviser in Italy. He also reassured him that the producers had made every effort to change the plot, avoid mistakes, and return "a correct vision of fascism from its latent state during the early days of the war to the triumph of the March on Rome." Caetani concluded his communication to Mussolini by mentioning that if screened in America's "twenty-five thousand movie theaters," the history of Fascism was bound to be watched by millions of people.[27] Meanwhile the ambassador had already requested assistance from several key figures in politics, film, and journalism who would support the shooting in terms of logistics (i.e., permits) and publicity.

Instead of overseeing the production from the Italian embassy in Washington, Caetani eventually took matters into his own hands and spent part of that summer in Rome. His goal was to assist his intermediaries, particularly di Robilant, not just with logistics, particularly for the large scenes featuring army and cavalry soldiers, but also and more significantly in securing the film's ideological integrity and controlling the publicity narrative.[28] Caetani wanted to have his name associated with a production that stressed the political novelty of the regime. On July 25, 1923, *Il Giornale d'Italia* described a production supervised by the "tireless Prince Caetani," that promised to offer "a clear and synthetic view of the fascist movement, in its ethical essence and in its patriotic and political goals." The promotional article highlighted the same figures that the ambassador had used in his communication with Mussolini: millions of spectators attending the country's *"twenty-five thousand movie theaters"* were bound to enjoy this most "efficacious propaganda of Italianness."[29]

Filming did not go smoothly. In mid-July the Italian chief of police, Emilio De Bono, informed Caetani that he was concerned about scenes showing wretched returning soldiers, widespread poverty, and communists spitting on the Italian flag.[30] Caetani must have shared his own concern with the filmmakers. In late July, Fitzmaurice reassured him by offering him the chance to "view the picture in New York upon its completion." The director also granted the ambassador the opportunity of correcting any error "to insure that our picture will be a true representation of your great movement."[31] The publicity machine was already active in America too, but here it was out of Caetani's direct control.

On August 28, 1923, a long article appeared in the *White Plains Reporter;* it included an interview with Fitzmaurice about filming *The Eternal City* in Fascist Italy. Variously edited, sections of the interview eventually made their way into the trade press. The director certainly said a few of the right things, including the fact that the filmmakers "received a great deal of help from the Government and were permitted to go everywhere." In a few instances, however, Fitzmaurice's answers were problematic, particularly when he revealed that Fascism had many detractors in Italy. "When we reached Rome," he noted, "some of the people were glad that we were to make a Fascist production, while others were opposed to the idea." Further, Caetani feared that the director's public insistence that the film did not constitute "good propaganda" was going to exert the opposite effect and hurt the film's commercial potential. His more disturbing statements pertained to Mussolini's participation. "I even photographed Mussolini in the picture," he boasted, "and in a sort of prologue, which we call a trailer, I have a picture of Mussolini in a scene in which *I am directing him how to act.*"[32] In effect, Fitzmaurice's statement reduced Mussolini to an actor working for a Hollywood director, a mere performer in a story that the Italian leader had not supervised and over which he exercised only indirect influence through his subordinates. This statement ran against all the publicity narratives that had made the Duce the cognizant and in-charge protagonist of a historical event.

In addition, *The Eternal City* itself did not match the Fascist officials' expectations. Caetani returned to Washington in late September and, upon Goldwyn's invitation, watched the film in New York on November 15.[33] Di Robilant had seen it a week before and had shared her disappointment with the ambassador. While she did not find much objectionable about the production—except for an intertitle that read "in a country famous for its vagabonds"—she nonetheless found it overall "dull." In her view "the whole [Fascist] movement appears entirely to have been censored as a strike-breaking organization." She added:

> Nothing of the history of spirituality of the movement itself appears, and this is all the more astonishing, when we remember how hard we all worked, exactly on that part. I have written pages and pages of history, we arranged for patriotic visions, and some of that material was actually photographed. For commercial reasons it has not been included in the picture.[34]

Her final impression was that *The Eternal City* "would not even be a financial success. There is no thrill, and the story is not exciting. The end falls entirely flat." Disappointed, she feared that upon seeing the film, Fascist officials would criticize her and the ambassador. She had expected much more "after having disturbed the Duce, the Army, the Police."[35]

Di Robilant's impression influenced Caetani's. After watching the film, he did not hesitate to convey his disappointment to Goldwyn. Caetani had many reservations about missing or incomplete intertitles that he felt were needed to explain the historical context. He also did not appreciate the scarcity of iconic images, whether related to World War I or "the fascists saluting with extended arms during the march on Rome." Revealing an unexpected understanding of film editing, he told di Robilant about his advice to Fitzmaurice that the Duce's "pictures *would not* be inserted in the play, but would *either precede or follow the film.*"[36] Eloquently emphasizing the political stakes, Caetani declared that he could not agree that

Mussolini should appear as "one of the actors of the Goldwyn Company."[37] This was also sensitive promotional issue that affected the Duce's standing in relationship to the film's narrative. Mussolini was the demiurge of the Fascist movement, after all, and his relevance could not be portrayed as secondary. The Duce was certainly an actor and a performer—as the anti-Fascist literature recognized early on and would continue to do for years—but in his own show, not someone's else's.

Caetani had ideas. "The picture of Mussolini at his desk," he wrote to di Robilant, "should be placed immediately after that of the King standing at the balcony. It could be preceded by a caption saying: 'This is Mussolini the man who organized the whole Fascisti movement and is now head of the Government.' "[38] The surviving copy of the film features the image of the Duce at his desk following that of the king, but not the suggested additional intertitle.[39] Secondly, to address the problem of "authorship," Caetani and the studio agreed to insert a statement from Mussolini that would have framed the entire film as overseen and approved by the Duce. *The Eternal City* premiered on January 20, 1924,[40] but four days later the ambassador was still working on tweaking the film's intertitles. On January 24, he informed Fitzmaurice that Mussolini had completed the "message to be used in connection with the exhibition" of the film. It read:

> Italy, by means of her gallant and strenuous fascisti youth has established order throughout towns and country; by a noble will effort she has gained civic peace which allows her to work and progress.

> Fascismo, in the history of Modern Europe, will remain an unparalleled example of moral energy and of spontaneous self-sacrifice devoted to the cause of civilization which is essentially the cause of order, of work and of national and social discipline. [Signed] Mussolini[41]

By then, the film had been distributed by First National and had premiered at the Strand Theater in New York City. It was an impressive production, with the theater's symphony orchestra playing Pietro Mascagni's popular *Cavalleria rusticana*. Naturally, Caetani was unnerved, fearing that a propaganda film qua propaganda would not work. He asked the consul general of Italy, Temistocle Filippo Bernardi, to have someone whom he trusted visit movie theaters where the film was being shown and report back to him.[42] He wanted to know whether the film's nonpolitical advertisements were having any impact on the film's reception in New York City. In early February, the consul communicated to the ambassador that *The Eternal City* was having some success with audiences, particularly when Mussolini and Fascist actions were on the screen. He also noted that early scenes featuring beggars and a robber would not help Italy's reputation. His short, lukewarm report did not bode well.[43]

Caetani seemed to have anticipated the film's reception: positive for the exposure of its key celebrity—the Duce—but negative for the film's obvious propaganda import.[44] On February 4, he wrote again to Mussolini repeating what he had written a few days earlier: distributors had asked that all the scenes in *The Eternal City* that had an obvious propaganda aspect be removed. He sought to reassure the Duce that the film maintained its ideological integrity and that it was doing well in the United States. But the message was clear to those who wanted to hear it: overt propaganda was not the proper way to broadcast the value of the regime in America.[45]

Meanwhile, the trade and general press published their reviews. Known for its coziness with the Mussolini regime, the *Saturday Evening Post* published a brief, celebratory review of the film, enriched by a few illustrations. "Sir Hall Caine modernized 'The Eternal City' for the screen," it reported, before adding that the film's "unforgettable characters are people of today. Fascists triumph where Caesars fell."[46] Other reviews, some laudatory and some critical, did not consider the recent historical context of Fascism's rise but, like the *SEP*, viewed Mussolini cinematically, so to speak, as a seasoned performer and a celebrity film actor. *Photoplay* began by describing *The Eternal City* as "one of the most beautiful pictures ever filmed" for its "views of Rome, taken from one of the hills; the shots in the Coliseum; the views along the beautiful roads shaded by Lombardy poplars."[47]

Some reviewers who were dismissive of the film's value singled out the Duce's presence. In the February 1924 issue of *Life* magazine, Robert E. Sherwood described the film as "nonsense on a heroic scale," lacking "a credible story." Still, although carried by "tidal waves of sonorous propaganda," the film showed the "Fascist Napoleon" exhibiting a "deportment on the screen [that] lends weight to the theory that this is just where he belongs."[48] While a few newspapers had branded Mussolini as an actor as early as November 1922, by 1924 this was an established trope, one that even Valentino's first unofficial publicity agent, Herbert Howe, could not resist. In one of his columns for *Photoplay*, he congratulated Fitzmaurice, "who made 'The Eternal City' with Barbara La Marr and Benito Mussolini. With Babbie and Benito in the cast the picture certainly should not be lacking in action."[49] Similarly, Agnes Smith of *Picture-Play Magazine* found that the film looked "like a news reel plus a fashion show," but even in her sarcastic tone she acknowledged that while "Barbara La Marr acts as the fashion model," Mussolini, as "Italy's pet fire eater, is the star of the newsreel sections."[50]

The reviews that emphasized the film's celebrity value appeared side by side with those that trashed its nationwide commercial potential due to its overt propagandistic content. "Pouf, pouf and a barrel of wind. Samuel Goldwyn (not now connected with Goldwyn Pictures) has a flop in 'The Eternal City,'" wrote an anonymous *Billboard* reviewer. "High-salaried actors, fares to Italy and expenses while there, $100,000 worth of publicity [. . .] subordinated into an outright plug for Mussolini." The result was that "because of its Roman flavor and the frequent references to Italy's new hero, 'The Eternal City' will find much favor with Italians. It is extremely doubtful if the general public will enjoy it, however."[51] Similarly, "Rush" (Alfredo R. Greason), the *Variety* reviewer, complained that the Goldwyn production sought "to tie up present day interest in the political upheaval of Italy [rather] than to develop the human interest of the story itself." As a result, the film was going to be "a special interest only to the Italian colony. Whether the rest of the United States will manifest enthusiasm over the alien political situation is something else again." The presence of Mussolini and the king at the film's end, concluded the review, killed the lovers' narrative climax, giving the "picture historic rather than romantic coloring."[52] Other reviewers complained that Hollywood had converted the original story, with its religious themes, into something completely different: "propaganda for the black-shirted forces of Mussolini."[53] Some even joked ironically that the new collaborative atmosphere between Hollywood and Rome would soon result in Mussolini playing *Ben Hur.*[54]

Beyond the reviewers' and exhibitors' lack of enthusiasm, the geopolitically sensitive quarters of the film industry deeply appreciated *The Eternal City* because it marked the first collaboration between Hollywood and a foreign country. In April 1924, in an article in the *New York Times,* Will Hays argued that "the first purpose of the producers is to make pictures that entertain, films in which costumes and customs of people are correctly portrayed, whether they deal with American, English or French life." He repeated his usual formula that films had to make a "contribution to international amity," and to support his case, he used the example of *The Eternal City.* Specifically, he referred to Caetani's role. "The Ambassador took the trouble to go over the scenario," he noted, "and satisfied himself that it would be a picture that would reflect Italy in a true light." Hays said that he hoped this would bode well for future productions. "This is perhaps the first instance of an Ambassador accredited to this country taking an interest in an American production to be produced in his own land."[55]

Caetani had different feelings. Following his disappointment over *The Eternal City,* he wondered whether the Italian embassy could further the Duce's cinematic exposure in a more controlled fashion. Mussolini himself wanted to play a more direct role and manage his image directly from Rome. Yet, once again, other mediators intervened and creatively reworked the Duce's image and message in the United States.

THE MAN OF THE HOUR

The speech in Italian should last three and a half minutes and the one in English the same so that the result would be of greatest impact.

INSTRUCTIONS FOR MUSSOLINI'S SPEECH FOR *THE MAN OF THE HOUR* (TRANS.)[56]

In Genoa, on May 11, 1927, a trusted officer of the *Biancamano* ocean liner received a box with seven film rolls and was asked to deliver it to Cortland Smith, president of Fox Newsreels, at the company's office on West 54th Street in New York City. The day after, an Italian government official in Rome reassured Mussolini's personal secretary Alessandro Chiavolini that the package was on its way to its American destination. Ten days later, on May 21, a telegram sent from New York arrived at the Plaza Hotel in Rome, addressed to Edgar L. Kaw, a Fox-Case film soundman. It was from Smith, complimenting Kaw and his colleagues in Fox's outfit no. 1, Ben Miggins and D. F. Whiting, on a job superbly done. "First test from can number 5 shows magnificent picture and perfect sound reproduction. Nothing better has ever been done in either pictures or sound. Will now develop balance and cable you results. Heartiest congratulations to you Miggins and Whiting = Courtsmith."[57]

In the spring of 1927, speaking of "picture" and "sound" together was not customary. The Fox-Case Corporation had pioneered a process by which sound could be physically recorded onto photographic film by adding a sound score along the strip of film frames. The sound-on-film process was a radical improvement over sound-on-disc technology, which required perfect synchronization between a phonograph and a movie projector during exhibition and inevitably led to embarrassing mistakes. With its Movietone sound system, the newly formed Fox-Case Corporation was declaring all-out war against its main competitor, Warner's Vitaphone system. "The kind of motion picture attraction chosen by the new company to introduce its system," Raymond Fielding has noted, "was the sound newsreel," or, we would specify, the celebrity newsreel.[58] The first Movietone sound film was presented on January 21, 1927, in New York City, eight months before the premiere of *The Jazz Singer*. But the first commercially significant Fox Movietone film premiered in New York on May 27, 1927, and it showed the most newsworthy person and event of the day: Charles Lindbergh's May 20 takeoff from Long Island for his historic transatlantic flight. While this sound film had no spoken parts, it was a cinematic event that opened the way for more. That was a period in which, to return to Frederic Lewis Allen, "every record for mass excitement and mass enthusiasm in the age of ballyhoo was smashed. Nothing seemed to matter, either to the newspaper or the people who read them, but Lindbergh and his story."[59]

To match the Lindbergh craze, the Fox-Case Corporation had already made plans for similar productions, all to be distributed by Fox. A few weeks before, it had allowed Jack Connolly and several technicians to leave for Europe with a mission: record the faces and voices of the most important celebrities of the day.[60] One of their first stops was Rome, where they had managed to film something unique that had to be kept secret so as not to ruin any promotional plan. Upon receiving the mysterious can no. 5, Fox's New York headquarters were quite pleased because they now had footage that offered a double novelty: for the first time it combined the image and the voice of Benito Mussolini making a speech in both Italian and English. Confidentiality had to be maintained. Kaw immediately telegrammed his mediator with the Italian government, J. P. Spanier, the Western Union Telegraph Company representative for Southern Europe, who was in Rome. In turn, Spanier

FIGURE 38. On the set of *Man of the Hour* (Movietone News, 1927), Villa Torlonia, May 6, 1927. From left: Prince Ludovico Spada Veralli Potenziani, governor of Rome; Augusto Turati, general secretary of the Fascist Party; Cornelio Di Marzio, secretary of the Fascists Abroad; Benito Mussolini; and U.S. ambassador to Italy, Henry P. Fletcher.

FIGURE 39. The operators of Fox-Case outfit no.1 filming *Man of the Hour*. Subfolder Fox Film: Pellicola di propaganda italiana, folder P.S.E. Varia 148, box 221, ACS, SPD-CO. Courtesy of Archivio Centrale dello Stato, Rome.

immediately relayed the message directly to the Duce's secretary, Chiavolini. The Duce's immediate circle had high hopes for this recorded speech that was directed at both American and Italian American audiences and could reach millions of people.

A few days earlier, on May 6, two weeks before the first Lindbergh recording, Fox Newsreels producer Jack Connolly, Ben Miggins (cameraman), and Edgar L. Kaw and D. F. Whiting (soundmen) had recorded Mussolini's speech in two languages at Villa Torlonia, the Duce's private residence in Rome (figures 38 and 39). The filming

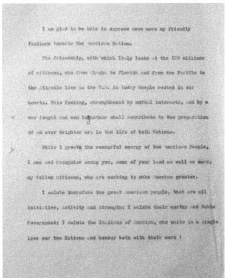

FIGURES 40 and 41. One of the initial drafts of Mussolini's speech, in Italian, to be reduced by 50%, and its final English version. Subfolder Discorso di S.P. per il "Movietone" della Fox Film, 16 August 1927 V, folder P.S.E. Varia 148, box 221, ACS-SPD-CO. Courtesy of Archivio Centrale dello Stato, Rome.

also included the U.S. ambassador to Italy, Henry P. Fletcher, whose role was to introduce the Duce to American audiences. In the footage, Mussolini sports riding breeches, and he was made to walk toward the camera and deliver his talk straight into it.[61] On the improvised set was also the former ambassador, Richard Washburn Child. Connolly allegedly helped Mussolini with his verbal delivery in English, and he and Child held a large card with the speech written on it for the Duce to read. The press later reported how Mussolini was willing to do multiple takes. During this same assignment, the crew also filmed images of Italian army soldiers on horseback, military bands, parading sailors, and a performance of the Vatican Choir, the latter in place of an interview with the Pope, who had declined their request.[62]

In addition to the challenge of speaking in English, Mussolini had to operate within another constraint—the limited length of his speech. He and his aides went through several drafts in Italian and English to abide by the specific instructions he had been given: "The speech in either in Italian or English could not last more than three and a half minutes." The Italian State Archive in Rome includes both Mussolini's initial, very long, typewritten versions—marked on the first page with what appears to be his penciled note "Ridurre del 50 per %" [Reduce by 50%]—and the final, shortened translation by J. P. Spanier, that best fit the newsreel format (figures 40 and 41). The final version reads:

I am glad to be able to express once more my friendly feelings toward the American Nation.

The friendship, with which Italy looks at the 120 millions of citizens, who from Alaska to Florida and from the Pacific to the Atlantic live in the U.S. is today deeply rooted in our hearts. This feeling, strengthened by mutual interests, and by a war fought and won together shall contribute to the preparation of an ever brighter era in the life of both Nations.

While I greet the wonderful energy of the American People, I see and recognize among you, some of your land as well as ours, my fellow citizens, who are working to make America greater.

I salute therefore the great American people, that are all initiative, activity and strength; I salute their worthy and Noble Government; I salute the Italians of America, who unite in a single love our two Nations and honour both with their work![63]

The Fox Movietone newsreel of Mussolini was in and of itself a special event. Even though William Fox paired it with another major attraction, the New York premiere of F. W. Murnau's first American picture, *Sunrise,* the filming of Mussolini's direct address was not going to be marginalized. Fox promoted it as "the first showing of the Mussolini Movietone, in which the Italian premiere will be seen and heard in a speech, the text of which has been copyrighted by the Fox Film Corporation."[64] The combination of art and political publicity may strike us for its "incongruousness" and seem "jarring and surprising," to use Bergstrom's words, but it was not a complete novelty for Fox.[65] According to Fielding, the exceptional footage of Lindbergh's takeoff had been paired four months earlier, on May 27, 1927, with Frank Borzage's masterpiece *Seventh Heaven* as part of an all-Movietone program.[66] Since evidence of Fox's in-house documentation about strategies and correspondence is largely absent for this period, one is left speculating about possible explanations. Fox had its own precedents to learn from. In March 1926, Ettore Villani, the Fox Newsreels Rome-based camera operator, had filmed the Fascist Party's seventh anniversary celebration. In the short memo he sent to New York with the footage, he transcribed part of Mussolini's speech and added the note "DUCE: leading captain." Pierluigi Erbaggio has argued that the fact that Villani volunteered this English translation of Mussolini's preferred attribute demonstrates that he knew how much his employer and, by extension, the Fox Newsreels audience obsessed about powerful leaders as worthy film subjects and how little they cared about Fascism as an undemocratic political movement.[67] It is thus possible to argue that Fox advertised the unusual combination of Murnau with Mussolini (and the other Italian footage) ultimately to promote the novelty of its wide-ranging offerings. Prior to the premiere, in fact, the company advertised the event as having three attractions:

3 Tremendous Features Combined in a Monumental Programme! [. . .] *Sunrise,* with Symphonic Movietone Accompaniment [. . .] the Vatican Choir, seventy voices of

sublime power and beauty on the Movietone! [. . .] See and Hear "The Man of the Hour," His Excellency Benito Mussolini, Premier of Italy. He speaks to you and lives before your eyes on the Movietone! Text copyrighted by Fox Film Corp.[68]

A preview was organized by Fox vice president and general manager Winfield Sheenan. *Variety's* founding editor Sime Silverman covered it on the front page, with a banner headline: "Mussolini's Hope in Screen." In his long review, Silverman did not just celebrate Mussolini's on-screen declaration of amity with the United States as a major political advancement but also praised the Duce for publicly recognizing the impact of the Movietone novelty on news communication. Allegedly, Mussolini had described Movietone as the medium that "can bring the world together, it can settle the differences; it can become the international medium, educator and adjuster; it can prevent war."[69] From the standpoint of the trade it represented, *Variety* appreciated that such an international figure had publicly celebrated the new frontier of cinematic news-making as it expanded its reach from mere coverage of exceptional events (i.e., Lindbergh's accomplishment) to more regular reporting on "politics, entertainment, propaganda, or any purpose that may be made appealing." The case of Mussolini was singular, even for Movietone—the "first demonstration of Fox's Movietone with a celebrity"—but it was also emblematic of the general power of the medium to communicate "directness and sincerity." His appearance on screen had the potential of changing people's minds about the dictator (figure 42). "If Movietone carries Mussolini to every incorporated village of this country[, . . .] millions of Americans will suffer altered opinions on Mussolini," Silverman argued. After all, thanks to the new medium, "a forceful character like Mussolini can go around the universe carrying conviction for whatever he may be discussing."[70]

For the New York premiere, Fox chose the Times Square Theatre on 42nd Street and Broadway. The studio also prepared a two-page, double-sided program that described the evening's attractions and sought to drum up excitement over the unprecedented deployment of prerecorded sound scores—a "Symphonic Movietone Accompaniment" for Murnau's film and Mussolini's actual voice for the Movietone News. In the Duce's case, the new technology allowed the premier to address film spectators directly: "He speaks to you, expressing, with his characteristic gestures, his sentiments toward the United States and the Italian-Americans in this country." The result, the program breathlessly claimed, was an unprecedented supply of liveliness and directness: Mussolini "lives before your eyes through MOVIETONE." (figure 43).

The reception was more than positive. The Movietone News featured a notable performance of the Vatican Choir, but the *New York Times* argued that "the subject that gave one of the most vivid conceptions of the potentialities of the sound and shadow features is that of Benito Mussolini making a speech."[71] *Moving Picture World* agreed. According to its reviewer, what mostly impressed the audience of the dual program "was the Movietone accompaniment for the picture and

C Benito Mussolini speaks to you through
the marvel of Movietone.

FIGURE 42. Published frames of Mussolini from *The Man of the Hour* (1927). "The Talking Pictures," *Screenland*, January 1928, 15.

the Movietone scenes, taken in Italy [through which] the audience saw and heard [. . .] the great Premier, himself, speaking in English and Italian, exactly as if he was actually in the theater."[72] The equally enthusiastic *Motion Picture News* found that "Movietone brings Mussolini face to face with Americans. [. . .] Lifelike it is: amazingly lifelike. A set speech, of course, but the illusion brings the Dictator right into the theatre."[73] What many found striking, as *Screenland* put it, was the "enormous close-up of the face of Mussolini. A most remarkable face."[74] The same magazine insisted a month later that such a film helps "us know our neighbors

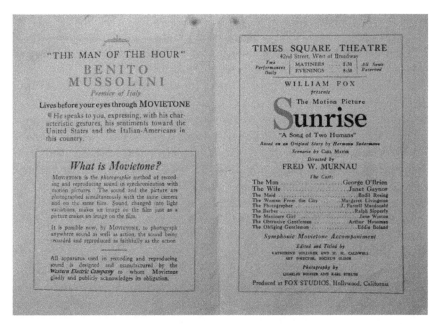

FIGURE 43. Program for double bill of *The Man of the Hour,* starring Benito Mussolini, and *Sunrise,* pages 2–3. Folder P.S.E. Varia 148, box 221, ACS-SPD-CO. Courtesy of Archivio Centrale dello Stato, Rome.

on this earth better" and turns distant leaders into "human beings [. . .] whom we better understand." This article celebrated the new medium with a photographic summary of its recent exploits. It featured frame enlargements from Movietone's footage of President Coolidge welcoming Charles Lindbergh, a close-up of the American aviator, and two medium close-ups of Mussolini, who, the caption read, "speaks to you through the marvel of Movietone."[75]

The pairing of Murnau with Mussolini lasted three months: by December 12, "the display ads for *Sunrise* no longer mention any Italian features."[76] When the program opened in Los Angeles on November 29, *The Man of the Hour* was not included. Bergstrom explains the absence of the Mussolini footage by pointing out that Los Angeles, unlike New York, did not have a large Italian immigrant population.[77] Another possible explanation is that the New York experience taught Fox that the combination of the two attractions was not working since they did not attract the same crowd. Fox's Sheenan seemed to have known that it was not possible to advertise both features at once properly. As Bergstrom acknowledges, his "press review a few days before the release of *Sunrise* directed all the attention to Mussolini and to Movietone." What could be more different than "a charismatic demagogue, speaking forcefully to the audience amid more than 20 minutes of Italian sound and fury" vis-à-vis "a film without dialogue and with an introverted, restrained acting style"?[78] Further, although popular culture had legitimized Mussolini on a grand scale, a few articles in the business press had been questioning Mussolini's notable experiments in governance on cultural grounds with their praise for the American values of individuality and freedom from state policies.[79]

Making the film happen had not been easy. On the Italian side, the archival record shows evidence of repeated requests to film the Duce by international companies and repeated denials or delayed permissions, a process that may be reminiscent of Wilson's situation before and during World War I. If Mussolini did not trust many of the Hollywood studios' Italian representatives, he had full confidence in his proven mediators, beginning with Child, who had been instrumental in coordinating contacts between the Fox Film Corporation and Mussolini. Not only was Child present during the filming in May at Villa Torlonia, but that summer he also promoted Mussolini's film performance for the readers of the *New York Times*.[80]

On the American side, the *Variety* review emphasized that the initiative to film notable Europe personalities with the new technology has been "Connolly's mission."[81] As *Variety* and other papers mentioned, Jack S. Connolly had been the MPPDA's Washington representative, a position that he had held until four months before, when he left to become European director of the Fox Movietone organization. A year after the premiere, he gave an interview to the *New York Times* on Movietone celebrities.[82] After the anonymous reporter praised Connolly for having persuaded George Bernard Shaw to be on camera, the conversation inevitably moved to the Duce. "When one first meets Mussolini," Connolly noted, "one is impressed with his vitality, his aggressiveness, his forcefulness and his power." The Fox executive described how Mussolini was willing to rehearse and correct his English pronunciation, demonstrating he was eager to improve himself. Connolly's conclusion about the Italian leader's modern personality shunned any political considerations and remained solidly in the Hollywood domain, primarily due to the Duce's personal style and cinematic appeal:

> In my opinion Mussolini is the best dressed man in Italy. His clothes look as if they had been molded on him. No motion picture actor in Hollywood is more careful about his appearance, and I would venture to say that if he ever decided to give up his present position which, incidentally, he likes very much, a dozen picture producers would be after him.[83]

Without referring to the newsreel, but still reverberating in its import, a few months later the New York monthly *The Mentor* dedicated one of its special issues to Mussolini, the "Man of Italy." Its main article did not hesitate to profile the Duce in the most celebratory manner as the leader of a popular plebiscite:

> Superficially Benito Mussolini, the outstanding figure in Europe today, appears to take the ancient Romans for his model. In point of fact, however, the extraordinary career of this modern man of Destiny is far more in the Napoleonic tradition.[84]

Similarly, other film periodicals underscored how the Movietone News show of Mussolini impacted both his standing and the future of news making and news reporting.[85] *Screenland* contended that "to introduce us to Mussolini, Calvin Coolidge, Bernard Shaw and Charles Lindbergh and at the same time hear their voices, is, so far, the most successful marriage of silence and sound."[86] *Picture-Play Magazine* noted that "Fox Movietone News quickly became a three-issue-a-week feature" for its ability to reveal "the vocal images" of famous personages, including Mussolini. More than depicting "their likeness," it was a matter of preserving "their living voices, their very personalities, for posterity."[87] For others, the Movietone News managed to reveal a novel dimension in its coverage of celebrities. "The sound cameras reflect unerringly the dynamic force of Mussolini," declaimed *New Movie Magazine*, "the quiet force of Henry Ford; the rugged conservatism of the good Calvin [Coolidge]."[88]

If the energy of the Duce's performance fueled widespread praise, it also fueled mockery. The British writer George Bernard Shaw had been an early admirer of Mussolini. In 1922 he had welcomed the Duce's rise to power in Italy, observing that amid the "indiscipline and muddle and Parliamentary deadlock," the Italian leader was "the right kind of tyrant."[89] In contrast, when on June 25, 1928 Fox released *George Bernard Shaw Talks to Movietone News*, the British writer gently made fun of Mussolini's performative oratory. Shaw posed with his arms around his waist to show what he called the "Mussolini stance," and he included the Fascisti salute. After expressing admiration for Mussolini's hair and brow, he ironically noted that while he could stop assuming the "terrifying Mussolini look" ("I can put it on, take it off, and do all sorts of things"), Mussolini could not. Instead, the Italian leader was "condemned to go through life with that terrible and imposing expression." Interviewed the same year by *Motion Picture Classic*, Shaw doubled down in irony, adding that "my imitation of Mussolini should have assured you of my ability at character roles." Indicating some of the cracks in the popularity of the Duce, the caption to one of the six film frames illustrating the article reads: "It has been said that there is but one thing funnier than George Bernard Shaw's imitation of Mussolini's expression, and that is Mussolini's expression."[90]

These commentaries reveal that if Bernard Shaw could appear as a great character actor, it was because Mussolini had become a character in the Olympus of Hollywood's celebrity-personalities and, as such, he was worthy of praise *and* ridicule. A December 1928 poster of the Movietone series prominently featured the Duce among the new cinematic format's exemplary subjects, together with Lindbergh and Shaw (figure 44). Similarly, a few months later Fox released a six-reel travelogue, *Chasing through Europe* (1929), which was devoted not to sites or historical monuments but to the Old World's modern personalities. Mussolini was obviously among them, together with another regular, the Prince of Wales. Reporting on the travelogue, *Screenland* conceivably reproduced Fox's

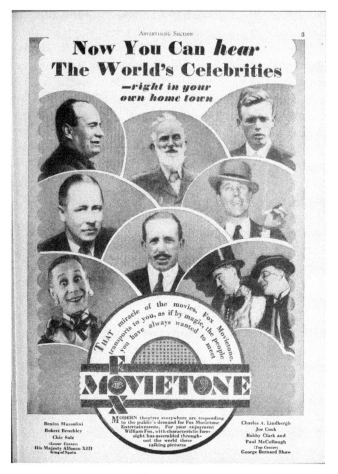

FIGURE 44. Fox Movietone ad featuring celebrities. *Picture Play Magazine*, December 1928, 3.

promotional slogan: "You will see a dozen celebrities on the screen[: . . .] two kings, two dictators, one royal prince, and one Sultan!"[91] The same year, in a celebratory volume on the history of motion pictures, Will Hays praised the Fox Movietone initiative for "bringing the world's personalities to the world's people" and thus offering "a very real contribution to the world's welfare."[92]

The bonds among cinema, news-making, and celebrities—no matter their domain of excellence—seemed to have reached a level of natural completion, with Mussolini as a fitting part in it. In truth, behind and before these celebrations were several modest, botched, and rarely successful initiatives by Italian companies, which sought to contribute to the promotion of Fascism and Mussolini's repute in the United States without fully understanding the American cultural marketplace.

CENSORING AND DISTRIBUTING

Throughout the 1920s and early 1930s, Italian officials in Washington, DC, were busy mediating between the MPPDA and Italian institutions or even private citizens, who often shared their concerns about negative film representations of Italians in Italian or American productions whether these were exhibited in the United States or elsewhere. This was a concern that had been central to the Italian government even before the days of the March on Rome.

One of the earliest documentable occurrences dates back to August 30, 1922, when Andrea Geisser Celesia di Vegliasco, secretary of the embassy of Italy, complained to Hays about a few films that had depicted Italians "in a very unflattering light" and about Hollywood's "regrettable habit of using the Italian type in filmmaking as an element of villainy, ferocity or grotesque vulgarity." The "belittling of our people," Geisser Celesia added, was "harmful to the bonds of friendship and esteem existing between our two countries."[93] Hays's response that MPPDA members generally did not intend to negatively portray the "life and character" of non-Americans and were instead interested in developing "the most cordial international relationship[s]" was prompt but general.[94] Two months after the March on Rome in late October 1922, an emboldened embassy wrote again to Hays requesting a resolution explicitly tailored to Italy.[95] The exchanges between the embassy and MPPDA about anti-Italian films continued for years, reaching an apex in the early 1930s, when the Italian diplomatic authorities were alerted about a group of Los Angeles–based Fascists who called themselves "legionaries" and were keen on protesting directly to the studios about the release of films perceived to be demeaning to Italy.[96] One of these films was *The Life of Giuseppe Musolino, the Italian Bandit*, which was devoted to the famous Calabrian brigand.[97] Others included *A Farewell to Arms, The Romance of a Dictator, This Is the Night,* and *The Guilty Generation.*[98] The complaints focused on these films' demeaning association of Italians with crime, laziness, and general ineptitude.[99] The film that received the most attention, at least according to the volume of the correspondence among diplomatic institutions, private individuals, and Italian American organizations, was Howard Hawks's *Scarface* (1932).[100] A case study of *Scarface* exceeds the framework of this study, but suffice it to say that the embassy's most explicit response consisted of two strategies: put pressure on the MPPDA, even when the producers of said offensive films were not its members, and mobilize Italian American communities at the local level. The second strategy posed the most challenges: the Italian embassy, in fact, was not only engaged in protesting negative representations of Italians in America but also in promoting positive ones.

As it had done before the March on Rome, throughout the 1920s and into the 1930s, the ambassador's office continued to serve as a sort of distribution center for educational productions about Italy to be exhibited in noncommercial outlets (i.e., cultural associations and aid societies). The obvious impetus was to promote a positive representation of the country, but another reason for the embassy's involvement was to avoid past mistakes that had occurred when private citizens had been allowed to make direct arrangements with the Italian government to legitimize their dubious commercial plans.[101] After October 1922, however, the new nationalistic ethos complicated the embassy's mission. Its distribution role faced a constant tension. One the one side were the productions that celebrated the safe image of old, touristic Italy, rich in historical and picturesque attractions but increasingly dated and unappealing. On the other were those that promoted an exciting image of a modern country, whose novel regime and protagonists, however, often attracted harsh criticism and were thus commercially risky.[102] For instance, after 1922 the Italian officials' attempts to distribute old educational shorts, mostly about Italian customs or the Italians' life during the Great War, were both unsuccessful and the cause of great concern. The new context made these productions appear dangerously propagandistic.[103]

Even after Caetani's tenure ended on February 7, 1925, the embassy's cautious position regarding the value of targeted propaganda, especially about Italian Americans, did not change. The embassy had to counter the misplaced ambitions of Italian-based Fascist officials and journalists who expected that the regime's "visual propaganda," as they labeled it, could overcome language barriers and reach the widest possible audiences.[104] The embassy felt that it also needed to curb the excesses of Fascist sympathizers in America. Since the Great War, Italy's most prominent citizens in America—the so-called *prominenti*—had largely become nationalistic, and a few of them had been quite receptive to the ethos of Fascism. The emergence in the United States even *before* the March on Rome of different nationalist groups, the so-called *Fasci di combattimento* (Italian Fasci of Combat), the Fascist League of North America, and the Sons of Italy, continued to pose striking challenges to the Fascist government's foreign policy due to the sensitive issue of Italy's war debt. As Caetani once wrote to Mussolini, the Fasci (just like the other groups) "will serve as an example with which to judge Italian Fascism." Caetani had then recommended that in the United States, Fascism "must limit itself to the ideological, philanthropic, and sports arena," arguing that "it cannot assume the character of an activist organization."[105] Americans were very sensitive to the "threat of political divisiveness among ethnic groups," as Philip V. Cannistraro put it, and Fascist militancy ran the risk of being perceived as meddling with American politics. Any perception of domestic interference by a foreign power would harm the Fascist regime's aspirations for a positive conclusion to the diplomatic negotiations about war debts.[106] Questions of diplomatic calculations and tact affected Mussolini's response to the new immigrations laws of 1924, which inspired him to consider immigrants as "vectors of *Italianità* in foreign lands," and to the remarkable press coverage of the Sacco and Vanzetti trial.[107]

The 1926 nationalization of Istituto LUCE complicated the embassy's mission.[108] In 1925, in fact, LUCE had made private, direct arrangements with the general secretary of the Italian Fasci Abroad (Fasci italiani all'estero) for the American distribution of Italian newsreels.[109] Now the embassy had to intervene to help control and centralize this flow of production by facilitating distribution and exchange agreements between the LUCE and American newsreel companies. These official operations were meant to curb the chaos of roles and distribution deals that the LUCE had contributed to.

By the early 1920s, American newsreel production companies competed for the approximately 16,500 American theatres that exhibited newsreels on a biweekly basis.[110] To enter this market, LUCE exchanged footage with American newsreel companies, especially with Fox Movietone and Hearst Metrotone, which had offices in Rome.[111] In turn, these companies broadcast Mussolini's image and biography in the United States, showcased his private and public life, and thus contributed to his standing as political and popular icon.[112]

LUCE IN AMERICA

Il Duce's facial expressions alone are worth the price of admission.
PHOTOPLAY, 1933[113]

Between April 1925 and August 1936, Fox's and Hearst's theatrically distributed newsreels featured Mussolini at least once a month as either a primary or secondary attraction.[114] Throughout that decade, the two companies' collaborations with the LUCE did not overlap exactly, at least according to the official documentation. In Erbaggio's careful research, "Mussolini is present in eighty-four Fox records between April 8, 1925, and October 22, 1935," while Hearst distribution listings refer to "the dictator in ninety-one newsreels issued between September 28, 1929, and August 31, 1936."[115] The archival record, as Erbaggio warns, is far from accurate: there is footage that is not referenced therein or that falls outside these dates. For instance, Fox's first related newsreel story, *Black Shirts,* dates back to February 28, 1923. It shows young and adult Fascist followers marching through the streets of Rome and convening at the monument to the Unknown Soldier on the steps of the Altare della Patria.[116] Similarly, Hearst released an International Newsreel devoted to the Duce before 1929, the brief 1926 *Mussolini Smiles!,* which presents the Duce as "Italy's strong man," who managed to survive assassination attempts— three in 1926 alone!—and maintain his good humor.[117] His titular smile indexed his strength in the face of adversity, and his intact charisma was made even more apparent when juxtaposed against the king's generally austere expression.

These assassination attempts were international knowledge, especially the first one, in which an Irish woman managed to nick the Duce's nose.[118] Hollywood was obviously intrigued by this incident since it offered one more opportunity to gossip about his popular biography and temperament. When Mussolini met with Fairbanks and Pickford in Rome in May 1926 and asked them to reassure the entire world that he was doing fine, he was referring to this episode. Film comedies, too, capitalized on this widespread knowledge to sustain their jokes. For instance, in Leo McCarey's 1926 *Mighty like a Moose*, starring the popular comedian Charley Chase, a married couple seeks the aid of plastic surgery to correct their unattractive physical traits. The husband (Chase) has protruding front teeth; the wife (Vivien Oakland), a large nose. To be effective, comedic routines and lines rely on social conventions and shared knowledge. After introducing Chase as a man who has been "secretly saving money for months—to take the detour out of his teeth," the film presents Oakland with an amusing parallel intertitle: "If Mussolini had had a nose like hers, his wound would have been fatal."

Even though Erbaggio could not examine the entirety of this newsreel production due to the lack of available footage, he was able to draw a few comprehensive and persuasive conclusions.[119] American newsreels tended to stress Mussolini's close relationship with symbols of modernity and technological progress and with the novelty of his political communication. Besides his known popular appeal, Fox's decision to make him the first "Movietoned" international political figure in 1927 was due to his image as a leader easily adaptable to the modern sound medium. Unsurprisingly, Fox experimented with this multilingual practice for two other sound newsreels, both released in 1931 and titled *Mussolini Promises Peace*. They recorded Mussolini speaking in English and French. The dictator affirmed Italy's willingness to pursue peace, "the chief problem which interests the whole humankind," and reinforced this idealistic message by praising the very cinematic technology that was recording him.[120] Mussolini defined cinema as "the most magnificent discovery of modern times," superior in his view even to the radio, even though, as Fox's synopsis sheet explained, his political statement was also broadcast over radio waves.[121] Shot while standing behind his desk in his office at Palazzo Venezia in Rome, the dictator was meant to exude, despite his difficulties with the English language, the calm competence of a charismatic modern leader, enamored of the modern film medium. This version of Mussolini looked very different from the man who gave frenzied speeches in front of massive crowds that other films had shown. As such, it was much closer to the image found in another source of visibility that Mussolini embraced mostly in the 1930s, and thus beyond the scope of this study—the eighty-two editorials that Sarfatti ghostwrote for him for Hearst's syndicated newspapers between 1928 and 1935.[122] Both Mussolini's sound films and editorials were meant to convey an image of a player in world politics and a national leader engaged with modernizing plans. Specifically, his press visibility was peppered with medical terminology, economic references, and concrete, but eloquent examples. Whatever the interests associated with the financial groups who were supporting investments in Italy, Mussolini was a topic of widespread appeal in the popular culture industry.[123]

The swan song of Mussolini's cinematic visibility before his dramatic decline in popularity was *Mussolini Speaks* (1933), which resulted from years of exchanges between the Istituto LUCE and American newsreel companies and thus constitutes a summation of his 1920s cinematic visibility. Produced by Harry Cohn of Columbia Pictures, the film revealed the longevity of the Duce's appeal and newsworthiness before his popularity declined following his imperialistic campaign in Ethiopia. The title of this seven-reel production resonates both with the previous *Mussolini Smiles* and with the sensational expectation of hearing Greta Garbo's voice as promised by the promotional slogan "Garbo Talks!" for her first sound film, *Anna Christie* (1930). Harry's brother Jack had assembled and edited footage of Mussolini and Italian life from different LUCE films.[124] Harry's idea for the film did not originate from an ideological affinity but from his interest in what one of his biographers calls "the trappings of monarchy."[125] Cohn's production was designed to be highly enjoyable: it sported a familiarly sensational screen introduction and voiceover by none other than famed radio commentator Lowell Thomas, the creator and promoter of Lawrence of Arabia and for years the voice of countless Fox Movietone newsreels.[126]

The film, which premiered on March 10 at the RKO Palace in New York and on August 11 at the Filmarte Theater in Los Angeles, tells the story of the Fascist leader through his public performances and historical achievements. It opens with the speech, translated in voiceover, that he gave in Naples to celebrate the tenth anniversary of the Fascists' March on Rome in 1922. To illustrate his speech but also to convey the modernity of his arrival on the Italian scene, the film intercuts his words and face with scenes of Italian life such as harvests, sporting events, and engineering projects and with views of typical landscapes, including an erupting volcano (figures 45 and 46). On the military side, there are also scenes of the Duce reviewing troops in North Africa and as he interacts with the Italian people.

The studio's promotional material praised how the film intertwined its dynamic rhythm with the Duce's rapid accomplishments. The film's style dovetailed perfectly with Mussolini's charismatic personality through strategic shot selection, fast editing, and celebratory sound commentary. The studio's own promotional weekly, the *Columbia Beacon,* opened its February 4, 1933, issue with a long homage to the film, calling it "an exclusive and authentic film autobiography" as if Mussolini had edited the movie himself.[127] The studio celebrated *Mussolini Speaks* as "a striking innovation in screen entertainment" with a simple but most eloquent rationale: "Never before has one of the leading figures in world affairs enacted his life's role on celluloid."[128] While this was an exaggeration, the film helped celebrate cinema itself. "Here, for the first time," the *Columbia Beacon* insisted, "are the true scope and power of the camera and microphone strikingly revealed."[129] Thus it was not just that Mussolini was so "cinematic" that a film about his life promised to be a success, but also that cinema, as a private enterprise, had become so relevant in public life that a film about Mussolini could play an important role in civic and political discourse.

The reviews followed the promotional tune. They praised the film as "more than a glorified newsreel" for its synthesis of sound and images. "Clever editing

FIGURES 45 and 46. Title screen and close-up of Mussolini in *Mussolini Speaks* (Columbia Pictures Corp. © 1933, renewed 1960 Columbia Pictures Industries, Inc.). All rights reserved. Courtesy of Columbia Pictures. Frame enlargements reproduced from the collections of the Library of Congress, Moving Image Section.

cuts in on his speech at short intervals," the *Film Daily* noted, "and shows in actual motion picture views the things that he discusses."[130] The most eloquent review came out in the *Motion Picture Herald*, which gave credit to Cohn for producing a "pictorial compilation" about "that genius of personality and leadership who was born Benito Mussolini, son of a laborer, and has become Il Duce, the leader." Interestingly, the review maintained that the political quality of his celebrity status made him worthy of promotional initiatives. Mussolini "is a phenomenon of modern governmental history, and as such is deserving, along those lines, of extensive ballyhoo."[131]

The RKO promotional material insisted on the isomorphism between Mussolini's life and his "moving picture autobiography," even suggesting the dramatic inadequacy of the latter. As a result, "no actor, no matter how gifted, is to be trusted with the gestures, actions, and speech of this international figure."[132] Similarly, the *New York American* praised Mussolini's performance for displaying "dramatic quality in speech and action that would be a credit to any motion picture star."[133] There were also negative reviews that focused on the film's quality rather than on the choice of the subject matter. "The picture lacks the cumulative power and sweep of an epic," cried the *New York Evening Post*.[134] Similarly, the *New York Herald Tribune* found the intercut scenes so "unintelligible and worthless" that the result was "entertainment and instruction not even bordering on the mediocre."[135]

Within a year, the tide was turning. The Duce's political novelty was expiring and so was the appealing originality of his personality. G. E. W. Johnson in the *North American Review* commented on the surprising accord between France and Italy by criticizing Mussolini as a bundle of contradictions. He thought that Mussolini was simultaneously a blustering warmonger and a skilled diplomat, "a bombastic pseudo-Caesar who is forever reenacting the crossing of the Rubicon, without having quite made up his mind what do after getting to the other side"[136] By the time American newspaper correspondent and journalism professor Edwin Ware Hullinger directed another biopic, *The Private Life of Mussolini* (1938), the interest in the Duce had faded.[137] A capable self-promoter, Hullinger wrote a long account for *Photoplay* in which he described the film as "the first screen biography, I believe, ever made of a living world statesman," but he could not but recycle the old slogans of Mussolini as a "star" and "marquee attraction" since these, by the late 1930s, had all but lost their weight.[138] The last *Time* magazine cover to feature Mussolini titled the drawing of his older, once gloriously young face, with a funeral-like epigraph, "Aging Dictator."[139]

Still, throughout the 1920s, many influential reporters, film critics, and even intellectuals condoned Fascism's un-American governance perversions, including the limitation of individual liberties, the one-party state's bureaucratic takeover, and the novel syndicalist and corporatist practices. Long believed to be popular in Italy, Mussolini's mode of mass-mediated plebiscitary governance had, at least for a while, appeared new, daring, and efficient. Many of those praising his leadership would have concurred with the view of Percy Winner, the former Rome-based

AP correspondent who in a 1928 *Current History* article argued that "Fascism succeeds not as a theory, a system, a regime or a government, but as a corporeal projection of a successful personality."[140] Critics and admirers could only agree, however, that with Mussolini a new season of mass-mediated governance had begun.

Conclusions

The public culture of a society is a forum where power in its various forms, including meaning and aesthetics, is elaborated and made authoritative.

THOMAS BENDER[1]

Politics is the Entertainment Branch of Industry

FRANK ZAPPA[2]

I opened this study with a photograph of Mary Pickford and Douglas Fairbanks giving the Fascisti salute while reminiscing about their May 1926 meeting with the Duce and the memory of his exemplary personal authority. After the discussions in later chapters about the many hagiographic profiles devoted to Mussolini, we can now recognize just how familiar with such views the two stars must have been. Even before meeting the Duce, Pickford praised his personality much more than his political successes. "He must be a true artist," she told a reporter that April, describing Mussolini's broad appeal. "You can tell that from his preface to the biography by Margaret [sic] Sarfatti, wherein he says he 'enjoys the feeling of universality that he belongs to all, and yet belongs to none.'"[3] The Hollywood couple never again met the Duce, but Pickford must have continued to appreciate other celebratory profiles of him. As late as 1934, she addressed a rally of Fascist sympathizers held in New York City on the anniversary of the March on Rome by reiterating her praise: "Italy has always produced great men," she declared, "and when she needed one most Mussolini was there. Viva Fascismo! Viva Il Duce!"[4]

In this work, I have argued that the two Hollywood icons' public encounter with Mussolini was more than an anecdotal occurrence. It signified, instead, the American public's growing fascination for authoritative popular and political actors. In past chapters, I have drawn the contours of this phenomenon by interlacing two 1920s case studies. I have researched and compared the ways in which the Italian dictator became seen as a charming and romanticized master of anti-Bolshevik governance in America with the ways in which, in the very same years, Hollywood actor Rudolph Valentino rose to fame as an exemplar of forceful and romantic leadership.

I initially availed myself mostly of press sources and films. American newspapers and periodicals, as well as film trade journals, extensively covered both men's meteoric rise to fame. Several Valentino films and a significant volume of newsreel footage of Mussolini were easily available. When venturing into the secondary literature directly related to the actor and the dictator, however, I looked in vain for passages that offered a substantial discussion of *both* figures. The duo's popularity has traditionally been explored by two separate disciplines, film history and political history, that have rarely engaged in a sustained or systematic dialogue about popular culture's relationship with dictators and autocrats—and vice versa. Specifically, existing studies of film stars and dictators have rarely taken a comparative approach, preferring instead to extract metaphors and anecdotes from the mines of film scenes, sober or sensationalized biographies, and all kinds of press reports.[5] The scarcity of such works is unsurprising. Historically, dictators do not appreciate sharing the spotlight in their own country, and they tend to discourage any competition, as the literature on film stardom in Fascist Italy reveals. More comparative in nature, a few studies have focused on different stars in a single national film culture,[6] or on two, or even three, dictators (or national leaders).[7] A wealth of studies in different languages has also become available on the "cinemas of dictators"—that is, on film productions under totalitarian regimes. These are typically classified by each individual nation's most dominant personality.[8] The literature on film stardom in autocratic regimes, however, may not appear entirely appropriate to the U.S. situation even though the abundance of authoritarian public figures who emerged in interwar America (e.g., Father Charles Coughlin, Huey Long) may suggest otherwise. In fact, the American popularity of Mussolini, observed vis-à-vis the rise of film stardom as a key instrument of public opinion management, prompted me to consider the extensive positive response to figures of charismatic authority in a democratic context.

Over the course of this work, I sought to document the historical intersections between the Divo and the Duce in pivotal moments, including their public confrontation over Valentino's plan to acquire American citizenship and the Fascists' belated attempt to attach themselves to Valentino's revered memory. No matter how telling such individual instances were, however, my most compelling finding was that attributes of political and romantic leadership extensively overlapped and even constituted each other. Discovered in articles, biographical profiles, interviews, and cartoons, these intersections reveal a commonality of personal traits that revolve around the notion of seductive authority. In spite of their antidemocratic and misogynistic pronouncements, or rather by virtue of them, both the film star and the dictator aspired to a degree of mass approbation that bordered on the plebiscitary.[9]

Even more remarkably, my research has revealed that the two men's appeal to American public opinion was a heavily mediated one. Valentino and Mussolini's American images were built up by scores of individuals operating on both sides of the Atlantic. These publicists came from a variety of institutional and personal backgrounds and worked, sometimes overtly and sometimes clandestinely, in the service of a diverse set of interests. They often operated across purposes. As a result, rather than describing as inevitable and systematic the emergence of a relationship of plebiscitarian approval between the Divo and the Duce on the one side and American moviegoers and citizens on the other, I found it more fitting and compelling to detail the accomplishments and missteps made by producers, publicists, journalists, financiers, and diplomats in advancing their popularity. While on screen, Valentino rarely played the role of the impenitent Sheik, but the imprint of his most commercially successful film turned out to be what made publicity campaigns either succeed or fail, even after his death. Similarly, when the regime's Italian and American handlers focused their promotion of Fascism on the Duce's bodily feats and personal leadership instead of his politics, they succeeded—at least for about a decade—in constructing an appealingly masculine model for American audiences.

This comparative lens has helped identify an instructive, if necessarily unsystematic, initial convergence of publicity practices involving mass cultural industries—film, publishing, and press—with financial and political institutions. The cultural and political *promotion* of Valentino and Mussolini's plebiscitarian consensus, in fact, achieved significant results. While their foreignness might have constituted, in theory, an impediment to the marketing of their charismatic and authoritarian personae, it created, in fact, unique promotional opportunities. The Divo's and the Duce's forceful personalities, made to convey Latin bluntness and the gravitas of ancient Roman history, facilitated a cosmopolitan and authoritarian reimagining of American male leadership. The simultaneous politicization of the Hollywood star and the aestheticization of the Italian dictator on American soil revealed the appeal that authoritarian leader-celebrities held over a diverse mass citizenry that was adjusting to the changes wrought by the war, by the extension of suffrage, and the advent of mass culture.

By bringing film and political history into close dialogue through the lens of publicity and public opinion management, the conclusions of this study pertain not only to either film or political history. Instead, they address both disciplinary camps within the domain of American public culture. *The Divo and the Duce* ultimately argues that celebrity culture in modern democracy grew out of the tension between expanded mass access to consumption, information, and civil rights and the well-promoted personal appeal of (male) leadership figures. The resonances between the two men's carefully crafted public personae have underscored the paradox that a public with expanded civic and consumer opportunities is also a public primed to embrace a celebrity's iconic authority.

Applied to the world's most exemplary democracy, this statement may sound disturbing. Celebrity studies has often linked celebrities' "distinctive discursive quality" to "the twinned discourses of modernity: democracy and capitalism."[10] But even though "the celebrity as public individual" and "as a marketable commodity" "serves as a powerful type of legitimation of the political economic model of exchange and value," the political economy of celebrity culture also rests on models of civic identity.[11] Stressing the link between celebrity and commodity in a liberal economy, in other words, does not exhaust celebrities' political dimension, though it may well end up masking it. Mussolini and Valentino, in their outspoken endorsement of nondemocratic governmentality, show that the authority that commercial society grants a celebrity affects much more than the dynamics of free economic exchange. It also affects public discourse about authority and citizenship.

Key civic consequences of such mass mobilization of film and political authority in American public culture included the insertion of private interests in public affairs and, attached to it, the spectacularization of political discourse. In *Liberty and the News* (1920), Walter Lippmann critiqued the emergence of a new balance of constitutional power in which the influence of the press on public opinion and, consequently, on the executive, resulted in a "plebiscite autocracy, or government by newspapers."[12] Since public opinion is collected and even manufactured by "special groups which act as extra-legal organs of government," the government is shaped far more by the pressure of these groups than by the elected representatives of the American people.[13] The result is a "shift in the locus of sovereignty" or, in other words, the effective marginalization of the public from government authority.[14]

Lippmann was articulating in eloquent form what others had been hinting at for some time. In the spring of 1906, the young journalist Richard Washburn Child, future U.S. ambassador to Italy, had discussed the same dramatic outcome in an *Atlantic Monthly* article. None other than Edward Bernays, in *Crystallizing Public Opinion* (1923), would refer to Child's insights appreciatively while wondering "whether the acts of men in commercial activity may ever become [. . .] so far reaching in their effect that they compel a universal public interest." "It may be said," Bernays continued, "that at no time have private industries become of such startling interest to the community at large as at present in the United States."[15] The pioneer of public relations practices closed the paragraph by noting, rhetorically, "How far present-day tendencies have born out Mr. Child's expectations of a growing and accepted public interest in important industrial enterprises, the reader can judge for himself."[16]

Bernays's currency was high in the 1920s, a decade of laissez-faire policies that under Presidents Harding and Coolidge were extremely favorable to American businesses. In applying the lessons learned from prewar Progressive muckraking, U.S. corporations sought a great deal of public acceptance by showcasing their espousal of public service and responsibility in their advertisements and public relations activities.[17] Talent moved around accordingly. The decade saw the consolidation of a revolving-door custom whereby public servants found lucrative positions in the corporate world, primarily as lobbyists. Will H. Hays's career move from the Harding administration to the chairmanship of the MPPDA—as Hollywood's master lobbyist and publicist—was one of the most visible of such transitions. Washington's strengthened alliance with the film industry also affected the degree of political leaders' modes of public presentation. Demand for publicity expertise grew in all domains. President Coolidge, despite his notorious aloofness, made himself repeatedly available for newsreels. His successor, Herbert Hoover, possibly outdid him through several stunts, including a celebrity-packed re-creation of the invention of the light bulb, starring Thomas Edison himself, which was broadcast live throughout the country and devised by none other than Bernays.

In the following years, the partnership between Hollywood persuasion and Washington power intensified. Through his contact with the Hoover administration, Louis B. Mayer had become by 1932, according to *Variety*, not just an "international statesman" but also "the only American holding that dual honor" of being "a national figure, of politics and the show business."[18] Mayer was not alone. Jack Warner competed with him on the same terrain, if on the opposite side, of presidential politics.[19] The mobilization of the vote for Franklin Roosevelt (Warner's candidate) and his subsequent victory turned studio executives' formerly rare practice of political advocacy into a rule. It was a New Deal in both government and business, with overlapping and cross-fertilizing public relations campaigns.[20] Once Roosevelt realized that Hollywood could sell his political agenda, showmanship became an essential quality of his government. Americans came to see Roosevelt as a celebrity, particularly through his starring role in newsreels and radio programs. Conversely, Roosevelt began to see Americans as movie audiences and radio listeners.[21]

At the same time, the migration to Los Angeles of New York cultural radicals, together with the arrival of European Jews, infused the movie capital with a leftist political culture that led to the unionization of the film industry, the creation of the Screen Actors Guild by the likes of Will Rogers and Joan Crawford, and the emergence of celebrity civic activism.[22] In 1934, California's hard-fought gubernatorial contest saw the conservative candidate Frank Merriam best former Socialist Party member (and MGM scenarist!) Upton Sinclair. Merriam's victory was helped by conservative-thinking studio heads like Mayer who led a most effective film campaign that helped build a decisive margin against their enthusiastic but less organized leftist opponents.[23]

In the fray of show business politics, one also encounters the familiar, eclectic profile of newspaper magnate, film producer, and gubernatorial hopeful William Randolph Hearst and the equally eclectic newcomer Joseph P. Kennedy. Hearst's background in filmmaking and yellow journalism made him appreciate "the theatricality of politics and the potential for political communication inherent in motion pictures." With equal showmanship, he used his press influence first to support the New Deal and eventually to do an about-face and oppose Roosevelt's domestic and internationalist policies. Similarly, Kennedy, the Irish banker with Harvard and Wall Street credentials, crossed many corridors of power from New York to Hollywood, where he shaped the trajectories of companies, actors, and executives while also enriching himself. It was in Hollywood that he "learned to perform as a public personality," something that his family members treasured as they entered public life.[24]

By the 1930s, the marriage of politics and showmanship provided a context in which the authoritarian style of governance and Mussolini's performative leadership could no longer appear to be utterly alien. The emergency of the Depression introduced Americans to a new level of emboldened executive power as shown in Roosevelt's famous inaugural address delivered on March 4, 1933. Only a shared sense of civic sacrifice and discipline could lead to effective leadership, he warned the crowd. And if Congress was unwilling to support his plan of action, he promised that

> I shall not evade the clear course of duty that will then confront me. I shall ask the Congress for the one remaining instrument to meet the crisis—broad executive power that would be given to me if we were in fact invaded by a foreign foe.[25]

Not paying any mind to the speech's commitment to democracy, the press welcomed it and described it accurately as a call for dictatorial powers. As Benjamin Alpers has shown, such general acceptance of exceptional authority lasted only a few months, but "the idea that America might need some kind of dictator appeared in a wide variety of places, including a pair of unusual Hollywood films": the aforementioned *Mussolini Speaks* (1933) and *Gabriel over the White House* (1934).[26] The period was also characterized by the public visibility of demagogic politicians and forceful radio personalities, including Father Coughlin and Huey Long (a regular in newsreels). Coughlin and Long feuded with many celebrities and moved from being strong supporters to vehement detractors of FDR and eventually became anti-Communist witch hunters. Neither man hesitated to express public admiration for the Fascist style of mass and personality-centered governance.[27]

While the 1930s is an obvious field of inquiry for the intersection of politics and mass media, we may also look beyond this decade, toward more contemporary challenges to the notion of popular sovereignty. Recent writings on the contemporary crisis of democracy brought about by the hegemony of mass media might be illuminating. As sociologist and political scientist Colin Crouch wrote in *Post-Democracy* (2004), although elections remain fundamental tools of political change, the staging of "public electoral debate is a tightly controlled spectacle, managed by rival teams of professional experts in the techniques of persuasion" and focused on a small and selective range of issues. While citizens play a passive role in the spectacle of the electoral competition, "politics is really shaped in private by interaction between elected governments and elites that overwhelmingly represent business interests."[28] Reduced to sound bites, empty rhetorical slogans, and growing personalization, political communication, for Crouch, does not enhance "true political discussion" but "is designed to be beyond the reach of scrutiny" by common voters. For years, Crouch adds, "only manipulative demagogues like Hitler, Mussolini, and Stalin" seemed to know "the secret of power through mass communication."

Not any longer: Lippmann's worst fears have become a daily reality. Today democratic politicians, especially in the United States, conduct their "personality-based election campaigning" by relying on a "persuasion business" that reaches from the advertising industry and commercial television to social media.[29] "Promotion of the claimed charismatic qualities of a party leader," Crouch remarks, "increasingly takes the place of debate over issues and conflicting interests."[30] In this climate, the news-making business reproduces the personalization of the candidate's political message with its "rapid, eye-catching banality." Echoing Lippmann's dystopian *Liberty in the News*, Crouch concludes that the "control over politically relevant news and information," is in the hands of "a very small number of extremely wealthy individuals."[31] In *Paradoxes of Democracy* (1999), sociologist Shmuel Noah Eisenstadt similarly remarked that the concentration of power over "the central nerves of the democratic process—the production and distribution of information," leads to "a 'technocratization' of knowledge" that excludes the public at large from the political process.[32]

The outcome for the destinies of the governed is not unforeseeable. First, liberal governments' policy making is largely shaped by lobbying, a much more secretive and less democratic mode of influence than traditional party politics.[33] Secondly, elite control over news and the political process leads to "withdrawal from political participation."[34] Historian Emilio Gentile has noted that as democracies are turned into theatrical representations, the state becomes the stage, politicians the leading players, and citizens the extras.[35] In a departure from the most famous passage from Lincoln's Gettysburg Address—"government of the people, for the people, by the people"—the voting public has become the real *idola*, in Francis Bacon's sense. What remains is not an "absent demos," to quote the *Economist*'s 2015 Democracy Index, but an "acting demos" that plays a role scripted elsewhere.[36]

Early-twentieth-century American celebrity culture ostensibly publicized the values of freedom and individualism. Yet, even in an inaugural phase, the popularity of iconic personalities diluted the ideals of direct democracy in favor of charismatic representation. Celebrity publicity is neither conservative nor progressive but constitutes a regular component of mass democracies, and as such has a history that deserves to be told. As cinema has been central to this historical dynamic, film historians may have a privileged vantage point in telling it, particularly in an epoch that is all too familiar with the convergence between celebrity culture and political leadership. This analysis of the encounter of film stardom and political leadership has shown that celebrity politics does more than merely promote a celebrity's political convictions, whether liberal or conservative; it also inspires a commanding form of social governance that has remained integral to modern democratic life.

ARCHIVAL SOURCES

ACS   Archivio Centrale dello Stato, Rome

          AP   Affari Politici, 1931–1945

          MCPG   Ministero della Cultura Popolare, Gabinetto

          MCP-DSP Ministero della Cultura Popolare, Direzione Generale Servizi della Propaganda

          NPE   Nuclei di Propaganda in Italia e all'Estero

          SPD-CO   Segreteria Particolare del Duce, Carteggio Ordinario

AMPAS   Academy of Motion Pictures Arts and Sciences, Margaret Herrick Library, Los Angeles, California

          CC   Core Collections

          SC   Special Collections

AP   Archivio Prezzolini (Lugano, Switzerland)

ASC   Archivio Storico Capitolino, Rome

ASMAE   Archivio Storico Diplomatico, Ministero degli Affari Esteri, Rome

          AIW   Ambasciata d'Italia in Washington, 1920–1924; and AIW, 1925–1943

          AP   Affari Politici, 1931–1945, Stati Uniti

          GMS   Gabinetto del Ministro e Segreteria Generale 1923–41

          MCP   Ministero della Cultura Popolare

          SAP   Serie Affari Politici, 1931–1945

BNCR   Biblioteca Nazionale Centrale, Rome

CMP	Charles Merriam Papers, Special Collections Research Center, University of Chicago
CMS	Center for Migration Studies, Staten Island, New York
GCP	George Creel Papers, Manuscript Division, Library of Congress
LOC	Library of Congress

	MD	Manuscript Division
	MP	Motion Pictures, Broadcasting and Recorded Sound Division

MIRC	Moving Image Research Collections, University of South Carolina

	FMNC	Fox Movietone News Collection

MNC	Museo Nazionale del Cinema, Turin

	FV	Fondo Valentino
	FB	Fondo Paolo Balboni

MoMA	Museum of Modern Art

	FSC	Film Study Center

NARA	National Archives and Records Administration, College Park, MD

	DS	General Record of the Department of State, Central Files
	IR	Italian Records
	MPSVRR	Motion Picture, Sound, and Video Research Room
	RCPI	Records of the Committee on Public Information
	RG	Record Group

NYPL	New York Public Library

	LC	Robinson Locke Collection, New York Public Library for the Performing Arts
	TC	Theater Collection, New York Public Library for the Performing Arts

OKP	Otto H. Kahn Papers, Firestone Library, Princeton University
RWCP	Richard Washburn Child Papers, Manuscript Division, Library of Congress
TWL	Thomas W. Lamont Collection, Baker Library, Harvard Business School
UCLA	University of California, Los Angeles

	SP	Special Collections, Library
	FTA	Film & Television Archive, Hearst Metrotone News Collection

VMSP	Victor Mansfield Shapiro Papers, Special Collections, UCLA Library
WLP	Walter Lippmann Papers, Sterling Memorial Library, Yale University
WWC	Woodrow Wilson Collection, Mudd Library, Princeton University
WWP	Woodrow Wilson Papers, Manuscript Division, Library of Congress

ABBREVIATIONS

AM	*Atlantic Monthly*
APSR	*American Political Science Review*
CHE	*Chicago Herald-Examiner*
CM	*Century Magazine*
CO	*Current Opinion*
CT	*Chicago Tribune*
CW	*Collier's Weekly*
EH	*Exhibitors Herald*
EM	*Everybody's Magazine*
FH	*Film History*
HM	*Harper's Magazine*
JAH	*Journal of American History*
JMH	*Journal of Modern History*
LAT	*Los Angeles Times*
LD	*Literary Digest*
LM	*Liberty Magazine*
MM	*McClure's Magazine*
MPC	*Motion Picture Classic*
MPH	*Motion Picture Herald*
MPM	*Motion Picture Magazine*
MPP	*Motion Picture Play*

MPW	*Moving Picture World*
MW	*Movie Weekly*
NAR	*North American Review*
NBIAS	*News Bulletin of the Italy America Society*
NM	*Il Nuovo Mondo*
NMM	*The New Movie Magazine*
NR	*The New Republic*
NYEP	*New York Evening Post*
NYH	*New York Herald*
NYHT	*New York Herald Tribune*
NYW	*New York World*
NYT	*New York Times*
NYTR	*New York Tribune*
PIA	*Progresso Italo-Americano*
PP	*Picture and Picturegoer*
PPM	*Picture-Play Magazine*
SEP	*Saturday Evening Post*
SFC	*San Francisco Chronicle*
TBIAS	*Trade Bulletin of the Italy America Society*

NOTES

Unless otherwise indicated, all translations from the Italian are my own.

INTRODUCTION

1. Max Weber, "Parliament and Government in Germany under a New Political Order," in *Weber: Political Writings,* ed. Pater Lassman and Ronald Speirs (New York: Cambridge University Press), 174 (italics in the original). The essay was published in book form in 1918 and was based on five articles Weber wrote for the *Frankfurter Zeitung* in the spring of 1917.

2. Bonnie Honig, *Democracy and the Foreigner* (Princeton, NJ: Princeton University Press, 2001), 4, 7 (italics in the original).

3. "Mrs. Doug. Mary Goes in for the Fairbanks-Sort-of-Thing," *MPM,* February 1927, 58. The title refers to two other images on top of the page showing Pickford launching the javelin and playing golf. Some of the friends in the photograph reproduced here would later emerge as leaders in the film business. Ted Reed, for instance, who had met Fairbanks during the third Liberty Loan drive, would serve as the Academy of Motion Picture Arts and Sciences' fifth president.

4. "Mary Pickford e Douglas Fairbanks in Italia," *La Tribuna illustrata,* April 26, 1926, 8.

5. "Douglas Fairbanks e Mary Pickford a Roma," *Il Messaggero,* April 28, 1926, 5.

6. "Le Giornate romane di Douglas," *La Tribuna,* April 29, 1926, 5. The state agency LUCE (L'Unione Cinematografica Educativa) made a newsreel of the Hollywood stars' Roman visit. It is now viewable on a DVD entitled *La Roma del LUCE,* directed by Nicola Caracciolo and Gianni Borgna (Rome: Istituto LUCE/Comune di Roma, 2004). Neither the LUCE footage nor any of the newspapers that I consulted included images of the three individuals together.

7. Both the Italian and the American press reported the stars' brief meeting with the Duce but did not mention the exact date. See "L'on. Mussolini riceve Mary Pickford and Douglas Fairbanks," *Il Tevere,* May 11, 1926, 3; "Film Stars See Mussolini," *NYT,* May 11, 1926, 29; "Mary Pickford and Douglas Fairbanks ricevuti da Mussolini," *Il Giornale d'Italia,* May 12, 1926, 3. Their meeting, first announced for early May, was postponed at least once.

8. Most biographical accounts tend to either ignore or downplay this meeting. Jeffrey Vance gives it a passing reference in *Douglas Fairbanks* (Berkeley: University of California Press, 2008), 225. The one partial exception is Eileen Whitefield's biography, which mentions that Pickford "had met Mussolini in the 1920s." *Pickford: The Woman Who Made Hollywood* (Lexington, KY: University Press of Kentucky, 1997), 315. Lorenzo Quaglietti discusses the stars' meeting with the Duce in *Ecco i nostri: L'invasione del cinema americano in Italia* (Rome: ERI, 1991), 41–44.

9. "L'on. Mussolini riceve Mary Pickford." See also "Impressioni di Mary Pickford e Douglas su Mussolini," *L'Impero*, May 22, 1926, 3.

10. To which Mussolini "smilingly" replied: "I don't know whether I like you better in the movies or in real life, but I certainly do both." "Film Stars See Mussolini," *NYT*, May 11, 1926, 29.

11. "Film Stars See Mussolini."

12. Thomas Doherty, *Hollywood and Hitler 1933–1939* (New York: Columbia University Press, 2013), 87, 91.

13. Alan R. Raucher, *Public Relations and Business, 1900–1929* (Baltimore: Johns Hopkins Press, 1968), 7.

14. Raucher, *Public Relations and Business*, 13, 15.

15. Raucher, 15.

16. My stress on World War I is indebted to, among others, Suzanne W. Collins, "Calling All Stars: Emerging Political Authority and Cultural Policy in the Propaganda Campaign of World War I" (PhD diss., New York University, 2008; forthcoming from Indiana University Press). Kathryn Cramer Brownell described the same phenomenon as "mass-mediated politics" but placed its key starting point in 1934, during the California gubernatorial campaign. *Showbiz Politics: Hollywood in American Political Life* (Chapel Hill: University of North Carolina Press, 2014).

17. Doherty rightly posits that these issues were "disputed without Hollywood stars manning the picket lines." *Hollywood and Hitler*, 111.

18. On Mussolini's diplomatic calculations, see Philip V. Cannistraro, "Mussolini, Sacco-Vanzetti, and the Anarchists: The Transatlantic Context," *JMH* (March 1996): 31–62.

19. Silas Bent (1882–1945) was a journalist, author, and lecturer. In his critical survey of newspaper practices entitled *Ballyhoo*, Bent adopted a lexicographer's definition of the term as "synonymous with barker in the slang sense of this word." *Ballyhoo: The Voice of the Press* (New York: Horace Liveright, 1927), unnumbered page before frontispiece. An excerpt from the book also appeared as "The Art of Ballyhoo," *HP*, September 1927, 485–94.

20. I am referring here to Daniel Boorstin's famous notion of "pseudo-events," introduced in his book *The Image*. Referring to pseudo-events, whose master architect was Edward Bernays, Boorstin defined them as "not spontaneous [, . . .] planted primarily [. . .] for the immediate purpose of being reported or reproduced [, . . .] ambiguous [, . . .] intended to be a self-fulfilling prophecy." *The Image: A Guide to Pseudo-Events in America* (1962; New York: Harper & Row, 1964), 11–12.

21. Graeme Turner, "Approaching Celebrity Studies," *Celebrity Studies* (March 2010): 16.

22. Randolph Bourne, "Trans-National America," *AM*, July 1916, 93.

23. "The Melting Pot," *Photoplay*, November 1918, 21.

24. For a discussion of transnational branding, see Turner, "Approaching Celebrity Studies," 15.

25. Italian historian Ferdinando Fasce's work, especially his *La democrazia degli affari: Comunicazione aziendale e discorso pubblico negli Stati Uniti, 1900–1940* (Rome: Carocci, 2016), has been foundational to my approach of grounding questions about social legitimacy into a concrete network of actors, interests, and investments.

26. For a critique of the culturalist approach to the study of Fascism, see Sergio Luzzatto, "The Political Culture of Fascist Italy," *Contemporary European History* (July 1999): 389–406.

27. *Mutual Film Corporation v. Industrial Commission of Ohio*, 236 U.S. 230 (1915) 244, quoted in Lee Grieveson, *Policing Cinema: Movies and Censorship in Early-Twentieth-Century America* (Berkeley: University of California Press, 2004), 201 (italics mine). Further, Justice Joseph McKenna added: "They are mere representations of events, of ideas and sentiments published and known; vivid, useful, and entertaining, no doubt, but, as we have said, capable of evil, having power for it, the greater because of their attractiveness and manner of exhibition."

28. Herbert Howe, "Hitting the Hookah with Rudie," *MPC*, December 1921, 19.

29. For a broad discussion of the attractiveness of Mussolini's authoritarian style of government in 1930s American political and popular culture, see Benjamin L. Alpers, *Dictators, Democracy, and American Public Culture: Envisioning the Totalitarian Enemy, 1920s–1950s* (Durham: University of North Carolina Press, 2003).

30. Josh Glick, "Wilson and the War Effort," in *Film and the American Presidency*, ed. Jeff Menne and Christian B. Long (New York: Routledge, 2015), 72–95.

31. Steven J., Ross, *Hollywood Left and Right: How Movie Stars Shaped American Politics* (New York: Oxford, 2011); and Brownell, *Showbiz Politics*.

32. Doherty, *Hollywood and Hitler*; and Ben Urwand, *The Collaboration: Hollywood's Pact with Hitler* (Cambridge, MA: Harvard University Press, 2013).

1. POPULAR SOVEREIGNTY, PUBLIC OPINION, AND THE PRESIDENCY

1. Alexis de Tocqueville, *Democracy in America* (New York: Library of America, 2004), 62, 292–93.

2. Tocqueville, *Democracy in America*, 139.

3. Woodrow Wilson, *Congressional Government: A Study in American Politics* (Boston: Houghton, Mifflin, 1885), 204–5, 332, 331, 324.

4. Woodrow Wilson, *An Old Master, and Other Political Essays* (New York: C. Scribner's Sons, 1893), 91.

5. Wilson, *An Old Master*, 80.

6. Woodrow Wilson, *Division and Reunion, 1829–1889* (New York: Longman, Green, 1894), 111.

7. Woodrow Wilson, *Constitutional Government in the United States* (New York: Columbia University Press, 1908), 110.

8. Similarly, the 1913 passage of the Seventeenth Amendment allowed for the direct election of U.S. senators for the first time. Up to that point they had been chosen by state legislatures.

9. George Kibbe Turner, "Manufacturing Public Opinion: The New Art of Making Presidents by Press Bureaus," *McClure's Magazine*, July 1912, 318.

10. Turner, "Manufacturing Public Opinion," 316, 322.

11. The film company's lawyers stressed cinema's educational role in "making or announcing publicly something that otherwise might have remained private and unknown," akin to the role and function of illustrated newspapers, magazines, and periodicals. Mutual Film Corporation v. Industrial Commission of Ohio, 236 U.S. 230 (1915), 243, quoted in Lee Grieveson, *Policing Cinema: Movies and Censorship in Early-Twentieth-Century America* (Berkeley: University of California Press, 2004), 199. Grieveson, who provides the best account of this decision and its impact (198–215), adds that the lawyers did not argue for First Amendment guarantees but instead relied on state guarantees of free speech "because it was not clear that the First Amendment was binding on the states" (310n30).

12. *Mutual Film Corporation,* 236 U.S. at 230 (italics mine). McKenna added: "They are mere representations of events, of ideas and sentiments published and known; vivid, useful, and entertaining, no doubt, but, as we have said, capable of evil, having power for it, the greater because of their attractiveness and manner of exhibition." *Mutual Film Corporation,* 236 U.S. at 244.

13. Arguably, the notion of film censorship itself did not impinge upon such clear-cut separation but instead relied on the appreciation of the intersection between private enterprise and public benefit due to their converging interest in public attention and consensus.

14. Charles Musser, "The Media Reconfigured: The US Presidential Elections of 1892 and 1896," in *Film and the American Presidency,* ed. Jeff Menne and Christian B. Long (New York: Routledge, 2015), 21. See also Charles Musser, *Politicking and Emergent Media: US Presidential Elections of the 1890s* (Berkeley: University of California Press, 2016).

15. Musser, "The Media Reconfigured," 34 (italics mine).

16. Kristen Whissel, *Picturing American Modernity: Traffic, Technology, and the Silent Cinema* (Durham, NC: Duke University Press, 2008), 63–116, 216–19.

17. Brian Neve, "The 'Picture Man': The Cinematic Strife of Theodore Roosevelt," in *Presidents in the Movies: American History and Politics on Screen,* ed. Iwan W. Morgan (New York: Palgrave, 2011), 65.

18. Especially close were the relationships between Roosevelt and the muckrakers affiliated with the weekly *McClure's Magazine.*

19. Kevin Brownlow, *The War, the West, and the Wilderness* (New York: Alfred A. Knopf, 1979), xv–xvi.

20. "Theodore Roosevelt—The Picture Man," *MPW,* October 22, 1910, 920.

21. Burton W. Peretti, *The Leading Man: Hollywood and the Presidential Image* (New Brunswick, NJ: Rutgers University Press, 2013), 38.

22. Wilson to Mary Hulbert, August 25, 1912, in *Papers of Woodrow Wilson,* ed. Arthur S. Link (Princeton, NJ: Princeton University Press, 1978), 25: 26.

23. James Startt, *Woodrow Wilson and the Press: Prelude to the Presidency* (New York: Palgrave Macmillan, 2004), 201.

24. "Phonograph to Give Wilson to All of U.S.," *NYT,* August 9, 1912, 1. One of these films was the one-reeler *The Old Way and the New* (Paramount, 1912). For several of the quotes below, I am indebted to Josh Glick, "Wilson and the War Effort," in Menne and Long, *Film and the American Presidency,* 75–76.

25. "Campaign Pictures," *Motography,* July 6, 1912, 25. See Startt, *Woodrow Wilson and the Press,* 203.

26. A few newspapers also initiated their own newsreel services, including the *Chicago Herald, Chicago Tribune,* and *Detroit Free Press.*

27. L. L. Gould, *Four Hats in the Ring: The 1912 Election and the Birth of Modern American Politics* (Lawrence: University Press of Kansas, 2009), 151–83.

28. A few sources use a different date, March 21, 1915, for the film's presidential screening, but the archival record about Wilson's early March response to the controversy contradicts this later date.

29. See for instance Lewis Jacobs, *The Rise of the American Film* (New York: Teacher's College Press, 1938), 1757.

30. Mark E. Benbow, "Birth of a Quotation: Woodrow Wilson and 'Like Writing History with Lightning,'" *Journal of the Gilded Age and Progressive Era,* October 2010, 509–33; and A. Scott Berg, *Wilson* (New York: G. P. Putnam's Sons, 2013), 349. Because the film's racist perspective on the Civil War and Reconstruction matched Wilson's views, his historical writings, and segregationist employment policies, other historians have not completely rejected the authenticity of the comment. Melvyn Stokes has recently argued that Wilson "*may* have said this" (italics in the original), while J. D. Keene has noted that "we may never resolve the dispute over whether Wilson uttered this phrase." Stokes, *D. W. Griffith's* The Birth of a Nation: *A History of "The Most Controversial Motion Picture of All Time"* (New York: Oxford University Press, 2007), 111; and Keene, "Wilson and Race Relations," in *A Companion to Woodrow Wilson,* ed. Ross A. Kennedy (New York: Wiley-Blackwell, 2013), 145.

31. Several companies had proposed their films on the basis of the country's national mission: Vitagraph for *The Battle Cry of Peace* and the American Correspondent Film Company for *The Battle of Przemysl.*

32. Ida Tarbell's popular serialized biography of Lincoln for *McClure's* had doubled the magazine's circulation. Dixon had variously depicted Lincoln as an icon of national brotherhood and reconciliation in three novels, including *The Southerner: A Romance of the Real Lincoln* (1913), which he dedicated to Wilson, "friend and college mate."

33. Stokes, *D. W. Griffith's* The Birth of a Nation, 188.

34. For multiple references to the event, see Arthur Lennig, "Myth and Fact: The Reception of *The Birth of a Nation,*" *FH* (June 2004): 117–41.

35. Wilson to Tumulty, undated but early March 1915, reel 332, series 4, file 2247, WWP. On April 24, 1915, Tumulty solicited Wilson to state publicly that "he did not approve the 'Birth of a Nation.'" The president agreed, but ultimately used the statement quoted in the chapter to handle his response to members of Congress. Letters of protests about the film kept coming to the White House until 1918.

36. "President Wilson Did Not Endorse Picture," *MPW,* May 15, 1915, 1122.

37. Berg, *Wilson,* 349.

38. See Robert Lang, ed., *The Birth of a Nation: D. W. Griffith, Director* (New Brunswick, NJ: Rutgers University Press, 1993).

39. Dixon to Tumulty, May 1, 1915, reel 332, series 4, file 2247, WWP.

40. Dixon to Tumulty, May 1, 1915 (emphasis in the original).

41. Charles Hirschfeld, "Nationalist Progressivism and World War I," *Mid-America* (July 1963): 139–57; and Ross A. Kennedy, "Preparedness," in Kennedy, *A Companion to Woodrow Wilson,* 273.

42. In 1917 alone, seventeen state legislatures threatened to present censorship bills.

43. Leslie Midkiff DeBauche, *Reel Patriotism: The Movies and World War I* (Madison: University of Wisconsin Press, 1997), 5.

44. One of the most forceful moguls to try to co-opt the president was Carl Laemmle, who kept pressing Wilson for short pronouncements to be used for newsreels' intertitles. In return for a special relationship with Universal against its archrival Hearst, Laemmle pledged "a million feet for the president during the Campaign." See Laemmle to Wilson, March 5, 1915, reel 198, series 4, file 72, WWP.

45. Kia Afra, *The Hollywood Trust: Trade Associations and the Rise of the Studio System* (Lanham, MD: Rowman & Littlefield, 2016), 33–49, especially 45.

46. Brady's charge was to fight censorship, but since he could not prevent the New York State legislature from passing a bill establishing a state censorship board in 1921, NAMPI was dissolved and replaced by the MPPDA (Motion Picture Producers and Distributors Association), led by Will H. Hays.

47. J. W. Binder [MPBTA's executive secretary] to Wilson, May 3, 1916, reel 199, series 4, file 72, WWP.

48. Suzanne W. Collins, "Calling All Stars: Emerging Political Authority and Cultural Policy in the Propaganda Campaign of World War I" (PhD diss., New York University, 2008; forthcoming from Indiana University Press), 184.

49. John H. Blackwood to Tumulty, April 10, 1916, reel 199, series 4, file 72, WWP; and "White House Showing for *Civilization*," *MPW*, July 22, 1916, 626.

50. Brian Taves, *Thomas Ince: Hollywood's Independent Pioneer* (Lexington: University Press of Kentucky, 2012), 96.

51. "Wilson Congratulates Ince," *Motography*, October 21, 1916, 936, quoted in Glick, "Wilson and the War Effort," 80.

52. Terry Ramsaye, *A Million and One Nights* (New York: Simon and Schuster, 1926), 728 (italics mine). Many more news services, including Hearst's International Film Service, Gaumont's Mutual Weekly, and Pathé News, jumped on the preparedness bandwagon.

53. Fox to Tumulty, March 4, 1916, reel 199, series 4, file 72, WWP.

54. Brady to Tumulty, July 31, 1916, reel 199, series 4, file 72, WWP.

55. Wilson to Tumulty, August 3, 1916, reel 199, series 4, file 72, WWP.

56. Karen Russell and Carl Bishop, "Understanding Ivy Lee's Declaration of Principles: U.S. Newspaper and Magazine Coverage of Publicity and Press Agentry, 1865–1904," *Public Relations Review* (June 2009): 98.

57. Lee made a name for himself by understanding "how 'corporate publicity' could also work in the corporation's favor." Russell and Bishop, "Understanding Ivy Lee's Declaration," 99. A pioneer in the field, Lee worked for the Pennsylvania Railway and Standard Oil. John D. Rockefeller had hired him in 1914 after his company violently repressed a coal mining rebellion (the Ludlow Massacre) in Colorado. For his work, Lee became known as the "prince of publicity men."

58. Wilson to Creel, July 21, 1918, box 2, GCP.

59. Elmer E. Cornwell Jr., "Wilson, Creel, and the Presidency," *Public Opinion Quarterly* (Summer 1959): 189.

60. The CPI's reach extended to Western Europe as well as parts of Asia and South America.

61. On June 30, 1919, Congress would legislate the CPI out of existence. All the files were hastily collected, moved to the basement of an old War Department building in Washington, and abandoned there. A Library of Congress staff member, Cedric Larson, located them in January 1937 and, in collaboration with NARA archivist James R. Mock, began to process them. See Larson and Mock, "The Lost Files of the Creel Committee of 1917–1919," *Public Opinion Quarterly* (January 1939): 5–29. Eventually, the CPI's official records and George Creel's papers were moved to their current locations: the National Archives (College Park, MD) and the Manuscript Division of the Library of Congress (Washington DC), respectively.

62. "Among the twelve million people who live in the United States, not a single one has yet proposed restricting the freedom of the press." Tocqueville, *Democracy in America,* 207.

63. Secretaries of State, War, and Navy, "Letter to the President," April 13, 1917, in box 1, volume 1, 1917–1918, 1931, GCP (italics mine). The same document was published in the *Official Bulletin* (May 10, 1917) but had already appeared in newspapers and periodicals: for instance, as "Two Appointments," *Outlook,* April 25, 1917, 725–26. The three secretaries were Robert Lansing, Newton D. Baker, and Josephus Daniels. Daniels had long been a journalist and had headed the publicity department for Wilson's 1912 presidential campaign.

64. "CPI: Preliminary Statement to the Press" n.p., in box 1, volume 1, 1917–1918, 1931, GCP. Slightly different from this archival copy, a printed edition "released for publication on May 28, 1917" appeared in the CPI booklet *Preliminary Statement to the Press of the United States* (Washington, DC: Government Printing Office, 1917).

65. CPI, *Preliminary Statement,* 6.

66. CPI, *Preliminary Statement,* particularly 4–5.

67. CPI, *Preliminary Statement,* 8 (italics mine); and Creel, *How We Advertised America* (New York: Harper & Brothers, 1920), 18.

68. Gustave Le Bon, *The Crowd: A Study of the Popular Mind* (New Brunswick, NJ: Transaction, 1995), 83, 87. First published in France in 1895 as *Psychologie des foules,* Le Bon's book appeared in English in 1896 and became a worldwide best seller.

69. Creel, *How We Advertised America,* 5.

70. For a detailed, but partisan assessment of the CPI activities, see *The Complete Report of the Chairman of the Committee on Public Information, 1917:1918:1919* (Washington: 1920; repr., New York: Da Capo Press, 1972), commonly known as the Creel Report; and Creel, *How We Advertised America,* also published in 1920. For more objective assessments, see James R. Mock and Cedric Larson, *Words That Won the War: The Story of the Committee on Public Information, 1917–1919* (Princeton, NJ: Princeton University Press, 1939); and Stephen L. Vaughn, *Holding Fast the Inner Lines: Democracy, Nationalism, and the Committee on Public Information* (Chapel Hill: University of North Carolina Press, 1980).

71. The poster design was indebted to an earlier British voluntary army recruitment poster entitled *Your Country Needs You,* designed in 1914 by Alfred Leete.

72. Mark Sullivan, "Creel—Censor," *CW,* November 10, 1917, 36. For a profile of Creel, see Mock and Larson, *Words That Won the War,* 52–66.

73. A native of Missouri, Creel entered journalism with stints first in Kansas, then in New York for Hearst's *Journal-American* and *Cosmopolitan,* and then in Colorado for the *Rocky Mountain News* (1911–1912). In Denver he developed ties with local reformist leaders.

Personal circumstances may have brought him to Wilson's attention. In 1912 he married a well-known former Belasco star, Blanche Lyon Bates, who was a close friend of president's oldest daughter, Margaret.

74. George Creel, *Chivalry versus Justice; Why the Women of the Nation Demand the Right to Vote* (New York: National Woman Suffrage Publishing, 1915).

75. George Creel, *Wilson and the Issues* (New York: Century, 1916), 9 (italics in the original). Creel dedicated *How We Advertised America* to Wilson as the "great and inspired leader in the fight for the moral verdict of mankind" (x).

76. George Creel, "Can Wilson Win?," *CM*, June 1916, 270.

77. George Creel, "A Close-Up of Douglas Fairbanks," *EM*, December 1916, 729.

78. In a private letter sent in 1939 to author-archivist Cedric Larson, Creel explained: "When we entered the war on April 6, 1917, and the papers carried the news that some rigid form of censorship would be adopted, I wrote a letter of protest to the President in which I explained to him that the need was for expression not repression, and urged a campaign that would carry our war aims and peace terms not only to the United States, but to every neutral country [. . .] . As for censorship, I insisted that all proper needs could be met by some voluntary methods. He sent for me after approving my proposal, drafted me to act as active chairman. No other person was considered for the place." Creel to Larson, July 18, 1939, quoted in Larson and Mock, "The Lost Files," 8.

79. Wilson to Tumulty, undated, box 3, volume 3 "1917–1918, 1931," GCP.

80. Secretaries of State, War, and Navy, "Letter to the President," April 13, 1917, box 1, GCP.

81. Paul Thompson, "Publicity Manager of the War," *The Independent*, April 28, 1917, 200; and "Creel: An Announcement," *EM*, January 1919, 25.

82. The Sedition Act forbade the use of "disloyal, profane, scurrilous, or abusive language" about the United States, its symbols, and its armed forces. It also applied to any expression of opinion that interfered with the sale of government bonds. It was repealed on March 3, 1921, but the original Espionage Act was left intact. Since then, the Espionage Act has since been repeatedly amended.

83. Brady to Tumulty, June 22, 1917, reel 199, series 4, file 72, WWP.

84. Wilson to Brady, June 27, 1917, reel 199, series 4, file 72, WWP.

85. Wilson to Brady, June 27, 1917 (italics mine). Creel was closely advising the president on the issue; see Creel to Tumulty, June 22, 1917.

86. Wilson to Brady, June 27, 1917.

87. This statement appeared in the United Kingdom in "Helping the Moving Pictures to Win the War," *Bioscope*, July 18, 1918, 8; quoted in Kristin Thompson, *Exporting Entertainment: America in the World Film Market, 1907–1934* (London: BFI, 1985), 94. In the United States, it appeared widely—for instance, on the contents page of the educational film magazine *Reel and Slide*, September 1918, 2. Thanks to Richard Abel for providing this reference.

88. Brady to Wilson (telegram), June 30, 1917, reel 199, series 4, file 72, WWP.

89. DeBauche, *Reel Patriotism*, 108–111. Universal's Carl Laemmle was possibly the most active in attempting to forge an independent relationship with Wilson.

90. See, for instance, "President Wilson Calls upon Film Industry," *MPW*, July 14, 1917, 217; and "Motion Pictures Mobilized for War," *MPW*, August 11, 1917, 918.

91. Lee Grieveson, *Cinema and the Wealth of Nations* (Oakland: University of California University Press, 2018), 76. See also DeBauche, *Reel Patriotism,* 135.

92. I borrow the expression from a letter that Brady sent to Creel in which Brady quoted Frank A. McDonald, president of the Theater Owners Association in Los Angeles. McDonald wanted the government to designate movie theaters as "temples of democracy." Brady to Creel, May 20, 1918, in RG 63, Records of the Committee on Public Information, Executive Division, CPI 1-A1, General Correspondence of George Creel, July 1917–March 1919, box 2, Brady, William A. #66, NARA-RCPI.

93. On the committee's activities, see "Industry Subscribes Over 2 ½ Million to Liberty Loan," *Exhibitor's Trade Review,* June 23, 1917, 173.

94. DeBauche, *Reel Patriotism,* 111–16.

95. I discuss Pickford and Fairbanks's involvement in the Liberty Loan campaigns in chapter 3.

96. See "War Achievements in the Motion Picture Industry Set Forth in Brief to Federal Officials by National Association," *Exhibitor's Trade Review* (July 20, 1918): 522; DeBauche, *Reel Patriotism,* 118–20; and Collins, "Calling All Stars."

97. Leo Braudy, *The Frenzy of Renown: Fame and Its History* (New York: Oxford University Press, 1986), 556.

98. See Mock and Larson, *Words That Won the War,* 136–37. For a concise and informative overview of the origins and activities of the Signal Corps, see Brownlow, *The War,* 119–130.

99. *Complete Report of the Chairman of the CPI,* 48.

100. On these films, see Mock and Larson, *Words That Won the War,* 137–38; and David H. Mould, *American Newsfilm 1914–1919: The Underexposed War* (New York: Garland Publishing, 1983), 260–62. Originally, *America's Answer* was a production of nine reels, eventually cut to five. *Under Four Flags* has apparently not survived.

101. The archival print of the film was severely edited by the Signal Corps in 1936 to about 56 minutes. I viewed a DVD copy of the incomplete version in NARA's Motion Picture, Sound, and Video Research Room (MPSVRR).

102. I drew the lines of the final intertitle from the scenario of *Pershing's Crusaders* (Official Film), no. 297, now readable in folder "Obsolete Misc. 200–299," box "111M Index to Obsolete Films 1–400," NARA-MPSVRR.

103. Mould, *American Newsfilm,* 263.

104. These films often showcased his serious temperament. For example, *America Goes Over* (Signal Corps, 1918) shows Wilson in his office writing the declaration of war. On Wilson's screen presence, see Glick, "Wilson and the War Effort," 84–89.

105. One of the most effective pro-Wilson commercial films of the period was Frank Borzage's drama *Whom the Gods Would Destroy* (1919), which *MPW* described as an "excellent argument for world leagues." "Wilson Ideas Form Picture's Basis," *MPW,* February 22, 1919, 1051.

106. Metro Pictures distributed the film with alternative titles: *Why Germany Must Pay, Wilson or the Kaiser,* and *The Fall of the Hohenzollerns.*

107. Intertitles transcribed during my viewing of the film at the Library of Congress.

108. Cornwell, "Wilson, Creel, and the Presidency," 189.

2. CULTURAL NATIONALISM AND DEMOCRACY'S OPINION LEADERS

1. Douglas Fairbanks, *Making Life Worth While* (New York: Britton, 1918), 87, 88, 89.

2. Walter Lippmann, *Public Opinion* (1922; New York: Free Press, 1997), 61.

3. As Charles Forcey remarked, "The outbreak of World War I was enough to reveal how thin was the liberal veneer over Roosevelt's nationalism." *The Crossroads of Liberalism: Croly, Weyl, Lippmann and the Progressive Era, 1900–1925* (New York: Oxford University Press, 1961), 313.

4. Herbert Croly, *The Promise of American Life* (1909; New York: McMillan, 1914), 154.

5. Forcey, *Crossroads of Liberalism*, v (italics mine).

6. Forcey, 270–71.

7. Randolph S. Bourne, "The War and the Intellectuals," *Seven Arts* 2 (June 1917), reprinted in *War and the Intellectuals: Collected Essays, 1915–1919*, ed. Carl Resek (New York: Harper & Row, 1964; Indianapolis: Hackett Publishing, 1999), 5.

8. *The Papers of Woodrow Wilson*, ed. Arthur S. Link (Princeton, NJ: Princeton University Press, 1983), 41:334.

9. Gregory S. Butler, "Visions of a Nation Transformed: Modernity and Ideology in Wilson's Political Thought," *Journal of Church and State* 39, 1 (January 1997): 36.

10. If his adviser Edward House kept in touch with the views of Wall Street and key industrialists and intellectuals, as well as with those of American and European leaders, his secretary Joseph Tumulty "was the President's interpreter of public opinion, his guide to mass psychology." John Morton Blum, *Joe Tumulty and the Wilson Era* (Boston: Houghton Mifflin, 1951), 60, quoted in Daniela Rossini, *Woodrow Wilson and the American Myth in Italy: Culture, Diplomacy, and War Propaganda* (Cambridge: Harvard University Press, 2008), 212n18.

11. Bishirjian, "Croly, Wilson, and the American Civil Religion," *Modern Age* (Winter 1979): 36–37. Bishirjian quotes a talk Wilson gave in 1919 (italics Wilson's).

12. Rossini, *Woodrow Wilson and the American Myth*, 61.

13. Rossini, 61.

14. Croly, *Promise of American Life*, 454.

15. Charles Hirschfeld, "Nationalist Progressivism and World War I," *Mid-America* (July 1963): 155.

16. Hans Vought, "Division and Reunion: Woodrow Wilson, Immigration, and the Myth of American Unity," *Journal of American Ethnic History* (Spring 1994): 26. As soon as he left office, Congress passed the Immigration Quota Act, followed by the Johnson-Reed Act in 1924, which restricted immigration to meager quotas.

17. Lloyd E. Ambrosius, *Wilsonian Statecraft: Theory and Practice of Liberal Internationalism during World War I* (Wilmington, DE: Scholarly Resources Books, 1991), 15.

18. "Peace at Any Price," *NR*, May 24, 1919, 101.

19. Croly, *Promise of American Life*, 310, 454.

20. Donna R. Gabaccia has recently stressed the rarely discussed relevance for global economic, political, and cultural history of the intersection between "immigrant foreign relations"—namely, the transnational linkages created "from below" by immigrants—and "the far-better-known history of American diplomacy." *Foreign Relations: American Immigration in Global Perspective* (Princeton, NJ: Princeton University Press, 2012), 3–4.

21. Horace M. Kallen, "Democracy versus the Melting Pot," *Nation*, February 25, 1915, 219.

22. Kallen, "Democracy versus the Melting Pot," 217.

23. Kallen, 219.

24. Kallen, 219.

25. Kallen, 220. Despite the apparent progressivism of his position, in 1927 Kallen met with Mussolini in Rome and wrote with admiration about the "vivid force and magnetism of the man." "Fascism: For the Italians," *NR,* January 12, 1927, 211.

26. Randolph S. Bourne, "Trans-National America," *AM,* July 1916, reprinted in Bourne and Resek, *War and the Intellectuals,* 117.

27. Bourne, "Trans-National America," 121 (italics mine).

28. Bourne, 121. Further, he argued that the melting pot ideology ("the Anglo-Saxon attempt to fuse") was akin to a "crusade" that would "only inflame the partial patriotism of trans-nationals, and cause them to assert their European traditions in strident and unwholesome ways" (122).

29. Bourne, 122.

30. Bourne, 123 (italics in the original).

31. Kallen and Bourne had been variously influenced by philosopher William James, who had deployed the notion of pluralism with respect to the variety of human experiences related to political institutions, personal and social identities, and international relations. See Kennan Ferguson, *William James: Politics in the Pluriverse* (New York: Rowman & Littlefield, 2007).

32. Bonnie Honig, *Democracy and the Foreigner* (Princeton, NJ: Princeton University Press, 2001), 3.

33. Honig, *Democracy and the Foreigner,* 7.

34. "The Pride and Fall of George Creel," *Chronicle,* May 1918, 1.

35. John Dewey, "The New Paternalism" *NR,* December 21, 1918, 216–17; William [Henry] Irwin, "An Age of Lies," *Sunset,* December 1919, 23–25, 54, 56; both quoted in J. Michael Sproule, "Social Responses to Twentieth-Century Propaganda," in *Propaganda: A Pluralistic Perspective,* ed. Ted J. Smith (New York: Praeger, 1989), 9–10. In 1928 Irwin would write a history of Paramount.

36. Hulet M. Wells, *Wilson and the Issues of Today: A Socialist Revision of George Creel's Famous Book* (Seattle: Socialist Party, 1918), 11–12 (words capitalized in the original).

37. A. Lawrence Lowell, *Public Opinion and Popular Government* (New York: Longmans, Green, 1913), 41.

38. Michael B. Grossman, "The Theory of Public Opinion from Bryce to Lippmann" (PhD diss., Johns Hopkins University, 1968), 6, 7.

39. Everett D. Martin, *The Behavior of Crowds* (New York: Harper, 1920), 243.

40. Martin, *Behavior of Crowds,* 285.

41. Ronald Steel, *Walter Lippmann and the American Century* (1980; New Brunswick, NJ: Transaction Publishers, 2009), 134.

42. Steel, *Walter Lippmann,* 144–46.

43. [Walter Lippmann], *NR,* May 17, 1919, cover.

44. Walter Lippmann, *Liberty and the News* (New York: Harcourt, Brace and Howe, 1920), 61.

45. Lippmann, *Liberty and the News,* 62–63.

46. Lippmann, 63, 70.

47. Lippmann, 82, 91.

48. Lippmann, 98, 99, 96–97.

49. Walter Lippmann, *Public Opinion* (1922; New York: Free Press, 1997), 173.

50. Lippmann, *Public Opinion,* 54–55.

51. Lippmann, 4.

52. Lippmann, 10, 11, 16.

53. "War and the Fifth Estate," editorial, *Photoplay,* September 1918, 17.

54. Lippmann, *Public Opinion,* 11.

55. Lippmann, 61, 60.

56. Lippmann, 61.

57. Lippmann, 59.

58. Lippmann, 19.

59. Lippmann, 195.

60. John Dewey, "Public Opinion," *NR,* May 3, 1922, 286.

61. Walter Lippmann, *The Phantom Public* (1925; New Brunswick, NJ: Transaction Publishers, 1999), 4.

62. Lippmann, *Phantom Public,* 187.

63. Lippmann, 61.

64. Lippmann, 137.

65. Lippmann, 9. Some of these works included Robert Michels, *Political Parties: A Sociological Study of the Oligarchical Tendencies of Modern Democracy,* trans. Eden and Cedar Paul (1911; New York: Hearst's International Library, 1915); A. Lawrence Lowell, *Public Opinion and Popular Government* (New York: Longmans, Green, 1914); and James Bryce, *Modern Democracies* (New York: Macmillan, 1921).

66. On elite theory, see Robert A. Nye, *The Anti-Democratic Sources of Elite Theory: Pareto, Mosca, Michels* (London and Beverly Hills: SAGE Publications, 1977).

67. John Dewey, *The Public and Its Problems* (1927; Athens: Ohio University Press, 1954), 69.

68. Dewey, *Public and Its Problems,* 146.

69. Dewey, 139.

70. In 1924 Merriam became the Social Science Research Council's first president.

71. In Rome from April to October 1918, Merriam practiced firsthand the power of propaganda. Once back to Chicago, he reflected on his experience from a methodological standpoint in "American Publicity in Italy," *APSR* (November 1919): 541–55. I return to his role in Italy in chapter 4.

72. Charles Merriam, "The Significance of Psychology for the Study of Politics," *APSR* (August 1924): 473.

73. Charles Merriam, *American Political Ideas: Studies in the Development of American Political Thought, 1865–1917* (New York: Macmillan, 1920), 453.

74. Charles Merriam, *Four American Party Leaders* (New York: Macmillan, 1926), viii. In the volume, he profiled Abraham Lincoln, Theodore Roosevelt, William Jennings Bryan, and Woodrow Wilson, with the premise that "leadership is one the basic factors in the organization of life, and its implications are everywhere of profound significance" (vii).

75. William Yandell Elliott "Mussolini, Prophet of the Pragmatic Era in Politics," *Political Science Quarterly* (June 1926): 161–92.

76. Grossman, *Theory of Public Opinion*, 3.

77. Trained in Chicago under Merriam, Harold Lasswell published in 1927 an influential study on war propaganda technique that, without the quantitative approach that defined his later works, sought "to expose to the most searching criticism our prevailing dogmas of sovereignty, of democracy, of honesty, and of the sanctity of individual opinion." *Propaganda Technique in the World War* (1927; New York: Peter Smith, 1938), 22. Lasswell went on to become one of the leading political scientists of his time with a wide range of contributions to the fields of communication theory, social psychology, and sociology. During World War II, he analyzed Nazi propaganda films as Chief of the Experimental Division for the Study of War Time Communications at the Library of Congress.

78. Sproule, "Social Responses to Twentieth-Century Propaganda," 12.

79. Jackson Lears, *Fables of Abundance: A Cultural History of Advertising in America* (New York: Basic Books, 1994), 221.

80. Daria Frezza, *The Leader and the Crowd: Democracy in American Public Discourse, 1880–1941* (Athens: University of Georgia Press, 2007), 139. Frezza quotes Ferdinando Fasce, *La democrazia degli affari: Comunicazione aziendale e discorso pubblico negli Stati Uniti, 1900–1940* (Rome: Carocci, 2016), 123.

81. Lears, *Fables of Abundance*, 230.

82. "Newspaper exposure of corporation affairs was called 'publicity,' but so was the corporation defense against criticism." Alan R. Raucher, *Public Relations and Business, 1900–1929* (Baltimore: Johns Hopkins Press, 1968), 7.

83. "Tainted News as Seen in the Making," *Bookman*, December 1906, 396, 402; "The Press Agents' War," *NYT*, September 9, 1914, 8; both quoted in Raucher, *Public Relations*, 141, 70.

84. In his critical review of Bernays's *Crystallizing Public Opinion* (1923), Ernest Gruening uses this expression to convey his distrust for the broad cultural shift that brought the public from being "damned" to be "bunked." "The Higher Hokum," *Nation* (April 16, 1924): 450.

85. Raucher, *Public Relations*, 141. See also Fasce's remarkable *La democrazia degli affari*.

86. His mother was Sigmund's sister Anna, and his father was Ely Bernays, brother of Freud's wife, Martha Bernays. For biographical and professional profiles, see Stuart Ewen, *PR! A Social History of Spin* (New York: Basic Books, 1996), especially 3–36; and Larry Tye, *The Father of Spin: Edward Bernays and the Birth of Public Relations* (New York: Crown Publishers, 1998).

87. Edward Bernays, *Crystallizing Public Opinion* (New York: Boni and Liveright, 1923); and Edward Bernays, *Propaganda* (New York: H. Liveright, 1928; repr., Brooklyn, NY: IG Publishing, 2005).

88. On his instrumental use of Lippmann's work, see Sue Curry Jansen, "Semantic Tyranny: How Edward L. Bernays Stole Walter Lippmann's Mojo and Got Away with It and Why It Still Matters," *International Journal of Communication* (January 2013): 1094–111. Bernays presumptuously included Lippmann's name as a like-minded thinker in the book's foreword.

89. Bernays, *Propaganda*, 54.

90. Edward Bernays, "The Minority Rules," *Bookman*, April 1927, 151, in folder "Writings File," box II:23, EBP.

91. Bernays, *Propaganda,* 37.

92. Bernays, *Crystallizing Public Opinion,* 78.

93. Bernays, *Propaganda,* 110, 109, 120.

94. Bernays, 48.

95. Edward Bernays, "Theda Bara in Cleopatra" in folder "Biography of an Idea: Notes. Theda Bara," box 457, Book File, EBP. Later on, he worked briefly with Samuel Goldwyn to promote an information bureau to help American companies gain a share of foreign markets through industrial films.

96. Edward Bernays, *Biography of an Idea: Memoirs of Public Relations Counsel Edward L. Bernays* (New York: Simon and Schuster, 1965), 149–50.

97. Bernays, *Biography of an Idea,* 77.

98. Bernays, 341–42.

99. Roger William Riis and Charles W. Bonner, *Publicity: A Study of the Development of Industrial News* (New York: J. H. Sears, 1926), 4, 10.

100. Riis and Bonner, *Publicity,* 10–11.

101. Carl Laemmle, "The Business of Motion Pictures," *SEP,* August 27, 1927, 10–11, and September 3, 1927, 18–19, in *The American Film Industry,* ed. Tino Balio (Madison: University of Wisconsin Press, 1976), 153–68; (quote) 161.

102. Silas Bent, *A Menace to Democracy: The Press in America—Is It Free?* (Philadelphia: n.p., 1929), 4. In the remainder of this study, I will refer to two of his most compelling works, *Ballyhoo* (1927) and *Strange Bedfellows* (1929), a critical survey of newspaper practices and a study of contemporary political leaders, respectively.

103. Bent, *Menace to Democracy,* 4.

104. Bent, 12.

105. Bent, 8, 12.

106. Bent, 12.

107. Kenneth McNaught, "American Progressives and the Great Society," *JAH* 53 (December 1966): 504, quoted in Raucher, *Public Relations,* v.

108. Raucher, 4–6.

109. Riis and Bonner, *Publicity,* 16. This rhetoric of alleged transparency and responsibility, however, was also used to protect monopolies, especially in conjunction with arguments that juxtaposed efficiency to excessive competition or government control.

110. Harper Leech, "Is American Business Entitled to the Rights of Free Speech?," *NELA* [National Electric Light Association] *Bulletin* (December 1927): 728, 730.

111. Raucher, *Public Relations,* 71, 74.

3. WARTIME FILM STARDOM AND GLOBAL LEADERSHIP

1. *The Complete Report of the Chairman of the Committee on Public Information, 1917:1918:1919* (Washington: 1920; repr., New York: Da Capo Press, 1972), 7.

2. DeBauche drew the expression "practical patriotism" from a June 1917 *NYT* advertisement that linked the exhibition of a film to the sale of Liberty Bonds. *Reel Patriotism: The Movies and World War I* (Madison: University of Wisconsin Press, 1997), 201n11.

3. Elizabeth Clarke, "War and the Sexes: Gender and American Film, 1898–1927" (PhD diss., Wilfrid Laurier University, 2007), 10. The First World War is not commonly adopted

as a historiographical divider for studies of gender in silent cinema. Detailing countless forgotten or rarely discussed films, Clarke has placed the conflict squarely at the center of her study of the "vital link between women, militarism, and American identity" in the silent period (10).

4. In light of the concomitant suffragist movement, the "depiction of active—and, more interestingly—*military* women" was not necessarily a sign of feminist advancement, as Clarke perceptively noted. Instead it "served the purpose of taming and directing women's growing political involvement towards contemporary nationalist aims." Clarke, "War and the Sexes," 3.

5. Clarke, 6.

6. "After April 1917, wartime heroism fell into two categories: women's sacrifice [. . .] and men's participation in battle." Clarke, 171.

7. Clarke has not considered at length the case of Mary Pickford, whose wartime popularity exceeded her screen roles.

8. DeBauche, *Reel Patriotism*, 38. In contrast, Kevin Brownlow has written that Wilson's declaration of war coincided with "torrents of war romances" on American screen. *The War, the West, and the Wilderness* (New York: Alfred A. Knopf, 1979), 131.

9. DeBauche, *Reel Patriotism*, 41.

10. Kristin Thompson, "Hearts of the World," in *The Griffith Project*, vol. 9, *Films Produced in 1916–1918*, ed. Paolo Cherchi Usai (London: BFI, 2005), 159.

11. "To exhibitors, Pickford films were meat and potatoes, while Chaplin was the seasoning." Scott Eyman, *Mary Pickford: America's Sweetheart* (New York: Donald I. Fine, 1990), 85.

12. Christel Schmidt, "American Idol: Mary Pickford, World War I, and the Making of a National Icon," in *Mary Pickford: Queen of the Movies,* ed. Christel Schmidt (Lexington: University Press of Kentucky, 2012), 147.

13. Anke Brouwers, "If It Worked for Mary . . . Mary Pickford's 'Daily Talks' with the Fans," in *Researching Women in Silent Cinema: New Findings and Perspectives,* ed. Monica Dall'Asta, Victoria Duckett, and Lucia Tralli (Bologna: DAR / Università di Bologna, 2013), 197–219.

14. Marion, who had a background in advertising, worked on the column between November 1915 and October 1916. Pickford oversaw each column. Cari Beauchamp, *Without Lying Down: Frances Marion and the Powerful Women of Early Hollywood* (Berkeley: University of California Press, 1997), 53.

15. Mary Pickford, "The Preparedness Parade," Daily Talks, *Dallas Morning News,* June 17, 1916, 11, quoted in Schmidt, "American Idol," 148.

16. Lasky to DeMille, March 5, 1917, quoted in *L'eredità Demille,* ed. Paolo Cherchi Usai and Lorenzo Codelli (Pordenone: Edizioni Biblioteca dell'Immagine, 1991), 517.

17. DeBauche, *Reel Patriotism*, 61.

18. R. E. Austin, "The Little American, Modern Movie Factor," *Duluth News-Tribune,* June 24, 1917, 1, quoted in Schmidt, "American Idol," 152.

19. Vachel Lindsay, "Queen of My People," *NR,* July 7, 1917, 280–81, quoted in Leslie Midkiff DeBauche, "Mary Pickford's Public on the Home Front," in *Film and the First World War,* ed. Karel Dibbets and Bert Hogenkamp (Amsterdam: Amsterdam University Press, 1995), 154.

20. DeBauche, *Reel Patriotism*, 61. In her memoir *Sunshine and Shadow* (Garden City, NY: Doubleday, 1955), Pickford claimed that San Francisco exhibitor D. J. "Pop" Grauman was the first one to call her "America's Sweetheart." Eileen Whitfield recounts that B. P. Schulberg, who had a background in publicity, was the one who came up with the phrase in response to the public's sentiment for the actress. Whitfield, "Laws of Attraction: Mary Pickford, Movies, and the Evolution of Fame," in Schmidt, *Mary Pickford*, 133; see also Schmidt, "American Idol," 147.

21. Chaplin underwent a remarkable transformation in wartime American perception. As Charles J. Maland has shown, the press "helped him establish the image of patriot" by publicizing that British and American soldiers would rather see him on screen than in the trenches. While his Britishness remained obvious to his American fans, he played a remarkable public role for the United States. He spoke to giant rallies, shot a promotional film, *The Bond*, for the Fourth Loan drive, and completed the iconic *Shoulder Arms* (1918). *Chaplin and American Culture: The Evolution of a Star Image* (Princeton, NJ: Princeton University Press, 1989), 37, 39.

22. Another active star was Theda Bara. Other notable female figures in the industry contributed to the war effort, including Lois Weber, who "was highly visible in Hollywood's war relief efforts, a sign of both her esteem in the industry and her continued embodiment of a Progressive Era feminine civic-mindedness." Shelley Stamp, *Lois Weber in Early Hollywood* (Berkeley: University of California Press, 2015), 174.

23. Austin, "The Little American," 1; and Grace Kingsley, "Mary Pickford Does Her Bit: Famous Actress to Help Liberty Loan," *LAT*, March 16, 1918, 12, quoted in Schmidt, "American Idol," 158.

24. Consider also *A Little Princess* (November 1917), where she played the role of a child. *The Little American* offered her a chance to explore the role of a grown woman.

25. Elizabeth Binggeli, "Blood and Sympathy: Race and the Films of Mary Pickford," in Schmidt, *Mary Pickford*, 190.

26. Binggeli, "Blood and Sympathy," 188.

27. Binggeli, 190

28. Binggeli, 189.

29. Gaylyn Studlar, *Precocious Charms: Stars Performing Girlhood in Classical Hollywood Cinema* (Berkeley: University of California Press, 2013), 30, 21.

30. Binggeli, "Blood and Sympathy," 189–91.

31. Binggeli, 191.

32. In *Less than the Dust* (1916), Pickford is an East Indian girl who, in love with a white British officer, seeks to make herself clean by wearing "English" clothes, only to discover in the end that she is indeed English. "The revelation has her literally rubbing the brownness from her dirty arm in disbelief." Binggeli, 194.

33. Binggeli, 198.

34. Warren Susman, *Culture as History. The Transformation of American Society in the Twentieth Century* (New York: Pantheon, 1984), 271–85.

35. John C. Tibbetts and James M. Welsh, *Douglas Fairbanks and the American Century* (Jackson: University Press of Mississippi, 2014), 150–51.

36. Tibbetts and Welsh, *Fairbanks and the American Century*, 10.

37. George Creel, "A Close-up of Douglas Fairbanks," *EM*, December 1916, 732.

38. Julian Johnson, The Shadow Stage: A Department of Photoplay Review, *Photoplay*, March 1917, 117 (italics in the original).

39. Michael Kimmel, *Manhood in America. A Cultural History* (New York: Free Press, 1997), 139–59; Gaylyn Studlar, *This Mad Masquerade. Stardom and Masculinity in the Jazz Age* (New York: Columbia University Press, 1996), 10–89; and Brian Faucette, "Afterword: The Makings of a Man, 1880–1927," in Tibbetts and Welsh, *Fairbanks and the American Century*, 333–38.

40. Alistair Cooke, MoMA program notes, quoted in Tibbetts and Welsh, *Fairbanks and the American Century*, 401n119. Cooke was a British film critic who worked with Iris Barry of MoMA on the first Fairbanks film retrospective in 1940.

41. Cooke, MoMA program notes, 401n119. Couéism, named after the psychologist Émile Coué, was a popular method of self-help that stressed autosuggestion.

42. Richard Schickel, *His Picture in the Papers: A Speculation on Celebrity in American Life Based on the Life of Douglas Fairbanks, Sr.* (New York: Charterhouse, 1973), 7.

43. Studlar, *This Mad Masquerade*, 72.

44. Studlar, 64.

45. On "wilderness cult," see Roderick Nash, *Wilderness and the American Mind* (New Haven, CT: Yale University Press, 1967).

46. In 1918 Fairbanks made short films to publicize war bonds, including *Swat the Kaiser* and *Sic 'Em, Sam* (distributed by the Federal Reserve).

47. Tracey Goessel, *The First King of Hollywood: The Life of Douglas Fairbanks* (Chicago: Chicago Review Press, 2016), 144.

48. Goessel, *First King of Hollywood*, 157; and Studlar, *This Mad Masquerade*, 25. When the western setting became too close to home, his characters dreamt of belonging to even more distant times and places, as in the Dumasian *A Modern Musketeer* December 1917).

49. Tibbetts and Welsh, *Fairbanks and the American Century*, 10.

50. Robert F. Martin, *Hero of the Heartland: Billy Sunday and the Transformation of American Society, 1862–1935* (Bloomington: Indiana University Press, 2002).

51. Alistair Cooke, *Douglas Fairbanks: The Making of a Screen Character* (New York: Museum of Modern Art, 1940), 17.

52. All the written material, including the *Photoplay* columns that appeared between November 1917 and April 1918, was ghostwritten by his secretary and publicist Kenneth Davenport.

53. Cooke, *Douglas Fairbanks*, 17.

54. Although in Shakespeare's *Julius Caesar*, Cassius is an envious character who lures Brutus into assassinating Caesar, in *Tales from Shakespeare* (1893–1894), the two-volume American supplement to the hugely successful prose abridgments of his plays, "Cassius and Brutus are figured as honorable patriots"—a solution "that better matches the idealized national history of colonial revolution." Maria Wyke, *Caesar in the USA* (Berkeley: University of California Press, 2012), 49.

55. Set in the fictional republic of Paragonia, the kingdom of Vulgaria, and the kingdom of Alaine, these three films adapt the "Ruritan romance" tradition of the late nineteenth century: "swashbuckling adventures of intrigue and mistaken identities set in imaginary kingdoms somewhere between Germany and the Balkans." Tibbetts and Welsh, *Fairbanks*

and the American Century, 80. Ruritania was a fictional country in central Europe that was the setting of three 1890s novels by Anthony Hope.

56. Tibbetts and Welsh, 89.

57. The tone of these films differed in remarkable ways from the popular war films of the time, such as Alan Crosland's *The Unbeliever* (February 1918) and Burton King's *The Lost Battalion* (September 1919), where the young male protagonists' war experiences lead them to acquire personal maturity and interclass and interethnic solidarity.

58. Tibbetts and Welsh, 89 (italics in the original). As Lary May put it, "[Fairbanks] mastered tyrants from above and revolutionaries from below who endangered foreign leaders sympathetic to the expansion of American interests." *Screening Out the Past: The Birth of Mass Culture and the Motion Picture Industry* (Chicago: University of Chicago Press, 1983), 117.

59. DeBauche, *Reel Patriotism*, 139.

60. Richard Koszarski, *An Evening's Entertainment: The Age of the Silent Feature Picture, 1915–1928* (Berkeley: University of California Press, 1994), 71.

61. See Michael J. Quinn, "Paramount and Early Feature Distribution: 1914–1921," *FH* (January 1999): 98–113.

62. Janet Wasko, *Movies and Money* (Norwood, NJ: Ablex, 1982), 21.

63. Loew had first acquired Metro Pictures Corporation in 1920, when the then-flagging company was producing *The Four Horsemen of the Apocalypse;* he merged it with Goldwyn Pictures Corporation in association with Louis B. Mayer, then a Metro executive, and his talented production head, Irving Thalberg.

64. Wasko, *Movies and Money*, 21.

65. Before the Triangle case, a notable precedent of Wall Street investment in the film industry had been that of the Mutual Film Corporation in 1912, also resulting in failure. See Koszarski, *An Evening's Entertainment*, 66; and Wasko, *Movies and Money*, 12.

66. Mary Nolan, *The Transatlantic Century: Europe and America, 1890–2010* (Cambridge, UK: Cambridge University Press, 2012), 54.

67. Nolan, *Transatlantic Century*, 54. See also Robert H. Zieger, *America's Great War: World War I and the American Experience* (Lanham, MD: Rowman and Littlefield, 2000), 16, 30.

68. Nolan, *Transatlantic Century*, 7.

69. Emily S. Rosenberg, *Financial Missionaries to the World: The Politics and Culture of Dollar Diplomacy, 1900–1930* (Durham, NC: Duke University Press, 2003).

70. Frank Costigliola, *Awkward Dominion: American Politics, Economic, and Cultural Relations with Europe, 1919–1933* (Ithaca, NY: Cornell University Press, 1984), 167–83.

71. Wasko, *Movies and Money*, 17, 12.

72. Kristin Thompson, *Exporting Entertainment: American in the World Film Market, 1907–1934* (London: BFI, 1985), 63–65.

73. "Wall Street Battle Seen in Finance's Film Invasion," *Variety*, February 6, 1920, 57.

74. According to a 1936 article, in the mid-1930s, Morgan owned and oversaw significant interests in four film companies: Fox, Paramount, RKO, and Warner Brothers. See "Whose Money Makes Movies?," *World Film News and Television Progress* (November 1936): 24–27. A. P. Giannini and his brother had founded the Bank of Italy in Northern California. By 1930 it was called Bank of America. The Gianninis were already active in

the film business in the 1910s and 1920s, lending money to studios but mostly backing individual films either featuring established stars or associated with trusted film professionals, including Cecil B. DeMille and Carl Laemmle. In 1926, Attilio Giannini wrote an assessment of the collaboration between banking and film industries, arguing that the film industry deserved "the attention and support of those who are seated in high places in the councils of our country." A. H. Giannini, "Financing the Production and Distribution of Motion Pictures," *Annals of the American Academy of Political and Social Sciences,* November 1926, 49. A. P. Giannini entertained relationships with Mussolini and several Fascist institutions.

75. The study was later published as "Gilmore, Field and Company: Investment Bankers," in *Cases on the Motion Picture Industry, with Commentaries,* ed. Howard T. Lewis (New York: McGraw Hill, 1930), 61–79. Connick's study used fictitious names for Famous Players–Lasky, renamed Gilmore, Field and Company. See also Wasko, *Movies and Money,* 18, 42n4.

76. "Gilmore, Field and Company," 68.

77. "Gilmore, Field and Company," 73.

78. "Publicity—What Is It?," *MPW,* July 20, 1918, 319–53.

79. James L. Hoff, "The Beginnings of Motion Picture Publicity," *MPW,* July 20, 1918, 319.

80. P. A. Parsons, "Doping It Out from the Papers," *MPW,* July 20, 1918, 327.

81. Otto Kahn, "The Motion Picture" (printed speech), folder 5, 77–The Motion Picture, box 300, Pamphlets 73–82, OKP.

82. Actually, Eliot had died the day before, on August 22, 1926.

83. Kahn, "The Motion Picture," 7.

84. Kahn, 7, 8.

85. Kahn, 12.

86. Kahn, 13.

87. Kahn, 15.

88. "Over There," *Photoplay,* March 1921, 119.

89. Wasko, *Movies and Money,* 21.

90. William Victor Strauss, "Foreign Distribution of American Motion Pictures," *Harvard Business Review* (April 1930): 309, 307.

91. Thompson, *Exporting Entertainment,* 100–147, and related tables; and Ruth Vasey, *The World According to Hollywood: 1918–1939* (Exeter, UK: University of Exeter Press, 1997), 29–62.

92. Cedric Larson and James R. Mock, "The Lost Files of the Creel Committee of 1917–1919," *Public Opinion Quarterly* (January 1939): 17.

93. Brady to Creel, August 29, 1917, in folder Brady, box 2, CPI 1-A1, Berenson to Brett, General Correspondence of George Creel, Chairman, July 1917–March 1919, Executive Division, NARA-RCPI.

94. *Complete Report of the Chairman of the CPI,* 7.

95. Larson and Mock, "The Lost Files," 29.

96. Lee Grieveson, *Cinema and the Wealth of Nations* (Oakland: University of California University Press, 2018), 76.

97. NAMPI, "Working Agreement Between the CPI and the Export Division of NAMPI," July 12, 1918, in folder Correspondences #7, box 2, Entry No. 62, General Bulletins, CPI 11A-A1, Division of Four-Minute Men, NARA-RCPI.

98. Helmuth Ortmann, "Film Europe II," *Reichfilmblatt* (April 24, 1926), quoted in *"Film Europe" and "Film America": Cinema, Commerce and Cultural Exchange, 1920–1939*, ed. Andrew Higson and Richard Maltby (Exeter, UK: University of Exeter Press, 1999), 1.

99. Kia Afra, *The Hollywood Trust: Trade Associations and the Rise of the Studio System* (Lanham, MD: Rowman & Littlefield, 2016), especially 159–63.

100. Thompson, *Exporting Entertainment*, 111.

101. "In a democratic commonwealth," he explained in his memoirs, "each business, each industry, and each art has as much right to, and as much duty toward self-regulation as has the general citizenry to self-government." Will H. Hays, *The Memoirs of Will H. Hays* (Garden City, NY: Doubleday, 1955), 327.

102. Press release, October 16, 1923, frame 1167, reel 19, Will Hays Papers, II (Rutgers University), quoted in John Trumpbour, *Selling Hollywood to the World: US and European Struggles for Mastery of the Global Film Industry, 1920–1950* (New York: Cambridge University Press, 2002), 17, 19.

103. Woodrow Wilson, "Men Are Governed by Their Emotions," public address, July 4, 1916, quoted in *The New Democracy: Presidential Messages, Addresses, and Public Papers (1913–1917) by Woodrow Wilson*, ed. Ray Stannard Baker and William E. Dodd (New York: Harper & Brothers, 1926), 2:225.

104. Will H. Hays, "What is Being Done for Motion Pictures" (speech), October 5, 1923, 8, Will Hays Papers, I, reel 12, quoted in Trumpbour, *Selling Hollywood to the World*, 17.

105. "Trade Follows the Motion Pictures," *Commerce Reports*, January 22, 1923, 191; and Edward Lowry, "Trade Follows the Film," *SEP*, November 7, 1925, 12; both quoted in Grieveson, *Cinema and the Wealth of Nations*, 6. Lowry was the MPPDA's European representative.

106. Hays, *Memoirs*, 334.

107. Trumpbour, *Selling Hollywood to the World*, 18–19, 64.

108. Victoria De Grazia, *Irresistible Empire: America's Advance through 20th-Century Europe* (Cambridge, MA: Belknap Press, 2005), 288.

109. Victoria De Grazia, "Mass Culture and Sovereignty: The American Challenge to European Cinema, 1920–1960," *JMH* (March 1989): 60.

110. Neil Gabler, *An Empire of Their Own: How the Jews Invented Hollywood* (New York: Doubleday, 1988), 189.

111. Jackson Lears, *Fables of Abundance: A Cultural History of Advertising in America* (New York: Basic Books, 1994), 222–23.

112. Emily Rosenberg, *Spreading the American Dream: American Economic and Cultural Expansion, 1890–1945* (New York: Hill and Wang, 1982) , 79–86.

113. Herbert Howe, "Is Mary Pickford Finished?," *LAT*, March 25, 1925, C7.

114. Howe, "Is Mary Pickford Finished?," C11.

115. Howe, C11.

116. "Mary Pickford Secretly Has Her Curls Shorn; Forsakes Little-Girl Roles to Be 'Grown Up,'" *NYT*, June 23, 1928, 1.

117. Zukor, quoted in Tibbetts and Welsh, *Fairbanks and the American Century*, 145. Chaplin also claimed to have come up with the moniker.

118. Tibbetts and Welsh, 187. The two *Zorro* films are *The Mark of Zorro* (1920) and *Don Q, Son of Zorro* (1925).

119. Siegfried Kracauer, *The Mass Ornament: Weimar Essays* (Cambridge, MA: Harvard University Press, 1995), 293, quoted in Tibbetts and Welsh, *Fairbanks and the American Century*, 91.

120. Studlar, *This Mad Masquerade*, 82–83.

121. Studlar, 81.

122. One notable exception was the darker *The Gaucho* (1928), which presents "a spiritual fervor and an element of seething sexuality the likes of which has never been seen before." Jeffrey Vance, *Douglas Fairbanks* (Berkeley: University of California Press, 2008), 227.

123. Goessel, *First King of Hollywood*, 190.

124. Richard Griffith, *The Movie Stars* (Garden City, NY: Doubleday, 1970), 151.

125. Griffith, *Movie Stars*, 151.

126. Mary Pickford, "Ambassadors," *SEP,* 23 Aug 23, 1930, 7, quoted in Whitfield, "Laws of Attraction," 167.

127. The 1921 Emergency Quota Act and the 1924 Johnson-Reed Act reduced the number of foreign newcomers to pitifully small quotas. But in truth, the war itself had sharply reduced the numbers of Europeans relocating to America.

4. THE DIVO, NEW-STYLE HEAVY

1. Adela Rogers St. Johns, "The Six Next Sellers," *Photoplay,* March 1922, 34.

2. Richard Abel, *Americanizing the Movies and "Movie-Mad" Audiences, 1910–1914* (Berkeley: University of California University Press, 2006), chapters 2 and 3.

3. Louella O. Parsons, "Propaganda! An Earnest Consideration of the Inestimable Part Being Played by the Motion Picture in the Great War," *Photoplay,* September 1918, 43.

4. Max Watson, "Making Americans by Movies," *Photoplay,* May 1921, 42.

5. "The Melting Pot," editorial, *Photoplay,* November 1918, 21.

6. Harry Carr, "The Hollywood Boulevardier Chats," *MPC,* June 1923, 74.

7. Gail Bederman, *Manliness and Civilization: A Cultural History of Gender and Race in the United States, 1880–1917* (Chicago: University of Chicago Press, 1995), 5.

8. Bederman, *Manliness and Civilization*, 13.

9. Bederman, 13.

10. In 1869 neurologist George Miller Beard had introduced the term *neurasthenia* as a condition showing symptoms of fatigue, anxiety, and depressed mood, whose cause he attributed to modern civilization.

11. The literature on the flapper is conspicuous. See Angela J. Latham, *Posing a Threat: Flappers, Chorus Girls, and Other Brazen Performers of the American 1920s* (Hanover, NH: University Press of New England, 2000). On youth, see Paula S. Fass's classic *The Damned and the Beautiful: American Youth in the 1920s* (New York: Oxford University Press, 1977).

12. Kevin White, *The First Sexual Revolution: The Emergence of Male Heterosexuality in Modern America* (New York: New York University Press, 1993), 26.

13. Carlos G. Groppa, *The Tango in the United States: A History* (Jefferson, NC: McFarland, 2004).

14. This possibility rested on a eugenic precondition: Italians were legally white even though their racialized representations persistently distanced them from the Anglo-Saxon core of American society. I have discussed Beban's films in *Italy in Early American Cinema:*

Race, Landscape, and the Picturesque (Bloomington: Indiana University Press, 2010), chapter 6.

15. See Giuliana Muscio, *Napoli/New York/Hollywood: Film between Italy and the United States* (New York: Fordham University Press, 2018), 100–156.

16. Hilary Hallett, *Go West, Young Women! The Rise of Early Hollywood* (Berkeley: University of California Press, 2013), 11.

17. In 1922, film productions made in Hollywood amounted to about 84 percent of the American film output and two-thirds of the international one. Hallett, *Go West, Young Women!*, 5, 7.

18. Hallett, 14. Some of the most important figures included actresses Clara Kimball Young, Alla Nazimova, Mary Pickford, Gloria Swanson, and Norma Talmadge; screenwriters Anita Loos, Frances Marion, and June Mathis; director-producer Lois Weber; and critics Adela Rogers St. Johns and Louella Parsons.

19. Both the industry and American mainstream culture sought to reassure fans that female filmmakers did not aim to subvert gender norms. According to *Photoplay,* they were "not temperamental 'artistes,' not short haired advanced feminists, not faddists, just regular women of good education and adaptability who have caught the trick of writing and understand the picture mind." "How Twelve Famous Women Scenario Writers Succeeded," *Photoplay,* August 1923, 31.

20. See Ben Singer, *Melodrama and Modernity: Early Sensational Cinema and Its Contexts* (New York: Columbia University Press, 2001), 221–87.

21. Shelley Stamp, *Movie-Struck Girls: Women and Motion Picture Culture after the Nickelodeon* (Princeton, NJ: Princeton University Press, 2000), 153, 152.

22. The question of women's crucial contribution to and eventual marginalization from early Hollywood has been the source of intense historiographical debates. See Jane Gaines, "Pink-Slipped: What Happened to Women in the Silent Film Industry?," in *Wiley-Blackwell History of American Film,* ed. Cynthia Lucia, Roy Grundmann, and Art Simon (Malden, MA: Wiley Blackwell, 2012), 155–77.

23. Shelley Stamp, "Women and the Silent Screen," in Lucia, Grundmann, and Simon, *Wiley-Blackwell History of American Film,* 181–206.

24. Stamp, "Women and the Silent Screen." Some of them are well known (i.e., Clara Beranger, Ouida Bergere, and Frances Marion), others are not (i.e., Sada Cowan, Jane Murfin, Olga Printzlau, and Eve Unsell).

25. Frederick Lewis Allen, *Only Yesterday: An Informal History of the 1920s* (1931; New York: Harper Perennial, 2000), 83.

26. See Warren I. Susman, "'Personality' and the Making of Twentieth-Century Culture," in *Culture as History: The Transformation of American Society in the Twentieth Century* (1973; New York: Pantheon, 1984), 271–86.

27. Lary May, *Screening Out the Past: The Birth of Mass Culture and the Motion Picture Industry* (Chicago: University of Chicago Press, 1983), 235; and Sumiko Higashi, *Cecil B. DeMille and American Culture: The Silent Era* (Berkeley: University of California Press, 1994), 142–78.

28. The myth of the Latin lover is a compound of different narrative strands, initially crystallized in the seventeenth-century Spanish play about Don Juan, a womanizer who before death repents all his wrongdoings, and in Giacomo Casanova's life story. The figure

of Don Juan pervaded the works of several writers and artists, from Molière and Lord Byron to Mozart, whose popular opera *Don Giovanni* (1787) influenced works by Hoffmann, Pushkin, Bernard Shaw, and Camus.

29. By comparison, the famous Neapolitan tenor Enrico Caruso, who died in August 1921, paid frequent and publicized visits to New York's Little Italy and played a struggling immigrant sculptor in the popular film *My Cousin* (1918).

30. *Motion Picture Studio Directory and Trade Annual* (New York: Motion Picture News, 1918), 193, quoted in Emily Leider, *Dark Lover: The Life and Death of Rudolph Valentino* (New York; Macmillan, 2004), 87.

31. While in New York, he worked as an extra in productions including *My Official Wife* (Vitagraph, 1914), *Seventeen* (Paramount, 1916), and *The Foolish Virgin* (Clara Kimball Young Film Corporation, 1916).

32. "Contemporary Dancing Has Evolved the Concave Man," *NYT,* January 14, 1914, S5: 11. See also Richard Barry, "Tango Pirates Infest Broadway," *NYT Magazine,* May 30, 1915, S5:16.

33. Colin Evans, *The Valentino Affair* (Guilford, CT: Lyons Press, 2014). Unlike Evans, Emily Leider located the court documents and accessed Valentino's divorce-hearing testimony. Leider, *Dark Lover,* 70.

34. "Dancing 'Count' Held in Vice Raid: Rodolpho Guglielmi Taken by Squad Headed by Swann Assistant," *NYT,* September 6, 1916, 4. See also Irving Shulman, *Valentino* (New York: Trident Press, 1967), 113.

35. A few newspaper retractions appeared on May 17, 1920, without, however, taking responsibility for journalistic wrongdoing. See Evans, *Valentino Affair,* 255–56.

36. Herbert Howe, "The Last Days of Valentino," *NMM,* n.d, 1928, 42, in MNC-RC. I am grateful to Paola Bortolaso and Silvio Alovisio for helping to locate this hard-to-find article.

37. Interestingly, to make ends meet, he sought a referral for a job in the Napa Valley vineyards from A. P. Giannini. He then received training to be a salesman for security bonds, only to find out that Americans were buying nothing but Liberty Bonds.

38. *Exhibitors Herald and Motography,* December 21, 1918, 51, lists the film among late December 1918 releases and indicates a length of seven reels. The AFI record suggests that the film's release was postponed due to the influenza epidemic. I inspected a six-reel restored version of the film, one reel shorter than the original, at the CINEMATEK (Brussels).

39. Shulman, *Valentino,* 98.

40. One of the film's final intertitles appealed to all possible authorities: "Marriage is not consummated *without* wedlock. The Church and State are one on this great point. You are not his wife—and never have been!"

41. Paramount, *The Married Virgin* ad, *MPW,* December 14, 1918, 1176.

42. His Italian first name also appeared in many foreign versions, including Rodolpho, Rudolph, Rudolf, and Rodolfo. Some of the initial combinations were M. Rodolpho De Valentina, Rudolph Volantino, and Rodolph (or Rudolph) Valentine.

43. While in *A Society Sensation* (1918), he is a good-natured American bachelor, in the comedy *All Night* (1918) and *Passion's Playground* (1920), he is respectively an aristocratic suitor and an Italian prince. The list of his credits also includes *Once to Every Woman* (1920), in which he is an Italian admirer who, rejected, attempts to murder his beloved before killing himself, and *Stolen Moments* (1920), in which he is a suave South American novelist.

44. "Eyes of Youth," *Variety,* November 7, 1919, 98.

45. Nazimova had established a social circle known as the Garden of Alla at her residence on Sunset Boulevard. Jean Acker and June Mathis were regulars, as Valentino and Natasha Rambova would be later.

46. Leider, *Dark Lover,* 103.

47. "June Mathis among Leaders in Advancement of Films," *LAT,* October 19, 1926, 24; and Thomas H. Slater, "June Mathis's *Classified:* One Woman's Response to Modernism," *Journal of Film and Video* (Summer 1998): 3.

48. "June Mathis Dies While at the Theatre," *NYT,* June 27, 1927, 1.

49. Donna Casella, "Feminism and the Female Author: The Not So Silent Career of the Woman Scenarist in Hollywood—1896–1930," *Quarterly Review of Film and Video* (September 2006): 232.

50. During the war, Mathis wrote daring female characters who fought against the enemy in *To Hell with the Kaiser* (1918) and *The Legion of Death* (1918).

51. Thomas H. Slater, "June Mathis's *The Legion of Death:* Melodrama and the Realities of Women in World War I," *Women's Studies* (September 2008): 833–44. Studlar wrote of 1920s Valentino as a representative figure of a "veritable obsession with the attainment of masculinity." *This Mad Masquerade: Stardom and Masculinity in the Jazz Age* (New York: Columbia University Press, 1996), 12–13. Hansen noted that "Valentino called into question the very idea of a stable sexual identity." *Babel and Babylon: Spectatorship in American Silent Film* (Cambridge, MA: Harvard University Press, 1991), 264.

52. Thomas H. Slater, "June Mathis's Valentino Scripts: Images of Male 'Becoming' after the Great War," *Cinema Journal* (Fall 2010): 100–101.

53. Slater, "June Mathis's Valentino Scripts," 102.

54. Carolyn Lowrey, *The First One Hundred Noted Men and Women of the Screen* (New York: Moffat, Yard, 1920), 118; and Jolo, "To Hell with the Kaiser," *Variety,* February 8, 1918, 39.

55. Lowrey, *Noted Men and Women of the Screen,* 118.

56. Lowrey, *Noted Men and Women of the Screen,* 118. In addition to Lowrey, others stressed Mathis's professional training and talent. In early 1923, for example, Barrett C. Kiesling noted: "After starting as a stage actress, she spent two years learning the art of writing stories and scripts." "June Mathis: Her Career," *Scenario Bulletin Digest* (March 1923): 5–6.

57. June Mathis, "Scenario Writers Must Find a Theme," *NYT,* April 15, 1923, S7: 3.

58. "Mathis," *Film Daily,* June 7, 1925, 115.

59. "Mathis," 115.

60. Years later *NYT* film critic Bosley Crowther gave credence to this story: "It was she who early insisted that Metro should make a picture from Blasco Ibanez' great popular novel. [. . .] The novel had been read and considered by virtually every producer in the business, and the general opinion was that it could not be made into a successful film. [. . .] But June insisted." Crowther, *The Lion's Share* (New York. E. P. Dutton, 1957), 55.

61. "Metro to Produce Ibanez's Novel 'Four Horsemen of the Apocalypse,' Author Will Aid in Making the Picture," *MPW,* December 20, 1919, 977. Terry Ramsaye also reported that Rowland bought the novel's filming rights against his studio's advice. *A Million and One Nights* (New York: Simon and Schuster, 1926), 799.

62. "Metro to Produce Ibanez's Novel," 977.

63. "June Mathis Confers with Ibanez on 'Four Horsemen of Apocalypse,'" *MPW,* January 17, 1920, 431. They appeared in a now lost promotional film to "be used as a pre-release trailer." See "Ibanez at Metro," *MPW,* February 21, 1920, 1233, 1249.

64. "Entry of Big Business Means New Blood, System, and Death of Waste," *MPW,* December 27, 1919, 1124.

65. "Entry of Big Business," 1124.

66. Edward Weizel, "Talking 'Shop' with June Mathis Brings Out 'Nothing But the Truth,'" *MPW,* December 27, 1919, 1141.

67. See A. Grove Day and Edgar Knowlton, *V. Blasco Ibáñez* (New York: Twayne Publishers, 1972), 79.

68. In 1926, the *Four Horsemen's* director, Rex Ingram, filmed another work of the Spanish novelist, the spy story *Mare Nostrum* (Metro-Goldwyn Corp., 1918). In 1926, MGM produced two ambitious Garbo vehicles, *The Torrent* and *The Temptress* from other Ibáñez works.

69. Day and Knowlton, *V. Blasco Ibáñez,* 95.

70. Santiago Maestro Cano, "Blasco Ibáñez: Un novelista para el cine," *Espéculo,* March–July 1997, 7. My thanks to Yeidy Rivero for help with this quote.

71. "Metro to Produce Ibanez's Novel," 977.

72. Blasco Ibáñez to Martínez de la Riva, Menton, October 15, 1921, in Ramón Martínez de la Riva, *Blasco Ibáñez: Su vida, su obra, su muerte, sus mejores páginas* (Madrid: Editorial Mundo Latino, 1929), 161.

73. See "June Mathis Confers with Ibanez," 431; and Liam O'Leary, *Rex Ingram: Master of the Silent Cinema* (London: British Film Institute, 1991), 113. Some of his themes and tone, most notably his anticlericalism and radical progressivism, were filtered out of his American reputation, but not his heavy-handed symbolism.

74. Benjamin B. Hampton, *History of American Film Industry* (1931; New York: Dover Publications, 1970), 310.

75. Joan M. Vale, "Tintype Ambitions—Three Vaudevillians in Search of Hollywood Fame" (PhD diss., University of San Diego, 1985), 74, 81, 80.

76. See *The Four Horsemen of the Apocalypse,* screenplay (in English), in Fondo Paolo Balboni, PABA0001, MNC. One of the film's intertitles also defines Julio as "our young tango hero." June Mathis, *The Four Horsemen of the Apocalypse,* title sheet, December 14, 1920, 80, file copy 86M, Turner/MGM Scripts, f.F.741, AMPAS.

77. Vicente Blasco Ibáñez, *The Four Horsemen of the Apocalypse,* trans. Charlotte Brewster Jordan (New York: E. P. Dutton, 1918), 76. Gavin Lambert writes that Mathis's addition of "a sword dance into one of the Tangier café scenes" in her script for *Eye for Eye* (1918), later retitled *L'Occident,* "anticipated Valentino's tango scene." Lambert, *Nazimova: A Biography* (New York: Knopf, 1997), 201–2.

78. Ibáñez, *Four Horsemen,* 76.

79. Ibáñez, 110, 111.

80. Ibáñez, 110.

81. Ibáñez, 111.

82. Ibáñez, 114

83. Ibáñez, 208, 210.

84. Ibáñez, 211–12.

85. Ibáñez, 223.

86. Ibáñez, 223. On his way to Paris, Julio experiences some form of internal turmoil and arrives in the capital aware that "a new impetus was going to fill the vacuum of his objectless existence." Ibañez, 295.

87. Ibáñez, 484–85, 488–89.

88. In the film's synopsis, Mathis writes: "Julio listened to his conscience, which convicted him of selfishness and told him he should fight for his father country's, for Marguerite's." "Synopsis (*The Four Horsemen*)," 3, file copy 1210, Turner/MGM Scripts, f.F.739, AMPAS.

89. "Entire French village had been built to be destroyed in Metro's *Four Horsemen*," *MPW*, September 11, 1920, 239. See also "Battle of Marne Shown on Screen in *The Four Horsemen of the Apocalypse*, *MPW*, September 25, 1920, 521.

90. "Metro Inaugurates Poster Contest to Exploit Ibanez's *The Four Horsemen*," *MPW*, December 25, 1920, 1051.

91. The caption below one of the photographs of Valentino in gaucho costume identified him as "Julio Desnoyers, in the Paris underworld," which indicates that the studio's publicity was following the novel's plot and not Mathis's script. "Putting Ibáñez on the Screen," *MPC*, March 1921, 62–63.

92. "Brilliant Throng of Spectators at Lyric Sees the Premiere of 'The Four Horsemen,'" *MPW*, March 19, 1921, 285. The film opened in Los Angeles on March 9.

93. "Brilliant Throng of Spectators," 285.

94. "'Four Horsemen,'" *MPW*, April 23, 1921, 852.

95. "Got the Pick of New York Windows for the 'Four Horsemen' Production," *MPW*, April 30, 1921, 961. Commercial arrangements among publishers, booksellers, and film distributors were not news. See "Tarzan Publishers Aid in Film Exploitation," *MPW*, October 19, 1918, 404.

96. "The Four Horsemen," *Motion Picture News*, March 5, 1921, 1859.

97. "The Four Horsemen," 1859.

98. Press sheet, *The Four Horsemen of the Apocalypse*, 28, 14–5, MFL, n.c. 31, no. 48 (microfilm), NYPL-TC.

99. "Metro Has Over 100 Road Companies Now Exhibiting 'The Four Horsemen,'" *MPW*, October 29, 1921, 1058. This article also notes that the film's special score, arranged by the prolific Hugo Riesenfeld, appealed to the country's "widely different audiences."

100. "Metro Has Over 100 Road Companies," 1058.

101. "*The Four Horsemen* Rides on the Screen," *LD*, March 26, 1921, 28.

102. Frederick James Smith, "The Celluloid Critic: The Newest Photoplays in Review," *MPP* (May 1921): 81.

103. "A Latin Lover," *Photoplay*, June 1921, 21.

104. Gordon Gassaway, "The Erstwhile Landscape Gardener," *MPM*, June 1921, 41.

105. Gassaway, "Erstwhile Landscape Gardener," 92. Here the reference to "pink powder" is invested with racial meaning, to cover up the swarthiness of his complexion. A few years later it famously stressed his difference in homophobic terms.

106. Gassaway, 92.

107. Gassaway, 92.

108. Ramsaye, *A Million*, 801.

109. Gassaway, "Erstwhile Landscape Gardener," 92.

110. Anthony Slide, *Inside the Hollywood Fan Magazine: A History of Star Makers, Fabricators, and Gossip Mongers* (Jackson: University Press of Mississippi, 2010), 78–79.

111. Herbert Howe, "Success—and the Morning After," *PPM*, August 1921, 30.

112. Howe ghostwrote letters for Valentino and distributed them to possible reviewers, especially columnists. One was Gladys Hall, who in April 1922 began a syndicated newspaper column, "The Diary of a Professional Movie Fan," for Copyright Metropolitan Newspaper Service. Gladys mentions one such letter from Valentino in the drafting of a column, "Me, Myself—Some Facts about R. Valentino," (August 7, 1922), now in Gladys Hall Papers, Scrapbook 1922–1923, AMPAS-SC.

113. Howe, "Success—and the Morning After," 30–31 (italics mine).

114. Howe, 31–32.

115. Howe, 96.

116. Jolo, "The Uncharted Seas," *Variety*, June 3, 1921, 41.

117. "Critics Say 'Conquering Power' Is Ingram's Greatest Picture," *MPW*, July 23, 1921, 422.

118. Rambova and Valentino had married in Mexico on May 13, 1922, even though a year had not passed since his divorce from his first wife. As a result, Valentino was briefly jailed for bigamy. They remarried on March 14, 1923. Rambova (whose real name was Winifred Kimball Shaughnessy) studied under the Russian ballet dancer and choreographer Theodore Kosloff in New York. For a profile, see Michael Morris, *Madame Valentino* (New York: Abbeville Press, 1991).

119. *Photoplay* was extremely critical of the film's "artificiality" but deemed Valentino's Armand to be "as good as it is permitted to be." "The Shadow Stage," *Photoplay*, December 1921, 62.

120. "Nazimova's Modern 'Camille' Uses Autos and Late Styles," *MPW*, August 20, 1921, 817.

121. Questions and Answers, *Photoplay*, October 1921, 76.

5. THE BALLYHOOED ART OF GOVERNING ROMANCE

1. Irving Shulman, *Valentino* (New York: Trident Press, 1967), 163.

2. Frederick Lewis Allen, *Only Yesterday: An Informal History of the 1920s* (1931; New York: Harper Perennial, 2000), 161.

3. Billie Melman, *Woman and the Popular Imagination in the Twenties* (London: Macmillan, 1988), 46, 90; Sarah Wintle, "*The Sheik*: What Can Be Made of a Daydream," *Women: A Cultural Review* 7, no. 3 (1996): 292; and Shulman, *Valentino*, 160.

4. "*The Sheik* by E. M. Hull," *Literary Review*, March 5, 1921, 12; and "Latest Works in Fiction," *NYT*, May 1, 1921, 25, both quoted in Shulman, *Valentino*, 160; and Patricia Raub, "Issues of Passion and Power in E. M. Hull's *The Sheik*," *Women's Studies: An Interdisciplinary Journal*, March 1992, 126.

5. In *The Sheik*, Diana's brother, Sir Aubrey, had called Sheik Ahmed a "damned nigger." E. M. Hull, *The Sheik* (Cutchogue, NY: Buccaneer Books, 1921), 134.

6. Evelyn Bach, "Sheik Fantasies: Orientalism and Feminine Desire in the Desert Romance," *Hecate* (January 1997): 11.

7. Bach, "Sheik Fantasies," 11.

8. Bach, 12.

9. Bach, 15.

10. Jesse L. Lasky, with Don Weldon, *I Blow My Own Horn* (Garden City, NY: Doubleday, 1957), 148–49, 147–48.

11. Joan M. Vale, "Tintype Ambitions—Three Vaudevillians in Search of Hollywood Fame" (PhD diss., University of San Diego, 1985), 85.

12. Hull, *The Sheik*, 134.

13. "The Shadow Stage," *Photoplay*, January 1922, 67.

14. "The Shadow Stage," 67.

15. Stephen C. Caton, "*The Sheik*: Instabilities of Race and Gender in Transatlantic Popular Culture of the Early 1920s," in *Noble Dreams, Wicked Pleasures: Orientalism in America, 1870–1930*, ed. Holly Edwards (Princeton, NJ: Princeton University Press, 2000), 114.

16. Bach, "Sheik Fantasies," 17.

17. Hull, *The Sheik*, 13.

18. "The Kashmiri Song! It makes me think of India." Hull, *The Sheik*, 13–14.

19. Bach, "Sheik Fantasies," 22.

20. Karen Chow, "Popular Sexual Knowledge and Women's Agency in 1920s England: Marie Stopes's 'Married Love' and E. M. Hull's 'The Sheik,'" *Feminist Review* (Fall 1999): 79.

21. Gaylyn Studlar, "'Out-Salomeing Salomé:' Dance, The New Woman, and Fan Magazine Orientalism," *Michigan Quarterly Review* (Fall 1995): 487–510.

22. Wintle, "*The Sheik*," 294.

23. Hull, *The Sheik*, 81, 57; and Bach, "Sheik Fantasies," 24.

24. Chow, "Popular Sexual Knowledge," 81.

25. Caton, "*The Sheik*," 112.

26. Even without availing herself of recent works in whiteness studies, Hansen made the same point clear in *Babel and Babylon: Spectatorship in American Silent Film* (Cambridge: Harvard University Press, 1991), 260.

27. His sudden control of a violent impulse recalls how Roberto in *The Married Virgin* could not continue his violent pursuit of Mary once her servant showed him a cross.

28. Caton, "*The Sheik*," 114 (italics in the original).

29. Caton, 115.

30. Bach, "Sheik Fantasies," 37.

31. "Paramount Plans Exceptional Publicity for Miss E. M. Hull, Who Wrote Novel, 'The Sheik,'" *MPW*, October 8, 1921, 685.

32. Marshall Frantz was a gifted illustrator whose paintings appeared on the cover of popular books as well as pulp magazines such as *Everybody's Magazine*.

33. "Paramount Plans Exceptional Publicity," 685. See also "Frantz Designs 'Sheik' Poster," *MPW*, September 24, 1921, 430.

34. "'The Sheik,' from Edith M. Hull's Novel, Completed: Paramount Says It Will Be the Sensation of the Year," *MPW*, October 1, 1921, 534. Decades later in his memoirs, Lasky instead stressed the exceptional degree of publicity work that went into promoting the film and "manufacturing a Valentino." Lasky, *I Blow My Own Horn*, 149.

35. *The Sheik*, advertisement, *MPW*, October 22, 1921, 830–31.

36. "53,629 See 'The Sheik,'" *Wid's*, November 10, 1921, 1.

37. "Desert Love," *MPC*, November 1921, 38.

38. Lawrence owed his celebrity to Lowell Thomas's illustrated lectures titled "With Allenby in Palestine and Lawrence in Arabia" and remained a popular subject of books, illustrations, and gossip throughout the 1920s. In 1934, as an expert on celebrity shows, Thomas served as on- and off-camera commentator in *Mussolini Speaks!* (Columbia Pictures).

39. I have discussed Italian immigrants' racial standing in the context of whiteness studies in Bertellini, *Italy in Early American Cinema: Race, Landscape, and the Picturesque* (Bloomington: Indiana University Press, 2010), 165–70.

40. H. H. Faulkner, "A Phrenological Study of Some Famous Stars," *Photoplay*, March 1922, 30–31.

41. The interview appeared only four months after Howe's first biographical profile of the Italian actor ("Success—and the Morning After," *PPM*, August 1921), which I discussed in the previous chapter.

42. Howe, "Hitting the Hookah with Rudie," *MPC*, December 1921, 19.

43. Howe, "Hitting the Hookah, 19, 72.

44. Howe, 72.

45. "Wife Accuses Valentino," *Variety*, May 20, 1921, 44; and Cal York, "Play and Players," *Photoplay*, August 1921, 92.

46. Howe, "Hitting the Hookah," 72.

47. Willis Goldbeck, "The Perfect Lover," *MPM*, May 1922, 94 (italics mine).

48. Goldbeck, "Perfect Lover," 41, 94. In this interview, he also railed against Prohibition, a patronizing practice that in his view established "class privilege" (40).

49. Herbert Howe, "What Are the Matinee Idols Made Of?" *Photoplay*, April 1923, 41.

50. Adela Rogers St. Johns, "The Six Next Sellers," *Photoplay*, March 1922, 34.

51. Regarding the volume of Valentino's fan mail as an indicator of spectators' spontaneous consensus, Cecil B. DeMille told *Photoplay*: "Women are now divided into two classes. Those who write letters to Rodolf Valentino and those who can't write." Cal York, "Plays and Players," *Photoplay*, June 1922, 53.

52. Herbert Howe, "Who Will the New Stars Be?" *MPM*, January 1922, 95.

53. Herbert Howe, "The Hollywood Boulevardier Chats," *MPC*, February 1922, 65.

54. Woodrow Wilson, *An Old Master, and Other Political Essays* (New York: C. Scribner's Sons, 1893), 62, 90.

55. Wilson, *An Old Master*, 85–86.

56. Woodrow Wilson, *Division and Reunion, 1829–1889* (New York: Longman, Green, 1894), 111.

57. Herbert Howe, "They Can't Fool the Public," *Photoplay*, June 1922, 47.

58. Howe, "They Can't Fool the Public," 111.

59. Biographer Emily Leider has maintained this in *Dark Lover: The Life and Death of Rudolph Valentino* (New York; Macmillan, 2004), 46. In 1994 Elinor Glyn's biographer Joan Hardwick had claimed, without offering much evidence, that Glyn ghostwrote these autobiographical installments. Hardwick, *Addicted to Romance: The Life and Adventures of Elinor Glyn* (London: Andrew Deutsch, 1994), 244. More recently, Anne Morey and Laura Horak have relied, with some caution, on Hardwick's position on this issue. See Morey, "Elinor Glyn as Hollywood Labourer," *FH* 18, no.2 (2006): 117n24; and Horak, "'Would You Like to Sin with Elinor Glyn?' Film as a Vehicle of Sensual Education," *Camera Obscura* 74 (2010): 111n49.

60. "The Most Talked of Man in America! / The Life Story of Rodolph Valentino, By Himself," *Photoplay*, January 1923, 86.

61. "An Open Letter from Valentino to the American Public," *Photoplay*, January 1923, 34.

62. Herbert Howe, Close-Ups and Long Shots, *Photoplay*, February 1923, 58.

63. Herbert Howe, "What Europe Thinks of American Stars," *Photoplay*, February 1923, 97.

64. *Blood and Sand* was released in the United States on August 5, 1922. It was released in Italy as *Sangue e arena* in January 1925.

65. Herbert Howe, "Mary Pickford's Favorite Stars," *Photoplay*, January 1924, 29.

66. Herbert Howe, Close-Ups and Long Shots, *Photoplay*, February 1924, 40.

67. Howe, Close-Ups and Long Shots, February 1924, 40.

68. Howe, 41.

69. "Speaking of Pictures," *Photoplay*, March 1924, 94.

70. Herbert Howe, Close-Ups and Long Shots, *Photoplay*, January 1925, 47.

71. Howe, Close-Ups and Long Shots, January 1925, 47.

72. Herbert Howe, Close-Ups and Long Shots, *Photoplay*, October 1924, 38.

73. Herbert Howe, "Inside Life Stories of *Photoplay* Staff Writers," *Photoplay*, July 1925, 55. Comparing individuals to Mussolini was common in Howe's columns.

74. Herbert Howe, "Here Are the Real Box Office Stars," *Photoplay*, June 1926, 29.

75. Lasky, *I Blew My Own Horn*, 140.

76. Hilary Hallett, *Go West, Young Women! The Rise of Early Hollywood* (Berkeley: University of California Press, 2013), 124, 129.

77. Horak, "'Would You Like to Sin with Elinor Glyn?,'" 75–76.

78. Elinor Glyn, *Romantic Adventure: Being the Autobiography of Elinor Glyn* (New York: Dutton, 1937), 299.

79. Hallett, *Go West, Young Women!*, 120 (italics mine).

80. Both Alexander Walker and Joan Hardwick claim that Glyn ghostwrote a few articles for Valentino, including this one. Walker, *Stardom: The Hollywood Phenomenon* (New York: Stein and Day, 1970), 163n; and Hardwick, *Addicted to Romance*, 244.

81. Rudolph Valentino, "Woman and Love," *Photoplay*, March 1922, 106.

82. Valentino, "Woman and Love," 42.

83. In the film's synopsis, Mathis wrote that as Doña Sol "makes violent love to him, [Gallardo/Valentino] loses his head." Synopsis of *Blood and Sand*, 3, Paramount Scripts File, B 557 #162, AMPAS-SC.

84. "*Blood and Sand* Going Big," *MPN*, September 9, 1922, 1281.

85. "*Blood and Sand* a Winner," *MPN*, August 26, 1922, 1053.

86. Peter Milne, "*Blood and Sand*," *MPN*, September 2, 1922, 1167.

87. "*Blood and Sand*," *Variety*, August 11, 1922, 32.

88. Michael Morris, *Madam Valentino: The Many Lives of Natascha Rambova* (New York: Abbeville Press, 1991), 99, 103.

89. Walker, *Stardom*, 168.

90. Gene Sheridan, "*Moran of the Lady Letty*," *Photoplay*, April 1922, 49.

91. Sheridan, "*Moran of the Lady Letty*," 102.

92. Sheridan, 102.

93. Sheridan, 103.

94. Maude Cheatham, "Fighters of the Screen," *MPC*, May 1923, 76.

95. Dick Dorgan, "Giving 'The Sheik' the Once Over from the Ringside," *Photoplay*, April 1922, 90–92.

96. Leider, *Dark Lover*, 169–170.

97. Dorgan, "Giving 'The Sheik' the Once Over," 90.

98. On Rogers's "commonsense humor," "rough-hewn wisdom," and "cowpoke identity" with regard to this film, see Mark Lynn Anderson, *Twilight of the Idols: Hollywood and the Human Sciences in 1920s America* (Berkeley: University of California Press, 2011), 151–54.

99. "The Vogue of Valentino," editor's introduction, *MPM*, February 1923, 27.

100. "Vogue of Valentino," 27–28.

101. "Vogue of Valentino," 28–29.

102. "Vogue of Valentino," 100.

103. Adela Rogers St. Johns, "What Kind of Men Attract," *Photoplay*, April 1924, 40, 110.

104. St. Johns, "What Kind of Men Attract," 110.

105. Dick Dorgan. "A Song of Hate," *Photoplay*, July 1922, 26.

106. Frederick James Smith, "Does Decency Help or Hinder?," *Photoplay*, November 1924, 38.

107. Cal York, "Gossip East And West," *Photoplay*, April 1924, 71.

108. Macfadden's publishing portfolio included the tabloid newspaper *New York Graphic* and *Movie Weekly* (1921–1924). For many years he relied on the public relations counseling of Edward Bernays, the self-professed master of the public relations business.

109. Rudolf Valentino, "The Romance of Rudolf Valentino's Adventurous Life," Parts 1 and 2, *MW*, February 18 and 25, 1922.

110. Rudolph Valentino, *Day Dreams* (New York: Macfadden Publications, 1923).

111. The link between the beauty firm and the Valentinos was not casual. Ullman was aware that Natacha Rambova was the stepdaughter of Richard Hudnut, who had founded a successful cosmetic firm. See Evelyn Zumaya, *Affairs Valentino: A Special Edition* (Turin: Viale Industria Pubblicazioni, 2015), 169; and Morris, *Madam Valentino*, 102, 117–18.

112. David O. Selznick directed a two-reel film of this beauty contest: *Rudolph Valentino and His 88 American Beauties* (1923).

113. A photograph appearing in early 1924 showed ironically the sister actresses Viola Diana and Shirley Mason impersonating the Valentinos while dancing the tango. "Natasha e Rudie!" *Photoplay*, January 1924, 67.

114. James R. Quirk, "Speaking of Pictures," *Photoplay*, September 1924, 27.

115. Cal York, "Studio News and Gossip East and West," *Photoplay*, September 1924, 50.

116. James R. Quirk, "Presto Chango Valentino!," *Photoplay*, May 1925, 36–37.

117. Zumaya, *Affairs Valentino*, 203. Several of her findings rely on the manuscript of the George Ullman memoir that apparently she had unprecedented access to. Zumaya published it together with a reprint of Ullman's 1926 biography of Valentino in *The S. George Ullman Memoir / The Real Rudolph Valentino by the Man Who Knew Him Best* (Turin: Viale Industria Pubblicazioni, 2014).

118. It was a very generous contract for two pictures with unprecedented conditions: he had to be consulted regarding the screenplays and was given final approval over the films' publicity. What he was denied was artistic control over the films. The first UA production

was *The Eagle* (November 8, 1925).

119. Divorce papers were filed in France on January 18, 1926. See Zumaya, *Affairs Valentino*, 307.

120. Victoria Carter, "Rudy, Be Free and Wild!," *Photoplay*, June 1926, 112.

121. Quirk, "Presto Chango Valentino!," 117.

122. "R. Valentino to Change His Act?," *NYW*, November 22, 1925, reel 16, RV Scrapbook 1921–1926, NYPL-TC.

6. STUNTS AND PLEBISCITES

1. Cal York, "Studio News and Gossip: East and West," *Photoplay*, February 1925, 61. Reichenbach had worked in Italy as an "advertising man" for the CPI during World War I.

2. Margaret Caroline Wells, "What!!! Valentino???," *Photoplay*, February 1925, 72.

3. Alma Whitaker "Secrets of Valentino's Life," *LAT*, December 21, 1924), n.p., quoted in Evelyn Zumaya, *Affairs Valentino* (Turin: Viale Industriale Pubblicazioni, 2015), 249.

4. Glendon Allvine, "The Press Agent Who is Paid $1,000 a Week," *Photoplay*, August 1926, 117.

5. E. M. Hull, *The Son of the Sheik* (New York: A. L. Burt, 1925), 4, 8, 7.

6. Miriam Hansen, *Babel and Babylon* (Cambridge, MA: Harvard University Press, 1991), 263.

7. Willis Goldbeck, "The Perfect Lover," *MPM*, May 1922, 40.

8. Mark Lynn Anderson, *Twilight of the Idols: Hollywood and the Human Sciences in 1920s America* (Berkeley: University of California Press, 2011), 89–90.

9. Anderson, *Twilight of the Idols*, 110.

10. Anderson, 85. "Male gender deviance and working-class coarseness," writes Anderson, "often functioned as indexes of each other" (99).

11. Anderson, 90. Anderson also posits that "fairies were an unexceptional sight on the Lower East Side and a familiar part of the vibrant working-class culture of the Bowery and its dynamic mix of immigrant populations" (192n50). The reference work is George Chauncey, *Gay New York: Gender, Urban Culture, and the Making of the Gay Male World, 1890–1940* (New York: Basic Books, 1994).

12. Konrad Bercovici, *Around the World in New York* (New York: Century, 1924), 144.

13. Bertellini, "Duce/Divo: Displaced Rhetorics of Masculinity, Racial Identity, and Politics Among Italian-Americans in 1920's New York City," *Journal of Urban History*, July 2005, 685–726.

14. "Pink Powder Puffs," *CT*, July 18, 1926, I:10, quoted in Emily Leider, *Dark Lover: The Life and Death of Rudolph Valentino* (New York; Macmillan, 2004), 371–72.

15. Rudolph Valentino, "To the Man (?) Who Wrote the Editorial Headed 'Pink Powder Puffs' in Sunday's *Tribune*," *CHE*, July 19, 1926, quoted in George S. Ullman, *Valentino As I Knew Him* (New York: 1926), 187–88.

16. Anderson, *Twilight of the Idols*, 93. For Anderson the easy condemnation of the piece has had a negative impact: "a diminution of the importance of queer identities and queer meanings in the development of mass cultural institutions such as the star system." (96). On the notion that Valentino enabled the circulation of "new forms of same-sex and cross-sex queer affiliation and relationality," see Susan Potter, "Valentino's Lesbianism:

Stardom, Spectatorship, and Sexuality in 1920s Hollywood Cinema," *Framework* (Fall 2015): 274.

17. In the late 1970s, Gene Siskel revealed that "according to *Tribune* archivist Harold Hutchings, the editorial was written by John Herrick." Herrick was a reporter and editorial writer for the *Tribune*, which he joined in 1924. His motivation and the proof that he was the author of the "Pink Powder Puffs" article remain unknown. See Siskel, "The Valentino Legend Stirs a Revival," *CT*, June 28, 1977, A2; and "John Herrick, Formerly with the *Tribune*, Dies," *Chicago Sunday Tribune*, December 25, 1955, I:10.

18. Anderson, *Twilight of the Idols*, 93, 94.

19. Anderson, 97.

20. At the time Shapiro was working for V-L-S-E (Vitagraph-Lubin-Selig-Essanay). Other founding members included Harry Reichenbach, Frohman Amusement Company; Wallace Thompson, Paramount Pictures; Terry Ramsaye, Mutual Film; Charles C. Burr, Paramount Pictures; and Ben Schulberg, Famous Players Film Company. See "Motion Picture Publicity Men Organize," *MPW*, August 19, 1916, 1256.

21. Shapiro collected dozens of newspaper clippings and event programs featuring Valentino, probably all linked to his UA publicity role. See folder 11, Valentino, Rudolph, box 2, VMSP.

22. Victor Shapiro, interview by Elizabeth Dixon, April–May 1966 (transcribed June 1966), transcript, p. 12, tape I, box 7, Oral History Project, VMSP.

23. Shapiro, interview, p. 13, tape I.

24. Shapiro, interview, p. 13, tape I.

25. Shapiro, interview, p. 159, tape IV.

26. Shapiro, interview, p. 160, tape IV.

27. Shapiro, interview, p. 14, tape I.

28. Shapiro, interview, p. 155, tape IV.

29. Shapiro, interview, pp. 160–61, tape IV.

30. The Shapiro Papers include typewritten pages "reproduced for the transcriber," which appear to be imperfectly copied texts of the "Pink Powder Puffs" piece and Valentino's first and second responses. They are identified respectively as Exhibit A, Exhibit B, and Exhibit C. See folder 8, Valentino 1966, box 4, VMSP.

31. At the bottom of Valentino's response, Exhibit B, there is the red-penciled name of Patricia Dougherty, who at the time working for the *CHE*. See folder 8, Valentino 1966, box 4, VMSP.

32. Shapiro, interview, p. 162, tape IV.

33. Shapiro, interview, p. 162, tape IV.

34. Shapiro, interview, pp. 163–64, tape IV.

35. Shapiro, interview, p. 164, tape IV.

36. Emily Leider reports it as an unsourced clipping in Valentino scrapbook, n.p., NYPL. *Dark Lover*, 375.

37. Shapiro, interview, pp. 167–68, tape IV.

38. Shapiro, interview, p. 168, tape IV. I have been unable to confirm the identity and profession of said John Glasscock.

39. Shapiro, interview, p. 168, tape IV.

40. Shapiro, interview, pp. 169–70, tape IV.

41. The expression "Lafayette, we are here" was allegedly uttered in 1917 by a U.S. military officer at the tomb of the Marquis de Lafayette, who fought for the United States in the Revolutionary War. It was a sentence meant in repayment and as homage to him and the French people in general. Some have identified the person who spoke those words as General John Pershing. Shapiro, interview, p. 170, tape IV.

42. Press statement, folder 8, Valentino 1966, box 4, VMSP. The response appeared in the *Herald-Examiner* on July 30, 1926, and it is reprinted in Allan R. Ellenberger, *The Valentino Mystique: The Death and Afterlife of the Silent Film Idol* (New York: McFarland, 2005), 155.

43. Shapiro, interview, p. 171, tape IV.

44. Shapiro, interview, pp. 172, 175, tape IV.

45. Shapiro, interview, p. 176, tape IV.

46. Shapiro, interview, p. 177, tape IV. Shapiro does not actually reveal whether and how UA managed the bulletins that the hospital was releasing several times a day.

47. For examples of 1926 newsreel coverage of the Divo's death, see *International News* 8, nos. 69, 70; and *The Passing of Rodolph Valentino,* now in Hearst Metrotone News Collection, UCLA-FTA.

48. Mia Fineman, *Faking It: Manipulated Photography Before Photoshop* (New York: Metropolitan Museum of Art, 2012), 144.

49. Frank Mallen, *Sauce for the Gander* (White Plains, NY: Baldwin Books, 1954), 74.

50. Many believed the published image to be true, to the extent that when a casket containing Valentino's body was removed from the hospital and transported to Campbell's, "they were certain it contained someone's else body to cover up a fast one Campbell had put over on them in favor of the *Graphic.*" Mallen, *Sauce for the Gander,* 75.

51. "Harry Klemfuss, Publicist, Is Dead: Pioneer in Public Relations Was Master of Stunts—Arranged Valentino Rites" *NYT,* February 17, 1961, 24; and Silas Bent, *Ballyhoo: The Voice of the Press* (New York: Horace Liveright, 1927), 127.

52. Bent, *Ballyhoo,* 127.

53. Mallen, *Sauce for the Gander,* 79.

54. Mallen, 79.

55. Bent, *Ballyhoo,* 128.

56. Mallen, *Sauce for the Gander,* 89; Bent, 127.

57. I have been unable to date the first one; the second one, entitled "Rudy Meets Caruso!," appeared in the *New York Evening Graphic,* March 17, 1927.

58. For an example of spiritualist poetry dedicated to the actor, see Humbert Wolfe, "Rudolph Valentino Comes to Heaven" (1927), in Mendel Kohansky, *The Disreputable Profession: The Actor in Society* (Westport, CT: Greenwood Press, 1984), 155–57.

59. Published in multiple issues, the biographical profiles started a day after his death in the *Chicago Daily News* and the *New York Evening World.*

60. Shapiro, interview, pp. 174, 185, tape IV.

61. Shapiro, interview, pp. 180–81, tape IV.

62. Mario Quargnolo, "Mussolini e il cinema," *L'Osservatorio politico letterario,* June 1967, 28–29. The actor visited Cinecittà. What survives of that visit is an image of him in the company of Ambrosio and German actor Emil Jannings on the set of the remake of *Quo Vadis?* (1924). The image appeared in *PP,* February 1925, 74.

63. "Valentino Seeks Citizenship Here," *NYT*, November 11, 1925, 15. The event was also accompanied by a press release from United Artists, insisting on his "honorary discharge" by the Italian government from all military duties," to stop rumors that he had failed to enlist.

64. A cable from the Associated Press reported that the Fascist paper *Il Popolo d'Italia* was publishing letters from anonymous Italians calling Valentino a "renegade Italian" and supporting a boycott of his films. See "Italians to Seek Valentino Boycott," *LAT*, December 7, 1925, 5; and "Valentino Taboo in Rome as Bad Italian," *New York World*, June 20, 1926, n.p., both in Scrapbook, T213, reel 3, NYPL-TC.

65. The letter is reprinted in Silvio Alovisio and Giulia Carluccio, *Intorno a Rodolfo Valentino* (Turin: Kaplan/MNC, 2009), 108–9; the quote is from p.108 (italics in the original). For a discussion of the letter, see Quargnolo, "Mussolini e il cinema," 28.

66. "Valentino, Here on Visit, Tells of Persecution by Fascisti," *SFC*, July 16, 1926, 1.

67. "Charlot in Rome," *NR*, October 13, 1926, 217. The *New York World* suspected that the boycott was an attempt on the part of the national film industry to "restore the Italian film to its old place," since "American films have been flooding the Italian market. "Valentino Taboo in Rome as Bad Italian," *NYW*, June 20, 1926, Valentino, Rudolph, Clippings, 1920–1929, MWEZ, n.c. 5654, NYPL-TC.

68. For a selection of these articles, see Alovisio and Carluccio, *Intorno a Rodolfo Valentino*, 136–45, 151–71, 226–27, 239–40, 291–93.

69. "L'estremo omaggio di N.Y. alla salma di Valentino," *PIA*, August 31, 1926, 3.

70. "Public Now Barred at Valentino's Bier," *NYT*, August 26, 1926, 1, 5.

71. On the episode, its interpretation, and even a few conspiracy theories regarding the authenticity of the Fascist guards' identity, see "Sciacalli, esibizionisti e bugiardi" and "Profanazione fascista alla salma di Valentino," *NM*, August 27, 1926; "Il pellegrinaggio di dolore alla salma di Valentino terminerà a mezzanotte," *PIA*, August 26, 1926, 3; "Crowds Still Try to View Valentino," *NYT*, August 27, 1926, 3. An unreferenced article published on August 26, 1926, titled "Valentino Bier Closed to View: 75,000 See It," mentions the names of the four members of the Fascist League local of New York who "were stationed at the coffin as a guard of honor." They were Umberto Barbani, a corporal in the organization; Frank Panico; Nichola [*sic*] Remati; and Guido Valenti, secretary of the local. See Valentino, Rudolph, Clippings, 1920–1929, MWEZ, n.c. 5654, NYPL-TC. A photograph of a man in black shirt making the Fascist salute by Valentino's casket appeared in *Life* magazine, June 20, 1938, 55.

72. It also reveals how imaginative other interpretations had been. Mallen had attributed the incident to Klemfuss, who in his view came up with the idea of Fascist guards and even with the "wide blue satin ribbon" reading "From Benito" across the wreath "to make news and pictures for the ubiquitous newspapermen covering the final Valentino curtain." Mallen, *Sauce for the Gander*, 83–84.

73. "Public Now Barred at Valentino's Bier," *NYT*, August 26, 1926, 1. The leftist New York–based *Il Nuovo Mondo* published a copy of Allegra's telegram to Ullman on its front page, while other articles denounced the "explicit order by Mussolini" to have Fascists standing guard at the sides of Valentino's bier and derided the Fascists' tasteless exploitation of Valentino's dead body, describing the Duce as a "clown and coward." See "Profanazione fascista alla salma di Valentino," *NM*, August 26, 1926, 2; and "Buffoni," *NM*, August 26, 1926, n.p., folder 667, Onoranze funebri per Rodolfo Valentino, box 65, ASMAE-AIW.

74. Emilio Axerio (Italian consul general) to De Martino, August 26, 1926, folder 667, Onoranze funebri per Rodolfo Valentino, box 65, ASMAE-AIW.

75. Axerio to De Martino, August 28, 1926, folder 667, Onoranze funebri per Rodolfo Valentino, box 65, ASMAE-AIW.

76. "Il plebiscito di dolore," *PIA*, August 29, 1926, 1; and "Plebiscito universale di cordoglio per Valentino," *Corriere d'America*, August 29, 1926, 1.

77. "Newspaper Opinions," *Wid's Daily*, August 8, 1922, 4.

78. While the topic of his postmortem celebrity life exceeds the subject of this study, it is important to emphasize the extent to which Valentino's afterlife remained profitable for the news and publishing industries. First came the sale of his estate, for which a special catalogue was printed in 1926. Then came the memorial tributes penned by stars, writers, poets, and regular devotees, collected in Charles Mank Jr., ed., *What the Fans Think of Rudy Valentino: A Memorial Book* (Staunton, IL: Charles Mank Jr., 1929).

7. PROMOTING A ROMANTIC BIOGRAPHY

1. Benito Mussolini, preface to *The Life of Benito Mussolini*, by Margherita Sarfatti (New York: Frederick A. Stokes, 1925), 9.

2. Ido Oren, *Our Enemies and United States: America's Rivalries and the Making of Political Science* (Ithaca, NY: Cornell University Press, 2003), 8.

3. On the role of the CPI in Europe and specifically in Italy, see Frank Costigliola, *Awkward Dominion: American Political, Economic, and Cultural Relations with Europe, 1919–1933* (Ithaca, NY: Cornell University Press, 1984); and Daniela Rossini, *Woodrow Wilson and the American Myth in Italy*, trans. Antony Shugaar (Cambridge, MA: Harvard University Press, 2008).

4. Paul O'Brien, *Mussolini in the First World War: The Journalist, the Soldier, the Fascist* (New York: Berg, 2005), 31. A Socialist leader since 1910, in 1912 Mussolini became editor of *Avanti!*, the organ of the Italian Socialist Party.

5. Louis John Nigro Jr., *The New Diplomacy in Italy: American Propaganda and U.S.-Italian Relations, 1917–1919* (New York: Peter Lang, 1999), 85. Other historians have linked the financing of *Il Popolo d'Italia* in 1914 and 1915 to French pro-war socialists and, in 1917, to the British secret service. See Anthony James Gregor, *Young Mussolini and the Intellectual Origins of Fascism* (Berkeley: University of California Press, 1979), 200.

6. Charles Merriam, "American Publicity in Italy," *APSR* (November 1919): 548, 555.

7. Merriam to Creel, "Weekly Report to Creel," June 1918, folder, Reports, box 4, 20-B2, Record Group 63, RCPI-NARA. See also Merriam, "Leadership in Italy," memorandum, April 30, 1918, folder, Reports, box 4, 20-B2, RG63, RCPI-NARA.

8. Gino Speranza, "Report Relative to Imperialist, Liberal and Social Revolutionary Forces in Italy," [n.d., but July 1918], Special Political Reports, Gino Speranza Papers, Hoover Institution on War, Peace, and Revolution, Stanford, CA, quoted in Nigro, *New Diplomacy in Italy*, 132n42. It is unlikely that Speranza was referring to the rather marginal Partito Socialista Riformista Italiano, which in the 1919 elections gained only 1.5 percent of the votes.

9. Wilson famously refused to allow Italy to annex Fiume (now Rijeka, Croatia), a city with an Italian majority population located in the recently formed Kingdom of Yugoslavia. In 1919, against the military plans of the inter-Allied occupying forces, the ultranationalist

writer Gabriele D'Annunzio had seized Fiume and declared it part of the Italian territory. A long stalemate with the Italian government and the Wilson administration eventually ended with the Italian army's bombardment of the city, which led to his defeat in January 1921. During the Fascist regime, Fiume returned and remained Italian.

10. Charles Merriam, *The Making of Citizens: A Comparative Study of Methods of Civic Training* (Chicago: Chicago University Press, 1931), ix, but also 223. Similarly, while reviewing Herbert W. Schneider's *Making the Fascist State* (1928), which was published in Merriam's series on comparative civic training, historian Charles Beard described the March on Rome as "amazing experiment." Beard, "A Review of *Making the Fascist State* by Herbert W. Schneider," *NR*, January 23, 1929, 278.

11. Gaetano Salvemini, *Memorie e soliloqui: Diario 1922–1923*, ed. Roberto Pertici (Bologna: Il Mulino, 2001), 370 (italics in the original).

12. Gaetano Salvemini, *The Fascist Dictatorship in Italy* (1927; New York: Howard Fertig, 1967), 113.

13. *St. Paul [MN] Pioneer Press*, October 31, 1922, quoted in John B. Carter, "American Reactions to Italian Fascism," 1919–1933, PhD diss., Columbia University, 1954, 13; and "Needed a Mussolini," *WSJ*, January 15, 1923, 1.

14. For instance, scholars as different as Roberto Vivarelli, Antonino Répaci, Adrian Lyttelton, and Giulia Albanese have variously stressed the key role of militia violence, the national scale of the event, and its significance for the history of the regime.

15. An exception to the general trend of the scholarship on early Fascism is Emilio Gentile, *E fu subito regime: Il fascismo e la marcia su Roma* (Rome-Bari: Laterza, 2012), which relies on David F. Schmitz, *The United States and Fascist Italy, 1922–1940* (Chapel Hill: University of North Carolina Press, 1988).

16. John P. Diggins, *Mussolini and Fascism: The View from America* (Princeton, NJ: Princeton University Press, 1972), 22–26, chapter 2.

17. Until 1923, the *Chicago Daily News* correspondent had been Edgar Ansel Mowrer (a former part-time CPI collaborator), who believed that the country's "admirable sense of civilization" could only make the possibility of a Fascisti revolution "somehow unnatural and comic." Mowrer, *Immortal Italy* (New York: D. Appleton, 1922), 397–98.

18. Later in the 1920s, George Seldes also denounced the activities of the Fascist secret police and state censors in the pages of *Liberty Magazine* and *Harper's Magazine*. He later critiqued both the Duce and American journalists' coverage of him in *Sawdust Caesar: The Untold History of Mussolini and Fascism* (New York: Harper & Brothers, 1935).

19. William Bolitho, *Italy under Mussolini* (New York: Macmillan, 1926), 29, 88.

20. "What Mussolini and the Fascist Mean to Italy," *CO*, October 1, 1922, 469–71. The article had the name Mussolini in the title, but its overall argument centered on what Fascism was and what political consequences it was going to entail for Italians. Similarly, before adopting a balanced and eventually anti-Fascist style of coverage of Fascism, in 1921 and 1922 the *Nation* had appeared intrigued by Fascists' leadership and use of violence.

21. Giuseppe Prezzolini, "The Fascist and the Class Struggle," *NR*, November 1, 1922, 243. Even the *New Republic* editorialists joined the American press that looked favorably on the March. They gave credit to the "politically youthful aspirants to glory" and to the Italian people in general for their good sense in avoiding a civil war between Fascists and Communists. See "The Week," *NR*, November 8, 1922, 263.

22. Gino Speranza, "Fascismo," *Independent,* November 1922, 258–59.

23. Gino Speranza, "A New Italian Renaissance," *Outlook,* February 1923, 351.

24. Anne O'Hare McCormick, "The Revolt of the Youth," *NYT,* June 5, 1921, S3:1. See also Federica Pinelli and Marco Mariano, *Europa e Stati Uniti secondo il New York Times: La corrispondenza estera di McCormick, Anne O'Hare, 1920–1954* (Turin: Otto Editore, 2000), 48. Eventually she changed her views of the country through a growingly negative assessment of the Blackshirts.

25. "A Black-Shirted Garibaldi," *NYTR,* October 31, 1922, 12.

26. "Fascisti Reported Seizing Control of Italian Cities," *NYT,* October 28, 1922, 1; and "The Fascisti in Power," October 31, 1922, 11.

27. For a detailed list of newspapers' reports and comments on Mussolini in North America, see Eugenio Coselschi, *Universalità del fascismo: Raccolta di giudizi di personalità e della stampa di tutto il mondo, 1922–1932* (Florence: Vallecchi, 1933); John P. Diggins, "Mussolini and America: Hero Worship, Charisma and the Vulgar Talent," *Historian,* August 1966, 559–85; and Mauro Canali's painstakingly researched *La scoperta dell'Italia: Il fascismo raccontato dai corrispondenti americani* (Venice: Marsilio, 2017).

28. Quoted in Carter, "American Reactions to Italian Fascism," 24.

29. Anne O'Hare McCormick, "The Swashbuckling Mussolini," *NYT,* July 22,1923, S3:1, 19.

30. McCormick, "Swashbuckling Mussolini," S3:1.

31. McCormick, S3:19.

32. McCormick, "The Old Woman in the New Italy," *NYT,* July 15, 1923, S3:6. Two years later, the *Herald* described him as "a modern Caesar, the Napoleon of 1925." *Herald,* November 21, 1925.

33. Consider *Rome or Death* (New York: Century, 1923), by American journalist, author, and historian Carleton Beals; *Mussolini as Revealed in His Political Speeches (November 1914– August 1923)* (New York: E. P. Dutton, 1923), edited and translated by the nationalist aristocrat Barone Bernardo Quaranta di San Severino; and *The Fascist Movement in Italian Life* (Boston: Little, Brown, 1923) by the Fascist popularizer Pietro Gorgolini, with a preface by Mussolini.

34. Basil Miles, "Italy's Black Shirts and Business," *Nation's Business,* February 1923, 22.

35. Unsurprisingly, labor and radical publications, including *The Advance* (Amalgamated Clothing Workers of America) and the socialist *New York Call,* were instead quite quick in denouncing the financing of Mussolini's undemocratic grip on power by Italy's industrialists and bankers.

36. Cover, *Time,* August 6, 1923; and cover, *Time,* July 12, 1926.

37. "Mussolini as Julius Caesar," *LD,* September 26, 1925, 21. The article reported the "essentially Caesarist character" of Mussolini's goals as they emerged in the British press.

38. "Mussolini Defines Fascism," *LD,* August 1925, 21.

39. Issac F. Marcosson, "After Mussolini—What?" *SEP,* May 29, 1926, 3–4, 135, 137. Interestingly, *SEP* also associated the Left with "vice" and Mussolini with "virtue," making the March on Rome a moral event with which the American public was to sympathize at once.

40. Anne O'Hare McCormick, "The People's Own Dictators," *NYT,* April 13, 13, 1924, S4:14. See also Charles W. Hollman, "Mussolini, Dictator for the People," *Outlook,* July 2, 1924, 348–51.

41. Following public denunciations of the regime and the publication of his book *The Fascisti Exposed: A Year of Fascist Domination,* Matteotti was murdered on June 10, 1924. Historians have claimed that Mussolini probably ordered the murder when Matteotti was about to make public incriminating documents proving that the Duce had sold exclusive rights to all Italian oil reserves to Sinclair Oil. See Mauro Canali, *Il delitto Matteotti* (Bologna: Il Mulino, 1997).

42. Richard Washburn Child to Horace Walter Child, October 31, 1922, in folder 1922, box 2, RWCP.

43. "Some of the Things That the Italy America Society Is Doing," *NBIAS,* May 1921, 2. In addition to cultural exchanges, IAS arranged for "collecting information on economic, commercial and industrial developments in Italy, and supplying it to banks, Chambers of Commerce, etc." At the end of World War II, it was renamed America-Italy Society.

44. The board of trustees included Cornelius Vanderbilt; William Guggenheim; Luigi Criscuolo, IAS founder; and Agostino de Biasi, writer, editor, and founder in 1915 of *Il Carroccio* (New York), a monthly periodical that openly served as a vehicle for Fascist propaganda in America.

45. IAS's first president was Charles Evans Hughes, the former New York governor (1907–1910), a 1916 Republican presidential candidate, and a prominent lawyer who argued before the U.S. Supreme Court numerous times between 1925 to 1930.

46. Douglas J. Forsyth, *The Crisis of Liberal Italy* (New York: Cambridge University Press, 2002), 264–65.

47. Forsyth, *Crisis of Liberal Italy,* 265.

48. Irene di Robilant, "Who Are the Fascisti?," *TBIAS,* October 1922, 1–3. In the next issue, the emphasis was on the Duce's immediate engagement with the national economy: "Italy's Financial Problems Faced by Mussolini's Cabinet," *TBIAS,* December 1922, 1–8.

49. "The Annual Election," *NBIAS,* April 24, 1920, 3.

50. "Annual Election," 3.

51. On Child, see Steven Wagler Bianco, "Richard Washburn Child: Italian-American Relations, 1921–1924" (MA thesis, University of Iowa, 1970); and Daniel E. Fausz, "Richard Washburn Child: America's Spokesman on Europe and Fascism 1915–1935" (MA thesis, Vanderbilt University, 1985).

52. In the mid- to late-1910s, he wrote war-inspired fiction, thrilling serials, and short stories about anarchists.

53. His political engagement, sympathies, and writings brought him close to powerful figures, beginning with Theodore Roosevelt, whom Child revered, and presidential politics.

54. Richard Washburn Child, *Potential Russia* (New York: Dutton, 1916).

55. *The Complete Report of the Chairman of the Committee on Public Information, 1917:1918:1919* (Washington: 1920; repr., New York: Da Capo Press, 1972; aka Creel Report) 75–76; and George Creel, *How We Advertised America* (New York: Harper & Brothers, 1920), 224–25.

56. Richard Washburn Child, "One, Two! The Goose-Step For You," *MM,* October 1919, 6.

57. Child, "One, Two!," 6. It is unclear when he also became member of its Committee on Economic Relations.

58. "Writers Dine Ambassador," *NYT*, July 8, 1921, 9. Among those present at his farewell dinner at the Hotel Astor were Edgar Sisson of *McClure's Magazine*, who had had a career as a journalist for Hearst before serving as the CPI's most prominent representative in Russia, and Martin Egan, PR director at J. P. Morgan & Co.

59. For an early and succinct example of the correlation between the excesses of the Bolsheviki's and the Fascisti's response as a popular reaction ("Going too far [Bolsheviki] alarmed people. [. . .] People revolt against revolt. [. . .] The Fascisti is the form this reaction has taken in Italy."), see "The Fascisti," *CO*, October 1921, 430.

60. Embassy Weekly Reports to State Department, 865.00, Microscopy 527 (hereafter M527), RG59, DS-NARA; and Schmitz, *The United States and Fascist Italy*, 51.

61. Child to Hughes, October 9, 1922, 865.00/1162, M527, RG59, DS-NARA.

62. Child to Hughes, telegram, Embassy-Department, October 26, 1922, 865.00/1164, M527, RG59, DS-NARA.

63. Gian Giacomo Migone reports that Child was still worried about Mussolini's "chauvinistic and reckless foreign policy." Child to Hughes, October 30, 1922, roll 10, M527, RG59, DS-NARA. I have been unable to find this communication. See Migone, *The United States and Fascist Italy: The Rise of American Finance in Europe,* trans. Molly Tambor (New York: Cambridge University Press, 2015), 37. This fundamental study was first published as *Gli Stati Uniti e il fascismo. Alle origini dell'egemonia americana* (Milan: Feltrinelli, 1980).

64. Mussolini to Hughes, October 31, 1922, 865.002/67, M527, RG59, DS-NARA. See also "Mussolini Tells Hughes He Seeks Collaboration," *NYT*, November 1, 1922, 1; and Carter, "American Reactions to Italian Fascism," 13–17.

65. Hughes to Mussolini, November 2, 1922, 865.002/67, M527, RG59, DS-NARA. See also "Hughes Felicitates Mussolini," *NYT*, November 4, 1922, 3.

66. Child to State Department, November 3, 1922, Records of the Department of State Relating to Political Relations between the United States and Italy, 1910–29, roll 1, 711.65/00, M527, RG59, DS-NARA.

67. Child to State Department.

68. Child to State Department.

69. Robert K. Murray, *The Politics of Normalcy: Governmental Theory and Practice in the Harding-Coolidge Era* (New York: Norton, 1973).

70. Embassy Weekly Reports to State Department, November 4, 1922, 865.00/1180, M527, RG59, DS-NARA.

71. "In Honor of Ambassador Richard Washburn Child," *NBIAS*, January 28, 1924, 4 (italics mine). Child's successor as U.S. ambassador to Italy until 1929 was Henry P. Fletcher.

72. Before his speech in New York, Child had given a similar one in Rome, on June 28, 1923, in front of Mussolini in which he stressed how "leaders of men" have the power to "teach humanity that it has power within itself to relieve its own distress. See Child, folder Discorso Luglio 1923 dell'Ambasciatore Child sul Fascismo, box 188, ASMAE-AIW, 1925–1943.

73. Following J. P. Morgan's death on March 31, 1913, in Rome, his son J. P. Morgan Jr. expanded the bank's business reach. During World War I, Morgan Bank became the sole munitions purchaser for the French and British governments and the agent for hundreds of banks underwriting Allied Bonds and after the war, directed loans in excess of $10 billion for European reconstruction work.

74. On Morgan in Italy, see Migone, *United States and Fascist Italy,* 15064.

75. Six months before the March on Rome, Child had reached out to Lamont asking about the executive's plans to visit Italy. In his response, Lamont mentioned his long-standing relationship with the Italian American banker Amadeo Giannini, who was Italy's "finance expert." Child to Lamont, March 18, 1922; and Lamont to Child, April 7, 1922, both in folder 12, Italy 1922, box 190, series IV, International Matters, TWL.

76. Ron Chernow, *The House of Morgan: An American Banking Dynasty and the Rise of Modern Finance* (1990; New York: Grove Press, 2010), 281.

77. Lamont had heard the editor of the *New York World* accusing Mussolini of dramatic gestures to cover up for a lack of policies. Asked for a response, Caetani reassured him: "Mussolini is not an actor for the purpose of acting. His actions have been in harmony with the extraordinary character of the fascist revolution and may appear dramatic to an Anglo-Saxon." Lamont to Caetani, April 21, 1924; Caetani to Lamont, April 24, 1924, both in folder 916 "Varie Fascismo 1922–1924," box 188, ASMAE-AIW, 1920–1924.

78. Chernow, *House of Morgan,* 279.

79. Migone, *United States and Fascist Italy,* 64; and Diggins, *Mussolini and Fascism,* 44.

80. D. W. M. [Dwight Whitney Morrow], "Confidential Memorandum for T. W. L. [Thomas W. Lamont] and R. C. L. [Russell C. Leffingwell]," November 12, 1925, p. 3, folder 17, Italy September–December 1925, box 190, series IV, International Matters, TWL. Morrow, a partner at J. P. Morgan & Co., was a powerful businessman and diplomat. Leffingwell was the chairman of the firm. According to Chernow, Lamont was the one person who ultimately helped Mussolini secure $100 million in credit for the regime. J. P. Morgan led the syndicate of creditors with a $50-million investment. Chernow, *House of Morgan,* 283. See also Migone, *United States and Fascist Italy,* 117–35, 150–64.

81. "Mr. Thomas W. Lamont Elected President," *NBIAS,* March 1925, 3. The nomination had occurred on January 26, 1925. The front page of the next issue (April 1925) carried a letter of congratulations to Lamont signed by President Calvin Coolidge—possibly an indication of how highly placed IAS was in the U.S. government.

82. Lamont to Fummi, December 11, 1925, in folder 17, box 190, TWL.

83. Carleton Beals, "Italian Fascism Developing a New Phase," *Current History,* May 1925, 229.

84. Edward P. Lamont, *Ambassador from Wall Street: The Story of Thomas W. Lamont, J. P. Morgan's Chief Executive* (New York: Madison Books, 1993), 335.

85. "Faith, Banks, and Panic," Business, *Time,* November 11, 1929, 46.

86. Otto Kahn, "Otto Kahn e il Fascismo," *Il Carroccio,* February 1926, 2–4, in folder 9 "Mussolini and Italy," box 299, OKP.

87. For a biographical account, see Robert Peele, *Gelasio Caetani: A Biographical Memorial* (New York: self-published, 1936).

88. "War Hero is Named Italy's Envoy Here," *NYT,* November 9, 1922, 18. His *NYT* profile summarized the regime's key aspirational traits: wartime heroism, agricultural reclamation and economic reform, and centuries-old noble family history. *Time* dedicated its cover to Caetani on April 28, 1924.

89. In attendance were Nicholas Murray Butler, president of Columbia University; Congressman Fiorello La Guardia: and several financial authorities including John D. Rockefeller Jr., Otto Kahn, and Felix Warburg.

90. "Address Delivered by H.E. Prince Gelasio Caetani before the Members of the Italy America Society," *NBIAS*, February 23, 1924, 3–4.

91. Embassy to Minister of Foreign Affairs (Mussolini), November 1, 1922, and November 7, 1922, in folder 916, Varie Fascismo 1922–1924, box 188, ASMAE-AIW, 1920–1924.

92. Mussolini to Caetani, August 28, 1923, in folder 916, Varie Fascismo 1922–1924, box 188, ASMAE-AIW, 1920–1924.

93. Mussolini to Caetani, August 11, 1923; unnamed embassy officer to Mussolini, August 17, 1923, both in folder 916, Varie Fascismo 1922–1924, box 188, ASMAE-AIW, 1920–1924.

94. "So mobile is [Mussolini's] face and so rapid its play of expression," Lee noted, "that the watching interviewer can get his meaning almost before the English words reach the ear." Ivy Lee, "Ivy Lee a-Visiting," *Time*, June 11, 1923, 12. Caetani had informed Mussolini about Lee's past publicity work for Standard Oil, J. P. Morgan & Co., and Otto Kahn.

95. See Caetani to Alberto De Stefani [Italy's finance minister], May 18, 1923, subfolder 17 Marcosson, Isaac, folder Accomandatizie M-Z, box 228, ASMAE-AIW, 1925–1943.

96. On Caetani's meeting with Child in the summer of 1923, see Maude Parker Child to RWC's parents, June 18, 1923 in folder 1923–1924, box 2, RWCP.

97. Caetani was adamant in his condemnation of Italian American Fascist organizations' use of violence. Given the "American psychology and the hypersensitivity of the American people," he wrote to the Duce in 1923, his embassy would discourage "in any shape or form" any connection between the activities of Italy's diplomatic institutions and the ones of the Italian American Fascists. Caetani to Mussolini, June 18, 1923, in subfolder 3, Fascismo negli Stati Uniti, folder 30, box 20, ACS-MCPG, Reports.

98. Caetani to All Consuls, October 20, 1923, in subfolder 2, Circular no. 4105 in relation to Mussolini's Portrait, 1923, folder 916, Varie Fascismo 1922–1924, box 188, ASMAE-AIW, 1920–1924.

99. Frederick L. Collins, "Is It Good-By Mussolini?," *Collier's*, June 27, 1925, 8.

100. The *Chicago Daily News*, the *Chicago Daily Tribune*, and the *NYW* were quite aggressive in their denunciation of Mussolini's responsibility. The *NYT* instead wrote of a "gray Fascism." "Matteotti Killing Traced to Five Men," *NYT*, July 6, 1924, 3.

101. Between 1924 and 1928, Child published several pro-Mussolini and pro-Fascism articles in the *SEP*, which, with a circulation of nearly three million, exerted a strong influence on middle-class America's sentiments of conservatism, isolationism, and fear of communism. See Douglas B. Ward, "The Geography of an American Icon: An Analysis of the Circulation of the *Saturday Evening Post*, 1911–1944," *American Journalism* (Summer 2010): 59–89.

102. Caetani to Mussolini, June 27 and July 12, 1924; Caetani to Child, June 28, 1924, both in folder 916, Varie Fascismo 1922–1924, box 188, ASMAE-AIW, 1920–1924.

103. In a telegram to Mussolini, Caetani reported the main points of his interview with the Associated Press, including his beliefs that "complete justice will be done" and that "the actual crisis will have the beneficial effect of cleansing and fortifying fascism." In early July, the Italian ambassador met with President Harding. Mussolini had advised him to report that the killers had been apprehended and that public opinion was satisfied. See Caetani to Mussolini, June 21, 1924, folder 914, Indagine Matteotti, 1924, box 188, ASMAE-AIW, 1920–1924.

104. See Child's view of the March on Rome: "'Open the Gates!'" *SEP*, July 12, 1924, 5, 55–56, 58.

105. Diggins, *Mussolini and Fascism*, 16–17.

106. "Favorites at Yale," *Chicago Daily Tribune*, June 20, 1931, 10. I thank Francesca Minonne for sharing this reference.

107. See Lloyd R. Morris, "Mussolini: A Benevolent Tyrant?" *Forum*, November 1923, 2067–74; and "Rome's New Caesar," *LD*, September 22, 1923, 15–16.

108. In the discussion of these biographical series, I am indebted to Pierluigi Erbaggio's superb doctoral dissertation, "Writing Mussolini: The Duce's American Biographies on Paper and on Screen, 1922–1936" (University of Michigan, 2016), especially chapter 2.

109. "Mussolini as Julius Caesar," *LD*, September 26, 1925, 21. See also "Mussolini Defines Fascism," *LD*, August 1, 1925, 20–21. An impressive discussion on the articulation of a fictional Mussolini through his numerous biographies in Italian, French, and English is in Luisa Passerini, *Mussolini immaginario. Storia di una biografia*, 1915–1939 (Rome-Bari: Laterza, 1991). Several biographical profiles rely on the exclusion of women from Mussolini's public dimension.

110. Child, *A Diplomat Looks at Europe* (New York; Duffield, 1925), chapter 6 ("Mussolini"), chapter 7 ("'Open the Gates!'"), chapter 8 ("A New State").

111. Child, *A Diplomat Looks at Europe*, 152.

112. Child, 169.

113. Child, 202.

114. Child, 208.

115. Child, "The President," *SEP*, April 17, 1926, 1.

116. When the Fascist regime became increasingly close to Nazi Germany, Sarfatti lost her clout with the Duce. Powerful party officials did not have difficulty marginalizing her—as a woman, as a Jew, and as a powerful party figure with outdated political views. See Philip V. Cannistraro and Brian R. Sullivan, *Il Duce's Other Woman: The Untold Story of Margherita Sarfatti, Benito Mussolini's Jewish Mistress, and How She Helped Him Come to Power* (New York: William Morrow, 1993); and Simona Urso, *Margherita Sarfatti: Dal mito del Dux al mito americano* (Venice: Marsilio, 2003).

117. Sarfatti's *The Life of Benito Mussolini* was published in London by Thornton Butterworth, in New York by Frederick A. Stokes, and in Italy by Mondadori. Sarfatti had her own ideas about the English version. Originally, the British publisher had invited writer and periodical editor Giuseppe Prezzolini to write the biography.

118. For discussions of *Dux*, see Victoria De Grazia, "Il fascino del Priapo: Margherita Sarfatti biografa del Duce," *Memoria: Rivista delle donne* 4 (1982): 149–54; Urso, *Margherita Sarfatti*. especially 160–177; and Cannistraro and Sullivan, *Il Duce's Other Woman*, 300–303.

119. Sarfatti, *The Life of Benito Mussolini* (New York: Frederick A. Stokes, 1925), 343.

120. Sarfatti, *Life of Benito Mussolini*, 56–57.

121. Sarfatti, 38.

122. Sarfatti, 15.

123. Sarfatti, 341.

124. Sarfatti, 302.

125. Mussolini, preface, in Sarfatti, *Life of Benito Mussolini*, 9–10; E. H. G., "'An Essential Element:' Mussolini the Force," *Illustrated London News*, October 21, 1925, 792.

126. John Carter, "Mussolini, Master of Italy," *NYT*, February 7, 1926, S3:1.

127. Carter, "Mussolini, Master of Italy," S3:24.

128. The series appeared in such widely distant newspapers as the *Chester Times* (Pennsylvania), the *Taylor Daily Press* (Texas), the *Anniston Star* (Alabama), and the *Oakland Tribune* (California). The *New York Sun* and the *New York Herald* published installments of the United Press Service autobiography simultaneously. See Erbaggio, "Writing Mussolini," 59n46.

129. Cannistraro and Sullivan, *Il Duce's Other Woman*, 355.

130. "Mussolini's Own Story of His Busy Life," *Chester Times*, January 5, 1927, 1. The first installment was entitled "My Twenty-Four Hours."

131. "Mussolini's Own Story," 1.

132. A box preceding the first-page article summarizes his "efficiency precepts," which include the following: "Never stay in bed after the instant of awakening. Read the newspapers while dressing. Shave. 'I am anti-whiskers.'" "Mussolini's Efficiency Precepts," *Chester Times*, January 5, 1927, 1. The Duce even advocates clean-shaven faces like Roman emperors—beards signal decadence and lack of discipline—and makes reference to the American lifestyle: "I have become rather skillful in the use of an American safety razor," Mussolini's "My Twenty-Four Hours," *Decatur (IL) Herald*, January 5, 1927, 14. Years later, writer Italo Calvino captured the novelty of Mussolini's youthful appearance by pointing out that nobody had "ever seen in Italy a statesman without a beard or a mustache." Calvino, "Il Duce's Portraits: Living with Mussolini," trans. Martin McLaughlin, *New Yorker*, January 7, 2003, 34; the article originally appeared as "Cominciò con un cilindro," *La Repubblica*, July 10–11, 1983.

133. Mussolini even offered insights into his dietary habits, which included small meals and four glasses of milk, said to provide "the greatest net results in health and productivity." Mussolini, "My Twenty-Four Hours," 5.

134. Benito Mussolini, "Mussolini Tells Details of Life," *Altoona Mirror*, January 8, 1927, 7.

135. I include these *SEP* installments in Selected Primary Sources under Mussolini's authorship. The single volume appeared as Mussolini, *My Autobiography* (New York: Charles Scribner's Sons, 1928; reprt., Mineola, NY: Dover Publications, 2006). All quotes will be from this edition.

136. See "Letter no. 62, Arnaldo to Benito: Milan, 10 Jan 1928," in *Carteggio Arnaldo-Benito Mussolini*, ed. Duilio Susmel (Florence: La Fenice, 1954), 128; Benito Mussolini, *Vita di Arnaldo* (Milan: Tipografia del Popolo d'Italia, 1932), 104; Diggins, *Mussolini and Fascism*, 28n9; and Cannistraro and Sullivan, *Il Duce's Other Woman*, 358.

137. Child mentioned the "Mussolini material" in letter from Rome to his father, November 23, 1927, in f. 1925–1930, b. 2, RWCP.

138. Richard Washburn Child, foreword to *My Autobiography*, by Mussolini, xi, x (italics mine).

139. Child, foreword, viii, ix. In Italy, where the same utopian rhetoric had blood on its hands, the same tone had a different ring. Unsurprisingly, Mussolini opted not to have *My Autobiography* published in Italy.

140. Child, foreword, xii, xiii.

141. Mussolini, "My Twenty-Four Hours," 14.

142. Alice Rohe, "Mussolini: Idol of Women," *LM*, September 17, 1927, 11.

143. There were obviously exceptions, including Mary Grey, "Mussolini Italian Patriot," *Canadian Magazine*, June 1925, 135, 157–58, 160.

144. In his report on the CPI's activities, Creel credits her journalistic skills in supplementing the CPI's news agency with "illustrated feature articles for the daily press and the periodical press." Creel, *How We Advertised America,* 300.

145. Her brother-in-law was Jack Howard, heir to the Scripps-Howard newspaper empire. She was also one of the first female journalists to complement her reporting with photographs. After a few years of traveling and other assignments, she returned to Italy in 1922, interviewing stage actresses Eleonora Duse and Sarah Bernhardt and playwright Luigi Pirandello. She had easy access to the new political celebrity Mussolini and, by her claim, became one of the first journalists to predict his rise to premier.

146. Alice Rohe, "Mussolini, Hope of Youth, Italy's 'Man of Tomorrow,'" *NYT,* November 5, 1922, S9:20. Years later Mussolini opened "his" serialized autobiography for the *SEP* with a chapter titled "Youth." *SEP,* May 5, 1928, 1.

147. Rohe, "Mussolini, Hope of Youth," S9: 20.

148. Alice Rohe, "Mussolini: Idol of Women: He Pours Contempt on the Softer Sex—And It Adores Him," *LM,* September 17, 1927, 9–11.

149. "In *Liberty* Next Week Read: Mussolini Idol of Women," *LM,* September 10, 1927, 17.

150. Rohe, "Mussolini: Idol of Women," 10.

151. Rohe, 9–10.

152. Rohe, 11. Rohe remembered quite well that Mussolini had displayed the same attitude a few years earlier during her first interview, when "his good-humored laughter had that tolerant, high disdain with which the Latin male regards woman."

153. Rohe, 11. After positing that "his pictures do not in the least exaggerate the tremendous force," she focused on his mouth: "Mussolini's mouth is well formed. It is the curved upper lip which explains much of the strain in his character that has developed a love of music, and which radiates that *je ne sais quoi* havoc among women."

154. Elinor Glyn, "Last Minute News from East and West," *Photoplay,* March 1927, 6.

155. Alice Rohe, "Mussolini, Lady Killer," *LD,* July 31, 1937, 27.

156. Rohe, "Mussolini, Lady Killer," 27 (italics mine). On a different level, for a discussion of Mussolini's private entanglements, actual or imaginary, with women, see Roberto Olla, *Dux: Una biografia sessuale di Mussolini* (Milan: Rizzoli, 2012).

157. Rohe, "Mussolini, Lady Killer," 27. She goes on to say, "Il Duce knows how to get what he wants from women, whether it is a grand passion or a grand propaganda. For, consciously or unconsciously, women respond to this 'x-quality,' call it what they may."

158. Brenda Ueland, "How to Pass the Screen Test," *LM,* April 9, 1927, 21.

159. Salvemini, *Memorie e soliloqui,* 370; Camillo Berneri, *Mussolini, gran actor* (Valencia: Mañana, 1934), Italian trans.: *Mussolini: Psicologia di un dittatore* (1937; Milan: Edizioni Azione Comune, 1966), 49, quoted in Stephen Gundle, "Mass Culture and the Cult of Personality," in *The Cult of the Duce: Mussolini and the Italians,* ed. Stephen Gundle, Christopher Duggan and Giuliana Pieri (Manchester: Manchester University Press, 2013), 78. George Seldes was possibly the American journalist who most frequently denounced Mussolini's dictatorial and comedic talent. Quoting a line from the Duce ("I wonder what would have become of me if I had been an American immigrant?"), he argued that "certainly his talent as an actor would not have been lost in the New World." Seldes, "Mussolini Actor Extraordinary," *LM,* August 2, 1924, 51.

160. Brenda Ueland, "Men I Would Be Afraid to Marry," *LM,* August 22, 1925, 37.

161. Ralph Barton, "News of the World," *LM,* January 16, 1926, 53.

162. Barton illustrated one of the 1920s most popular books, *Gentlemen Prefer Blondes* (1925). Upon Rex Ingram's invitation, he worked, uncredited, on the sets and costumes of Valentino's *The Conquering Power.* He was known to despise Mussolini.

163. The military outfits that Mussolini began sporting in the 1930s were still not part of his public wardrobe. At the time he was still wearing bourgeois clothes.

164. Calvino, "Il Duce's Portraits," 34.

165. Barton, "News of the World," 35.

166. Warren Nolan, "Those Who Wear the Toga of Publicity," *NYT,* July 15, 1928, 6. Nolan also says, "Whenever [Mussolini] opens his mouth six cameras click and ten pencil points break. It may be believed that he is not unmindful of the political advantages accruing to a Fascist statesman through provocation of publicity."

167. It also continued in the press. For an example of the intertwined praise for Mussolini's charm, justification of his violent ruling as a dictator ("Has any people ever followed a leader who simply called 'Here, kittykittykitty!' or its equivalent, to them?"), and awe at his acting skills ("If by actor you mean a man who so thoroughly knows human nature that he can exact the desired response from it"), see Katharine Dayton, "Mussolini at Close Range," *North American Review,* December 1928, 646, 655, 659.

168. *Birmingham Age–Herald,* November 3, 1922, 1, quoted in Carter, "American Reactions to Italian Fascism," 13.

169. In Italian cinema, the confrontation between Mussolini and Valentino was arguably dramatized in the film *Maciste contro lo sceicco* (Maciste against the Sheik, 1926), starring Maciste, Italian silent cinema's strong man par excellence. The lack of research on the film's production circumstances prevents a definitive answer. However, the long-standing parallel between Mussolini and Maciste's heroic body type suggests that the film staged an allegorical rivalry between the Divo and the Duce. Jacqueline Reich has argued that the ways the film configures the sheik's "compound, with its desert setting, tent, as well as his costume, acknowledges the most famous of Arab screen incarnations at the time." Furthermore, several scenes, including one of an attempted rape, reveal the film's "striking, structural resemblance" to *The Sheik.* Jacqueline Reich, *The Maciste Film of Italian Silent Cinema* (Bloomington, IN: Indiana University Press, 2015), 229.

8. NATIONAL LEADER, INTERNATIONAL ACTOR

All documents and correspondence cited through note 46 come from folders held in Archivio Storico Diplomatico, Ministero degli Affari Esteri (Rome), Ambasciata d'Italia in Washington, 1920–1924 (ASMAE-AIW). All the correspondence quoted from note 57 on, unless otherwise specified, is from Archivio Centrale dello Stato (Rome), Segreteria Particolare del Duce, Carteggio Ordinario (ACS-SPD-CO).

1. Quoted in "Romans Help Director in 'The Eternal City,'" *White Plains Reporter* August 28, 1923, n.p., in folder 917, Propaganda Cinematografica sul film *The Eternal City,* 1923–1924, box 189, ASMAE-AIW, 1920–1924.

2. Agnes Smith, "The Screen in Review," *PPM* (February 1924): 55.

3. The most recent and synoptic publication is Steven Ricci, *Cinema and Fascism: Italian Film and Society, 1922–1943* (Berkeley: University of California Press, 2008).

In Italian, the literature is massive. For recent bibliographic references, see Lorenzo Quaresima, ed., *Storia del cinema italiano*, vol. 4, *1924–1933* (Venice: Marsilio; Rome: Edizioni di Bianco & Nero, 2014). I will refer to most specific works later in the chapter.

4. On newsreels in general and on the Istituto LUCE, see Ernesto G. Laura, *Le stagioni dell'Aquila: Storia dell'Istituto LUCE* (Rome: Ente dello spettacolo, 2000); and, in English, Pierluigi Erbaggio, "Istituto Nazionale LUCE: A National Company with an International Reach," in *Italian Silent Cinema: A Reader*, ed. Giorgio Bertellini (New Barnet, Herts: John Libbey, 2013), 221–31. On Italian newsreels' construction of Mussolini's image, see Francesco Pitassio, "I cinegiornali LUCE e la creazione del 'divo' Mussolini," in Quaresima, *Storia del cinema italiano*, 446–454. For an overview of the Duce in Italian cinema, see Pierre Sorlin, "A Mirror for Fascism: How Mussolini Used Cinema to Advertise His Person and Regime," *Historical Journal of Film, Radio and Television*, January 2007, 111–17. On Mussolini's impact on Italian film culture, see Stephen Gundle, *Mussolini's Dream Factory: Film Stardom in Fascist Italy* (New York: Berghahn Books, 2013).

5. On the cult of the Duce, see the recent work done in Great Britain by Stephen Gundle, Christopher Duggan, and Giuliana Pieri. This includes an art exhibit at the Estorick Collection of Modern Italian Art (2010); the DVD *Mussolini: The Story of a Personality Cult* (2011); a special issue of *Modern Italy* (2013); and the edited volume *The Cult of the Duce: Mussolini and the Italians* (Manchester, UK: Manchester University Press, 2013).

6. See particularly Renzo De Felice, *Mussolini il fascista: La conquista del potere, 1921–1925* (Turin: Einaudi, 1966); and De Felice, *Mussolini il fascista: L'organizzazione dello Stato fascista, 1925–1929* (Turin: Einaudi, 1969).

7. In Italy, he often succeeded in controlling his own image. See Sergio Luzzatto, "'Niente tubi di stoffa sulla testa': L'autoritratto del fascismo," in *L'Italia del Novecento: Le fotografie e la storia*, ed. Giovanni De Luna, Gabriele D'Autilia and Luca Criscenti (Turin: Einaudi, 2005), 1:117–201.

8. "Italian Pictures: Mussolini Reported behind Financing Interests," *Variety*, May 21, 1924, 2.

9. With great difficulty, *Messalina* was eventually distributed in the United States as both *Messalina* and *The Fall of an Empress*. Other Italian epic films circulated in America in 1924 and 1925, including a reissued copy of *Quo Vadis?* and a remake of *The Last Days of Pompeii* (1926). On Italian films as international propaganda in the United States, see Gian Piero Brunetta's pioneering essay "Il sogno a stelle e strisce di Mussolini," in *L'estetica della politica*, ed. Maurizio Vaudagna (Rome-Bari: Laterza, 1989), 39–48; and Guido Tintori, "Tra luce e ombra: Una storia della propaganda cinematografica fascista nel Nuovo Mondo," in *L'ombra lunga del fascio: Canali di propaganda fascista per gli "italiani d'America,"* ed. Stefano Luconi and Guido Tintori (Milan: M&B Publishing, 2004), 61–84. Beyond the 1920s, see Roberto Vezzani, "Reframing Italianness: Circulation of Italian Fiction Films in the United States During the 1930s" (PhD diss., University of Michigan, 2016). Vezzani has compiled a list of over 120 Italian fiction films distributed in the United States between 1931 and 1941 and discussed the context of their circulation in "Fascist Indirect Propaganda in 1930s America: The Distribution and Exhibition of Italian Fiction Films," *The Italianist* (August 2018): 156–73.

10. Will H. Hays, *The Memoirs of Will H. Hays* (Garden City, NY: Doubleday, 1955), 511.

11. Long ignored, the film has gained recent notoriety thanks to the work of film scholar Giuliana Muscio, who has called attention to the film's only known surviving copy,

preserved at the Museum of Modern Art. It was screened at the 2015 silent film festival in Pordenone. The MoMA print is incomplete: it includes the added-on opening credits and only reels 6 and 7, amounting to about 28 minutes of the original 81 minutes. I was able to inspect the surviving footage at MoMA/Film Study Center on October 31, 2016.

12. Lillian Gish had filmed *The White Sister* (1923) a few months before Fitzmaurice arrived in Italy for *The Eternal City*. That October the Goldwyn company began filming *Ben Hur* in Italy. June Mathis had written the original script. A few months later, once the Goldwyn Company's incorporation with MGM was complete, the production moved to Hollywood. On American companies' filming in Italy, see Giuliana Muscio, "Il 'Grand Tour' cinematografico: Produzioni americane in Italia negli anni Venti," in *A nuova luce*, ed. Michele Canosa (Bologna: Clueb, 2000), 89–102.

13. A. Scott Berg, *Goldwyn: A Biography* (New York: Riverhead Books, 1989), 113.

14. Mary Hammond, "Hall Caine and the Melodrama on Page, Stage and Screen," *Nineteenth Century Theatre & Film* (May 2004): 39.

15. Berg, *Goldwyn*, 116.

16. Mussolini to Regi agenti diplomatici e consolari all'estero, March 1, 1923, folder 917, Propaganda Cinematografica sul film *The Eternal City*, 1923–1924, box 189, ASMAE-AIW, 1920–1924.

17. Courtland to Caetani, January 27, 1923, folder 923, Films 1922–1924, box 189, ASMAE-AIW, 1920–1924.

18. Caetani to Mussolini, January 27, 1923; Caetani to Sinigaglia, January 27, 1923, both folder 923, Films 1922–1924, box 189, ASMAE-AIW, 1920–1924.

19. Caetani to Federzoni, handwritten letter, n.d., folder 917, Propaganda Cinematografica sul film *The Eternal City*, 1923–1924, box 189, ASMAE-AIW, 1920–1924.

20. Caetani had been reassured first in this regard by Undersecretary of State William Phillips, whose involvement reveals the well-documented closeness between the Hays Office and the State Department. See Trumpbour, *Selling Hollywood to the World: US and European Struggles for Mastery of the Global Film Industry, 1920–1950* (New York: Cambridge University Press, 2002), 63–90. Between 1936 and 1941 Phillips would become U.S. ambassador to Italy, welcoming Hays during his trip and arranging his meeting with Mussolini. Hays, *Memoirs*, 511, 517. Phillips's predecessor as Undersecretary of State had been Henry P. Fletcher, who also preceded Phillips as American ambassador to Italy (from 1924 to 1929).

21. Hays to Caetani, April 28, 1923, folder 917, Propaganda Cinematografica sul film *The Eternal City*, 1923–1924, box 189, ASMAE-AIW, 1920–1924.

22. Hays to Caetani, April 28, 1923.

23. Caetani to Hays, May 14, 1923, folder 917, Propaganda Cinematografica sul film *The Eternal City*, 1923–1924, box 189, ASMAE-AIW, 1920–1924 (italics mine). Four days later Caetani reiterated that he needed full assurance from the Hays Office that the studios were not going use "our country as a background for their films." Caetani to Hays, May 18, 1923, folder 917, Propaganda Cinematografica sul film *The Eternal City*, 1923–1924, box 189, ASMAE-AIW, 1920–1924.

24. Hays to Caetani, May 25, 1923, folder 917, Propaganda Cinematografica sul film *The Eternal City*, 1923–1924, box 189, ASMAE-AIW, 1920–1924. Hays also communicated to Goldwyn about the necessary presence of Irene di Robilant.

25. Caetani to Hays, May 31, 1923, folder 917, Propaganda Cinematografica sul film *The Eternal City*, 1923–1924, box 189, ASMAE-AIW, 1920–1924. All the American parties involved, including Fitzmaurice, knew of the project's diplomatic and political stakes and possibly went out of their way to reassure all the parties involved that they wanted to represent "the Fascist cause, the Italian government and the Italian people in a true and favorable light." Fitzmaurice to Goldwyn, May 21, 1923, folder 917, Propaganda Cinematografica sul film *The Eternal City*, 1923–1924, box 189, ASMAE-AIW, 1920–1924.

26. Caetani to Mussolini, June 8, 1923, folder 917, Propaganda Cinematografica sul film *The Eternal City*, 1923–1924, box 189, ASMAE-AIW, 1920–1924.

27. Caetani to Mussolini, June 8, 1923.

28. The press was made cognizant of their mediating role. On October 5, 1923, the *Elmira (NY) Star-Gazette* explained that it was thanks to di Robilant ("chief location adviser") and Ambassador Caetani that a foreign film company could get permission to film Mussolini giving a speech, "the first ever issued for any amusement venture." Clipping, n.p., folder 917, Propaganda Cinematografica sul film *The Eternal City*, 1923–1924, box 189, ASMAE-AIW, 1920–1924.

29. "L'amb. Caetani per la conoscenza del fascismo negli Stati Uniti," *Il Giornale d'Italia*, July 25, 1923, 5 (italics in the original).

30. De Bono to Caetani, July 19 and 20, 1923, folder 917, Propaganda Cinematografica sul film *The Eternal City*, 1923–1924, box 189, ASMAE-AIW, 1920–1924. De Bono made it clear that he had no hesitation in subjecting the completed film to heavy censorship.

31. Fitzmaurice to Caetani, n.d. but received on July 26, 1923, folder 917, Propaganda Cinematografica sul film *The Eternal City*, 1923–1924, box 189, ASMAE-AIW, 1920–1924.

32. "Romans Help Director in 'The Eternal City'" (italics mine). Excerpts from the same interview also appeared in Constance Palmer Littlefield and Helen Lee, "The Listening Post," *Screenland*, November 1923, 83.

33. Goldwyn to Caetani, November 10 and 12, 1923; Caetani to Goldwyn, November 13 and 14, 1923, both in folder 917, Propaganda Cinematografica sul film *The Eternal City*, 1923–1924, box 189, ASMAE-AIW, 1920–1924.

34. Di Robilant to Caetani, November 8, 1923, folder 917, Propaganda Cinematografica sul film *The Eternal City*, 1923–1924, box 189, ASMAE-AIW, 1920–1924.

35. Di Robilant to Caetani, November 8, 1923.

36. Caetani to di Robilant, November 19, 1923, p. 2, folder 917, Propaganda Cinematografica sul film *The Eternal City*, 1923–1924, box 189, ASMAE-AIW, 1920–1924 (italics mine). This is a three-page summary of his communication with Goldwyn.

37. Caetani to di Robilant, November 19, 1923.

38. Caetani to di Robilant, November 19, 1923. Caetani's correspondence seems to anticipate the exchanges between the German consul in Los Angeles, Dr. Gustav Struve, and the Hays Office (particularly when its foreign manager was Frederick Herron) regarding scenes to be cut or reedited from *All Quiet on the Western Front* (Universal, 1930). See Ben Urwand's controversial *The Collaboration: Hollywood's Pact with Hitler* (Cambridge, MA: Harvard University Press, 2013), 21–39, especially 35.

39. Instead, they introduced single intertitle preceding the scenes of the king at the balcony and Mussolini at the desk. It read: "It was fortunate for Italy that it had a really great and sensible King who received the liberator and tended to him the Premiership."

40. The *AFI Catalog* indicates December 17, 1923, which, according to the archival evidence I have located, seems incorrect. The reviews from the time and Berg's research indicate January 20, 1924, as the film's premiere (at the Strand). Berg, *Goldwyn*, 117.

41. Caetani to Fitzmaurice, January 24, 1924, folder 917, Propaganda Cinematografica sul film *The Eternal City*, 1923–1924, box 189, ASMAE-AIW, 1920–1924. Mussolini had sent his much wordier message, in Italian, to Caetani on January 20. The MoMA print does not include this intertitle.

42. Caetani to Consul General Bernardi, January 23, 1924, folder 917, Propaganda Cinematografica sul film *The Eternal City*, 1923–1924, box 189, ASMAE-AIW, 1920–1924.

43. Bernardi to Caetani, February 5, 1924, folder 917, Propaganda Cinematografica sul film *The Eternal City*, 1923–1924, box 189, ASMAE-AIW, 1920–1924.

44. On the day of the film's opening and just before the planned American release of another pro-Fascist film, *Il grido dell'aquila* [The Eagle's Cry, 1923], Caetani sent a cable to the Fascist Institute of National Propaganda. "Americans," he wrote, "see with absolute horror anything that even remotely may be appear to be foreign propaganda." He also reminded the Institute that when the American distributors saw *The Eternal City*, they "refused to accept it unless some the sections about the war were cut, and the sequences of the Congress in Naples, Mussolini speeches, and the March on Rome be reduced." In the future, he added, "every work of propaganda in America has to be carried out *indirectly* in a way that prevents audiences from realizing that one is exercising pressure on them." Caetani to Delegazione di Roma/Istituto Fascista di propaganda nazionale, January 24, 1924, folder 917, Propaganda Cinematografica sul film *The Eternal City*, 1923–1924, box 189, ASMAE-AIW, 1920–1924. As the first film about the March on Rome, *Il grido dell'aquila* does not appear to have circulated in the United States.

45. Gaetani to Mussolini, February 4, 1924, folder 917, Propaganda Cinematografica sul film *The Eternal City*, 1923–1924, box 189, ASMAE-AIW, 1920–1924.

46. This undated *SEP* clipping, possibly from 1924, is in folder 917, Propaganda Cinematografica sul film *The Eternal City*, 1923–1924, box 189, ASMAE-AIW, 1920–1924

47. "The Eternal City," *Photoplay*, January 1924, 68.

48. Robert E. Sherwood, "The Silent Drama: 'The Eternal City,' 'Wild Oranges,' 'The Dramatic Life of Abraham Lincoln,'" *Life*, February 14, 1924, 24.

49. Herbert Howe, Close-Ups and Long Shots, *Photoplay*, February 1924, 41.

50. Agnes Smith, The Screen in Review, *PPM*, February 1924, 55.

51. "The Eternal City," *Billboard*, February 2, 1924, 57–58.

52. "Rush" [Alfred R. Greason], "Pictures: The Eternal City," *Variety*, January 24, 1924, 26, 27. The reviewer also reported that the largely Latin audience "received the picture quietly up to the introduction of poses of the real Mussolini. Then it burst into a demonstration" (27).

53. Frederick James Smith, "New Screenplays in Review," *Screenland*, February 1924, 52–53.

54. Constance Palmer Littlefield and Helen Lee, "The Listening Post," *Screenland*, March 1924, 79.

55. "Will Hays' Two Years," *NYT*, April 6, 1924, S10:5. The *NYT* article does not include any quotation marks, but the observations seem to come from Hays rather than from the anonymous reporter.

56. "Pro Memoria," unsigned typewritten document, in subfolder Fox Film: Pellicola di propaganda italiana, folder P.S.E. Varia 148, box 221, ACS-SPD-CO. The original document reads: "Il discorso in italiano dovrebbe durare 3 minuti e mezzo e quello in inglese lo stesso perchè così si avrebbe il massimo rendimento."

57. Kaw to Spanier, telegram, May 21, 1927, subfolder Fox Film: Pellicola di propaganda italiana, folder P.S.E. Varia 148, box 221, ACS-SPD-CO. On the composition of the crew, see also E. I. Sponable, "Historical Developments of Sound Films," *Journal of the Society of Motion Picture Engineers* (May 1947): 409, quoted in Raymond Fielding, *The American Newsreel: 1911–1967* (Norman: University of Oklahoma Press, 1972), 164. For some of the following English-speaking references, I am indebted to Janet Bergstrom's remarkable essay, "Murnau, Movietone and Mussolini," *FH* (October 2005): 187–204.

58. Fielding, *American Newsreel*, 161. Interestingly, Fielding also reports, "as early as July 25, 1924, Case produced an experimental sound-newsreel interview in which President Calvin Coolidge and Senator Robert F. La Follette appeared."

59. Frederick Lewis Allen, *Only Yesterday: An Informal History of the 1920s* (1931; New York: Harper Perennial, 2000), 188–89. Movietone News crews also photographed Lindbergh's return to the United States—in Washington, DC, on June 11, 1927. The final result was a full sound reel of ceremonies that allowed filmgoers to hear Lindbergh's speech and see him next to President Coolidge. Fielding, *American Newsreel*, 162.

60. Jerome Beatty, "Shooting the Big Shots," *American Magazine*, February 1931, 68–69, 138–41.

61. Chiavolini to Kaw, May 5, 1927, subfolder Fox Film: Pellicola di propaganda italiana, folder P.S.E. Varia 148, box 221, ACS-SPD-CO.

62. Sime Silverman, "Mussolini's Hope in Screen," *Variety*, September 21, 1927, 1, 20. See also Bergstrom, "Murnau, Movietone and Mussolini."

63. The typewritten pages are in a thin folder, Discorso di S.P. per il "Movietone" della Fox Film, 16 August 1927 V, included in the subfolder Fox Film: Pellicola di propaganda italiana, folder P.S.E. Varia 148, box 221, ACS-SPD-CO. The same subfolder includes the text of a telegram sent on August 16, 1927 by Pavolini to Spanier in which Mussolini's secretary thanks the representative for the Western Union Telegraph Company for "today's well-done English translation of the speech." A very short and incomplete online version of the Movietone News episode is available on YouTube, https://youtu.be/lUhJEfTFMoI (accessed August 30, 2018).

64. Projection Jottings, *NYT*, September 18, 1927, S7:5. Since the speech was copyrighted, newspapers could not reproduce it and the Duce's address could be experienced only by purchasing a movie ticket. Bergstrom, "Murnau, Movietone and Mussolini," 192.

65. Bergstrom, 192.

66. Fielding, *American Newsreel*, 162. Unfortunately, I have found no evidence of this pair. The *NYT* column Projection Jottings, a usual site for well-placed promotion, does not mention it. *Sunrise* was possibly the first film release with an original synchronized score.

67. Pierluigi Erbaggio, "Writing Mussolini: The Duce's American Biographies on Paper and on Screen, 1922–1936" (PhD diss., University of Michigan, 2016), 12. Erbaggio found this detail in News Story B1904, Dope Sheets, MIRC-FMNC.

68. Fox film advertisement, quoted in Bergstrom, "Murnau, Movietone and Mussolini," 187.

69. Silverman, "Mussolini's Hope in Screen," 1.

70. Silverman, 1. The difference with how American newsreels dealt with Hitler could not be more striking. Because of his combustible effect in U.S. movie theaters, where his appearance was met by storms of boos and applause, vitriol and defiant shouts of "Heil" from audiences, newsreel editors in 1933 were "all dodging Hitler close-ups." "Pix Reaction Is Anti-Hitler," *Variety*, May 16, 1933, 1, quoted in Thomas Doherty, *Hollywood and Hitler, 1933–1939* (New York: Columbia University Press, 2013), 89.

71. Mordaunt Hall, "Murnau's Drums and Fifes of Life," *NYT*, October 2, 1927, S8:7.

72. Phil M. Roe, "At the World's Crossroads," *MPW*, October 2, 1927, 299.

73. "Sunrise and Movietone," *MPN*, October 7, 1927, 1046.

74. Helen Ludlam, "What's Doing in Times Square," *Screenland*, December 1927, 98.

75. "The Talking Pictures," *Screenland*, January 1928, 15.

76. Bergstrom, "Murnau, Movietone and Mussolini," 191.

77. Bergstrom, 192.

78. Bergstrom, 201.

79. The most articulate rebuff was by Julius H. Barnes, who juxtaposed the "power of individual initiative" against "the "stifling atmosphere of state bureaucracy" in "An Answer to Mussolini's Challenge," *Nation's Business*, September 1927, 15, quoted in Bergstrom, "Murnau, Movietone and Mussolini," 194. That March, a special issue of *Survey* [*The Graphic Number*] had been dedicated to Mussolini's regime. It sought to offer a balanced assessment of Fascism by asking, "Can we both organize creative energy and conserve liberty?" There were stern critics, including Gaetano Salvemini and William Bolitho, but also defenses of the regime, including Alfredo Rocco's interpretation of its theory, Edmondo Rossi's discussion of its corporate structure, and Lamont's exposure of its accomplishments. See "An American Look at Fascism," *Survey*, March 1, 1927, 678–765, 678.

80. "Child Sails to See Mussolini," *NYT*, July 10, 1927, 8.

81. Silverman, "Mussolini's Hope in Screen," 1.

82. "Movietone Celebrities: Filming Mussolini. Italy's Beau Brummell," *NYT*, November 18, 1928, S9:6.

83. "Movietone Celebrities," 6.

84. Paxton Hibben, "The Man of Italy: His Life, His Personality, His Activities as a Leader of the People," *Mentor*, November 1927, 3.

85. Similarly, the cabinet chief of the Italian Ministry of Foreign Affairs, Francesco Giorgio Mameli, foresaw Movietone News's impact on world diplomacy: "This invention offers the opportunity and the pleasure of introducing the great statesman who gives a new vision to Italy, a new spirit to all classes of Italians, and a new conception and soul to the art of governance." Unsigned and undated typewritten document, subfolder Fox Film: Pellicola di propaganda italiana, folder P.S.E. Varia 148, box 221, ACS-SPD-CO.

86. It also warned that "these particular triumphs, however, are straight newsreel reporting and have nothing to do with art." "Rob Wagner Asks: What About Art?," *Screenland*, June 1929, 44.

87. "Our Changing World Now Turns to Movietone," *PPM*, August 1929, 8.

88. Louis Reid, "The Newsreel Comes into Its Own," *NMM*, December 1930, 108.

89. Michael Holroyd, *Bernard Shaw*, vol. 3, *1918–1950: The Lure of Fantasy* (London: Penguin, 1993), 143. In 1927, anti-fascist intellectual Salvemini engaged in a harsh polemic

against Shaw in the pages of the *Manchester Guardian* and elsewhere. Their exchange is now included in Gaetano Salvemini, *Polemica sul fascismo* (Rome: Ideazione, 1997).

90. Henry William Hanemann, "Oh Shaw," *MPC*, November 1928, 49.

91. Anne Bye, "In New York," *Screenland*, February 1929, 104.

92. Will H. Hays, *See and Hear: A Brief History of Motion Pictures and the Development of Sound* (New York: MPPDA, 1929), 55.

93. Embassy [Andrea Geisser Celesia di Vegliasco] to Hays, August 30, 1922, subfolder Cinematografie anti-Italiane (azione Will Hays), folder 923, Films 1922–1924, box 189, ASMAE-AIW, 1920–1924. The two films mentioned were *Fair Lady* (Bennett Pictures, 1922) and, especially, *The Truthful Liar* (Realart Pictures, 1922).

94. Hays to Geisser Celesia, September 7, 1922, subfolder Cinematografie anti-Italiane, folder 923, Films 1922–1924, box 189, ASMAE-AIW, 1920–1924.

95. Geisser Celesia to Will H. Hays, December 11, 1922, subfolder Cinematografie anti-Italiane, folder 923, Films 1922–1924, box 189, ASMAE-AIW, 1920–1924. The MPPDA also assured the embassy that it would act quickly in case it was alerted to any production demeaning to Italians.

96. Ministry of Foreign Affairs to Embassy, October 8, 1932, telegram, in folder Cinematografie anti-Italiane, box 12, ASMAE-SAP.

97. Ministry of the Interior to Ministry of Foreign Affairs, July 10, 1932, in folder Film *The Life of Giuseppe Musolino,* ASMAE-SAP.

98. De Martino to Minister of Foreign Affairs, October 20, 1932, in folder Italia nel cinema americano: *Scarface,* ASMAE-SAP.

99. As Vezzani has documented, ASMAE-SAP holds several documents showing the extent to which exponents of the Italian regime critiqued American films. Vezzani, "Reframing Italianness," 145–47.

100. The documentation on *Scarface* includes private letters, institutional exchanges among diplomatic and governmental entities, and clippings from American and Italian American newspapers. Comparatively, references to *Little Caesar* (1931) are surprisingly modest. See folder Italia nel cinema americano *Scarface* e altri, box 12, ASMAE-AP. For a study of the reception of *Scarface* in Italy, see Carla Mereu Keating, "'The Italian Color:' Race, Crime Iconography and Dubbing Conventions in the Italian-Language Versions of *Scarface* (1932)," *Altre Modernità* [S.I.], (February 2016): 107–23.

101. The most notable example was that of *Gloria: Apoteosi del Soldato Ignoto* (Apotheosis of the Unknown Soldier; Federazione Cinematografica Italiana e dall'Unione Fototecnici Cinematografici, 1921), a two-reel war film commonly referred to as *Gloria,* aimed at exciting a sense of patriotism among Italian Americans. In January 1922, the office of the premier had sent several copies of the film to Washington and stipulated contracts with business representatives. It never received any information regarding their distribution and reception, or any compensation. See folder 920, Film *Gloria* 1922–1924, box 189, ASMAE-AIW, 1920–1924.

102. On the strategies and challenges of Italian fascist culture in America, see Luconi and Tintori, *L'ombra lunga del Fascio;* Matteo Pretelli, "Culture or Propaganda? Fascism and Italian Culture in the United States," *Studi Emigrazione,* March 2006, 171–92; and Stefano Luconi, *La "Diplomazia parallela:" Il regime fascista e la mobilitazione politica degli Italo-American* (Milan: Franco Angeli, 2000).

103. See folder 922, Films 1920, box 189, ASMAE-AIW, 1920–1924.

104. Alessandro Salvo, "La propaganda 'visiva,'" *Il Legionario*, October 10, 1925, 1. *Il Legionario* was a magazine created and addressing Italian communities abroad.

105. Caetani to Mussolini, January 28, 1923, folder 18, box 163, Report 71, ACS-MCPG, quoted in Philip V. Cannistraro, *Blackshirts in Little Italy: Italian Americans and Fascism, 1921–1929* (West Lafayette, IN: Bordighera Press, 1999), 26, and Emilio Gentile, "I Fasci Italiani all'Estero: The 'Foreign Policy' of the Fascist Party," in *The Struggle for Modernity: Nationalism, Futurism, and Fascism*, ed. Emilio Gentile (Westport, CT: Praeger, 2003), 152. An earlier and longer version of this essay is Emilio Gentile, "La politica estera del partito fascists. Ideologia e organizzazione dei Fasci Italiani all'Estero (1920–1930)," *Storia Contemporanea* (December 1995): 897–956.

106. Cannistraro, *Blackshirts in Little Italy*, 24–44.

107. See Monte S. Finkelstein, "The Johnson Act, Mussolini and Fascist Emigration Policy: 1921–1930," *Journal of American Ethnic History* (Fall 1988): 38–55, 47; and Philip Cannistraro, "Mussolini, Sacco-Vanzetti, and the Anarchists: The Transatlantic Context," *JMH* (March 1996): 31–62.

108. In 1926, an executive order of the Duce had put the once-private newsreel agency Istituto LUCE, founded in 1924, under the power of the government, specifically the Ministry of Foreign Affairs.

109. See folder Propaganda Italiana all'Estero, Bastianini a tutte le delegazioni fasciste all'estero e nelle colonie, 20 settembre 1925, box 749, ASMAE-MCP.

110. This figure and other newsreels exhibition details are reported in Doherty, *Hollywood and Hitler*, 79.

111. The two companies had offices in London and Paris as well. After 1919, and after gaining international clout following World War I, a handful of American companies came to dominate the world's newsreel market—Pathé, Fox, Hearst, and Universal. In 1927, they were joined by Paramount. To gain a sense of these companies' reach, note that Fox employed cameramen in fifty countries and had production centers in nine others.

112. The UCLA Film and Television Archives holds several 1920s newsreels by Hearst Metrotone News and International News distributed respectively by MGM and Universal.

113. "Mussolini Speaks," *Photoplay*, June 1933, 96.

114. For several of these references I am in debt to Erbaggio, "Writing Mussolini," particularly 109–13 122–32, and Appendix B (146–49).

115. Erbaggio, "Writing Mussolini," 111.

116. *Black Shirts* (Fox, February 28, 1923), preserved at MIRC-FMNC.

117. These attempts occurred on April 7, September 11, and October 31.

118. "Italy: Mussolini Trionfante," *TM*, April 19, 1926, 12–14.

119. The Fox and Hearst archives at the University of South Carolina and UCLA hold material from several filmed newsreels from the 1920s, including outtakes, synopsis and dope sheets, and cameramen's written records of their work. In addition, the National Archives and Records Administration (NARA) holds much of the Universal News footage covering the period 1929–1967 in its MCA/Universal Pictures Collection, 1929–1967.

120. *Mussolini Promises Peace* (Fox, January 10, 1931) is preserved at MIRC-FMNC.

121. Release no. 32., v. 4, synopsis sheets, MIRC-FMNC. Radio was a medium that Fascist officials wanted to employ extensively in the United States to broadcast news about Fascism.

Due to the Duce's own linguistic limitations, his radio programs in Italian were mainly used to communicate with Italian Americans, mostly in the 1930s. See Stefano Luconi, "Radio Broadcasting, Consumer Culture, and Ethnic Identity among Italian Americans in the Interwar Years," *Italian Americana* (Summer 2002): 150–59.

122. Erbaggio examines a good selection of these editorials in "Writing Mussolini," chapter 4.

123. In the conclusion to his dissertation ("Writing Mussolini," 133–41), Erbaggio looks at the documentable links from the 1930s between studios and financial powers such as J. P. Morgan, New York National City Bank, and Bank of America, all engaged in shaping public opinion by financing Hollywood vertical integration. These financial firms issued Italian bonds on the American financial market. Erbaggio uses the scant available documentation to hypothesize that these financiers' activities benefitted from supporting Mussolini's uncritical popularity in America as an exemplary leader. While my work points in the same direction for the 1920s, more research is needed regarding the post-Depression years.

124. Jack had acquired two reels of Mussolini giving speeches on the tenth anniversary of the March on Rome. Then, "a young worker in the New York office of Columbia, Harry Forster, proposed illustrating the speech with footage of the Mussolini accomplishments." Bob Thomas, *King Cohn: The Life and Times of Harry Cohn* (New York: G. P. Putnam's Sons, 1967), 102.

125. Bernard F. Dick, *The Merchant Prince of Poverty Row* (1993; repr., Lexington: University Press of Kentucky, 2009), 72–73. Biographers have stressed Cohn's personal fascination with Mussolini and utter ignorance of Fascism. His attraction to the Duce was not reciprocated: Mussolini banned the film in Italy "because Italy's idol doesn't think the picture is timely enough for current showing in his country." "Il Duce Nixes Mussolini Pic," *Variety*, December 12, 1933, 5.

126. Universal had been one of the first studios to introduce the practice of using an off-screen narrator, and "Fox Movietone employed the most prestigious of all the vocal hosts." Doherty, *Hollywood and Hitler*, 79.

127. "Il Duce, Italy's Man of the Hour, 'Stars' in Film Record of Achievements, Produced by Columbia," *Columbia Beacon*, February 4, 1933, 1, 3, in folder Columbia Picture Corporation, box 218, Stati Uniti 1934, part 2, ACS-MCP-DSP. In addition to describing the usual array of posters, lobby display cards, and miniature insert cards, another company publication destined for exhibitors, the *Columbia Showman*, mentioned that the studio had sent "publicity stories" in both English and Italian to American newspapers and that it had created tie-ins with Italian restaurants and stores by printing film advertisements on menus and paper bags. See *Columbia Showman* 6 (March 1933): n.p., in "*Mussolini Speaks!* (Cinema 1933) Press Book," MFL n.c. 182 #09 and #20, NYPL-TC.

128. "Il Duce, Italy's Man of the Hour," 1.

129. "Il Duce, Italy's Man of the Hour," 1.

130. "Mussolini Speaks!," *Film Daily*, March 11, 1933, 4. See also "Mussolini Speaks," *Photoplay*, June 1933, 96.

131. "Mussolini Speaks!" *MPH*, March 18, 1933, 34.

132. *RKO Newsletter*, March 11, 1933, 2, in Clippings, *Mussolini Speaks* (Cinema 1934), NYPL-TC.

133. "Film of Mussolini's Life is Fascinating," *New York American*, March 13, 1933, n.p., in "*Mussolini Speaks* (Cinema 1934), Clippings," NYPL-TC (card catalog).

134. Thornton Delehanty, "The New Film: 'Mussolini Speaks,'" *NYEP,* March 13, 1933, n.p., in *"Mussolini Speaks* (Cinema 1934), Clippings," NYPL-TC (card catalog). In the same period MGM was promoting *Gabriel over the White House,* which twisted Thomas Jefferson's notion of democracy to enhance the totalitarian governance of its sympathetic protagonist by launching it as "The Birth of a NEW Nation!" *MPH,* April 1, 1933, 21.

135. Lucius Beebe, "'Mussolini Speaks'—Palace," *NYHT,* March 13, 1933, n.p., in Clippings, *Mussolini Speaks* (Cinema 1934), NYPL-TC.

136. Gerald Johnson, "Will France and Italy Make Up?," *NAR,* January 1935, 52.

137. In 1928, Hullinger collected and reedited his articles as *The New Fascist State: A Study of Italy under Mussolini* (New York: Rae D. Henkle, 1928).

138. Edwin Ware Hullinger, "Mussolini Movie Star," *Photoplay,* August 1938, 24.

139. Cover, *Time,* June 9, 1941, 1.

140. Percy Winner, "Mussolini—A Character Study," *Current History* (July 1928): 517.

CONCLUSIONS

1. Thomas Bender, "Wholes and Parts: The Need for Synthesis in American History," *Journal of American History* (June 1986): 126.

2. Frank Zappa, with Peter Occhiogrosso, *The Real Frank Zappa Book* (New York: Simon & Schuster, 1987), 322 (capital letters and italics in the original).

3. "Douglas and Mary Turn Rome Topsy-Turvy on their Arrival," *NYH,* April 29, 1926, 3.

4. "Mary Pickford Salutes," *NYT,* March 24, 1934, 18.

5. See the otherwise impressive studies by Stephen Gundle, *Mussolini's Dream Factory: Film Stardom in Fascist Italy* (New York: Berghahn, 2013); and Jacqueline Reich, *The Maciste Films of Italian Silent Cinema* (Bloomington: Indiana University Press, 2015), particularly 187–237.

6. The important studies on film stardom within dictatorial regimes, from Gundle's *Mussolini's Dream Factory* to Antje Ascheid, *Hitler's Heroines: Stardom and Womanhood in Nazi Cinema* (Philadelphia: Temple University Press, 2003), mainly, and admirably, focus on stars' filmic presence and performances. By design, they do not engage in full-fledged cultural comparisons with either Italy's or Germany's culture of charismatic dictatorship.

7. Recent examples include Allan Todd, *The European Dictatorships: Hitler, Stalin, Mussolini* (Cambridge: Cambridge University Press, 2002); Richard Overy, *The Dictators: Hitler's Germany and Stalin's Russia* (New York: Norton, 2004); and Robert Gellately, *Lenin, Stalin, and Hitler: The Age of Social Catastrophe* (New York: Knopf, 2007). Wolfgang Schivelbusch compares dictators and democratic leadership in *Three New Deals: Reflections on Roosevelt's America, Mussolini's Italy, and Hitler's Germany, 1933–1939* (New York: Picador, 2006).

8. Renzo Renzi, ed., *Cinema dei dittatori: Mussolini, Stalin, Hitler* (Bologna: Grafis, 1992); and Raphaël Muller and Thomas Wieder, *Cinéma et régimes autoritaires au XXe siècle écrans sous influence* (Paris: Presses Universitaires de France, 2008).

9. History can teach us a lesson about the contradictions inherent in deploying such democratic options to impose an authoritarian will. In 1852, a year after his coup d'état had made him president of France, Napoleon III reintroduced universal suffrage and, through a referendum meant to ascertain French people's stance on his proposed institutional arrangements, took away their sovereignty and declared himself emperor.

10. P. David Marshall, *Celebrity and Power: Fame in Contemporary Culture* (Minneapolis: Minnesota University Press, 1997), 4.

11. Marshall, *Celebrity and Power*, 10.

12. Lippmann, *Liberty and the News* (New York: Harcourt, Brace and Howe, 1920), 61.

13. Lippmann, *Liberty and the News*, 61.

14. Lippmann, 62.

15. Richard Washburn Child, "The Critic and the Law," *AM*, May 1906, 620–29, quoted in Edward Bernays, *Crystallizing Public Opinion* (New York: Liveright, 1923), 66–67.

16. Child, "The Critic and the Law," 67.

17. Roland Marchand, *Creating the Corporate Soul: The Rise of Public Relations and Corporate Imagery in American Big Business* (Berkeley: University of California Press, 1998), 88–201.

18. "Louis B. Mayer a National Figure," *Variety*, June 21, 1932, 4; Kathryn Cramer Brownell, *Showbiz Politics: Hollywood in American Political Life* (Chapel Hill, NC: University of North Carolina Press, 2014), 23; and Scott Eyman, *Lion of Hollywood: The Life and Legend of Louis B. Mayer* (New York: Simon & Schuster, 2005), 169. Earlier in the decade, Mayer had also become vice-chairman of the Republican Party in California.

19. Brownell, *Showbiz Politics*, 21.

20. Trade and general interest periodicals celebrated the profession: "Press Agentry Now Refined Art in Boosting Stars, Studios," *Daily Variety*, September 24, 1936; and Mary Peace, "Ballyhoodlums," *SEP*, August 15, 1936, 16–17, 60. For an assessment, see Edgar Dale, "Motion Picture Industry and Public Relations," *Public Opinion Quarterly*, April 1939, 251–62.

21. Brownell, *Showbiz Politics*, 23.

22. Brownell, 23–26.

23. Greg Mitchell, *The Campaign of the Century: Upton Sinclair's Race for Governor of California and The Birth of Media Politics* (New York: Random House, 1992), 62–63. For the coverage of this event from the film industry side, see Steven J. Ross, *Hollywood Left and Right: How Movie Stars Shaped American Politics* (New York: Oxford University Press, 2011), chapter 2; and Brownell, *Showbiz Politics*, chapter 1. Interestingly, the conservative victor, Frank Merriam, was a cousin of the aforementioned political scientist Charles E. Merriam, who had served as CPI director in Rome in 1918.

24. Burton E. Peretti, *The Leading Man: Hollywood and the Presidential Image* (New Brunswick, NJ: Rutgers University Press, 2012), 76 and Cari Beauchamp, *Joseph P. Kennedy's Hollywood Years* (London: Faber & Faber, 2009), xvii.

25. FDR, "Inaugural Address, March 4, 1933," quoted in Benjamin Alpers, *Dictators, Democracy, and American Public Culture: Envisioning the Totalitarian Enemy, 1920s–1950s* (Chapel Hill: University of North Carolina Press, 2003), 27.

26. Alpers, *Dictators, Democracy, and American Public Culture*, 28.

27. Another forceful voice of the time was the radio personality and daily columnist Walter Winchell. Though he too turned against FDR, he always opposed the Fascist turn of European politics. On Winchell, see Neal Gabler's masterful *Winchell: Gossip, Power and the Culture of Celebrity* (New York: Vintage Books, 1994).

28. Colin Crouch, *Post-Democracy* (Malden, MA: Polity Press, 2004), 4.

29. Crouch, *Post-Democracy*, 24.

30. Crouch, 26.

31. Crouch, 50.

32. Shmuel Noah Eisenstadt, *Paradoxes of Democracy: Fragility, Continuity, and Change* (Baltimore and Washington: Johns Hopkins University Press / Woodrow Wilson Center Press, 1999), 90.

33. On the end of party politics, see also Peter Mair, *Party System Changed: Approaches and Interpretations* (New York: Oxford University Press, 1997).

34. Eisenstadt, *Paradoxes of Democracy,* 90.

35. Emilio Gentile, *"In democrazia il popolo è sempre sovrano" Falso!* (Rome-Bari: Laterza, 2016), xii. I am indebted to Gentile's work for many of this conclusion's references. Gentile has discussed the notion of *democrazia recitativa,* or staged democracy, in other works, including *Il capo e la folla: La genesi della democrazia recitativa* (Rome-Bari: Laterza, 2016).

36. *Democracy Index 2015: Democracy in an Age of Anxiety* (London: The Economist Intelligence Unit, 2016), 11–12.

SELECTED PRIMARY SOURCES

Aikman, Duncan. "American Fascism: A Plea for American Liberalism." *Harper's Magazine,* April 1925, 513–19.

"L'amb. Caetani per la conoscenza del fascismo negli Stati Uniti." *Il Giornale d'Italia,* July 25, 1923, 5.

Barnes, Julius H. "An Answer to Mussolini's Challenge." *Nation's Business,* September 1927, 15–17.

Beals, Carleton. "The Dictatorship of Benito Mussolini." *Current History Magazine,* May 1923, 208–17.

———. *Rome or Death.* New York: Century, 1923.

Bent, Silas. "The Art of Ballyhoo," *Harper's Magazine,* September 1927, 485–94.

Bernays, Edward L. *Crystallizing Public Opinion.* New York: Boni and Liveright, 1923.

———. *Propaganda.* New York: Horace Liveright, 1928.

"The Black and White Brotherhood." *Literary Digest,* November 11, 1922, 13.

Bourne, Randolph. "Trans-National America." *Atlantic Monthly,* July 1916, 86–97.

Brooklyn, Peter. "Mussolini vs. Fascism." *New Republic,* December 8, 1926, 65–66.

Carter, John. "Mussolini, Master of Italy." *New York Times Book Review,* February 7, 1926, S3:1, 24.

Child, Maude Parker. *The Social Side of Diplomatic Life.* Indianapolis: Bobbs-Merrill, 1925.

Child, Richard Washburn. "Are We Imperialists?" *Saturday Evening Post,* September 7, 1929, 33.

———. "The Critic and the Law." *Atlantic Monthly,* May 1906, 620–29.

———. "Deluding Democracies." *Saturday Evening Post,* February 7, 1925, 10.

———. "Dictators on Trial." *Saturday Evening Post,* February 21, 1925, 14.

———. *A Diplomat Looks at Europe.* New York: Duffield, 1925.

———. Foreword. *My Autobiography,* viii–xiii. New York: Charles Scribner's Sons, 1928.

———. "Government by Blackmail." *Saturday Evening Post,* August 23, 1924, 3.

———. "Low Tide in Politics." *Saturday Evening Post,* April 24, 1926, 22.

———. "Majority Man." *Saturday Evening Post,* March 28, 1925, 29.

———. "The Making of Mussolini." *Saturday Evening Post,* June 28, 1924, 3–4, 156–58.

———. "Mussolini Now." *Saturday Evening Post,* March 24, 1928, 29, 133–35, 137.

———. "One, Two! The Goose-Step For You." *McClure's Magazine,* October 1919, 5–6, 51–52.

———. "Our American Diplomat." *Saturday Evening Post,* November 1, 1924, 3.

———. "Our Foreign Policy." *Saturday Evening Post,* December 13, 1924, 6.

———. *Potential Russia.* New York: E. P. Dutton Co., 1916.

———. "The President." *Saturday Evening Post,* April 17, 1926, 1–3.

———. "A United States of Europe." *Saturday Evening Post,* December 25, 1926, 3.

———. "What Does Mussolini Mean?" *Saturday Evening Post,* July 26, 1924, 23, 87–90.

———. "What Europe Thinks." *Saturday Evening Post,* April 4, 1925, 35.

Cobb, Irving S. "A Big Little Man." *Cosmopolitan,* January 1927, 145–46.

Corsi, Edward. "Benito Mussolini." *Outlook,* November 29, 1922, 574–75.

———. "From Mine Worker to Ambassador at Washington." *Outlook,* May 2, 1923, 801–3.

Cortesi, Arnaldo. "Faith in Fascism Shown by Works." *New York Times,* May 8, 1927, 6.

Creel, George. *How We Advertised America.* New York: Harper & Brothers, 1920.

———. *The War, the World and Wilson.* New York: Harper, 1920.

———. *Wilson and the Issues.* New York: Century, 1916

Dayton, Katharine. "Mussolini at Close Range." *North American Review,* December 1928, 653–59.

Dewey, John. "Public Opinion," *New Republic,* May 3, 1922, 286–87.

———. *The Public and Its Problems: An Essay in Political Inquiry.* New York: Holt, 1927.

Di Robilant, Irene. "Who Are the Fascisti?" *Trade Bulletin of the Italy America Society,* October 1922, 1–3.

Dorgan, Dick. "A Song of Hate." *Photoplay,* June 1922, 22, 26.

"Douglas and Mary Turn Rome Topsy-Turvy on their Arrival." *New York Herald,* April 29, 1926, 3.

"Douglas Fairbanks e Mary Pickford tra le rovine del Foro Romano." *Il Lavoro d'Italia,* April 30, 1926, 3.

"Douglas ricevuto dal Duce." *La Tribuna,* May 12, 1926, 5.

"Il duce supremo dei liberi popoli ha risposto." *Il Popolo d'Italia,* October 10, 1918, 1.

Elliott, W. Y. "Mussolini, Prophet of the Pragmatic Era in Politics." *Political Science Quarterly,* June 1926, 161–92.

"The Eternal City." *Billboard,* February 2, 1924, 57–58.

"The Eternal City." *Photoplay,* January 1924, 68.

"The Fascisti." *Current Opinion,* October 1921, 430.

Faulkner, H. H. "A Phrenological Study of Some Famous Stars." *Photoplay,* March 1922, 30–31.

"Film Stars See Mussolini." *New York Times,* May 11, 1926, 29.

"The Four Horsemen." *Motion Picture News,* March 5, 1921, 1859.

Frothingham, Arthur Lincoln. "Mussolini Acquitted of Despotism." *Current History,* July 1923, 561–65.

Gassaway, Gordon. "The Erstwhile Landscape Gardener." *Motion Picture Magazine,* June 1921, 41.

Gerould, Katharine Fullerton. "Hollywood: An American State of Mind." *Harper's Magazine,* May 1923, 690–92.

Giannini, Attilio H. "Financing the Production and Distribution of Motion Pictures." *Annals of the American Academy of Political and Social Sciences,* November 1926, 46–49.

Glyn, Elinor. *It.* New York: Macaulay, 1927.

———. "Rudolph Valentino as I Knew Him." *Modern Screen Magazine,* May 1930, 26.

Goldbeck, Willis. "The Perfect Lover." *Motion Picture Magazine,* May 1922, 40–41, 94.

Gorgolini, Pietro. *The Fascist Movement in Italian Life.* Boston: Little, Brown, 1923.

Hays, Will H. *See and Hear: A Brief History of Motion Pictures and the Development of Sound.* New York: MPPDA, 1929.

Hibben, Paxton. "Man of Italy: His Life, His Personality, His Activities as a Leader of the People," *Mentor,* November 1927, 1–8.

"The Hollywood Boulevardier Chats." *Motion Picture Classic,* June 1923, 74.

Hollman, Charles W. "Mussolini, Dictator for the People." *Outlook,* July 2, 1924, 348–51.

Howe, Herbert. Close-Ups and Long Shots. *Photoplay,* February 1924, 41.

———. "Hitting the Hookah with Rudie." *Motion Picture Classic,* December 1921, 18–19, 72.

———. "The Hollywood Boulevardier Chats." *Motion Picture Classic,* February 1922, 65.

———. "The Last Days of Valentino." *New Movie Magazine,* 1928, 41–43, 128.

———. "What Europe Thinks of American Stars." *Photoplay,* February 1923, 97.

Hullinger, Edwin Ware. *The New Fascist State: A Study of Italy under Mussolini.* New York: Rae D. Henkle, 1928.

"In Liberty Next Week Read: Mussolini Idol of Women." *Liberty Magazine,* September 10, 1927, 17.

"Italian-American Press on the Mussolini Regime." *Literary Digest,* January 30, 1926, 14–15.

"Italy's New Leader." *American Review of Reviews,* December 1922, 649–50.

Kahn, Otto. "Otto Kahn e il Fascismo." *Il Carroccio,* February 1926, 3–7.

Kallen, Horace M. "Democracy vs. the Melting Pot." *Nation,* February 25, 1915, 190–94, 217–20.

Kelly, T. Howard. "Red Blood and Plenty of Sand." *Physical Culture,* February 1923, 27.

Kornfield, Louis D. "Benito Mussolini, Italy's Man of Destiny." *Current History,* January 1923, 574–78.

Lamont, Thomas W. "The Effect of the War on America's Financial Position." *Annals of the American Academy of Political and Social Science,* July 1915, 106–12.

Laski, Harold Joseph. *Authority in the Modern State.* New Haven, CT: Yale University Press, 1919.

———. *Studies in the Problem of Sovereignty.* New Haven, CT: Yale University Press, 1917.

"A Latin Lover." *Photoplay,* June 1921, 21.

Lee, Ivy. "Ivy Lee a-Visiting." *Time,* June 11, 1923, 12.

Leech, Harper. "Is American Business Entitled to the Rights of Free Speech?" *National Electric Light Association Bulletin,* December 1927, 728–30, 757.

Lippmann, *Liberty and the News.* New York: Harcourt, Brace, and Howe, 1920.

———. *The Phantom Public,* New York: Harcourt, Brace, 1925.

———. *Public Opinion,* New York: Harcourt, Brace, 1922.

Marcosson, Isaac F. "After Mussolini—What?" *Saturday Evening Post,* May 29, 1926, 3–4, 135, 137.

Martin, Charles E. "Growth of Presidential Government in Europe." *American Political Science Review,* November 1924, 567–83.

"Mary Pickford e Douglas Fairbanks in Italia." *La Tribuna Illustrata,* April 25, 1926, 8.

"Mary Pickford e Douglas Fairbanks ricevuti da Mussolini." *Il Giornale d'Italia,* May 12, 1926, 3.

McCormick, Anne O'Hare. "Italy and Popes and Parliaments." *New York Times,* July 24, 1921, S3:8–9.

———. "The People's Own Dictators." *New York Times,* April 13, 1924, S4:1, 14.

———. "The Revolt of the Youth." *New York Times,* June 5, 1921, S3:1, 17.

———. "The Swashbuckling Mussolini." *New York Times,* July 22, 1923, S3:1, 19.

———. "The Women March on Mussolini." *New York Times,* June 17, 1923, S3:6, 11.

"The Melting Pot." *Photoplay,* November 1918, 21.

Merriam, Charles E. "American Publicity in Italy." *American Political Science Review,* November 1919, 541–55.

———. "The Significance of Psychology for the Study of Politics." *American Political Science Review,* August 1924, 469–88.

Michels, Robert. "Some Reflections on the Sociological Character of Political Parties." *American Political Science Review,* November 1927, 753–72.

Miles, Basil. "Italy's Black Shirts and Business." *Nation's Business,* February 1923, 22.

Montgomery, Roselle Mercier. "Mussolini, the Idol of Italy." *Current History,* April 1926, 740–42.

Morris, Lloyd R. "Mussolini, a Benevolent Tyrant?" *Forum,* November 1923, 2067–74.

Mowrer, Edgar Ansel. *Immortal Italy.* New York: D. Appleton, 1922.

"Mrs. Doug: Mary Goes in for the Fairbanks-Sort-of-Thing." *Motion Picture Magazine,* February 1927, 58.

Munro, William Bennett. "The Resurgence of Autocracy." *Foreign Affairs,* July 1927, 605.

"Mussolini as Julius Caesar." *Literary Digest,* September 26, 1925, 21.

Mussolini, Benito. "The Death Struggle of a Worn-out Democracy." *Saturday Evening Post,* June 23, 1928, 3–5, 141–42, 145–46.

———. "Dictatorship Defended by Benito Mussolini." *Los Angeles Times,* November 17, 1929, 7.

———. "Fascism Wrote a Bloody and Magnificent Page in History, Says Duce." *Washington Post,* October 23, 1927, M1.

———. "Five Years of Government." *Saturday Evening Post,* August 25, 1928, 6–7, 130, 133–34, 137–38, 141–42.

———. *My Autobiography.* New York: Charles Scribner's Sons, 1928.

———. *Mussolini: As Revealed in His Political Speeches, November 1914-August 1923.* New York: Howard Fertig, 1976.

———. "Mussolini's Own Story of His Busy Life." *Chester Times,* January 5–15, 1927.

———. "Mussolini Speaks of Peace." *San Antonio Light,* May 5, 1929, 4.

———. "Mussolini Surveys American Tariff, Trade Situation." *Galveston Daily News,* July 21, 1929, 7.

———. "New Paths." *Saturday Evening Post,* September 8, 1928, 3–5, 76, 80.

———. Preface to *The Life of Benito Mussolini,* by Margherita Sarfatti. New York: Frederick A. Stokes, 1925.

———. "Thus We Took Rome." *Saturday Evening Post,* August 4, 1928, 6–7, 105–6, 109.

———. "Toward Conquest of Power." *Saturday Evening Post,* July 21, 1928, 6–7, 121–22, 125–26.

———. "Youth." *Saturday Evening Post,* May 5, 1928, 3–5, 117–18, 121.

"Mussolini Declares Friendship for Us." *New York Times,* October 31, 1922, 5.

"Mussolini Defines Fascism." *Literary Digest,* August 1, 1925, 20–21.

"Mussolini, Garibaldi or Caesar?" *Literary Digest,* November 18, 1922, 17–18.

"Mussolini's Hope in Screen." *Variety,* September 21, 1927, 1, 23.

"Mussolini's Method with the Press." *Literary Digest,* January 19, 1929, 16.

"Mussolini: The First Man in Italy." *Nation,* November 15, 1922, 534–36.

"Needed: A Mussolini." *Wall Street Journal,* January 15, 1923, 1.

"L'on. Mussolini riceve Mary Pickford e Douglas Fairbanks." *Il Tevere,* May 11, 1926, 3.

"Our Changing World Now Turns to Movietone." *Picture-Play Magazine,* August 1929, 8–9.

Parsons, Louella O. "Propaganda! An Earnest Consideration of the Inestimable Part Being Played by the Motion Picture in the Great War." *Photoplay,* September 1918, 43–45, 110.

"Plans of the Fascisti." *New York Times,* October 20, 1922, 13.

Prezzolini, Giuseppe. "The Fascist and the Class Struggle." *New Republic,* November 1, 1922, 243–45.

———. "Mussolini's First Year." *New Republic,* October 31, 1923, 251–53.

Quaranta di San Severino, Bernardo, ed. *Mussolini as Revealed in His Political Speeches (November 1914-August 1923).* New York: E. P. Dutton, 1923.

Rambova, Natacha. *Rudy: An Intimate Portrait of Rudolph Valentino by His Wife.* London: Hutchinson, 1927.

"Il ricevimento in onore di Douglas Fairbanks e Mary Pickford." *L'Impero,* May 1, 1926, 5.

Roberts, Kenneth L. *Black Magic.* Indianapolis: Bobbs-Merrill, 1924.

Rohe, Alice. "Mussolini, Hope of Youth, Italy's 'Man of Tomorrow.'" *New York Times,* November 5, 1922, S9:20.

———. "Mussolini: Idol of Women: He Pours Contempt on the Softer Sex—And It Adores Him." *Liberty Magazine,* September 17, 1927, 9–11.

———. "Mussolini, Lady Killer." *Literary Digest,* July 31, 1937, 27.

"Romans Help Director in 'The Eternal City.'" *White Plains (NY) Reporter,* August 28, 1923.

"Rome's New Caesar." *Literary Digest,* September 22, 1923, 15–16.

Ross, Edward Alsworth. "Italians in America." *Century Magazine,* July 1914, 444–45, 619.

"Rush" [Alfred R. Greason]. "Pictures: The Eternal City." *Variety,* January 24, 1924, 26.

Salvemini, Gaetano. *The Fascist Dictatorship in Italy.* New York: Holt, 1927.

———. "Who Opposes Mussolini?" *New Republic,* February 9, 1927, 324–25.

Sarfatti, Margherita. *The Life of Benito Mussolini.* New York: Frederick A. Stokes, 1925.

———. *Dux.* Milan: Mondadori, 1926.

Schneider, Herbert Wallace. *Making the Fascist State.* New York: Oxford University Press, 1928.

Seldes, George. "Fascism (Alias Bolshevism) in Italy." *Liberty Magazine,* September 19, 1925, 15.

———. "Mussolini: Actor Extraordinary." *Liberty Magazine,* August 2, 1924, 50–51.

———. "The Truth about Fascist Censorship." *Harper's Magazine,* November 1927, 732–43.

Sherwood, Robert E. "The Silent Drama: 'The Eternal City' 'Wild Oranges' 'The Dramatic Life of Abraham Lincoln.'" *Life,* February 14, 1924, 24.

Shuler, Marjorie. "Mussolini at Close Range." *Review of Reviews,* October 1923, 395–97.

Sicari, Gian Franco. *Rodolfo Valentino.* Milan: Gloriosa, 1926.

Silverman, Sime. "Mussolini's Hope in Screen." *Variety,* September 21, 1927, 1, 20.

Speranza, Florence Colgate. *The Diary of Gino Speranza: Italy, 1915–1919.* New York: Columbia University Press, 1941.

Speranza, Gino. "A New Italian Renaissance." *Outlook,* February 1923, 351.

St. Johns, Adela Rogers. "Valentino: The Life Story of the Sheik." *Liberty,* September 21, September 28, October 5, October 12, 1929.

St. Johns, Ivan. "Fifty-Fifty," *Photoplay,* October 1926, 46, 123.

Stoddard, Lothrop. "Realism, the True Challenge of Fascism." *Harper's Magazine,* October 1927, 578–79, 581.

"Sunrise and Movietone." *Motion Picture News,* October 7, 1927, 1046.

Ueland, Brenda. "How to Pass the Screen Test." *Liberty Magazine,* April 9, 1927, 16–18, 21.

———. "Men I Would Be Afraid to Marry." *Liberty Magazine,* August 22, 1925, 35–37.

Ullman, George. *The Estate of Rudolph Valentino to Be Sold at Public Auction: Catalogue, Dec. 10, 1926.* Los Angeles: Eureka Press, 1926.

———. *Valentino as I Knew Him.* New York: Macy-Masius Publishers, 1926.

Valentino, Rudolph. *Day Dreams.* New York: Macfadden, 1923.

———. *How You Can Keep Fit.* New York: Macfadden, 1923.

———. "Motion Picture Novel." *Bookman,* February 1923, 724–26.

———. *My Private Diary.* Chicago: Occult Publishing, 1929.

———. "To the Man (?) Who Wrote the Editorial Headed 'Pink Powder Puffs' in Sunday's Tribune." *Chicago Herald-Examiner,* July 19, 1926, 1.

———. "Woman and Love." *Photoplay,* March 1922, 42, 106.

Warren Nolan, "Those Who Wear the Toga of Publicity." *New York Times,* July 15, 1928, 6, 23.

Watson, Max. "Making Americans by Movies." *Photoplay,* May 1921, 42.

"What Mussolini and the Fascisti Mean to Italy." *Current Opinion,* October 1, 1922, 469–71.

"Why Mussolini Charms the American Business Man." *Literary Digest,* June 9, 1923, 72–74.

"Why Our Bankers Like Mussolini." *Literary Digest,* February 13, 1926, 11–12.

Wilson, Woodrow. *An Old Master, and Other Political Essays.* New York: C. Scribner's Sons, 1893.

———. *Congressional Government: A Study in American Politics.* Boston: Houghton, Mifflin, 1885.

———. *Constitutional Government in the United States.* New York: Columbia University Press, 1908.

Winkler, J. K. "I'm Tired of Being a Sheik." *Colliers,* January 16, 1926, 28.

Winner, Percy. "Mussolini, a Character Study." *Current History,* July 1928, 517–27.

CPSIA information can be obtained
at www.ICGtesting.com
Printed in the USA
FFHW020848040519
52285548-57650FF